Literary Communication in Song Dynasty

Based on first-hand historical materials, this book explores the various aspects of literary communication during the Song Dynasty in China.

The book investigates the single-channel dissemination of poetry and *ci* works, the dissemination of literary collections, the dissemination through wall inscriptions, the oral dissemination of Song *ci*, the remuneration and commercialization of literature in the Song Dynasty, the paths to fame for Song writers, the non-literary factors in the dissemination of literature and the dissemination of literary works through paintings and songs. The author provides insights into the six major questions in the study of literary communication: Who disseminates, where, how, what, to whom and the effects of dissemination. The author also seeks to provide detailed answers to the following questions. What was the role of female singers in both domestic and official entertainment? What were the costs and prices of the books? Who paid the authors? What methods did writers use to gain fame and social recognition?

This work will be essential reading for scholars and students of Chinese studies, communication studies and media and cultural studies.

Wang Zhaopeng is the president of China Society of Literature of the Song Dynasty. He is Chair Professor of Humanities at Sichuan University, China, and Professor of the School of Literature and Journalism at South-Central Minzu University, China. His works in Chinese include *Historical Materials of ci Studies*.

Zhu Wei is an associate professor in the School of Foreign Languages, South-Central Minzu University, and currently a Ph. D. candidate of School of Foreign Languages and Cultures, Chongqing University, China. Her research interest include translation studies and modern translation technology.

Li Minjie is a professor in the School of Foreign Languages, South-Central Minzu University, China. His research interest includes literary translation and comparative literature.

China Perspectives

The *China Perspectives* series focuses on translating and publishing works by leading Chinese scholars, writing about both global topics and China-related themes. It covers Humanities & Social Sciences, Education, Media and Psychology, as well as many interdisciplinary themes.

This is the first time any of these books have been published in English for international readers. The series aims to put forward a Chinese perspective, give insights into cutting-edge academic thinking in China, and inspire researchers globally.

To submit proposals, please contact the Taylor & Francis Publisher for the China Publishing Programme, Lian Sun (Lian.Sun@informa.com)

Titles in media communication currently include:

Visual Culture in Contemporary China I
Zhou Xian

New Media Users in China I
A Nodes Perspective
Peng Lan

New Media Users in China II
A Mediatization Perspective
Peng Lan

Infodemic in the Era of Post-Truth
Yan Su

Attraction of Knowledge Celebrities
How They Motivate Users to Pay for Knowledge
Xiaoyu Chen

Literary Communication in Song Dynasty
Wang Zhaopeng, Translated by Zhu Wei and Li Minjie

For more information, please visit https://www.routledge.com/China-Perspectives/book-series/CPH

Literary Communication in Song Dynasty

Wang Zhaopeng

Translated by Zhu Wei and Li Minjie

LONDON AND NEW YORK

First published 2024
by Routledge
4 Park Square, Milton Park, Abingdon, Oxon OX14 4RN

and by Routledge
605 Third Avenue, New York, NY 10158

Routledge is an imprint of the Taylor & Francis Group, an informa business

© 2024 Wang Zhaopeng

Translated by Zhu Wei and Li Minjie

The right of Wang Zhaopeng to be identified as author of this work has been asserted in accordance with sections 77 and 78 of the Copyright, Designs and Patents Act 1988.

All rights reserved. No part of this book may be reprinted or reproduced or utilised in any form or by any electronic, mechanical, or other means, now known or hereafter invented, including photocopying and recording, or in any information storage or retrieval system, without permission in writing from the publishers.

Trademark notice: Product or corporate names may be trademarks or registered trademarks, and are used only for identification and explanation without intent to infringe.

British Library Cataloguing-in-Publication Data
A catalogue record for this book is available from the British Library

ISBN: 978-1-032-69742-0 (hbk)
ISBN: 978-1-032-71253-6 (pbk)
ISBN: 978-1-032-71251-2 (ebk)

DOI: 10.4324/9781032712512

Typeset in Times New Roman
by SPi Technologies India Pvt Ltd (Straive)

Contents

Preface: An Interview on the Imaginative Space of Literary Communication Studies   *vi*

Translators' Preface and Acknowledgements   *xxiv*

Introduction: Issues in Literary Communication Studies   1

1   The Spread of Single Pieces of Poems in Song Dynasty   16

2   The Spread of Poetry Anthologies in Song Dynasty   42

3   The Spread of Wall-Inscribed Poems in Song Dynasty   56

4   The Spread of Poems by Singing and Dancing Girls in Song Dynasty   90

5   The Remuneration for Writers in Song Dynasty   125

6   Dissemination Effects of Obtaining Recognition from Prominent Figures   140

7   Non-literary Factors for the Communication Effect of Literature   147

8   The Communication of Poetry through Paintings and Songs   168

    Epilogue   198

    Index   *199*

Preface: An Interview on the Imaginative Space of Literary Communication Studies

An interview between **Xiao Peng** and **Wang Zhaopeng**

Xiao: Prof. Wang, I carefully read your manuscript of *Literary Communication in Song Dynasty* and found it very enlightening. There were many things that I didn't know before or only had a vague understanding of. You have done pioneering work in describing the ecosystem. The social environment and cultural soil in which Tang and Song literature grew are presented clearly, at least to a certain extent, to the readers. In terms of television terminology, you have provided the readers with a "reproduction of scenes".

Wang: Thank you for the encouragement. You have been working in the media industry and have been researching mass communication for many years, so you are very familiar with modern media. By looking back at the ancient literary communication from the perspective of modern communication, there will certainly be deeper thinking and new discoveries. I would like to hear your opinions and also exchange some ideas with you.

Xiao: It feels quite surreal that we discuss communication of the distant history through modern communication technologies such as email and the messaging software QQ. Different from the older generations who sit together face-to-face for academic exchanges, we can communicate with each other from afar, asking and answering questions through written correspondence. This is a phenomenon in the field of communication studies.

Wang: As a fellow scholar, I am especially eager to hear your criticisms and suggestions.

Xiao: I noticed that many chapters in your manuscript end with an unfinished topic. For example, at the end of Chapter 3, you mentioned, "This chapter provides a compilation of historical materials and an analysis of the phenomenon, and a more in-depth theoretical interpretation awaits future research". And at the end of Chapter 5, you mentioned, "Further exploration is needed to understand other manifestations of literary commercialization and their impact on Song

	Dynasty literature". In Chapter 7, when discussing non-literary factors in the dissemination of Li Qingzhao and Zhu Shuzhen's fame and status, you said, "As for the changes in fame and status of Li Qingzhao and Zhu Shuzhen since the Qing Dynasty, they will be discussed in the future". Are you trying to tell the readers that many aspects of communication for Song Dynasty literature have not been fully explored in this book, and there is more to be studied?
Wang:	You are right. This is a collection of essays, and the individual chapters were not written in the same period. The time span between the beginning and the end of the writing process is about 20 years. Song Dynasty literary communication is a large subject, and there are many areas that I haven't touched upon, and even if I have, I haven't thought through them thoroughly. What is discussed in this book is just some important and macroscopic points of observation in Song Dynasty literature. The discussions of individual cases are just examples. These research findings are, at best, a phased display and exploratory thinking, far from being a comprehensive and systematic observation and study.
Xiao:	Please allow me to speak frankly. There are many important observations and hot topics in academia that I believe you have not addressed. For example, the dissemination of literary anthologies, the dissemination of poetry and *ci* works and the dissemination of block printing in bookstores are not discussed in your book. In terms of case studies, you chose two cases that no one had paid attention to before: the comparison of dissemination of the works by Li Qingzhao and Zhu Shuzhen and the transmission of Wang Wei's "Three Farewells of Yang Guan (*Yang Guan san die*)" in the history. However, you did not touch upon classic cases like the dissemination of Liu Yong's works. Did you intentionally avoid the familiar and try to explore new research areas, or is it an expression of the curiosity and desire for novelty in your academic studies?
Wang:	Indeed, this book only explores several issues related to the ways in which Song Dynasty literature was communicated. It cannot be considered a comprehensive and systematic study of Song Dynasty literary communication. In my scholarship, I have a tendency of "getting tired of the old and seeking the new". I always want to explore new topics, try new methods and find new directions, so I constantly shift my "battlefields". After exploring a specific topic for some time, I often discover new questions and new areas and then "change my focus" to explore the newly discovered issues and fields. Because I engage in multiple battles and attacks, each point and facet is not fully developed and systematic. I know that there are gains and losses in doing so, but my academic research is based on interest. I want to enjoy the interest and pleasure of academic research. Therefore, I let my interests guide the shift of my research field and research direction.

	Life is already full of constraints, and if academic research is also "restricted by formalities" instead of following one's own interests, then the research would become boring.
Xiao:	I know that your student, Prof. Tan Xinhong, has recently published a book entitled *A Study on the Dissemination of ci Works in Song Dynasty*. His research mainly focuses on *ci* works of the Song Dynasty, and some chapters in his book overlap or resemble yours, such as the discussion of songs sung by girls, inscriptions on walls and stone inscriptions, collections of poems and copying and transcribing. Some chapters are unique to him, such as the recitation of *ci* works of the Song Dynasty, the inscription on paintings, the anthologies of poems, prefaces and postscripts to collections, personal book collections, sales and trade of books, book prices, postal system, mail dissemination and miscommunication or loss of transmission. Some aspects are approached from a different perspective compared to yours. For example, you talk about printing and publication, while he discusses the evaluation of poems. Overall, they are roughly discussions of the same cultural phenomenon.
Wang:	Tan Xinhong's work is an important achievement in the research of Song Dynasty poetry dissemination, covering a wider range of topics in comparison to mine. I do hope that he can forge his own path by developing his own academic features and advantages instead of duplicating my approach.
Xiao:	Apart from Tan Xinhong, do you have any other academic teams around you that conduct researches on literary communication? Do you play different academic roles among the team members? Exploring a new academic field like this requires a long-term commitment.
Wang:	Yes. As to literary communication, I have personally done some exploratory work, just like a geological surveyor who explores mineral resources. Once I find a deposit, I would let others develop it. When I explore or become aware of areas that have potential for further studies, I would assign my doctoral students to dig deeper into those areas. Because I have so many things to do, my academic research areas keep shifting. I also realize the disadvantage of this approach is that no topic is fully developed. I haven't kept a balance between continuous innovation and making each innovation substantial and fruitful. For me, an individual person, my capabilities and energy are limited, so I increasingly realize that research in the humanities, like in natural sciences, also requires teamwork. My team mainly consists of my students. For example, for the dissemination of literary collections, I assigned my doctoral student Deng Jian to work on it. His doctoral thesis focuses on Song Dynasty literary collections and dissemination. Stone engravings were an important cultural medium during the Song Dynasty, so I had another doctoral student, Wang Xing, work for the doctoral thesis on Song Dynasty stone engravings

and literary communication. As for the awareness of literary communication of the literati in the Tang Dynasty and the changes in the dissemination of *ci* works in the Ming Dynasty, I assigned my doctoral students Huang Junjie and Wang Chao to work on them respectively (in recent years, the topics for the doctoral dissertations of the students I have supervised have been mostly designed by me). These doctoral dissertations have been well appraised by the reviewers and members of the defence committee. Therefore, I plan to publish these doctoral theses, along with my own book, in a series entitled *Research on the History of Chinese Literary Communication*. My academic research involves deepening key points first, advancing on multiple fronts and gradually forming lines and planes of research. Once the key points, lines and planes are clear, we can have a more complete understanding and thorough insight into the dissemination conditions and processes at a certain era or multiple eras.

Xiao: I admire your strategic abilities. Traditional academic research has mostly been a solo endeavour, just as the scholar Qian Zhongshu said, "Academic pursuits are akin to the cultivation and exchange of knowledge in an old, deserted house by a few sincere individuals". The capacity to integrate advantageous resources into a whole requires special coordination skills and a macro perspective. Sima Guang's compilation of "Comprehensive Mirror to Aid in Government" (*Zizhi Tongjian*) involved several top-notch historians and was an example of collective achievement. This is different from the collective writing of literary histories and appreciation dictionaries in 20th-century academia.

Wang: Yes. Academic research in agrarian societies has mainly relied on individual scholars' intellectual labour. With the development of modern science and technology, almost all fields now require scaled social cooperation. The production and assembly of Boeing aircraft components and the large-scale collaboration in the Human Genome Project are typical examples. Research on ancient literature, such as ours, should also gradually adapt to this trend, moving from individual labour to collaborative and scaled cooperation. However, each individual should still be a leading expert in their respective field.

Xiao: We coincidentally both strive to restore history to its fullest and explore the original academic path of history. In my work *A Comprehensive History of ci Works in Song Dynasty*, I mentioned the narrative historiography of the German historian Leopold von Ranke and his famous quote: "History must be recorded as it really happened". In your book, you also emphasized that in studying Song Dynasty literature, or ancient Chinese literature as a whole, we need to examine the broader background of society, politics and economy, as well as the individual writers' livelihoods, so as to understand their sources of income and their living conditions. In discussing remuneration, which was one of the sources of income for Song Dynasty writers, we need to understand the remuneration system and its influence. Discussing income sources and living conditions allows us to have a clearer and more realistic understanding of the distant past. This is an area that has been overlooked by the academic community. Nevertheless, fundamentally speaking, this kind of historical restoration still upholds the empirical academic tradition valued by Tang Guizhang and his predecessors.

Wang: It seems that you focus more on the individual *ci* poets' living conditions, such as their health, outer appearance, marriage, personality, social communication, hobbies, diseases and psychological conditions. I am more interested in exploring the living conditions of various groups in that era, the primitive aspects of social culture and economy, and their ways of life and entertainment. It aims at re-creating the overall scene.

Xiao: I would say you take a more macroscopic and closer approach to history. I, like a film director, focus more on the characterization of the actors, while you pay more attention to the environmental settings, social customs and daily lives. After reading your manuscript, I had a question for you: Could your book be understood as a brief introduction to the history of literary communication in the Song Dynasty?

Wang: I'm afraid not. Communication studies serve as an observational perspective and a theoretical tool for understanding history. It can be utilized to narrate and analyse history. But if it becomes history itself, it would be too vast and wide. To write *A History of Literary Communication in the Song Dynasty* would encompass all major areas, main subjects and significant cases of communication. We discussed this topic before and found that it covers a vast amount of content. Considering that there are still many unexplored fields, and there is a lack of clear understanding of the data preservation, it would…we think it would be too impulsive and impractical to discuss the history of literary communication or write a general introduction for that. If *A History of Literary Communication in the Song Dynasty* were written in this way, readers would not accept it. I think that writing such a work would require a collective effort of the academic community for at least ten or eight years. To write *A History of Communication for Chinese Literature*, it would require an even longer time for academic accumulation and exploration.

Xiao: Talking about this, I have a question to consult with you. Your new work contains a wealth of historical materials and documents, but such a large amount of factual statements might leave readers the impression of being merely narration and antiquarianism. Does your study of literary communication, which makes full use of the advantage of bibliographical research, focus on the collection of historical

	materials? Lu Xun once criticized Zheng Zhenduo's work of literary history as a long compilation of materials which lacks historical narration. Does your research also have this problem? Please forgive me for my scepticism.
Wang:	Your question is sharp but true to the fact, or "hits the nail on the head" in the words of Xin Qiji, a famous poet in the Song Dynasty. My book does indeed focus on the mining and compilation of bibliographical materials. Tan Xinhong's work, *A Study on the Dissemination of ci Works in Song Dynasty*, is similar to mine in this aspect. I don't know how long this process of mining bibliographical materials will continue. It is perhaps a considerably long period of time in the future, and the mining and compilation of such bibliographical materials will remain a research focus for me. However, as mentioned before, this is not the entirety of our research or the final result; it is only part of the achievement for a stage of the research. Especially for the second part of this book, it is even more so. Originally, I planned to compile a comprehensive catalogue of the collections of poetry for the Song Dynasty before conducting a macroscopic analysis of the concepts, modes and processes of literary communication. However, as my research plan continued to change, I didn't have enough time to complete the original ideas and plans. The second part was supposed to be the foundation work before conducting macroscopic theoretical analysis, but since this foundation work is not yet completed and the macroscopic analysis didn't have the opportunity to be carried out, it gives you the impression of mere narration. Ultimately, there is still a gap between readers' expectations and our research progress and academic capabilities.
Xiao:	Paying special attention to literature exploration is your academic specialty in research, as well as the academic style you have adhered to over the years. There are different choices in research methods and academic styles. Can we use theoretical deduction, general examples or purely narrative approaches to study the communication of ancient literature? For your insistence on literature exploration, do you have any other considerations?
Wang:	I have indeed a sense of rectification. In the new century, research on the communication of ancient Chinese literature has gained considerable achievements and progress. However, there is also a worrisome phenomenon, which includes the lack of empirical evidence and a reliance on preconceived frameworks of literary communication. For example, some researchers simply apply communication theories or adopt a few superficial and seemingly relevant historical materials to prove a certain point. Instead of investing great effort in reading through vast original literature, they use subjective assumptions to deduce the history of literary communication. It is difficult to say whether the conclusions drawn in this way conform to the truth of history.

When I study literary communication, I start with historical materials and strive to possess them as much as possible. I try to explore the true history of literary communication through the induction and analysis of materials. In my papers on this topic, I aim to solve specific problems in literary communication and provide new historical materials for further exploration. Some of these materials are directly quoted from original texts, while others provide leads to historical sources.

Xiao: The concerns you have raised remind me of many scholars in the past who scoffed at the reckless application of new concepts and methods from the West to interpret ancient Chinese literature. It is precisely because of this mechanical application of Western theories without solid exploration of documentary evidence that history had to conform to their theories. The result was always a superficial theory and vague history that did not support each other. Your research on communication intentionally emphasizes empirical evidence, integrating traditional and local academic approaches. It is both traditional and modern. Nowadays, electronic literature resources are becoming increasingly abundant and convenient. It is not too hard to fully possess these materials. Some young scholars do not pay enough attention to using first-hand materials, and instead, they engage in superficial research. It seems to be an issue of academic attitude, right?

Wang: The digitization of ancient texts has indeed brought us a wealth of resources that surpass what our predecessors could have imagined. However, the existing digitized copies still have limitations in terms of searching functions. They can only perform keyword-based searching, lacking intelligent retrieval capabilities. For example, searching for "dissemination" as a keyword in the electronic version of the *Complete Library of the Four Treasuries* (siku quanshu) yields only 691 entries. In fact, there are countless materials related to communication contained within the *Complete Library of the Four Treasuries*! Materials that are relevant to literary communication but do not directly contain the term cannot be retrieved. Compared to existing physical books, the digitized books that can be fully searched are still quite limited. More importantly, the retrieved literature is fragmented and disjointed instead of being organic materials extracted from the "on-sites" of the literature. Therefore, without extensive reading of original texts and a careful study of the primary source materials, it is difficult to have a thorough understanding of the "real scenery" and the background of the materials. Consequently, it is challenging to truly "reconstruct" historical scenes and ecological contexts. Therefore, I repeatedly remind my students to make full use of the retrieval capabilities offered by digitized texts but not to rely solely on the retrieved materials. At present, digitized texts of ancient

	literature can only serve as an auxiliary means and should not be the main reliance for studying the history of literary communication.
Xiao:	What specific plans do you have for exploring research materials on literary communication?
Wang:	I have roughly outlined a "three-step" map. The first stage involves massive literature collection and compilation, with which we thoroughly clarify the original ecological scenes of literature and obtain complete first-hand data. We aim to publish a comprehensive collection of literary communication materials, followed by narrative descriptions and theoretical development. Without comprehensive data, any theoretical judgements and observations would be unreliable and incomplete. The second stage of our research project involves theoretical studies. Only in the third stage would we consider compiling various types of specialized histories.
Xiao:	It is a great idea to publish a comprehensive collection of literary communication materials. Do you have any concrete plans or progress in this regard?
Wang:	We have not yet formulated specific operational plans because the scope of literary communication is quite broad, and determining its boundaries is a challenge. Materials about literary communication can be direct or indirect and explicit or implicit. If we look at literary texts from the communication perspective, it seems that there are traces of communication in all of them. For example, a poem presented as a tribute, a letter or a preface written for a book all embody acts and a sense of communication. Is it necessary to collect and collate all these poems and letters? I am still undecided on how to define the scope of literary communication materials. Do you have any suggestions?
Xiao:	I'm not an expert in this field, so I haven't thought deeply about it. But if I were to embark on studying literary communication, it would naturally occur to me that certain categories of reference documents are needed. In other words, document compilation should consider the needs and possibilities of researchers. The first things to choose would be, of course, the most narrow and essential areas, such as imperial decrees and prohibitions related to the communication of literary works, institutional systems, records of literary communication in official histories and unofficial histories, collections of customs and social practices, media forms, important prefaces and postscripts, significant literary events, political events, influential figures in literary communication, recitation activities, book versions, technological processes and so on. Broad and peripheral materials are not unimportant, but they are difficult to define in scope and can be taken later when the research has reached a certain depth. Alternatively, they can be left to later scholars to explore freely.

Wang: Given the limited research capacity, I think it would be best to start with the period-specific communication of Tang and Song literature, which means compiling the materials on the communication and reception of Tang and Song literature during that time. If we were to include the communication history of Tang and Song literature throughout the dynasties, the volume would be too massive, and each category could become an independent book. When choosing between taking a broad or narrow approach and studying across dynasties or within specific time periods, I believe a narrow approach within a specific time period would be more valuable. This issue requires further in-depth argumentation and cannot be hastily concluded.

Xiao: I have been engaged in television media research for many years and I particularly appreciate how you use modern media phenomena as a reference to depict and evaluate the distant past. For instance, when discussing the practice of wall inscriptions during the Song Dynasty, you compared it with posting online today and stated, "The act of inscribing poems on walls in the Song Dynasty was analogous to posting online today, exhibiting four key characteristics: openness, freedom, immediacy and non-commercial nature. It also had three main effects: talent discovery, reflecting social demands and advertising and promotion. Similar to how people today post and comment on online forums, there were often responses and harmonizations to the inscribed poems in the Song Dynasty". Such descriptions bridge the gap between the past and present ecosystems, giving readers a refreshing and compelling feeling.

Wang: The inspiration for using analogy with contemporary phenomena occurred to me while giving lectures to students. Later, it evolved into an article which readers found quite interesting. After finishing that article, I increasingly realized that wall inscriptions and the act of reading wall inscriptions were a natural part of the daily life of Song Dynasty literati, or you can say it was a cultural norm. It is similar to how we go online every day to follow social and cultural information. This issue requires further expansion and deepening. This approach of bridging the past and the present through analogies and comparisons is one that I will apply to the study of other communication phenomena as well. For example, a comparative study may be conducted between ancient girl lyrics and contemporary performances of singing and dancing or the study of the communication effects of celebrity recognition may be compared with contemporary celebrity endorsements and prefaces by renowned scholars. The comparison between the past and the present and the interdisciplinary references are both meaningful. For research on the communication of Song Dynasty *daqu* (grand plays) and *zhuanta* (modified dance), we can combine literary and dramatic studies, forming an interdisciplinary

	area. The numerous works praising the sacrificial rituals in suburban temples mentioned in the "History of Song" were often composed by officials of the imperial music bureau. The study of court rituals and ceremonies also holds value for the field of communication studies.
Xiao:	Modern media have undergone significant changes compared to media in ancient times. For example, books and stone carvings are no longer considered as media. Modern media mainly refers to broadcasting, television, internet, newspapers, outdoor advertisements and social media and so on. Timeliness is the core element of modern media. Timeliness determines whether a medium is a sunrise industry or a sunset industry, whether it has space of living or not. Does this concept of timeliness have relevance to the study of literary communication in ancient times?
Wang:	Of course it has. In my introduction of the book, I discuss the levels of literary communication, dividing the content of communication into contemporary works and works of the past. Disseminating works of the past is a form of inheritance and dissemination, similar to the re-broadcasting of television programmes. Republishing of printed books does not emphasize timeliness. On the other hand, the dissemination of contemporary works is contemporary dissemination. It is closer to the scene of creation and has stronger flavour of timeliness. Some even have real-time dissemination, such as impromptu poetry composed at banquets. Of course, it is still not possible to achieve live broadcasting. In addition to these two forms of communication, the subsequent communication of these works by future readers is part of the history of literary communication. For example, in my book, I discuss the communication process of "Three Farewells of Yang Guan (*Yang Guan San Die*)". The textual research of the Song Dynasty version only focuses on the communication at that time, which covers the situation of block printing and copying by people of the Song Dynasty. The spreading of versions from the Yuan, Ming, Qing Dynasties and modern times is something that Mr. Tang Guizhang had previously studied. Of course, we can continue to study them to make further additions. The timeliness of different modes communication of is one of the important factors we observe in our research.
Xiao:	What about participation? Participation is the primary element of contemporary mass communication. Without interactive participation, it is considered outdated media. The media that can provide the maximum degree of people's participation is the "king" of today's media. Social media has become the most popular form of media due to its unmatched user-generated content platform. Examples include Twitter, Weibo, text messages, forums (BBS), MSN, QQ, Facebook, blogs, YouTube, Tudou, Youku, Plurk and so on. Does this have any inspiration for your research on literary communication?

Wang: The wide-range participation is also enlightening. Interaction between writers and disseminators is a common phenomenon in ancient literary communication. In the Song Dynasty, the lyricists would listen to songs at the singing sites and be inspired or requested to compose impromptu lyrics. This is a form of interactive participation. In my research on the pictorial communication of "Yangguan Qu", I mentioned that Song Dynasty literati would often gather to appreciate paintings and then engage in poetry composition and singing, which can also be considered as participatory interaction. Of course, the scale and speed of such interaction cannot be compared with modern electronic media platforms like Weibo, forums (BBS), MSN, QQ. When I wrote this book, I only considered the interactive nature of creation, communication and reception, but I did not pay attention to participation, especially the effect of widespread participation. This is a direction that can be further explored in the future.

Xiao: Many scholars who study Tang and Song poetry tend to quote the opinions of predecessors in their literary criticism. Quoting the opinions of Qing Dynasty critics is not a serious problem, but when quoting the opinions of Song Dynasty critics, we often find discrepancies. In the conclusion of Chapter 1, you stated, "Therefore, today, when interpreting and analysing the viewpoints of literary critics of Song Dynasty (or even other eras), it is crucial to carefully check whether the critic had access to the writer's complete works and whether they referred to specific works or complete works, so as to avoid misunderstandings". In other words, the information we see at the end of communication may be different from what the ancients saw. Is that right?

Wang: Yes, this is a very important phenomenon of literary communication. Many poetic works that we see today are far different from what the ancient people evaluated at that time. The ancients may have only seen the initial drafts, or only single pieces of works, or versions that were not edited. Whereas what we see are works that have been transmitted, edited and transformed for thousands of years as the result of countless people's selections. This creates difficulties in the dialogue between the ancients and the present people. The number of works, types of works, stylistic appearances, values and moral criteria of both sides are different. Therefore, when people quote the evaluations of the ancients to achieve interaction between the past and the present, it is simply like "chicken speaking with a duck" (talking without communicating), and there would be discrepancy of context. In the face of such situations, the analysis of communication studies becomes very important. Otherwise, our literary critiques will be blind disputes.

Xiao: The sixth chapter in your book, which is entitled "The Dissemination Effects of Obtaining Recognition from Prominent Figures in the Song Dynasty", includes only 4,000 words, but it's a great topic in

Preface xvii

literary studies. It's a pity that so many aspects were not explored. It only talks about the communication effect and does not touch upon the effect on social cohesion, the causal effect on the trend of paying respects by literati, or the impact on the mentality of literati and officials. Zhang Yuangan carefully collected the inscriptions of celebrities, and Jiang Kui also carefully collected evaluations by famous critics. They were both great connoisseurs. But these typical phenomena were not thoroughly analysed in your work. From the perspective of social psychology and for a comparison between ancient and modern times, we can discover the superstition and worship of idols by the masses. What a great topic!

Wang: Your words are very insightful. When I was contemplating the communication effect, I also considered related issues, but not in a comprehensive way. My main focus was on the communication process. The subsequent affects you mentioned are indeed valuable topics. In fact, every form of communication we discuss will always have subsequent effects, whether positive or negative. By analysing their gains and losses, we can gain a deeper understanding of the society. This is what we refer to as the theoretical research in the second stage.

Xiao: After reading your manuscript, I have come up with many ideas. The concept of communication has both a broad and narrow definition. The broad definition of communication should include some peripheral literary communication phenomena, such as changes in morning papers, the practice of paying respects by literati, private schools or academies, the imperial court's gifting of new poems and songs to foreign countries, the communication by government officials to foreign countries, Da Sheng Fu[1] and the Jiaofang institution[2], and the imperial court's decrees to collect books from all over the country. These all possess the nature of literary communication. Broadly speaking, literary communication is a form of cultural communication, isn't it?

Wang: Yes, you are right. Broadly speaking, studies on literary communication should also cover the phenomena of counter-communication, such as communication taboos, literary inquisition (imprisonment or execution of an author for writing something considered offensive by the imperial court), moral boundaries in the society, technological barriers, wartime destruction, fires and so on. In the early Southern Song Dynasty, Cao Xun (1098–1174), a *ci* poet, planned to personally finance the engraving printing of the poems written by his father, Cao Zu. Emperor Song Gaozong, hearing of the plan, issued a decree for the bookshops in Yangzhou to destroy the engraving boards. The court considered Cao Zu's witty and insolent poetry as something that trampled on societal moral boundaries. Interestingly, Emperor Song Huizong didn't care about them at all and enjoyed Cao Zu's witty and insolent poems very much. On the other hand,

	Moqi Yong was quite the opposite. He thought his own seductive poems were too vulgar and deliberately removed them when compiling his collection entitled "Da Sheng Ji". Analysing such opposite phenomena is an interesting approach for studies.
Xiao:	You previously mentioned cross-text communication, saying that it is a prominent cultural phenomenon worthy of attention. I'm not familiar with this aspect, and I would love to hear more details.
Wang:	This expands the scope of literary communication to the entire domain of art. When a poem or composition from ancient times is transformed into a painting by an artist, written as a calligraphic work by a calligrapher or composed into a song by a musician, the communication effect is much greater than that of a simple written text. In my analysis of the communication of "Three Farewells of Yang Guan (*Yang Guan San Die*)", I wanted to explore the cross-text communication among poetry, painting and music. There is still much-uncharted territory in this field. The poems on paintings were generally regarded as a specific genre of poetry in the past. If we analyse them from the perspective of communication, new discoveries can be made. Similarly, analysing the chanted poems with music from the perspective of literary communication will also yield many new insights.
Xiao:	Copying, engraving, wall inscriptions, stone carving, selected editions, singing and other different forms and mediums of communication each have their own advancement and backwardness, convenience and trouble. They can be assessed based on their interactivity, durability, security and stability. Singing is the most vivid form, but it is also easily forgotten. Stone carving is the most stable, while paper documents are the least secure. This is somewhat similar to various forms of modern art like drama, sculpture, painting and gardens, which have different forms of expression. Of course, there is a distinction between advanced and traditional media, as well as new and old media. After the advent of photography, traditional landscape and portrait paintings faced great challenges. After the emergence of film, shadow puppetry and drama declined in popularity. When television appeared, it posed a threat to the survival of film. With the emergence of the modern internet, other mass media such as television, newspapers and radio became sunset industries. The same literary work, when disseminated through different media, will ultimately produce distinct effects. Comparative studies between media are also meaningful topics of investigation.
Wang:	Block printing emerged during the Northern Song Dynasty and was the most advanced medium of communication at that time. However, block printers initially used it to print Buddhist scriptures, historical texts and religious books, while private collections and poetry collections were block-printed much later. Single works were more

freely printed. Inscribing on walls was the best choice for fashionable and popular literature, as no one would write serious content from Buddhist scriptures or historical texts on walls. This shows the influence of content on the medium of communication. I recently discovered that image dissemination during the Song Dynasty was also a noteworthy form of communication. Folk daily necessities and decorations also served propagative functions. For example, since the Song, Jin and Yuan Dynasties, literati from all periods of history liked to produce porcelain pillows. Artisans in the Song Dynasty used calligraphy to decorate porcelain pillows in unique ways, inscribing them with poetry, lyrics, songs, prose, maxims and auspicious phrases in various script styles such as seal style, official script, regular script, running script and cursive script. It provides valuable material evidence for the study of folk literature and customs. Folk riddles, couplets, auspicious phrases related to weddings and funerals, among others, also are valuable for researches. Of course, these belong to relatively peripheral observation areas.

Xiao: Since block printing is the main means of literary communication, the bookstore system of the Song Dynasty should also be a key research focus. The academy system of the Song Dynasty, of course, served as a place for literary communication and group gathering. The system of imperial libraries and their book collections, as well as large-scale book compilation projects organized by the court during the early Northern Song and Southern Song Dynasties, all hold significance in the field of communication studies.

Wang: You mentioned many inspiring ideas and suggestions. If you were to write a work on literary communication in the Tang and Song Dynasties, which perspectives and aspects would you start with? What would be your ideal communication of Tang and Song literature in your mind? What other new issues and perspectives can be taken regarding literary communication?

Xiao: As a scholar, I didn't conduct research in this field and cannot produce such a work. However, as a reader, I have many different desires for reading and imagination in this field. In your introduction of the book, you have already elaborated on the subjects, environments, methods, content, recipients and effects of literary communication in detail. This is powerful and persuasive narration, just like the dignified and imposing army Chen Liang talked about. In addition to that, from the perspective of modern media, I think we can analyse some other aspects. For example, conducting data surveys on sample households is a challenge that studies on literary communication in history cannot take, but it can be accomplished by studying contemporary communication of ancient literature. In the case of contemporary communication of Song lyrics, we can design questionnaires to investigate the popularity, loyalty, satisfaction, brand image, communication effects, value evaluation, readership scale and image recognition of poets and their poetic works among sample households through interviews. By these means, we may obtain a large amount of data from the market and scholars, and then we may make a comparison between communication in ancient and modern times. In ancient societies, the competition between different media and the rise and decline of each can also be observed as today, so is the influence of competition among literati and scholars. In my mind, there are many interesting topics for research: How big was the literary consumption market? What was the class structure of consumers? What is the distribution of high-rank consumers and low-rank consumers? How did the will of the market and the royal court affect the creations of the poets? Was there a competition strategy for literary communication? Did poets intentionally cater to societal needs in their creations? Did they take the strategy for mass communication or communication for specific groups of people? What were the commercial ethics and political risks for literary communication? I think they are all interesting topics.

Wang: Drawing inspiration from modern media research is indeed enlightening. However, we must also be cautious, as there are significant differences between ancient and modern societies. In remote agricultural societies, most people had limited opportunities for spiritual lives and entertainment. Therefore, they had stronger desire for literature than modern people. A piece of the poem could possibly bring them happiness for many days. And even the accompaniment of a singing girl was considered a luxurious enjoyment. Rare and precious experiences naturally left a deep impression. Today, we have a highly developed material life with various entertainment choices readily available, such as movies, television, music, karaoke, bars, internet and tourism. This has diverted our attention towards literature. Literary consumption is just one form among many cultural consumption options, and it is a more traditional and increasingly marginalized one, making it difficult to generate passion. This is a reality that we have to face. I believe that studying the communication of ancient literature and summarizing its spiritual significance for modern individuals and society should be one of our important goals and responsibilities.

Xiao: I know that you started researching literary communication as early as the early 1990s. Today, research on the communication of ancient literature has become a very hot topic in academic circles, and there have been many similar works and articles. I don't mean to praise you excessively, but instead, I want to know why you made such a choice. In the 1980s, when we were in graduate school, the academia circle was crazed with "methodology fever". New methods such as system theory, control theory and information theory became hot topics of discussion among scholars. Today, it seems like an unsuccessful attempt to break through and perhaps a desperate move in times of crisis. In the late 1980s, you introduced the paradigm theory from the West to interpret the works of Song Dynasty poets, which gained widespread attention and acclaim in the academic community. Later, you tried using quantitative statistical methods to study Song Dynasty poems. And now, you are fully focused on the communication and reception of literature of Tang and Song Dynasties. Is this an extension of your methodological thinking? You have inherited the documentary research methods of the older generation of scholars, which have achieved remarkable results and are widely recognized in the academic community. At the same time, you are also enthusiastically seeking new breakthroughs. Do you feel a sense of anxiety about being outdated in your mind?

Wang: It is true that I was once enthusiastic about various new Western thoughts and methods, hoping to find new breakthroughs for traditional research of ancient literature. "Paradigm criticism" was one of my attempts. It could solve some important problems, but not all of them, nor could it replace other research methods. Chinese scholars, like most intellectuals in China, dream of finding a method or idea from the West that could completely solve all social and academic problems. This is impossible. Any ideological method or theoretical model can only solve part of the problems, as there is no panacea in the world. Recognizing this, we need to broaden our horizons and learn from others.

Xiao: I fully agree with you in this point. Rejecting foreign scientific culture is not the right approach, nor is just taking a sip. The study of literary communication is just one of the many wonderful methods. It is trendy and has a vast academic space. I should say that your academic sensitivity has led you to make the right choice.

Wang: In my research on literary communication, there is a process from being spontaneous to being conscious. Inspired and influenced by communication studies when I studied as a student, I found some interesting phenomena and cases for communication of ancient literature and felt the need to research them. At that time, however, I didn't really understand the value and significance of studying literary communication. After a long period of contemplation, I realized that literary communication is an essential link in the process of generating and realizing literary value. It is an important dimension in literary research. In 1998, I wrote a short essay entitled "Communication and Reception: Two Additional Dimensions of Literary History Research" (published in the *Journal of Jianghai*, the third issue of 1998), discussing the study of Chinese literary history in the 20th century. The article pointed out that literary research in the 20th century focused on two aspects: qualitative analysis of writers and works and positioning and evaluation of writers and works. However, the positioning of the value, significance and influence of writers and works was primarily a static observation based on the value concepts and aesthetic standards of modern researchers, without revealing the different roles and impacts of a writer or a work in different eras, and the fluctuation of value and significance of writers and works over time. Therefore, the study of literary history should gradually shift from the two-dimensional study of writers and works to the four-dimensional study of writers, works, communication and reception. Since then, I have devoted a lot of energy to the study of literary communication. In 2000, after I transferred to Wuhan University, I established the Research Center for Chinese Literary Communication and Reception. I believe that communication and reception are just one of the many modern academic research areas and should not replace traditional research areas, nor should other research areas be underestimated. Mr. Tang Guizhang's academic studies inherited the tradition of *Xiaoxue* scholars of the Qian-Jia school[3] and represent the development and magnification of the Jiang-Zhe *ci* poetry school. I understand that the mainstream characteristic of this academic tradition is "*Xiaoxue*" (Elementary Learning), including studies of editions, chronologies, textual criticism and discussions on *ci* poetry. However, the future mainstream of *ci* poetry research may be "Ecology of *ci*". In addition to the foundation of "*Xiaoxue*" tradition, it may also include studies of regional culture, family culture, customs, statistics, communication, reception, etc. Your exploration of personality psychology is also an important method. All of these should be seen as emerging topics in academic research, manifesting the development of researches on classical literature towards modernization.

Xiao: I hope that in the future, academic research in China will gradually develop its own style and academic characteristics. Similar to literary creation, it can truly develop its own characteristics and Chinese style, showing the academic charm of our Eastern culture.

Wang: We look forward to and strive for it together!

Notes

1 *Dasheng Fu*, also known as Dasheng Mansion, was an official institution in the Northern Song Dynasty. It was responsible for managing music and rituals. *Dasheng Fu* was established in 1105 and abolished in 1120.
2 *Jiaofang* (education workshop) was an organization responsible for music, dance and theatre performances in the imperial courts from the Tang Dynasty to the Qing Dynasty. On one hand, the *Jiaofang* nurtured a large number of talented musicians and contributed to the development of ancient Chinese music. On the other hand, when these performers returned to the civilian population for various reasons, they also contributed to the development of folk music. Therefore, the role of the *Jiaofang* was evident and significant.

3 The *Qianjia School*, also known as "Qianjia studies", was an academic school during the early Qing Dynasty. During the reigns of Emperor Qianlong and Emperor Jiaqing in the Qing Dynasty (1736–1820), the scholarly school emerged that emphasized textual criticism and textual research. The scholars of this school devoted themselves to the compilation of ancient texts and the study of language and writing. Initially, their focus was on collating and correcting Confucian classics, but later they expanded their scope to include historical records, works of various philosophers and study of history, geography, astronomy and calendars, music theory and ceremonial systems. The main founder of the Qianjiajia School was Gu Yanwu, a prominent Confucian scholar from the late Ming and early Qing Dynasties. Other notable representatives of the school include Yan Ruqiu, Qian Daxin, Duan Yucai, Wang Niansun, Wang Yinzhi and others. After the Jiaqing reign, the imperial government of the Qing Dynasty, facing internal and external challenges, had to loosen its strict control over intellectual and academic activities. Subsequently, scholars abandoned the stance of solely dedicating themselves to the classics and disregarding worldly affairs. As a result, the Qianjia School gradually faded away. Although the school had limitations in suppressing new ideas and detaching from society, over the span of a century, a considerable number of dedicated scholars immersed themselves in the study of traditional Chinese culture, thus playing a very positive role in research, summarization and preservation of traditional classics.

Translators' Preface and Acknowledgements

We feel extremely honoured to translate Professor Wang Zhaopeng's work. Professor Wang is a renowned expert in the field of Chinese verse studies. After graduating from university, he studied Chinese ancient literature, particularly Tang and Song literature, under the guidance of Professor Zeng Zhaomin and Professor Tang Guizhang and made great achievements. He has presided over several academic projects funded by the National Social Science Funds of China and published dozens of articles in important academic journals, receiving widespread acclaim from the academic community. Professor Wang is the president of China Society of Literature of the Song Dynasty. He is a chair professor at Sichuan University in humanities and a professor at the School of Literature and Journalism at South-Central Minzu University. He has published works such as *Historical Materials of ci Studies*, *Lectures on Famous Tang and Song ci Works* and *Ten Lectures on Methods of ci Study*. We feel both honoured and pressured to have the opportunity to translate Professor Wang's work. Throughout the translation process, Professor Wang has provided us with a lot of guidance and assistance, for which we are deeply grateful.

Due to the specific characteristics of English and Chinese languages and the cultural differences between the two, it is a challenging task for translators to accurately convey the content while maintaining the readability of the translation. During the translation process, we extensively consulted relevant literature, aiming to understand the content of the book as comprehensively and deeply as possible. We sought to grasp the themes of the original poems, understand the background and personalities of the poets and comprehend their thoughts and motivations during the writing process. This laid a solid foundation for our understanding of the original text. To ensure the readability of the translated text, we employed methods such as paraphrasing, literal translation with annotations and adaptation for certain unique expressions in the Chinese text to make the language expressions smooth and natural for the readers to facilitate their understanding of the text.

This book was translated by Zhu Wei, with proofreading and revisions done by Li Minjie. We would like to express our gratitude to all those who have provided us with tremendous help throughout the process of translating and publishing. Special thanks go to Ms. Sun Lian and Ms. Luo Jingran from Routledge and Mr. You Jinghai from Wuhan University Press for their generous help and patience during the process. My thanks also go to the graduate students Li Yan, Qin Qian, Chen Xuelian, etc., for their assistance to the translators during the translation process.

Due to the differences between the English and Chinese languages and the extensive use of classical Chinese in the original work (such as quantities of poems and *ci* works of the Song Dynasty and literary commentaries in classical Chinese), translating this book was indeed a great challenge to the translators. If there are any mistranslations caused by wrong understanding, we welcome readers to contact us.

Zhu Wei and Li Minjie
South-Central Minzu University

Introduction
Issues in Literary Communication Studies

The study of literary communication and reception is one of the well-developed topics in literary research in the 21st century. At present, many achievements have been made in studies of literary reception, but we are just at the initial stage in studies of literary communication. The research methods, research objects and research scope for the latter are still obscure. So far, for studies on literary communication for ancient Chinese literature, there is no consensus in academic circles on what issues should be addressed and how to conduct the research. The author holds that in studies on the communication of ancient Chinese literature, the following six issues should be addressed.

0.1 Communication Subjects

The first issue to be addressed is the subject of the communication, i.e., who spreads the literature or which people or institutions spread the literature.

In Chinese history, subjects of literary communication were different in various periods. Some were individuals, while others were groups of people. There were non-government institutions, such as family clans, bookstores, guilds and temples, as well as government institutions, such as government offices and schools. In the Song Dynasty (960–1279 A.D.), families, bookstores, *Mi Shu Sheng*,[1] *Guo Zi Jian*[2] and governments at various levels, as well as schools in states and counties, had already compiled and printed literary books. The schools not only published books but also collected books and lent books to the public in the same way as contemporary libraries. Although few literary books were published at temples, those who were responsible for the stone inscriptions were mostly Buddhist or Taoist abbots (*Zhang Lao*) of the temple. Celebrities such as Su Shi (1037–1101 A.D.), Huang Tingjian (1045–1105 A.D.) and Qin Guan (1049–1100 A.D.) of the Northern Song Dynasty often sent their poems to the *Zhang Lao*, or elder of Buddhist Monastery in Hangzhou for stone inscriptions. This is similar to authors today who submit their articles to publishing houses or newspapers. The monks in temples also asked for poetic works from the famous poets at the time. This is similar to publishers today, who make arrangements in advance with authors for their contribution. Temples in the Tang Dynasty performed dual functions: the educational function as

DOI: 10.4324/9781032712512-1

schools and the cultural function as libraries. Many literati at the time lived in temples for a long time. The functions and contributions of ancient temples in literary communication are worthy of our attention and research.

The purpose, motivation and conception of communication were different among different communication subjects. Some spread literary works randomly and spontaneously, while others had their specific purposes. Some spread literary works for profit, while others did not. Some were professional publishers, while others were non-professional or amateur ones. For example, the singing girls of the Song Dynasty; the dramatists in the Yuan, Ming and Qing Dynasties; and the traditional storytellers in the Song and Yuan Dynasties were all professional communication subjects. Those who travelled between different vassal states during the periods before the Qin Dynasty, in their composition of poems in diplomatic situations, were amateur communication subjects. Those who spontaneously copied, recited and chanted poems were also non-professional literary communicators.

Different communication subjects played different roles due to their different identities, social status and social influence. In some specific periods and fields, the influence of official institutions was greater than that of non-government institutions. Professional profit-making institutions such as bookstores, with professional management personnel who had rich experience in publishing affairs, published literary works with higher quantity, higher speed and wider coverage of readers than non-commercial institutions and individuals.

From the perspective of the history of literary communication, we should study not only the literary communication subjects in the specific historical period but also the changes among them; we should not only analyze the characteristics, identities, conceptions and purposes of the communication subjects from the synchronic perspective but also explore the differences and changes of the communication subjects at different periods from a diachronic perspective.

0.2 Communication Environment

The second issue to be addressed is the communication environment, i.e., the situation in which literary works are spread.

The environment can be divided into two categories: hard environment and soft environment. Hard environment refers to the explicit and visible communication settings: official places such as schools run by the governments, public places such as temples and villages, entertainment places such as singing halls and brothels, performance sites such as markets and theatres, places of business such as bookshops, private setting such as family gatherings and friends' gatherings. We need to answer the following issues: What are the relatively fixed places and provisional places for literary communication in each historical period? Which literary works are communicated in certain places? What are the special functions and influences of the literary works? What are the restrictions or negative effects of literary communication?

Soft environment refers to the implicit and invisible conditions such as the economic environment, political environment and relevant technical conditions. Different economic and political environments have different driving forces and impact on literary communication. The advanced economy is beneficial for literary communication in that people not only have the economic power to spread literary works but also have better material conditions to receive and consume them. The increase in the power of literary consumption will, in return, promote literary communication. The degree of openness and freedom in the political environment and the looseness or strictness of communication policies and publishing regulations also have a direct impact on literary communication. Generally speaking, loose policies and liberal politics would accelerate literary communication, while a harsh political environment would hinder literary communication. But the complexity of the matter should also be paid due attention. In some conditions, harsh policies potentially stimulate literary communication. For example, in the context of political struggles between different parties in the Northern Song Dynasty, the banning of literary works of political opponents, on the one hand, restricted the spread of works of those banned writers, while on the other hand, it stimulated the curiosity and desire among the public for ownership of the banned works. Su Shi's poems used to be priced by gold in Emperor Huizong's reign (1082–1135 A.D.). This was partly caused by the officially strict prohibition at the time.

0.3 Communication Mode

The third issue to be addressed is communication mode, i.e., the way in which literature is communicated. In ancient China, when the mass media was underdeveloped, which media, methods and means were adopted by the people in their spread of literature? What are the characteristics, main achievements and changes in literary communication at each historical period? According to the means of communication, communication modes may be divided into two categories: oral communication and written communication.

Oral communication includes chanting, singing, talking with singing, performance and so on. As is recorded in *Mo Zi*,[3] "(Some use the gap period between) mourning to recite the three hundred odes, to play the three hundred odes on stringed instruments, and to sing the hundred odes".[4] These are examples of oral communication. Other typical examples include the chanting of *Han Yuefu*,[5] the chanting by singing girls in Tang and Song Dynasties, the talking-singing of *Dunhuang Bianwen*,[6] the talking-singing of *Huaben*[7] in Song and Yuan Dynasties and the drama performance in Yuan, Ming and Qing Dynasties. The specific situation, function, characteristics and development of each communication mode need further investigation.

As to written communication, it has various forms such as hand-copying, wall inscriptions, stone inscriptions and engraving printing. Although hand-copying is a relatively primitive and backward way of communication, it has played an important role in the long history of Chinese literary communication.

4   Introduction

Of course, its communication functions are various at different times. By the Tang Dynasty and the Five Dynasties, it was the mainstream mode of communication; since the Song and Yuan Dynasties, it was an auxiliary instead of a mainstream mode of communication. For literary works spread by hand-copying, the channels and ways of communication might vary at different times. Wall inscriptions gradually became popular in the middle and late Tang Dynasty and were widely adopted in the Song, Jin and Yuan Dynasties. At the time, wall inscriptions became a convenient and important medium for publishing literary works, as well as a medium for readers' reading and acceptance. Wherever the literati at the time went, they would have a look at the poems inscribed on the local walls. In the poem "Reading Yuanshen's Poem at Pavilion of Blue Bridge Courier Station" written by Bai Juyi, there are the following lines: "Whenever I go to the Pavilion of Courier Station, I dismount the horse first. I look around for his poem along the wall and around the columns".[8] In "Poem to the Tune of *Huan Xi Sha*" by Zhou Bangyan during the Northern Song Dynasty, there is a similar line: "Whenever I get off the horse, I look for the inscribed poems on the walls first".[9] In the poem "Recalls of a Traveler" by the poet Lu You of the Southern Song Dynasty, there is a line, "I leisurely read the poetic lines of others inscribed on walls".[10] Zhao Bingwen of the Jin Dynasty and Yu Ji of the Yuan Dynasty, respectively, wrote the poetic lines: "Dismounting the horse, I look for inscribed poems on the walls; sweeping off the dust, I read the tablet inscriptions in the humble cottage",[11] and "The fellow countrymen invite me to appreciate the inscribed poems on the walls, and the monks from temples in mountains ask me to see the *Shetian* Tablet".[12] Stone inscription is a fixed way of literary communication.[13] Further studies should be conducted around the relevant policies and regulations in the Tang, Song, Jin and Yuan Dynasties, as well as the main subjects, location, management modes and communication channels. As a type of communication media, the stone inscription was firstly adopted in the era of Emperor Qin Shihuang (259 B.C.–210 B.C.), the first emperor of the Qin Dynasty. In the Song Dynasty, it became an important mode of literary communication, and there were professional operators at the time. Stone rubbings are not only the carrier of calligraphy art but also the carrier of literary works with special communication function and value. So far, there are some relatively in-depth studies on the production and historical value of stone inscriptions. However, few of them are conducted to explore the characteristics, functions and management of stone inscriptions from the perspective of literary communication. Engraving-printed anthologies used to be the object of research on textual bibliography, publishing history and printing history. It needs to be further explored on how to give a new interpretation from the perspective of literary communication.

0.4   Communication Content

The fourth issue to be addressed is the content of communication. They answer the following questions: What is communicated? Whose works, as well as which works, are communicated? Whose works are spread in time after they are finished? Which kind of work is more popular at the time or in the time afterwards?

The spread of ancient literature demonstrates a great "time gap". For some poets, especially those well-known ones, their poetic works were spread rapidly and widely once finished. For example, the poems of Su Shi and Huang Tingjian, two famous poets in the Song Dynasty, were read and recited as soon as they were finished. However, for some other writers, especially those less known ones, their works could hardly be spread in time. These works, "hidden in the remote mountains while waiting to be handed down to later generations", needed several decades or even hundreds of years before they were finally accepted by the readers. Many of the poetic anthologies in the Song Dynasty were published and circulated by descendants, relatives and friends of the poets decades or even hundreds of years after the poets' death. The "time gap" in literary communication would inevitably lead to the "delay" of the writers' influence on others. In other words, a poet whose works lagged behind in influence could not exert much influence on other poets at the time. Only when their works were finally spread widely could they impose an impact on others. Generally speaking, the popularity of poets is directly proportional to the speed and range of literary communication. The higher the popularity of a writer, the greater the desire of readers to read his works; the greater the demand of the readers, the more editions are available in the world.

The speed and range of literary communication are not only related to the popularity of the writers but also to the aesthetic values embedded in the works themselves. The works which cater to the current aesthetic tastes are usually rapidly spread and widely accepted by the people. On the contrary, the works that don't conform to the aesthetic fashion of the time are generally denied by the people; therefore, they cannot be rapidly spread. For example, the *ci* works of Liu Yong, a poet in the Northern Song Dynasty, conformed to the aesthetic taste of the public at that time, so they were spread rapidly and widely. The popularity of his poems is reflected in the following lines: "Where there is a well that supplies drinking water, people are heard chanting out Liu Yong's *ci*".[14] However, it is quite different for Huang Chang, the *Zhuangyuan* (number one scholar in the imperial examination in ancient China) in Emperor Shenzong's reign in the Northern Song Dynasty. Though Huang Chang enjoyed a high reputation in society, he didn't care about the entertaining function of his works and didn't cater to the aesthetic taste of the readers at the time. In his works, there are lots of elegant words which are of his own interest; thus, the works are "gentle and upright, but rarely satisfying the common readers".[15] Therefore, his works were not widely spread and accepted by the common readers, except that they were admired by the poet himself.

The spreading process for literary works is usually not of linear type but of curve type. There are periods of oblivion, as well as periods of popularity, periods of downs, as well as periods of ups.

The works of some writers have been spread continuously without stopping. For example, the works of Ouyang Xiu, Su Shi and Xin Qiji in the Song

Dynasty were continuously printed and circulated among the public. However, the works of some other writers were intermittently spread. After being popular for some time, the works would go out of people's horizons and gradually sink into oblivion. After a long history of neglect, they would rise up and come back into people's horizons. For example, Li Qingzhao's[16] works were very popular in the Southern Song Dynasty. At the time, the published collections of her works included the 12 volumes of *Collections of Li Yi'an*[17](*Li Yi'an Ji*), 7 volumes of *Literary Works of Yi'an Jushi* (*Yi'an Jushi Wen Ji*), 6 volumes of *ci Works of Yi'an* (*Yi'an ci*) and *Collections of Washed Jade* (*Su Yu Ji*) in the form of 1 volume, 3 volumes and 5 volumes. In the Ming Dynasty, almost all works of Li Qingzhao fell into oblivion. Even Yang Shen, a scholar of great learning in the Ming Dynasty, never saw collections of Li Qingzhao's *ci*. In modern society, with the rise of Li Qingzhao's status in literary history, her works have been re-compiled and widely spread. Since the 20th century, there have been so many anthologies and complete collections of her works that are published. The number is so great that few *ci* writers can catch up with her in contemporary China. Zhu Shuzhen, a female poet who lived about the same time as Li Qingzhao, left her only collection of poems, *Broken-Hearted Collections* (*Duanchang Ji*), which were compiled by Wei Zhonggong of the Southern Song Dynasty, to a later generation of readers. Her works were not widely circulated, thus exerting little influence on others. Since the Ming Dynasty, with the rise of Zhu Shuzhen's reputation, her poetry anthologies have been widely spread. Even in some popular Chinese novels, Zhu Shuzhen's poetry collections were put at the desk of the heroines.

The spread of literary works is sometimes featured by "abruptness". For some time, a literary work is not so popular. Then, for some reason, some years later, it abruptly becomes popular and is widely spread. And then its influence gradually declines. For example, *Additional Yuefu Poetry* (*Yuefu Buti*), a collection of chanting *ci* by Zhou Mi, Zhang Yan and Wang Yisun in the late Song Dynasty, was rarely spread at that time. It was nearly totally lost in the Yuan and Ming Dynasties. During the reign of Emperor Kangxi in the Qing Dynasty, Zhu Yizun accidentally discovered the anthology and had it published in Beijing; then, it became popular and was widely spread in China. There was a trend of imitating the style of the work at the time; thus, the poetic style in Beijing was greatly influenced. Afterwards, although *Yuefu Buiti* was still in print, its spread was limited, so much so that there was not even a formally proofread edition in the 20th century. Compared with other *ci* anthologies of the Song Dynasty, this work has limited influence nowadays. This is not a unique phenomenon in the history of literature. The spread of the *Anthology of Thatched Cottage Poems* (*Caotang Shiyu*), compiled in the Southern Song Dynasty, is roughly similar to it. This book was rarely circulated in the Southern Song Dynasty. However, in the Ming Dynasty, it was in full flourish for a certain period. It became the most important model of *ci* poetry in the Ming Dynasty. No other *ci* anthology was comparable to this one in the number of published editions. Mao Jin, a bibliophile and litterateur of the late Ming Dynasty, once sighed,

> The number of *ci* anthologies totals at several hundreds in Song and Yuan Dynasties, but only *Caotang Shiyu* has been widely spread for hundreds of years. Whether in pavilions or restaurants, the chanting with music may be heard. Even the humble scholars in poor conditions have strong desire for the work. I don't know why it's so moving![18]

In the Qing Dynasty, Zhu Yizun, the leader of the school of *ci* poetry in Western Zhejiang, was greatly dissatisfied with the poetic style of *Caotang Shiyu* and made severe criticism of it. Since then, *Caotang Shiyu* has been neglected and fallen into oblivion.

During a historical period, contemporary works are spread and so are the works in the previous era. A literary work is spread not only at the present time but also in later years. Therefore, the study of literary communication in the Song Dynasty may involve the following issues: How many literary works of the Song Dynasty were spread at the time? How many literary works of the Tang Dynasty (or before the Tang Dynasty) were spread in the Song Dynasty? Which works were most influential in the Song Dynasty? Between Du Fu and Li Bai, whose works were spread more widely? What are the changes in different historical periods?

0.5 Communication Object

The fifth issue to be addressed is the object of communication, i.e., who is the literary work spread to? The literary works ultimately affect readers, and the value of the works can be realized only after the recipients accept them. The value orientation of the recipients also has an important influence on the spread of literary works.

There are three types of recipients: The first type is consumer-readers. If subdivided, consumer-readers may be further divided into two categories: ordinary readers and professional literati. Ordinary readers generally read for entertainment and recreation. Those works suitable for their entertainment demands are easier to spread. For example, *ci* of the Song Dynasty is more entertaining than the poetry of the dynasty; therefore, *ci* enjoys a higher speed and wider breadth in literary communication than poetry. The storytelling novels were more entertaining than those documentary-style novels at the time, so the former were spread in a wider range. The storytelling novels were so popular among the public that there were professional book clubs and editors. During the reign of Emperor Jiajing and Emperor Wanli in the Ming Dynasty, people's strong interest in and great demand for popular novels promoted the prosperity of popular novels at the time. However, restricted by traditional literary ideas, the known literati at the time were ashamed of writing novels. For economic benefits, booksellers had to write novels themselves or hire

8 Introduction

others to write novels for them. These led to the publishing of large quantities of popular novels and the widespread of them. Different from the ordinary readers, literati at the time read to satisfy their cultural and aesthetic demands. Therefore, works with rich cultural implications and high artistic value would be favoured and highly valued by the literati, and they were relatively spread in a wider range. For example, Du Fu's poems corresponded with the cultural psychology and met the aesthetic needs of the scholar-officials in the Song Dynasty, so they were widely spread at the time. In the dynasty's history, there was even a grand phenomenon that "scholars from thousands of schools make annotations to Du Fu's poems". Literary works, out of certain social classes, are finally accepted by certain social classes. The recipients of storytelling novels in the Song and Yuan Dynasties were mostly common citizens at the time, while the recipients of the poetic works of Du Fu and Han Yu were mainly literati. Readers from different social classes at different historical times have different preferences on the style and content of the works based on their reading purposes and aesthetic tastes. Therefore, it is worthy of attention and discussion to the following issues in our study of certain historical periods: Which genre is more popular? What are the subject matters of the popular works? What is the social status of the readers?

The second type of readers are critic-readers. The consumer-readers read literary works mainly for entertainment. Though they have their own specific aesthetic understanding, they don't make comments to the public. However, the critic-readers read with critical eyes in the whole reading process. After reading a literary work, they would make comments, evaluations or interpretations to the public from the perspective of their own literary conceptions. Their positive or negative comments would directly or indirectly influence the spread of the literary work. Those works that win unanimously favourable comments tend to attract the recipients' attention and arouse their interest, which further promotes the circulation of the work. On the contrary, those works that get negative comments from the critics, and those left out by the critics, would arouse little interest from the readers, and thus the literary communication is negatively influenced. In the Song Dynasty, people attached importance to the recommendation of celebrities. Once a literary work was recognized and recommended by some famous critics, it enjoyed such overwhelming popularity and sold so well that there was even a shortage of printing paper in the city. Those works that failed to get the critics' favourable recommendation would sink into oblivion.

The third type of readers are creative writers. Writers and poets generally read literary works to draw useful elements for reference in their own creations. As far as poetry is concerned, poets would read others' poems to follow their rhyme patterns or imitate their styles. "Tune: Charm of a Maiden Singer Memories of the Past at Red Cliff" (*Nian Nu Jiao: Chibi Huai Gu*) by Su Shi, and "Green Jade Cup: Never Again Will She Tread on the Lakeside Lane" (*Qingyu An: Ling Bo Bu Guo Heng Tang Lu*) by He Zhu, have been repeatedly imitated in rhyme patterns.[19] The more imitative the works are, the more the readers are interested in the imitated poems, especially the imitation by famous poets would arouse readers' aspiration to read the original. For example, Su Shi's "Tune: Water Dragon's Chant, After Zhang Zhifu's Lyric on Willow Catkins, with the Same Rhyming Patterns" (*Shui Long Yin: ci Yun Zhang Zhifu's Yanghua ci*) has always been regarded as a masterpiece work by critics. After reading this poem, people naturally desire to appreciate Zhang Zhifu's original poem so as to make a comparison between the two to see whether the original one or the imitating one is better. This invisibly promotes the spread and influence of the original poem. In fact, the aforementioned poem of Su Shi was included in some anthologies which took in one by Zhang Zhifu together. Similarly, the poems imitating those of Tao Yuanming by Su Shi and others in the Song Dynasty not only promoted Tao Yuanming's status among poets of the time and even in the history of poetry but also accelerated the spread of Tao Yuanming's poems. The poems imitating those of Shan Gu (Huang Tingjian), Su Dongpo (Su Shi), Li Bai, Meng Jiao, Jia Dao and Han Changli (Han Yu) in the Song Dynasty and the *ci* imitating those of Liu Yong, Li Yi'an (Li Qingzhao), Xin Jiaxuan (Xin Qiji) and Jiang Yaozhang (Jiang Kui), etc., are all products of imitative-creative activities, as well as reading activities. The imitative activity usually takes place after the reading process. Such imitative-creative activities often arouse readers' interest in the imitated text, thereby promoting the communication of the original.

Another type of imitative activity similar to this is that, after reading a piece of inspiring work of others, the writer is motivated with the desire to create a new one in order to have a competition. For example, after reading Cui Hao's poem "Yellow Crane Tower" (*Huanghe Lou*), Li Bai decided to write a new one. However, he thought that it was difficult to surpass the previous one to write a poem with the same title. As is expressed in his lines: "There is such beautiful scenery here, but I cannot write any line because Cui Hao has already composed verses before". Therefore, he wrote another poem entitled "On Phoenix Terrace at Jinling" (*Deng Jinling Feng Huang Tai*). The competitive poem and high praise of Li Bai greatly promoted the fame of Cui Hao's poems and accelerated the spread of Cui Hao's poems.

To sum up, different types of recipients have different expectation horizons. The difference in their reading interest and choice of reading materials decide that they have different impacts on the spread of the literary works. The influence of recipients upon literary communication is to be further investigated with empirical studies as well as theoretical studies.

0.6 Communication Effect

The sixth issue to be addressed is the communication effect. The following questions should be answered: What is the function and effect of literary communication? Why does it have such an effect? Which one plays the decisive role in communication, the content of the work, the method or channel of communication?

The effect of literary communication, first of all, depends on the artistic quality of the literary work itself. But the same piece of work would have different communication effects if it is spread in different ways. For example, for Tang poetry, the written ones are not as inspiring and appealing as those sung out with music. Wang Wei's poem, "Seeing Off Yuan'er on His Mission to Anxi" (*Song Yuan Er Shi Anxi*), after being composed in tunes, became a classic song with enduring popularity in the Tang and Song Dynasties. It was spread more widely and was more popular than other poems of the poet. Similarly, the sung-out *ci* in the Song Dynasty had a better communication effect than the written ones. The *ci* works of the Song Dynasty were mostly sung by singing girls. The pretty faces of the singing girls were pleasing to the eyes, and so were their tender voices and beautiful melodies to the ears. Compared with the traditional reading of poetic texts, the singing performed two "pleasing" functions, one to the eyes and the other to the ears. In addition, people in the Song Dynasty generally gathered in banquets and listened to the songs together. The warm atmosphere and "sense of being on the spot" in the gatherings made it more attractive than individual reading and personal appreciation.

For handwritten copies, those written by famous calligraphers were more eye-catching than those written by ordinary people and the printed copies because the calligraphy would turn them into works of art. The literary works that were calligraphed by famous calligraphers are the crystallization of literary art and calligraphy art. For example, Ouyang Xiu's work "Record of the Old Tippler's Pavilion" (*Zui Weng Ting Ji*), handwritten by Su Dongpo, was a perfect combination of such art. It was greatly cherished by readers of later generations and was spread widely. Yuan Jie's poem "Ode to the Resurgence of the Tang Dynasty" (*Da Tang Zhong Xing Song*), calligraphed by the famous calligrapher Yan Zhenqing and inscribed on the stones in Qiyang, Hunan Province, is also a classic masterpiece handed down to the later world. In the Song Dynasty, it was often rubbed and sold in the markets. In ancient China, there were many "Three Wonders Monuments", on which the poems inscribed were written by famous poets and calligraphed by well-known calligraphers. For example, the inscription on the tombstone of Yuan Dexiu, a famous poet in the Tang Dynasty, was written by the famous litterateur Li Hua of Tang Dynasty, calligraphed by the great calligrapher Yan Zhenqing, and carved with seal characters by the famous calligrapher Li Yangbing. It was imitated by people of later generations, thus getting the name "Three Wonders Monument". During the Three Kingdoms period, Cao Zhi[20] wrote poetic texts for the Temple of Confucius, which were later calligraphed by Liang Hu[21] and carved by Zhong Yao. Thus, the tablet is called the "Three Wonders Tablet". These exquisite treasures (rubbings) with high literary and calligraphic values were still widely spread in the Ming and Qing dynasties and stored by some collectors.

The effect of literary communication is not only affected by different communication modes and communication media but also by non-literary factors, such as the writer's social and political status, status in literary circles, family background and personal identity.

Generally speaking, a writer with a higher political status enjoys a higher social reputation, and his works would attract more attention at a certain period of time. Therefore, his works are spread more timely and widely. Most of the anthologies published by the local governments in the Song Dynasty included works of well-known officials with high political status. Works of authors whose names were not so well-known were rarely collected and published. For example, after the death of Wang Anshi, a prime minister of the Northern Song Dynasty, the imperial government appointed some scholars to edit and publish his collections, as was related to his special political status and social influence.

The literary works by writers who enjoy a higher reputation in the literary world are often spread faster and more widely than those of ordinary writers. In the Northern Song Dynasty, Ouyang Xiu was a leader of the literary circle, and his works were generally spread quickly. "Once his 'Record of the Old Tippler's Pavilion' (*Zui Weng Ting Ji*) was completed, it was spread and read all over the country. Its overwhelming popularity caused shortage of printing paper for a time".[22] Sometimes, his manuscripts were spread out before they were revised and finalized; therefore, it was too late for the author to take them back and revise them. Su Shi and Huang Tingjian's poems were also eagerly spread in this way.

The writer's family background also has a certain impact on the spread of his works. If the writer grows up in a family with a literary background, his works are easier to enter the literary circle and attract people's attention. Otherwise, it is very difficult for his works to enter the literary circle, which would eventually be ignored. Li Qingzhao and Zhu Shuzhen in the Song Dynasty are two typical examples. Li Qingzhao's father, Li Gefei, was a literary celebrity who had close contact with Su Shi and his four students – namely, Huang Tingjian, Qin Guan, Chao Buzhi and Zhang Lei. Because of such relationships, Li Qingzhao was highly praised by Chao Buzhi and Zhang Lei, and her works were gradually known in the literary world and were spread widely. However, Zhu Shuzhen grew up in an ordinary family far away from the literary circle. Without the recommendation of literary celebrities, it was difficult for her works to be widely noticed, so they were only spread in a limited field.

The writer's special identity also affects the spread of his works. In ancient China, the works of loyal officials and righteous men attracted more attention from the readers, while the works of treacherous officials and base men were rejected and cast aside. For example, "Ode to Plum Blossom" (*Mei Hua Fu*) by Song Jing, an official and poet in the Tang Dynasty, was a poem with graceful and splendid style. Because the author was a famous minister with a resolute and stern personality, the poem was highly praised and sought after by readers of later generations. Many men of letters at the time would like to read the poem as soon as possible. Fan Zhongyan, a famous politician in the Northern Song Dynasty, was an upright and noble man; therefore, his poems were also cherished by readers of later generations. The poetry of Yue Fei, one of China's greatest generals and national heroes, was recited even more widely.

However, the works of Cai Jing and Qin Hui, two treacherous officials who harmed the country and the people, were rarely circulated. Yan Song, an official in the Ming Dynasty, wrote some poems with high artistic levels. Because he was a treacherous official, his works were spread in a limited range.

The non-literary factors that influence the effect of literary communication are not limited to the aforementioned points, and further studies are necessary.

When studying the effect and influence of literary communication in ancient China, we should not only focus on the influences in the past but also the influences on present cultural life and literary development; we must not only pay attention to the "past perfect tense" of the literary communication in ancient China but also to the "present tense" and even the "future tense". We should answer the following questions: What kind of literary works do contemporary people prefer to read? Which types of works are more popular? Are they original works or adapted works which meet the aesthetic, entertaining, practical and worldly demands of nowadays readers? What are the communication modes that work best? In the 1980s and 1990s, dictionaries that helped readers to appreciate Tang poetry and Song poetry were popular in China. The same dictionary might be printed with hundreds of thousands or even millions of copies. Why did these books sell well at the time but sell slowly later? Recently, books with pragmatic interpretations of classic works, such as "Boiled Three Kingdoms" (*Shui Zhu San Guo*) and "The Monkey King Is a Good Employee" (*Sun Wukong Shi Ge Hao Yuan Gong*), have become bestsellers in China. What enlightenment does it provide to our research on the spread and acceptance of ancient literature? The research on the spread and acceptance of ancient Chinese literature should step out of the academic walls to analyse the diverse needs of current readers.

Notes

1 *Mishu Sheng* (Secretarial Department) is the official central institution in charge of national collection of books in ancient China. In the late Eastern Han Dynasty (25–220 A.D.), the government set up *Mishu Jian* (secretarial supervisor), which was later promoted to *Mishu Sheng* in the Northern and Southern Dynasties (420–589 A.D.). In the Jin Dynasty (266–420 A.D.) and Yuan Dynasty (1271–1368 A.D.), it was degraded to *Mishu Jian* again. In the early Ming Dynasty (1368–1644 A.D.), it was totally abolished by the central government due to the rapid development of printing and publishing technologies and widespread of books. *Mishu Sheng*, or *Mishu Jian*, has a history of over 1,200 years. Their rise and fall reflects the development of the official library in ancient China.

2 *Guozijian* (Imperial College or Imperial Academy) is the highest educational administration and top ranking academic body in ancient China until its closing in the Qing Dynasty. Its history can be traced back to the Sui Dynasty (581–618). In ancient times, scholars who could do studies in imperial academy were regarded as sons of fortune (*Guo Zi*). The *Guozijian* in Beijing, built in 1306, was the highest administrative organ to the educational management, as well as the top one seat of learning during the Yuan (1271–1368), the Ming (1368–1644) and the Qing (1644–1911) Dynasties. It has also served as an advanced research institute for top researchers and scholars, including scholars from foreign countries.

3 *Mo Zi*(or Mo Tzu, 468 B.C.–376 B.C.) is a thinker of the pre-Qin period and founder of Mohism. His main work is Mozi.
4 The "three hundred odes" are taken to be the 305 poems of the *Shi Jing* (*The Books of Songs*). The translation is adapted from Ian Johnston: *The Mozi—A Complete Translation*. Hongkong: Chinese University Press, 2009: 685.
5 *Han Yuefu*, or *Yuefu Poetry*, were poems written in the Han Dynasty. Originally, *Yuefu* was a government office set up by the imperial court to train musicians, collect folk songs and ballads, compose music and match musical instruments to it. It later refers to folk songs and ballads collected, matched with music and played by court musicians. Poems of this style represented a new creation of ancient folk songs and ballads in the years after The *Book of Songs* was compiled, and equalled *The Book of Songs and Odes of Chu* in importance. About 50 to 60 *Yuefu* poems have been handed down to this day. They truthfully depicted various aspects of society at the time and revealed genuine emotions, thus creating a literary tradition reflecting ordinary people's sentiments. In particular, *Yuefu* poems were noted for their vivid depiction of women's life. All poems that could be chanted or were written with *Yuefu* themes were collectively called Han Yuefu in later times.
6 *Bianwen*, shortly called *bian*, was a literary genre popular during the Tang period (618–907). It is a type of literature that was influenced by the Buddhist *changdao* (lit. "guidance [to enlightenment] by [publicly performed] singing") and advanced the literary tradition of the *songs of the Music Bureau* (*yuefu shi*), *tales of strange events* (*zhiguai*) and *rhapsodies* (*fu*) that were very popular during the Han (208 B.C.E.–220 C.E.), *Wei* (220–265) and *Southern Dynasties* (420–589) periods. According to the monk Huijiao (497–554), Buddhist missionaries urgently needed a kind of vernacular literature that could be understood by everyone. Songs and verses helped to entertain the audience and to express easily even complicated matters. The genre of *bianwen* literature includes Buddhist stories as well as tales about anecdote in Chinese history. The meaning of the term *bianwen* is approximately the same as that of *yanyi* (lit. "extended meaning/morale [of an episode]"), a term often used for historical novels. This means that an historical event is narrated in a new form that was more attractive than historiographical reports. *Bian* can thus either mean that the historical content is "changed" into a popular form (hence the common translation as "transformation texts"), or that there is a plot with a history "developing" in the course of the story. *Bianwen* is a genre that was long forgotten and only came into remembrance with the discovering of manuscript novellas in the famous grottoes of Dunhuang. In some *Dunhuang bianwen* texts, there are marks indicating the mode of the voice in which a certain passage has to be spoken or chanted, like *ping* "even", *ze* "inclined" or *duanjin* "emotionally". The artistic level of the *bianwen* performances resulted in a combination of music, narration and illustration and so attracted the masses from all levels of society. The *bianwen* texts preserved in Dunhuang include two different types of texts, namely Buddhist stories and profane stories. Buddhist stories mainly served to propagate the religion of Buddhism and were mainly directed towards the moral sensitivity of the audience. Some stories also appeal to national loyalty and filial piety, moral attributes rather uphold by Confucianism.
7 *Huaben*, the script for storytelling in Song and Yuan folk literature.
8 Bai, Juyi. 1979. *Bai Juyi ji* ("The Collected works of Bai Juyi"). Zhonghua Book Company (15): 312.
9 Tang, Guizhang. 1965. *Quan song ci* ("The Complete Collection of *ci* Works in Song Dynasty"). Zhonghua Book Company (2): 615.
10 Lu, You. 2011. *Jiannan shigao* ("Jiannan Poetry Manuscript"). In Zhonglian Qian and Yazhong Ma, eds. *Lu You quanji jiaozhu* ("Complete Works of Lu You with Annotations") (6): 386.

14   *Introduction*

11 Zhao, Bingwen. 1995. *You caotang ershou (qi yi)* ("Two Poems on Visiting the Humble Cottage (No. 1)"), in Ruizhao Xue and Mingzhi Guo eds. *Quan Jin Shi* ("A Complete Collection of Jin Poetry"), Vol. 73, Nankai University Press (2): 503.
12 Yu Ji. 1983. *Zi Renshou hui Chengde* (Returning from Renshou to Chengdu). *Daoyuan yigao* (Daoyuan manuscripts), Vol. 3, *Siku Quanshu* (Complete Library in Four Branches of Literature, Wenyuange edition), Vol. 1207, Taiwan Commercial Press, 745.
13 There is no civilization that has relied so much as the Chinese on carving inscriptions into stone as a way of preserving the memory of its history and culture. Records of important events were inscribed on bone and bronze as early as the second millennium B.C., and brick, tile, ceramics, wood and jade were also engraved to preserve writings and pictorial representations, but the medium most used for long inscriptions was stone. The most extensive of several large projects to preserve authoritative texts was the carving of the Buddhist canon on 7,137 stone tablets or steles –over 4 million characters – in an undertaking that continued from 605 to 1096. Earlier, from 175 to 183, the seven Confucian Classics in over 200,000 characters were carved on 46 steles, front and back, to establish and preserve standard versions of the texts for students, scholars and scholar-officials of the Eastern Han Dynasty. The Confucian Classics were also inscribed by six successive dynasties, with the last engraving, by the Manchu Ch'ing Dynasty, completed at the end of the 18th century. At sacred sites, cliffs and rock faces were also used for large religious inscriptions. By the beginning of the 7th century, or perhaps much earlier, the Chinese found a method of making multiple copies of old inscribed records using paper and ink. Rubbings (also known as inked squeezes) in effect "print" the inscription, making precise copies that can be carried away and distributed in considerable numbers. To make a rubbing, a sheet of moistened paper is laid on the inscribed surface and tamped into every depression with a rabbit's hairbrush. (By another method, the paper is laid on dry, then brushed with a rice or wheat-based paste before being tamped.) When the paper is almost dry, its surface is tapped with an inked pad. The paper is then peeled from the stone. Since the black ink does not touch the parts of the paper that are pressed into the inscription, the process produces white characters on a black background. (If the inscription is cut in relief, rather than intaglio, black and white are reversed.) This technique appeared simultaneously with, if not earlier than, the development of printing in China. Many scholars contend that block printing derived from the technique of making impressions with carved seals: in printing, a mirror image is carved in relief on a wood block; the surface that stands in relief is then inked and paper pressed onto it – the reverse of the method used for making rubbings. A rubbing, by accurately reproducing every line of the inscription in a white impression on black ground, provides a sharper and more readable image than the original inscription or a photograph of the original. The advantage of this technique is that it may be applied to any hard surface, including rock faces or cliffsides, pictorial reliefs or even bronze vessels and figurines. As long as the object inscribed is in good condition, a rubbing of it can be made, regardless of its age or location. And by providing an accurate replica of the surface of a given inscription or relief, a rubbing gives the scholar, and especially the student of calligraphy, insights that simple transcriptions or freehand copies, subject to scribal errors and the copyist's skill, cannot. Rubbings made a century ago preserve a far better record of the inscription than the stone itself, which might have suffered from natural erosion, not to mention damage caused by having been tamped in the process of taking thousands of rubbings. Early rubbings, therefore, are invaluable sources, preserving impressions of countless inscriptions now defaced or completely lost. Paradoxically, it is paper, usually thought of as a fragile medium,

that preserves unique copies of inscriptions that were conceived of as permanent records in stone. See https://www.lib.berkeley.edu/EAL/stone/rubbings.html.
14 Ye, Mengde. 1990. *Shilin bishu luhua* (Records of Cummer Resort in Stone Forest), Vol. 3, Shanghai Bookstore Publishing House. 1.
15 Huang, Chang. 1983. *Yanshan Jushi xinci xu* (preface of Yan Shan Ju Shi's new poems). *Yanshan ji* (A Collection of Yanshan), Vol. 20, *Siku Quanshu* (Complete Library in Four Branches of Literature, Wenyuange edition), Commercial Press of Taiwan, Vol. 1120, 149.
16 Li Qingzhao (1084–1155 A.D.) was a remarkable Chinese female poet of the Song Dynasty (960–1279 A.D.). During her lifetime, Li made great achievements in the field of lyrics. Born in present-day Ji'nan of Shandong province, Li shared her artistic and academic interests early on with her husband Zhao Mingcheng, a notable poet at the time. The style of her lyrics changed dramatically after she fled south following the invasion of the Jin Kingdom in present-day North China. Her lyrics predominantly reflected leisure and life before the invasion. After fleeing to the south, she endured great hardships in life and the style and lyrics of her poetry turned pessimistic and sorrowful, expressing nostalgia. Li Qingzhao's lyrics were created according to "delicate restraint". Her poems first merge intense passion with literary images to create artistic conceptions in which feelings and scenery are well blended. Secondly, the poems use simple yet original language, which is natural and expressive. Her lyrics are easy to recite and are also filled with spoken language and common sayings.
17 Li Yi'an, the literary name (*hao*) of Li Qingzhao. She is also called "*Yi'an Jushi*" (Hermit Yi'an).
18 Mao, Jin. *Caotang Shiyu Ba* (Postscript of Caotang Shiyu). *Ciyuan Yinghua* (Essence of *ci* World).
19 Further reading: Wang, Zhaopeng. 1999. "*Mingzuo*" *yu* "*hezuo*" (Famous Works and Imitative Works). *Xue Lin Man Lu* (Rambling in the Forest of Study), Vol. 14, Zhonghua Book Company.
20 Cao Zhi (192–232), son of Cao Cao, a noted poet and calligrapher.
21 Liang Hu, a calligrapher in the East Han Dynasty.
22 Zhu, Bian. 2002. *Quwei jiuwen* ("Old Stories at the Winding Wei River"), Vol. 3. Zhonghua Book Company, 120.

1 The Spread of Single Pieces of Poems in Song Dynasty

The anthologies in the Song Dynasty were usually compiled and printed in the authors' later years or after their deaths (a detailed study will be found in Chapter 2). However, for those famous poets such as Su Shi and Huang Tingjian, their poems were often "spread right on the day they are finished"[1] and "pursued by all once finished".[2] What are the communication tools that were adopted to spread the work so quickly? In addition to traditional handwriting, there are three other modes – namely, engraving printing, stone inscriptions and wall inscriptions.

1.1 Engraving Printing

Engraving printing in publishing was firstly adopted in the Sui and Tang Dynasties and was widely applied during the Five Dynasties (709–960 A.D.).[3] As for the publishing and sales of engraving-printed books of single poems, it firstly appeared in the late Tang Dynasty. The poet Xu Kui of the late Tang Dynasty commented in his poem "Ten Poems for Myself" (*"Zi Yong Shi Yun"*): "My humble rhyme-prose (*fu*) are heard to have been engraving-printed and sold, my dull poems are found to have been shown in paintings". Xu Kui's "humble rhyme-prose" and "dull poems", which were "engraving-printed and sold", are all single pieces of poems.

In the Song Dynasty, with the development of printing technologies, the engraving printing and sales of single poems became more and more popular. The poems of famous writers were engraved and published once they were finished. For example, when Ouyang Xiu's "Record of the Old Tippler's Pavilion" (*"Zui Weng Ting Ji"*) was completed, "it was spread and read all over the country. Its overwhelming popularity ever caused shortage of printing paper at a time. Once Song Zijing got a copy, he read it again and again".[4] Sometimes the poems were circulated even without revision by the poet:

> When Ouyang Xiu served as an official in Chuzhou, he had a subordinate officer named Du Bin, who was good at playing the *pipa*.[5] Whenever Ouyang Xiu drank alcohol, he would have Du Bin play the *pipa*. Therefore, his poem goes with the following lines: "Who is the most virtuous among

DOI: 10.4324/9781032712512-2

the drunken people? Du Bin plays *pipa* with such beautiful melodies." Once this poem was circulated, Du Bin was much sick of it. Though he prayed for Ouyang Xiu to do away with his name from the poem, he failed in the end due to the fact that the poem had already been widely spread.[6]

Wang Anshi also sighed at such "incapacity for revision of poems due to the fast circulation".[7] Ouyang Xiu's poems were quickly spread once they were finished. Though he made some revisions later, the original texts had already been widely circulated. Therefore, various versions of the same poem were found among the people. Some editions were compiled based on the first drafts, while others were compiled based on the revised versions. As is found in the revision notes to Volume 39 of "*Ouyang Wenzhong Gong Ji*" ("Collected works of Ouyang Xiu") in photocopied "*Sibu congkan*" ("Four series books"):

> The two poems in this volume, "Zhixi Pavilion in Xiazhou" (*Xiazhou Zhixi Ting Ji*) and "Gucheng Confucian Temple" (*Gucheng Fuzi Miao Ji*), in comparison, are different from those in "Literary Essence of Song Dynasty" (*Song Wen Cui*) published in the fourth year during Emperor Qingli's reign. In addition, "Study at Jizhou" (*Jizhou Xue Ji*), in comparison, is different in wording from that in the common versions published in Fujian. It is believed that the first drafts had already been widely spread before their publication.

In the revision notes to Volume 46 of the same book, there are the following words:

> "Pleading Letters" (*Yan Shi Shu*) is adopted from "An Anthology of Northern Song Writings" (*Shen Song Wen Hai*) compiled by Jiang Tian. It is supposed to be the first draft, which is not as good as the revised one in later anthologies.

It is easy to find different versions of the same poem from the Song Dynasty. Possibly, the differences were not caused by publishers' intentional alteration or engraving with mistakes but by the difference between the authors' first drafts and final versions. If the first drafts and the final versions were printed and spread out through different channels, the texts were different in various versions.

Su Shi's poems, once finished, were spread and engraved quickly. As is shown in his letter "Reply to Chen Chuandao":

> I don't write poems lately, the reason for which will be told when we gather together. Instead I write some epigraphies and epitaphs at people's invitation to which I cannot say "no". I want to present them to the inviters, but I am too busy to do so. Then I hear that the book sellers have already had them printed. I think that you have already read them.[8]

As is stated here, when Su Shi finished the epigraphies and epitaphs, they were immediately "printed" by the booksellers in Bianjing (present Kaifeng). At that time, "Su Shi's poems collected by people are numerous, among which about half are fake ones. Many poems are tampered with by vulgar people, thus the reading of these works made people feel unfair".[9] The poems of Su Shi collected by people were all single pieces that were engraved and published. As Zhu Bian wrote,

> When Lu Huiqing, a political reformer in Northern Song Dynasty, was relegated, it should have been Liu Ban's task to draft the edict. Su Shi said: "You have been potentially an executioner for so long, till you have the opportunity to kill someone today." Liu Ban rushed away with the excuse of being sick. Su Shi drafted the edict at one go, which was passed on and spread in the capital city rapidly. Its overwhelming popularity even caused shortage of printing paper in the city.[10]

Thus it can be seen that Su Shi's works spread so fast at the time. The rapid and wide spread of literary works increases the authors' influence in the literary circle. Zhu Bian further wrote,

> The poems of Su Dongpo (Su Shi), once finished, are passed on and spread among the people. Whenever a poem written by Su Dongpo is available, Ouyang Xiu feels pleasant all the day. The predecessors are mostly like this. One day, when Ouyang Xiu talks with his son about Su Dongpo's poetry, he sighs: "Keep this in mind, that thirty years later, people in this world will not talk about me!" During the years of Congning (1102–1106 AD) and Daguan (1107–1110 AD) in Emperor Huizong's reign, the poems of Su Dongpo written in his exile at Hainan are very popular among the readers, who really don't talk about Ouyang Xiu any more. At the time, though the imperial court tries to ban the Su Dongpo's poems by increasing the pecuniary reward to 80,000 coins. However, the stricter the ban is, the wider the poems are spread. People with a large storage of Su Dongpo's poems would take pride in it. The literati who have no access to Su Dongpo's poems would feel depressed, and would be criticized by others as "not being elegant".[11]

Li Bai and Du Fu, two great poets of the Tang Dynasty, did not have such extensive influence in the poetry circle or among readers at the time. This has a lot to do with the limits of the communications media at that time. Li and Du lived in an era in which engraving printing wasn't popular, and poetry works were mainly copied by hand, hence the limitation in the speed and range of the spread of their literary works.

Individual booksellers and bookstores generally had a profit-making purpose in their engraving printing and sales of poems. Su Shi once said, "The businessmen crave for gains in publishing my poetic works. I plan to have their engraving blocks destroyed, however it turns out that even more copies are published".[12] In Wang Pizhi's "Fleeting Gossip by the River Sheng" (*Shengshui Yan Tan Lu*), there are the following words:

> At that time, when Cai Junmo (1012–1067) wrote the poem "Four Virtuous Men and One Mean Man" (*Si Xian Yi Bu Xiao Shi*) and had it posted in the capital city, people competed in copying the work. The book sellers made a lot of money by selling them. Foreign envoys also purchased them and brought them back to their countries.[13]

Here Cai Xiang (with the courtesy name[14] Junmo) had his own poem posted in the capital city, which was competitively copied by the people. The booksellers found the opportunity for profits, so they had the poems printed and made a lot of money. Even some poems that were not written by famous poets were printed and "sold in the markets".[15]

The extensive printing and reading of poems requires relatively concentrated and specialized book markets. The book markets ("bookshops") are generally believed to appear in the Western Han Dynasty (206 BC–24 A.D.). In Yang Xiong's "*Fa Yan: Wuzi Pian*" ("Words to Live By"), there are the following words: "For those who enjoy reading, if they don't follow the teachings of Confucius, they're just like bookshops in chaos". In the book "*San Fu Huang Tu*" ("Three Districts of the Capital City"), there is a description of Imperial College students' purchase of books at markets during the reign of Emperor Pingdi:

> In the fourth year, the students' lodging houses, which amount to 30, were constructed. The trading markets were also built along hundreds of rows of locust trees. The students went shopping here on the 1st day and 15th day of each month. They brought here the books published at their hometowns and had them traded with others. They discussed freely and frankly under the trees in groups.[16]

Some bookstores in Luoyang in the Eastern Han Dynasty even "opened book shelves" for public reading. Wang Chong "often visited the bookstores in Luoyang city and read books on sale, which he could recite after reading only once".[17] The bookshops of the Tang Dynasty and Five Dynasties are also mentioned in historical records.[18] The book markets in the Song Dynasty were larger and more common than ever. Xiangguo Temple in Kaifeng, the capital city of the Northern Song Dynasty, was a big book market at that time, to which scholars and men of letters paid frequent visits. Volume 2 of Wu Chuhou's "*Qingxiang Zaji*" ("Miscellaneous Records of the Blue Box") shows that the author "once paid a visit to bookstores of Xiangguo Temple,[19] and turned back home with a volume of poems published under the supervision of Feng Yingwang".[20] Huang Tingjian also frequently visited the bookstores at the Great Xiangguo Temple. He once wrote, "I got a copy of Song Zijing's

"*Tang Shi Gao*" ("Drafts of Tang History") at a bookstore. Returning home, I read the book several times, which greatly improved my writing".[21] Li Qingzhao and her husband were also regular visitors to the bookstores at Xiangguo Temple.[22]

Bookstores at Xiangguo Temple include stores that had run for many years, as well as temporary stalls:

> (Taoist Cripple Liu) lives for 30 years at Zhangpo Dian by the gate of the capital city, and everyday sits in a bookstore at the east of the Xiangguo Temple.[23]
>
> (Mu Xiu) once obtained a copy of "*Liu Zongyuan Ji*" ("Collection of Liu Zongyuan's Works"). He hired workers to engrave and print hundreds of copies. Then he brought them to Xiangguo Temple in the capital city, and set up book stalls to sell the books.[24]

The "bookstore" in which Cripple Liu sits is a shop specializing in sales of books, while the "book stalls" where Mu Xiu sells "Collection of Liu Zongyuan's Works" is temporarily set. The bookstore at Xiangguo Temple even delivered books to the doors of the buyers. For example, in the eighth year of Yuan You in Emperor Zhezong's reign, the Korean envoys were sent to Bianjing (Kaifeng), where they wanted to buy some books. "Chen Xuan, a government official, and other escorts, asked the bookstores at Xiangguo Temple to arrange book exhibitions in the embassy, waiting for the envoys to buy the books".[25] The delivery of books to the doors by the booksellers was not a particular case. In Bianjing, there were also floating booksellers who travelled around to sell books.

In the Southern Song Dynasty, there were even more bookstores in Hangzhou, the capital city at the time, than in any other city in the country. Orange Garden Bookstore (*Ju Yuan Ting Shu Fang*), Zhang's Bookstore (*Zhang Guanren Zhu Shi Zi Wen Ji Pu*) and Yin's Bookstore by Imperial Ancestral Temple (*Taimiao Qian Yin Jia Wen Zi Pu*) were all well-known professional bookstores in Lin'an city.[26] In Jianyang and Masha of Fujian, similar bookstores were "well popular for some time".[27] These bookstores and bookshops sold literary anthologies as well as single poems.

By printing and selling poetic works, publishers and booksellers could make a lot of money. Did they have to pay a certain amount of money to the authors? In the existing documents, there is no record that any author obtained payment from the booksellers or publishers. Some authors sometimes got some remuneration (payment for articles). But they were not paid by publishers or booksellers but by some special recipients and those who invited the authors to write pragmatic articles, such as epigraphies and epitaphs.

Poets could also get some remuneration by writing poems, but they are not "regular" ones. In some cases, poetry lovers bought poems from famous poets with money. For example, Mei Yaochen (1002–1060 A.D.) was famous for writing poems, so a kinsman of the emperor bought poems from him. Chen Shidao (1053–1102 A.D.) was also famous for his poems, so Zhao Shiwei, a member of the royal house, once asked him to write the poem "Gao Xuan Guo Tu" for the price of "hundreds and thousands". At the end of the Song Dynasty, the poet Fang Hui also "labelled the price" of writing poems for others. In Zhou Mi's "*Guixin Zashi*" ("Miscellaneous Records of Guixin Years"), there are the following words:

> A man asked Fang Hui to write a piece of poetic preface and promised to pay him five coins. Fang Hui demanded to obtain the payment first. With the money in hand, he wrote some lines with a casual air. Seeing that the words were finished in such hast, the man was unhappy and demanded to take back the money while returning the lines. They quarrelled with each other and even fought with fists.[28]

Of course, there were few poets who demanded payment, like Fang Hui at the time. Most poets didn't accept any money or other sort of payment when they were invited to write poems. For example, Su Shi, at the firm invitation of Yao Chun of Suzhou, wrote the poem "Poem to Sanrui Hall" (*San Rui Tang Shi*). Yao paid him "eighty pots of eupatorium (*Huixiang*)", while Su Shi "entrusted others to return them".[29] This shows that it is not popular among the poets to write poems for others to make money.

Another case is that when a poet presented his poems to high officials or noble lords, the recipients would reward him with money or other payment. Generally, the rewards depended on the quality of the poems.

The printing and sales of a single poem and remuneration to poets reveal the commercialization of literature in the Song Dynasty, although the "commerce consciousness" of poets has not yet formed. The commercialization of literature plays a positive role in promoting the development of literature. First of all, it helped to develop a group of "professional" poets who made a living by writing poems. In Bianjing, the capital city of the Northern Song Dynasty, there was a man named Zhang Shou Shan Ren who "made a living" by writing poems for others for "more than 30 years".[30] In the Southern Song Dynasty, such "followers who sponged on others" were predecessors of professional writers for later generations. In the dynasty, there was a group of literati who made a living by writing poems for others. In the article "Idler" in Volume 19 of "Record of Millet Dream" (*Meng Liang Lu*), there are the following words:

> Some talk about the past and the present, some recite poems and chant songs, some play chess and zither, some play the game of throwing arrows to pots and other chess games, and some draw bamboos and orchids. They are all named "followers who sponge on others".[31]

Liu Xiang, a composer of *ci* works,[32] is one of such "followers" who "write poems and chant songs". He seemed to be a common man who wore coarse clothes, but he was famous for his poems. "Unrestrained in Jin Chu, he made a living by following feudal officials". He once contributed a poem entitled "To the Tune *Qin Yuan Chun*" (*Qin Yuan Chun*) to Xin Qiji, who bestowed him "hundreds and thousands of coins" and "urged him to stay at home for several months". When departing, Xin also gave him "thousands of strings of coins".[33]

Secondly, the commercialization of literature accelerated the spread and consumption of literary works and expanded the influence of writers in literary circles and readers. It not only promoted the development of literature in the local region but also facilitated cultural exchanges between various ethnic groups. Su Shi's poems had already spread as far as the eastern part of Liaoning and other remote places before they were compiled into anthologies. Volume 7 of "Fleeting Gossip by the River Sheng" (*Shengshui Yan Tan Lu*) contains the following descriptions:

> Zhang Yunsou (Zhang Xunmin), on his way to Liao Dynasty as an envoy, once lived in an inn of Youzhou.[34] He found "Old Man's Walk", one of Su Shi's poems, inscribed on the wall. He also learned that some bookstores in Fanyang had published the anthologies, entitled "Collections of Great Poet Su Shi's Poems" (*Da Su Xiao Ji*), which included dozens of poems written by Su Shi. Astonished by the fact that Su Shi was deeply loved by the remote "barbarians", Zhang Yunsou wrote the following lines after the inscribed poem: "Who has ever written the beautiful lines at Youzhou? I am inquired about Su Shi whenever I meet the local Hu people".[35]

The poems of Wei Ye (960–1020 A.D.), a poet of the Northern Song Dynasty, were also spread to Qidan.[36] In "Elegant Sayings in Yuhu" (*Yu Hu Qing Hua*, Vol. 7), there are the following words:

> In Xiangfu Years,[37] diplomats of Qidan were sent to the capital city of Song Dynasty. They said their men were fond of reading Wei Ye's poems. However, they had only the upper part of anthologies of Wei Ye's poems, so they asked for the latter half. It was only then that Emperor Zhenzong learned about the poet Wei Ye. The emperor decided to call in the poet, who had already passed away some years before. He ordered his men to have Wei Ye's poems collected, which were compiled in the ten volumes of "Humble Cottage Collections" (*Cao Tang Ji*). The anthologies were then granted to the diplomats of Qidan.[38]

The cross-border trade between the Northern Song and the surrounding ethnic groups was active. In addition, some envoys and merchants bought collections of poems inland China and brought them back to their homes. As a result, the poems of the Song Dynasty were quickly spread to various parts of the Liaodong and Qidan regions, which exerted significant influence on the local literary circles.

1.2 Stone Inscription

Stone inscription is another important medium for literary spread in the Song Dynasty.

The origin of the stone inscription can be traced back to early primitive societies.[39] The earliest application of stone inscriptions in literary communication is the recording, with stone inscriptions of the achievements of Emperor Qing Shihuang (259–210 B.C.), the first emperor of the Qin Dynasty. In "Inscriptions at Zhi Fu" (*Zhi Fu Ke Shi*), there are the following words: "The courtiers sang high praise of Qing Shihuang's great achievements, and proposed to have them inscribed on stones as monuments to later generations".[40] The inscription of Qing Shihuang's achievements on stones demonstrates "self-consciousness" in communication. In Emperor Pingdi's reign in Western Han Dynasty, Wang Mang commanded Zhen Feng to inscribe classic works on stones which would be handed down to later generations. The inscribed works include *The Books of Changes* (*Yi Jing*), *The Book of Songs* (*Shi Jing*), *The Book of Books* (*Shu Jing*) and *The Commentary of Zuo* (*Zhuo Zhuan*). In the year 175, during Emperor Lingdi's reign in the Eastern Han Dynasty, Cai Yong[41] wrote the calligraphy of the "Six Confucian Classics" and ordered "chisellers to cut the characters into the surface of the stones, which were erected in the court of the National Academy (*taixue*). All scholars were allowed to take rubbings from the Stone Classics". This is an example of purposeful literary communication. In "Biography of Cai Yong" (*Caiyong Zhuan*) in the later part of Volume 6 of "Book of the Later Han" (*Hou Han Shu*), there are the following words: "Once the stone slabs were erected, thousands of carriages brought those people who desired for a look or to take rubbings. People and carriages crowded all the streets and lanes".[42] Here the significance of the stone inscriptions is obvious in literary communications.

As an important medium of literary communication, stone inscriptions were applied a little later than other media. According to the historical records, there were less than ten poems inscribed on stones during the Six Dynasties (of course, the actual number may be larger than the figure in the records). It gradually became popular only since the Tang Dynasty. According to Yang Dianxun's "Index of Prefaces and Postscripts of Stone Inscriptions" (*Shi Ke Ti Ba Suo Yin*), poems inscribed on stones, which were handed down from the Tang Dynasty and categorized in "poems and *ci*" in the book, amounted to 167 pieced only. If further subdivided, there were only 33 stone-inscribed poems during the 144 years from the early Tang Dynasty to the year 762, the first year of the Baoying Period during Emperor Suzong's reign, while there were 134 stone-inscribed poems during the 144 years of the middle and late Tang Dynasty (from the first year of the Guangde Period of Emperor Daizong's reign to the end of the Tang Dynasty). The number in this period is more than four times that of the previous one. Judging from this statistical figure, we learn that stone inscriptions of poems gradually flourished in the Mid-Tang Dynasty. However, the Song Dynasty witnessed the great popularity and rapid development of stone inscriptions. In "Index of Prefaces and Postscripts of Stone Inscriptions" (*Shi Ke Ti Ba Suo Yin*) alone, there is a record of over 900 stone-inscribed poems in the Song Dynasty, which is over five times the number of the Tang Dynasty.

The adoption of stone inscriptions as communication tools was deeply rooted among people in the Song Dynasty. To the people at the time, stone inscriptions could not only cross the barriers of time to have the literary works spread to "infinite day" but also overcome the limits of space to have the works "spread all over the country". Precisely because stone inscriptions could spread the works extensively and for a long time, some unknown poets in the Song Dynasty, in order to have their works "published" to extend their influence, had their own poems inscribed on stones. Song Qi[43] once commented, "On the left bank of the river, some people, incompetent in writing poems, have their poems inscribed on stones. They are generally called 'infatuated poets'".[44] Some other people have their poems inscribed on stone in fear that their works would fall into oblivion in the long run of history. For example, "Chen Wuyou, the magistrate of Zhenghe County, was afraid that his poems would fade away over the long history, so he had them inscribed on stones".[45]

The poems engraved in stones in the Song Dynasty were generally single pieces, but sometimes several poems were engraved together. For example, Ouyang Xiu's several poems were engraved together by Lu Jing:

> At first, Lu Zilü (Lu Jing) collected my thirteen poems entitled "Missing Yingzhou" (*si ying shi*), which were finished during the years when I stayed in the Yingtian Prefecture (*Yingtian Fu*, the auxiliary capital of the Northern Song Dynasty and first capital of the Southern Song Dynasty, present Shangqiu city in Henan Province) and later when I took the position in *Zhongshu Sheng* (the Imperial Secretariat). They were engraved on the stones. Now, I have finished seventeen more poems in Bozhou and Qingzhou, which will be added as an attachment.[46]

Several poems were engraved together. And when they were topped out, they turned into a volume or a book of poems, equivalent to a small anthology. When Lu You engraved Han Ju's poems on the stone, he also engraved Han's poems together.[47]

There are no limitations on the scope of stone engravings. Works of any form or genre can be engraved on stones. Poems, *ci*, *fu* (descriptive poem), odes, records, praises, argumentations, reports, prefaces, postscripts, letters and epitaphs, etc., were all engraved on stones. One simply needs to have a look at the stone carvings from different dynasties, such as those in Wang Chang's "*Jinshi Cuibian*" (Selected Rubbings of Ancient Inscriptions) and Lu Zengxiang's "*Baqiongshi Jinshi Buzheng*" (Supplements to Epigraphy in Eight Jade Chambers), to understand this point.

The texts produced by rubbings of stone carvings during the Song Dynasty have specific naming terms, such as "*bei ben*" (tablet inscription) and "*tie ben*" (copy inscription), or "*shi ben*"(stone inscription) and "*mo ben*" (ink inscription) or simply "*mo ben*" (imitating inscription) and "*ta ben*"(rubbing inscription).

From the perspective of the subjects (or participants) of the stone carvings, there is a distinction between "the founders of the stone tablets" and "the engravers of the stone tablets". On some stone tablets, the names of both "the founders of the stone" and "the engravers of the stone" are generally inscribed together. For example, at the end of the stone carving "Record of Hunan Tower" of the Song Dynasty, there are the following words:

> In the fourth month of the first year of *renwu* in Emperor Chongning's reign (1102 AD), written by Li Yanbi of Luling, handwritten by Zhou Mian of Huayuan, inscribed in the seal style by Cheng Lin of Poyang, and erected by Zhang Guan of Zhugong…engraved by Long Bian and Long Shi of Guizhou.[48]

In comparison, the founders of the stone tablets were temporary and non-professional, while the engravers of the stone tablets (stone carvers) were professionals. Let's look at an example to illustrate further:

> There was a master stonecarver named Li Zhongning in Jiujian Prefecture. His skill in engraving characters was exceptional, and Huang Tingjian, the royal historian, named his residence *"zuo yu fang"* (Jade Carving Workshop). In the early Chongning period, an imperial edict was issued to compile the names of conservative loyal officers. The prefect summoned Li Zhongning and urged him to engrave the names. Zhongning replied, "I come from a humble home, and it was only through my skill in engraving the poems by Su Shi and Huang Tingjian that I managed to make a decent living. But today, to be associated with treacherous individuals, I truly cannot bear to do it".[49]

Li Zhongning would rather engrave the poems of Su Shi and Huang Tingjian on stones, which ensured he would be able "to make a decent living". This reveals that he made a living by engaging in this profession. It also suggests that large quantities of the works by Su and Huang be engraved on stones. In the book "*Dongpo Shihua Lu*" ("On Poems of Su Dongpo") written by Chen Xiuming of the Yuan Dynasty, there are the following words: "'*Man Ting Fang*' (To the tune *Man Ting Fang*) of Su Dongpo (Su Shi) was widely spread across the country through stone engravings".[50] From this, we can learn that the wide spread of Su's poems through stone engravings.

During the Song Dynasty, there were two types of inscriptions on stone tablets: "self-engraved inscriptions" and "inscriptions engraved by others", with the latter being the most common. In the fifth year of Chongning (1106), Huang Jing engraved ten poems of "Poems to the Tune *Jiu Quan Zi*", which were written by the poet Pan Lang of the Song Dynasty, on stone tablets by the West Lake of Hangzhou, with the purpose of "spreading and preserving the works".[51] This is a typical example of "inscriptions engraved by others".

From the perspective of those who erected the stone tablets, "inscriptions engraved by others" may further be divided into those under official requests and those for private purposes. From the perspective of the nature and purpose of the inscriptions, there is a distinction between commercial inscriptions (for-profit) and non-profit inscriptions. Non-profit inscriptions aim to spread works and expand the influence of the authors or the people involved rather than making money from selling them. Commercial inscriptions, on the other hand, primarily focus on selling and making a profit but also serve the purpose of spreading the works. Commercial inscriptions are more complex: whether they are official or private ones, as long as they are reproduced and sold for a profit, they fall into the category of commercial inscriptions. Among these, the most notable are the temple monks who specialized in stone engraving. In the historical records and works on stone engravings of the Song Dynasty, the majority of inscriptions were carved by monks. This is mainly because temples were frequented by literati, travellers and worshippers, making the poems on the stones in the temples easy to spread or copy. The monks in charge of the temples, mountain lodging and monastic institutions were primarily responsible for managing and selling the stone inscriptions.[52] Such stone engravings by specialized monks were often driven by profit motives.

Literati often had their literary works engraved on stones by monks in the temples. In Wei Tai's work "*Dong Xuan Bi Lu*" ("Written records at Dong Xuan"), there are the following words:

> When Chen Shugu obtained the poem (i.e. Li Shu's poem "*ti zhougongdi ling*", or On the Tomb of Emperor Zhougong), he quickly asked temple monks to engrave it on a stone and made a hundred copies, which were then distributed in the capital. Soon after, Emperor Renzong heard about the poem and sent it to the Imperial Academy.[53]

Qin Guan's poems, on the other hand, were often sent to monks in Hangzhou to be engraved on stones. In a letter to Huang Tingjian, Qin Guan wrote,

> You have kindly handwritten my works "Longjing" and "Xuezhai", and your calligraphy and painting were exceptionally exquisite, far beyond what my humble literary skills could deserve. I have already sent them to monks in Qiantang to be engraved in stone tablets.[54]

Stone engraving became an important platform for poets of the time to "publish" their works.

In some cases, monks in temples would request literary works from literati to be engraved on stones, which is similar to the modern practice of "articles written on invitation" for newspapers and magazines. For example, in the preface of Huang Shang's "*Yaochi Yue*" (moon of the heaven), there are the following words: "I wrote two poems '*Yunshan*' (mountains in clouds) and '*Yanbo*' (mist-covered waters) to the Tune '*Yaochi Yue*'. The monk in Jingyan Temple requested them to be engraved on stones, so I sent him these works".[55] Su Shi's literary works were also often taken by monks of Hangzhou temples to be engraved on stones.[56]

One of the ways stone inscriptions were spread was the rubbing and sales. Copyright didn't seem to be a problem for stone inscriptions during the Song Dynasty. Especially for the inscriptions on cliffs (texts directly engraved on natural cliffs), anyone could go to "print" them for sale. What Zhang Lei read of "*Zhongxing Song*" (The Resurgence of Tang Dynasty) was a copy sold by a "peddler" ("Someone brings this poem from stone tablets into my room, and I open my dizzy eyes immediately and have a look at it"[57]). In the early Southern Song Dynasty, Hu Zai visited Wuxi and bought a poem of Yuan Jie's "Einai Qu" with a hundred coins, which was also a copy of the inscriptions sold by a "peddler".

For stone engravings (raw stones are processed into stone tablets with different sizes and shapes, which were then engraved with texts), in theory, the "copyright" belongs to those who erected the stones. However, most stone tablets were placed outdoors or in the wild, and visitors could freely make rubbings of them, so there is no ownership or "patent rights". At most, there is a "first rubbing" right. Let's take a look at an anecdote about Fan Zhongyan, the Chinese poet, politician, philosopher, writer, military strategist and notable scholar-official of the Song Dynasty:

> When Fan Wenzheng (Fan Zhongyan) was guarding Poyang, a scholar presented him with a poem. The poem was written beautifully and won the favor of Fan Zhongyan, who extended his courtesy to the scholar. The scholar claimed that he had never had enough to eat in his life, and there was no one in the world colder and hungrier than him. At the time the calligraphy of Ouyang Xun was highly popular in the capital, with each rubbing of Inscriptions at Jianfu Temple selling for one thousand coins. Fan Zhongyan prepared paper and ink for him, intending to have him transcribe the inscriptions at Jianfu Temple and sell them in the capital.[58]

Obviously, the tablet of Jianfu Temple with Ouyang Xun's inscriptions was not erected by Fan Zhongyan or the scholar. It was just a popular one at the time, so Fan Zhongyan prepared paper and ink for the scholar to make a thousand rubbings to sell in the capital to make ends meet.

Of course, if someone claims ownership of a stone tablet, then they naturally have the right to sell rubbings of the stone inscriptions. During the Song Dynasty, there were frequent incidents of stealing tablets to obtain illicit wealth. Liu Kezhuang once said that someone named Xue stole an old stone tablet and used it to make rubbings, and the relevant books collected by scholars and sold by book vendors in the capital were all produced by Xue.[59] At the end of the Xuanhe period, Miao Zhongxian, the prefect of Xuzhou, monopolized the stone tablet inscribed with Su Shi's "*Huang Lou Fu*" ("Ode to the Yellow Tower") and made a fortune by selling rubbings. This also illustrates the phenomenon of monopolizing the "right to sell rubbings" at that time:

> During Su Dongpo's exile to the south, there was a demand from the public to completely destroy all the poems written by Su Dongpo, and

the emperor issued a decree to execute this order. As a result, the literary works of Su Dongpo stored in the homes of scholars and officials were not dared to be brought out. Officials were afraid of causing trouble, and most of the stone inscriptions were destroyed. The Yellow Tower of Xuzhou was constructed by Su Dongpo himself. Su Zhe, the younger brother of Su Dongpo, wrote a *fu* poem for that and Su Dongpo personally inscribed it on a stone tablet. The Prefect of Xuzhou at that time couldn't bear to destroy the tablet, so he threw it into the moat and changed the name of the tower to "Observing the Wind." In the later years of Emperor Huizong's reign, the ban was somewhat eased. At that time, it became fashionable for nobles and aristocrats to possess articles by Su Dongpo, and those who sold his works made a fortune. Therefore, gradually, artisans began to make rubbings of the stone inscriptions from the moat. There was a man named Miao Zhongxian, who was the Prefect of Xuzhou at the time. Miao ordered the subordinates to dig out the stone tablet. Day and night, they made rubbings and produced thousands of copies. But suddenly, Miao Zhongxian said to his subordinates, "The ban on Su Dongpo's works still is valid, so why should this stone tablet be preserved? It should be immediately destroyed." When people heard that the stone tablet had been destroyed, they were eager to get the copies and the prices of rubbings and imprints increased even more. When Miao Zhongxian's term of office ended, he brought all the rubbings to the capital and sold them, making an immeasurable amount of money.[60]

Miao Zhongxian was shrewd as a businessman (although he was overly cunning and committed the grave sin of destroying cultural relics). He successfully took advantage of the public's desire to acquire Su Dongpo's writings. He first claimed ownership of the stone tablet with inscriptions of the "Ode to the Yellow Tower", made thousands of rubbings and imprints and then destroyed the tablet, cutting off the source of the rubbings. As a result, the prices of the original rubbings skyrocketed. True to his plan, he brought thousands of ink copies to the capital for sales, reaping profits beyond calculation.

The selling price of rubbings from stone tablets generally fluctuates depending on the fame and status of the author and calligrapher of the inscription. We may take a look at what is recorded in Volume 2 of *"Xiangshan Yelu"* ("Records of Xiangshan"):

Ouyang Xiu wrote the epitaph for Shi Manqing's tomb, and Su Zimei wrote the calligraphy, while Shao Yu wrote the seal scripts. The poet and monk Mi Yan[61] from Shandong repeatedly urged Ouyang Xiu to quickly finish it. The work was completed. ... Ouyang Xiu and Su Zimei told Mi Yan, "Thought the tablet is finished, we are not yet to have it rubbed and printed." Mi Yan couldn't deny the beauty of the poem. One day, Ouyang Xiu unexpectedly saw the rubbing at the Liyuan Temple and asked the monk, "Where did you get it?" The monk replied, "I bought it with five hundred *wen* of money" Ouyang Xiu was angry. He turned to Mi Yan upon his arrival, saying, "Why did you sell my work to a commoner for five hundred coins? Don't you have any sense?" Mi Yan humorously replied, "the present price is 383 coins more than other copies." Ouyang Xiu became even angrier and asked, "What is this?" Mi Yan said, "Don't you remember that when you took the first in the imperial *jinshi* exam, a commoner copied your new *fu* works and sold them on the streets with the price 2 *wen* or 12 coins. Today the price is 500 *wen* for each, which is much more expensive than those of the earlier ones." At the words, Ouyang Xiu felt at ease.[62]

In the early years, though Ouyang Xiu was No. 1 in the provincial examination and became a *jinshi*, he did not have a high literary reputation. Therefore, a rubbing of his "*xin fu*" (new *fu* work) was sold for only "two *wen*". However, when he became a master in the literary world, a copy of his epitaph for Shi Manqing's tomb was sold by the monk Miyan at a price of "five hundred *wen*". Ouyang Xiu thought it was sold too cheaply, which degraded his status and the value of his literary work. It seems that Ouyang Xiu was quite familiar with the market price of inscriptions. His poems and writings were often published and sold, so it was only with a comparison of prices that he criticized the lower price set by Mi Yan. Moreover, from the phrase "sold them on the streets", we learn that at the time, the sellers of stone rubbings called out and sold them along the streets, similar to the "newsboys" who sell newspapers nowadays.

For the cultural exchanges between China and foreign countries at that time, the sales of stone rubbings were also an important channel. Koreans often came to China to purchase stone inscriptions. "*Pan Zi Zhen Shi Hua*" records that "a set of stone tablets with inscriptions of Yu Xiulao's poem was placed at Jinshan Temple. Whenever Gyerim (Korea) people pay tribute in China, they would purchase several hundred model copies before their return".[63]

A second way of spreading stone inscriptions was the mutual presentation of gifts among friends. There are many records of this practice, such as "carving poems on stones to leave them to friends";[64] "obtaining the letter of Yan Lugong (Yan Zhenqing) to Li Guangbi asking for loan of rice, he personally copied it onto a stone and sent the rubbings to relatives and friends";[65] "sending rubbings from stone inscriptions to show the admiration";[66] "sending poetry rubbings from stones inscriptions for appreciation";[67] and "subsequently ordering stone rubbings to be made as gifts to fellow enthusiasts".[68]

The third way of spreading stone inscriptions is the self-rubbing and copying by passers-by. For example,

> In the Daguang period, Liu Qi (courtesy name Sili) from Wenyang went to the peak of Mount Tai, where he saw inscriptions on all four sides of

a stone stele. He then made rubbings of the inscriptions and took them home.

At the beginning of the Zhenghe period, I (Zhao Mingcheng) personally went to Mount Tai and obtained the inscriptions of two stone tablets, which I included in my collection".[69]

Liu Zihui also said, "Once during my travels between Qin Luo, Zhao, and Wei, I encountered numerous magnificent and fragmented stone steles. Many were beautifully written, but some were damaged and unidentifiable. Nonetheless, I still made rubbings and took them home".[70]

The spread of stone inscriptions has its unique value and function. Oral transmission (singing, reciting, etc.) is generally limited by time and space, making it prone to distortion and easy to be lost to the world. Hand copying is time-consuming and slows down the dissemination process. As Ju Yizun, a Qing Dynasty scholar, once stated, "With the appearance of more and more poems, people get tired of hand-copying. Then they are published".[71] This serves as the evidence. On the other hand, the spread of stone inscriptions is characterized by convenience, reproducibility, wide distribution, longevity, authenticity and appreciation value.

Convenience means the quick and convenient process of stone rubbing, allowing readers to rub and copy as much as they need. Readers can even do it themselves. Reproducibility means that even if the rubbings are lost after many years, they can be reproduced based on the original stone inscriptions. If the original stone is worn out or destroyed, it can be re-engraved on a new stone (although replication from rubbings may result in some distortion). Wide distribution means that stone inscriptions are not limited by space and can be spread far and wide. Longevity means that stone tablets can be permanently preserved, unlike woodblocks, which are easily damaged. Even if the rubbings are damaged or lost, they can still be reproduced based on the original stones after thousands of years, ensuring endless transmission. As was stated in Su Shi's poem *"Lanxiu Ting"* (Lanxiu Pavilion): "Poems are written and engraved on stone tablets, and they will be passed down for thousands of years".[72] It highlights the longevity nature of stone inscriptions.

Because of the aforementioned reasons, to prevent the loss and disappearance of works, the people of the Song Dynasty first chose to engrave them in stones for permanent preservation. For example, when Su Shi read the poem "Palace Lyrics" by Lady Huarui of the Later Shu Dynasty, he found it to be very remarkable, which was comparable to Wang Jian's work. Deeming the poem indispensable, he had it engraved on stones.[73] When Wu Zeng travelled to the southern part of the Yangtze River, he read Pan Lang's *"Ti Shijing Jueju"* (Four-Character Quatrain on Stone Well). Fearing it would be lost, he hoped that "Master Fa Zhen could carve it in stone".[74] Many lost poems and lyrics that were not recorded in anthologies or collections were preserved through stone inscriptions. Tang Guizhang's work, *"Ci of Song Dynasty Inscribed on Stones"*, is a compilation of works from 14 different poets. None of the poems were taken from selected anthologies of poems of the Song Dynasty but were merely found in stone inscriptions.[75] This demonstrates the unique value and function of stone inscriptions.

The convenience, reproducibility and longevity of stone inscriptions surpassed those of woodblock printing at that time (especially single-piece woodblock printing). Therefore, the Song Dynasty seemed to attach more importance to stone inscriptions than woodblock printing. When Shu Dan accused Su Shi, he said that "Su Shi's short works were engraved on wooden boards, and longer works were engraved on stones, which were widely spread domestically and internationally".[76] This reflects the attitude of people in the Song Dynasty towards stone inscriptions. Sometimes, people of the Song Dynasty considered wooden blocks easy to damage and lost, so they transferred the text from woodblocks to stone inscriptions in the hope of its ever-lasting transmission.

The authenticity and appreciation value of stone inscriptions pertain to the calligraphy of the inscribed poems. Most of the inscriptions were written by famous calligraphers. For example, Ouyang Xiu's "Record of the Old Tippler's Pavilion" (*Zui Weng Ting Ji*) was inscribed by Su Shi,[77] while his "Preface to the Collection of Ancient Inscriptions" (*Ji Gu Lu Zi Xu*) was engraved by the renowned calligrapher Cai Xiang.[78] Calligraphy itself is a precious art. Therefore, stone inscriptions possess a dual artistic value (both literary and calligraphic value). Only stone inscriptions could maintain the original style and spirit of the calligraphy (i.e., authenticity), which other media of the time could not replace. At that time, when readers appreciated or copied the calligraphy of their contemporaries or predecessors, they primarily relied on stele rubbings and reproductions. Hence, people of the Song Dynasty had a strong inclination towards storing stele rubbings. When several pieces were compiled into a volume, they served as both reading materials for literary works and calligraphy models for appreciation and copying.

Stone inscription is not only a medium for the communication of literary works but also a carrier of calligraphy art. Due to the widespread dissemination of stone carvings during the Song Dynasty, scholars and literati collected, organized and studied stone inscriptions, which led to the emergence of a specialized field of study called "*jinshi xue*" (study of (inscriptions on) metal (mostly bronze) and stone) or epigraphy. Stone inscriptions combine literary value, calligraphic value and historical value, making special contributions to Chinese cultural history.

1.3 Wall Inscriptions

Wall inscriptions refer to those poems that authors or "enthusiasts" wrote on the walls of buildings, such as post stations, mansions, temples and bridges, for pedestrians to view and copy.

Compared to dynamic woodblock printing and stone engraving, wall inscription is a static means of communication. As an information carrier, walls themselves cannot circulate and spread like printed books or engraved stone tablets. They can only be transmitted through the reading and copying by pedestrians. Therefore, the speed and breadth of dissemination through wall inscriptions are not as fast as woodblock printing and stone engraving.

However, wall inscriptions are "free", non-commercial and effortless means of communication. Poets can freely and publicly publish their works on various buildings without the need for printers or stone engravers, let alone printing plates, stone tablets or carving tools. People can simply use a brush to write on the walls or even use tools like pomegranate peels for writing.[79] Readers of the poems could recite, memorize and transcribe the poems without the cost of money. Of course, the range of dissemination is also limited, as one cannot read the poems without personally seeing them.

The practice of wall inscriptions started to be popular in the Tang Dynasty. By the middle Tang Dynasty, Bai Juyi's poems were already "inscribed on the walls of imperial ministries, Taoist and Buddhist temples, post stations, and city walls".[80] Li Bai's original inscriptions on the walls of Hill Peak Temple in Shuzhou during the glorious age of the Tang Dynasty[81] and Luo Yin's inscriptions on the walls of Ganlu Temple in Zhenjiang in the late Tan Dynasty[82] were both preserved until the Song Dynasty.

During the Song Dynasty, wall inscriptions became a platform for poets to freely "publish" their works. As long as they had the inspiration for poetic creation, the poets would inscribe their poems on walls for public display. In the book "*Qingxiang Zaji*" (Vol. 8), there is such a recording:

> Zhang Shixun had a fondness for landscapes. When he was the magistrate of Shaowu, he often visited Buddhist temples, where he would be inspired to compose poems and leave them inscribed on the walls. He often visited Xian Temple, and once wrote a poem there: "Xian Temple is nestled deep in the Western Mountains…". He also visited Baogaiyan Temple when he left a poem: "As a distinguished guest…". Furthermore, during his journey to Jianning County by way of the Luoyang Village, he encountered treacherous and breath-taking steep mountain paths that defied description. He composed two verses at the village temple: "When the Basil flowers are in full blossom, how many times I get drunken".[83]

In Huang Sheng's "*Zhongxing Cihua*", there are similar records:

> A man from Longxi, known as You Zixi, travelled to Jiangxi to participate in the imperial examination. As he ascended the stairs of a tavern, he encountered a group of young men sitting together, unaware of his literary background. In the midst of their revelry, the young men started composing poems on the wall, each filled with arrogance and disregard for others. You Zixi stood up and asked to write a poem, which was met with ridicule from the young men. However, as he began writing, his verses revealed profound meaning and brilliance. Upon reading his poem, the young men quietly slipped away, humbled by its excellence.[84]

These "young men" who had some literary skills wanted to inscribe their poems on the wall for public display, indicating the prevailing trend of wall inscriptions at the time.

Wall inscription was a fixed and popular form of literary communication at the time. Therefore, during the Song Dynasty, literati would always pay attention to the poems written on walls whenever they arrived at a new place. Zhou Bangyan, in his *ci* work entitled "Huan Xi Sha", wrote the following lines: "Dismounting from the horse, I firstly search for inscribed poems on the walls; going out of home, I casually memorize the names of villages". Yan Shu and Huang Tingjian also mentioned that they had the experience of "dismounting from the horse" to search for inscribed poems on the walls:

> Yan Shu once passed by Yangzhou on his way to Hangzhou. When he rested at the Daming Temple, closing his eyes, he strolled slowly. He instructed his attendants to recite the poems on the walls but reminded them not to mention the names and ranks of the authors. As there were few poems worth reading in their entirety, only few poems were recited from the beginning to the end. Yan Shu then asked the attendant to recite another poem, which read "the music composed by Emperor Yang of Sui Dynasty to the tune *shuidiao*...." Appreciating the quality of the poem, Yan Shu asked who was the author of the poem, and learned that it was a poem of Wang Qi, a magistrate in Jiangdu.
>
> On his way back from the south, he arrived at Nanhua Bamboo Pavilion. He instructed his attendants to recite the poems on the walls, again cautioning them not to mention the names and titles of the authors. After a long time, the attendant recited a quatrain: "There is no need for the monks in the mountain to hold banquets to welcome...". Singing high praise of the poem, Yan Shup looked at the name on the wall and said, 'Indeed, this is a poem written by Ge Minxiu.'[85]

According to records, poets at the time would generally sign their titles and names when writing poems on walls.

Since the literati of the Song Dynasty had the habit of seeking, reciting and transcribing poems on walls wherever they went, many poets would "publish" their poems by writing them on walls to gain recognition from famous critics and increase their reputation. Wang Qi, Qin Guan, He Zhu and others from the Northern Song Dynasty became famous because of their poems on the walls. As illustrated earlier, "after reading Wang Qi's poem on the wall, Yan Shu invited him to have a meal together and go sightseeing" and "even promoted him for official position as his own subordinate". Qin Guan admired Su Shi's literary fame and was eager to meet him but had no opportunity to get acquainted with him. So he intentionally imitated Su Shi's writing style and wrote poems on the walls that Su Shi would pass by, hoping to gain Su Shi's recognition. When Su Shi saw it, he was indeed pleased. From then on, Qin Guan became a friend of Su Shi and made a name for himself.[86]

People of the Song Dynasty valued the preservation of poems on the walls to ensure that more people could recite and copy them. Those poems written by famous poets were particularly cherished and rarely rubbed away. For example, when Kou Zhun, the famous politician and poet of the Northern Song Dynasty, visited a monk's residence in Shanfu, each poem he wrote was protected with a green silk cover by the local people.[87] However, there is also an exception:

> Xie Wuyi once wrote a poem "To the tune *Jiang Cheng Zi*" at the wall of an inn of Apricot Flower Village in Huangzhou, which read as "the wine flags float in Apricot Flower Village, …". Passersby would always demand a brush from the innkeeper, which caused the innkeeper great trouble, so he smeared it with mud.[88]

This anecdote also demonstrates how eye-catching and beloved Xie Wuyi's poem on the wall was at that time, as well as the Song Dynasty people's love for copying poems on the walls.

To preserve the literary works, the authors of poems, *ci* works, anecdotes and historical records in the Song Dynasty paid attention to collecting and recording wall inscriptions, thereby expanding their field of communication. Almost all poetic anthologies and lyrical anecdotes include poems on the walls. In Volume 16 and Volume 17 of "*Nenggai Zai Man Lu*" ("Notes of Neng Gai Studio"), there is "To the Tune *Lang Tao Sha*" "written on the walls of an inn in Shanfu" by a lady, "To the Tune *Dian Jiang Chun*" written by an anonymous person who "carved with a double-edged fine-toothed knife" on the "Mud Wall" in Caizhou, "To the Tune *Dian Jiang Chun*)" on the walls of the South Zen Temple in Fengcheng and "To the Tune *Yu Lou Chun*".[89] In Volume 59 of Hu Zai's "*Tiaoxi Yuyin Conghua* (Series of poetic notes by the recluse of the Brook Tiao)", there are also records of "poems on the walls of the post stations" which are "coarse and bold in language but admirable in tone", written by an anonymous person who imitated Su Shi's "Thoughts on the Red Cliff".[90] A large number of poems of the Song Dynasty were preserved and recorded in poetic and lyrical anecdotes and historical records through wall inscriptions. The famous poem "To the Tune *Pu Sa Man*" written by Li Bai, a poet of the Tang Dynasty, was passed down because it was "written on the walls of the Cangshui Post Station in Dingzhou" during the Northern Song Dynasty.[91]

Due to the popularity of single-page woodblock printing, stone engraving and wall inscriptions, the literary works of Song Dynasty writers were able to be widely and promptly circulated. Readers and writers in the Song Dynasty primarily relied on single-page engraved editions and stone tablet editions to read and familiarize themselves with contemporary writers' literary works. This is similar to how we read and gradually understand the works of contemporary poets and writers through scattered newspapers and magazines nowadays. It was often during their later years or after their death that one could access a writer's complete collection. For example, in Ouyang Xiu's reading of Su Shi's poetry and prose, most of them were single-page editions (rubbings). In "*Qu Wei Jiu Wen*", there are the following words, "Dongpo's poetry and prose, once finished, were soon circulated. Every time when a poem arrived, Ouyang Xiu would be delighted all day long". When Wang Anshi read Su Shi's stones inscription of "*Biao Zhong Guan* Stele", he exclaimed, "This is great as Sima Qian's '*San Sheng Shi Jia*' ('Conferring Royal Titles to The Three Princes') in *Shiji* ('Records of the Historian')". What Wang Anshi read was also a single-page stele edition shown by others.[92] In Zeng Jili's "*Tingzhai Shihua*" ("Talks on Poetry in Tingzhai"), the author made a comparison between Huang Tingjian's poem "Wuxi Stele" and Zhang Lei's poem:

> On Reading "*Zhongxing Song*" ("The Resurgence of Tang Dynasty"), and stated: "with the popularity of rubbing poems from stone inscriptions, it is easy for us to make a clearer comparison of their merits". In comparison with Huang Tingjian's poems, Zhang Lei's work is a giant in the presence of a super-giant – to feel dwarfed in comparison.[93]

What Zeng Jili read was also a copy of rubbings from stone tablets. Huang Tingjian also explicitly stated in his poem, "Half my life I've read rubbing editions".[94] This reveals that the poets of that time often read the works of others in the form of single-page "rubbing editions", similar to today's loose-leaf editions.

There is an important issue worth our attention. In the Song Dynasty, there were both single-page dissemination and book publication. So today, when we analyse the comments of literary critics in the Song Dynasty, we must carefully check whether the critics have obtained the entire works they commented on or whether their comments were based on partial works. For example, in the early Southern Song Dynasty, Wang Zhuo wrote "*Biji man zhi* (Commentary from Biji Lane on *ci* works')", which provided many critiques on ancient and contemporary *ci* poets. However, some of the contemporaneous *ci* poems written by living poets were not yet collected and published. In Chao Buzhi's "Assessments of the Poems in Current Dynasty",[95] there are discussions about Huang Tingjian's *ci* poems, but at that time, Huang's *ci* works had not been collected and published yet. Li Qingzhao, in her "Critique of *ci* Poems", evaluated the strengths and weaknesses of *ci* poets in the Northern Song Dynasty, but she may not have read their complete works. Therefore, today, when interpreting and analysing the viewpoints of literary critics of the Song Dynasty (or even other eras), it is crucial to carefully check whether the critic had access to the writer's complete works and whether they referred to specific works or complete works, so as to avoid misunderstandings.

Notes

1. Wang, Mingqing. 2001. *Hui Zhu lu* ("Swaying Deertail Whisk"), Vol. 7. Shanghai Bookstore Publishing House, 134.
2. Hui, Hong. 2001. *Lengzhai yehua* ("Night Talk in the Studio of Coldness"), Vol. 10. *Song Yuan biji xiaoshuo daguan* (Grand View of Story-Telling Novels in Song and Yuan Dynasties). Shanghai Chinese Classics Publishing House, 2223.
3. Ye, Dehui. *Shu you keban zhishi* ("The Beginning of Engraving-Printed Books"), *Keban sheng yu wudai* ("Popularity of Engraving Printing in the Five Dynasties"), *Shulin qinghua* ("Thoughts on Books"), Vol. 1. Liaoning Education Press, 1998; Zhang, Zhaokui, Section 2 of Chapter 3, *Zhongguo chuban shi gaiyao* ("Outline of Chinese Publishing History"). Shanxi People's Publishing House, 1985. "Five Dynasties" or "Five Dynasties and Ten Kingdoms" (907–960) was an era of division and political disturbance in 10th century imperial China in between the Tang Dynasty and the Song Dynasty, two highly successful dynasties. During that brief era, when China was truly a multistate system, five short-lived regimes succeeded one another in control of the old imperial heartland in northern China, hence the name *Wudai* (Five Dynasties). During those same years, 10 relatively stable regimes occupied sections of southern and western China, so the period is also referred to as that of the *Shiguo* (Ten Kingdoms). See https://www.britannica.com/place/China/The-Five-Dynasties-and-the-Ten-Kingdoms.
4. Zhu, Bian. 2002. *Quwei jiuwen* ("Old Stories at the Winding Wei River"), Vol. 3. Zhonghua Book Company, 120.
5. *Pipa*, a plucked string instrument with a fretted fingerboard; four-stringed Chinese lute.
6. Ye, Mengde. 1990. *Shilin bishu luhua* ("Records of Summer Resort in Stone Forest"), Vol. 2, Shanghai Bookstore Publishing House, 16.
7. Hu, Zai. 1962. *Tiaoxi yuyin conghua* ("Series of Poetic Notes by the Recluse of the Brook Tiao"). *Gaozhai Shihua* ("Poetic Notes in Elegant Study"), Vol. 34. People's Literature Publishing House, 229.
8. Su, Shi. 1986. *Sushi wenji* ("A Collection of Su Shi's Works"), Vol. 53. Zhonghua Book Company, 1575.
9. Su, Shi. 1986. *Da Liumian Tuchao shu* ("Reply to Du Chao Liumian"), *Sushi wenji* (A Collection of Su Shi's Works), Vol. 49, Zhonghua Book Company, 1429.
10. Zhu, Bian. 2002. *Quwei jiuwen* ("Old Stories at the Winding Wei River"), Vol. 7. Zhonghua Book Company, 186.
11. Zhu, Bian. 2002. *Quwei jiuwen* ("Old Stories at the Winding Wei River"), Vol. 8. Zhonghua Book Company, 204–205.
12. Su, Shi. 1986. *Da Chen Chuandao* ("Reply to Chen Chuandao"), *Sushi wenji* ("A Collection of Su Shi's Works"), Vol. 53, Zhonghua Book Company, 1574.
13. Wang, Pizhi. 2001. *Shengshui yan tan lu* ("Fleeting Gossip by the River Sheng"), Vol. 2, *Song Yuan biji xiaoshuo daguan* ("Grand View of Story-Telling Novels in Song and Yuan Dynasties"). Shanghai Chinese Classics Publishing House, 1237.
14. A courtesy name (*zi*; lit. "character"), also known as a style name, is a name bestowed upon one at adulthood in addition to one's given name. This practice is a tradition in the East Asian cultural sphere, including China, Japan, Korea and Vietnam. A courtesy name is not to be confused with an art name, another frequently mentioned term for an alternative name in East Asia, which is closer to the concept of a pen name or a pseudonym. See https://www.definitions.net/definition/courtesy%20name.
15. Zhou, Mi. 1988. *Guixin zashi* ("Miscellaneous Records of Guixin Years"). Zhonghua Book Company, 19.
16. Ouyang, Xun. 1965. *Yiwen leiju* ("A Collection of Art and Literary Works"). Vol. 88, Shanghai Chinese Classics Publishing House, 1517.

17 Fan, Ye. 1965. *Wang Chong zhuan* (Biography of Wang Chong), *Houhan shu* ("History of the Later Han Dynasty"), Vol. 49, Zhonghua Book Company, 1965: 1629.
18 Ye, Dehui. 1998. *Shushi zhi yuanqi* ("The Beginning of Bookstores"). *Shulin qinghua* ("Thoughts on Books"), Vol. 2. Liaoning Education Press, 27.
19 The Great Xiangguo temple is located in the centre of the city of Kaifeng, the capital city of Northern Song Dynasty. The temple was a royal temple and is one of the ten famous temples in history. During Northern Song Dynasty, the temple was worshipped and respected by emperors, and became one of China's most vibrant centres of arts and calligraphy; a hub for poets, artists and musicians; and a meeting place for all classes of society.
20 Wu, Chuhou. 1985. *Qingxiang zaji* (Miscellaneous Records of the Blue Box), Vol. 2, Zhonghua Book Company, 20.
21 Zhu, Bian. 2002. *Quwei jiuwen* ("Old Stories at the Winding Wei River"), Vol. 4. Zhonghua Book Company, 142.
22 Li, Qingzhao. 1979. *Jinshilu houxu* (afterword to Records of Bronze and Stone Inscriptions). Wang, Zhongwen (eds.). *Li Qingzhao ji jiao zhu* ("Collated and Annotated Complete Works of Li Qingzhao"). People's Literature Publishing House, 177.
23 Hu, Zai. 1962. *Tiaoxi yuyin conghua* ("Series of Poetic Notes by the Recluse of the Brook Tiao"), Vol. 58. People's Literature Publishing House, 401.
24 Wei, Tai. 1983. *Dongxuan bilu* ("Written Records at Dong Xuan"), Vol. 3, Zhonghua Book Company, 30; Zhu, Bian. 2002. *Quwei jiuwen* ("Old Stories at the Winding Wei River"), Vol. 4. Zhonghua Book Company,142.
25 Su, Shi. 1986. *Lun Gaoli maishu lihai zhazi sanshou* ("Three Poems on Sales of Books to Korean Convoys"), *Sushi wenji* ("A Collection of Su Shi's Works"), Vol. 35, Zhonghua Book Company, 995.
26 Wu, Zimu. 1982. *Tuan xing* ("Guilds"), *Pu xi* ("Shops and Stalls"). *Meng liang lu* ("Records of Dreams of Glory"), Vol. 13. China Business Press, 104–107; Zhou, Mi. 1988. *Guixin zashi* ("Miscellaneous Records of Guixin Years"). Zhonghua Book Company, 167.
27 Ye, Dehui. 1998. *Shushi zhi yuanqi* ("The Beginning of Bookstores"). *Shulin qinghua* ("Thoughts on Books"), Vol. 2. Liaoning Education Press, 27.
28 Zhou, Mi. 1988. *Guixin zashi* ("Miscellaneous Records of Guixin Years"). Zhonghua Book Company, 252.
29 Su, Shi. 1986. Yu Tong zhanglao ("To Monastery Tong"). *Sushi wenji* ("A Collection of Su Shi's Works"), Vol. 61. Zhonghua Book Company, 1877.
30 Wang, Pizhi. 2001. *Shengshui yan tan lu* ("Fleeting Gossip by the River Sheng"), Vol. 10, *Song Yuan biji xiaoshuo daguan* ("Grand View of Story-Telling Novels in Song and Yuan Dynasties"). Shanghai Chinese Classics Publishing House, 1306–1307.
31 Wu, Zimu. 1982. *Meng liang lu* ("Records of Dreams of Glory"), Vol. 19. China Business Press, 169.
32 *ci* (lyric) originated in the Tang and the Five Dynasties, and developed to maturity as a new literary form in the Song Dynasty. Also known as "lyric with a melody", "*yuefu* poetry" or "long and short verses", *ci* developed from poetry. Its main feature is that it is set to music and sung. Each piece of *ci* has a name for its tune. There are strict requirements for the number of lines and the number of characters as well as tone pattern and rhyming in different tunes. In terms of length, *ci* is divided into short lyrics, medium lyrics and long lyrics. In terms of musical system, a piece of *ci* is usually divided into two stanzas of *que* or *pian*, as ancient Chinese called them. Occasionally, it consists of three or four stanzas, or just one. Thus, the music can be played once or many times. In terms of style, *ci* falls into the graceful and restrained school and the bold and unconstrained school. The former is delicate and sentimental, often describing family life and love, while the latter is bold and free, often expressing one's vision about major social issues like the fate of the nation. Many literati and

scholars of the Song Dynasty composed *ci* lyrics, which played a significant part in promoting its development. Today, *ci* is generally not set to music and sung. Rather, it is a literary form composed in accordance with the requirements of a music tune. See https://www.chinesethought.cn/EN/shuyu_show.aspx?shuyu_id=3440.

33 Yue, Ke. 1981. *Ting shi* (History at Rectangle Table), Vol. 2, Zhonghua Book Company, 23.
34 Youzhou, one of the nice states (zhou) in ancient China. The region covers the present Liaoning, Beijing, Tianjing and northern part of Hebei.
35 Wang, Pizhi. 2001. *Shengshui yan tan lu* ("Fleeting Gossip by the River Sheng"), Vol. 7, *Song Yuan biji xiaoshuo daguan* ("Grand View of Story-Telling Novels in Song and Yuan Dynasties"). Shanghai Chinese Classics Publishing House, 1284.
36 *Qidan* or Khitan, ethnic group in ancient China, a branch of the Eastern Hu people inhabiting the valley of the Xar Murun River in the upper reaches of the Liao River.
37 Xiangfu Years (1008–1016 A.D.), the years in Emperor Song Zhenzong's reign.
38 Wen, Ying. 1984. *Yuhu qinghua* ("Elegant Sayings in Yuhu"), Vol. 2. Zhonghua Book Company, 66.
39 Li, Falin. 1988. *Zhongguo gudai shike conghua* (*Essays on Stone Inscriptions in Ancient China*). Shandong Education Press, 11–16.
40 Sima, Qian. 2000. *Qing Shihuang Benji* ("The First Emperor Qing Shi Huang"). *Shi ji* (*Records of The Grand Historian*), Vol. 6. Zhonghua Book Company, 177.
41 Cai Yong (132–192) was a Confucian scholar and writer of the Late Eastern Han Dynasty. He was famous for his vast knowledge in literature, history and science that he had acquired during his youth. He therefore entered the service of Grand Mentor (*taifu*) Hu Guang and was appointed gentleman of the interior (*langzhong*) as editing clerk (*jiaoshu*) in the Dongguan Archives (*dongguan*), and later promoted to court gentleman for consultation (*yilang*). A memorial by him criticizing the court caused his dismission. During his time at the court of the Han dynasty, he was one of the promoters of China's first project of incising the Six Confucian Classics – namely, *The Book of Songs* (*Shijing*), *The Book of Documents* (*Shujing*), *Rites and Ceremonies* (*Yili*), *The Book of Changes* (*Yijing*), *The Book of Music* (*Yuejing*) and *The Spring and Autumn Annals* (*Chunqiu*), into 46 stone slabs, the so-called "Stone Classics from the Xiping reign (172–177 CE)" (*Xiping shijing*). He also wrote the calligraphy for this project. One aim of this project was to propagate the correct wording of the Classics. Emperor Ling (*Han Ling Di*, 167–189) therefore ordered Cai Yong to determine the correct words and characters and to write it in the Official Chancery Script (*litizi*) on the slabs. Chisellers then cut the characters into the surface of the stone. It was finished in 183 C.E., and the slabs were erected in the court of the National Academy (*taixue*). All scholars were allowed to take rubbings from the Stone Classics, and disputes about the correct text of the Classics were ended. A situation as before, when scholars wrote their versions in lacquer on the Lantai Pavilion (*lantai*), could be avoided. On the other hand, the creation of an orthodox text also contributed to the extinction of different versions of the Classics. Cai Yong is also known as a famous writer and composer of a lot of poems and rhapsodies, like the *Shuxing fu* that laments about the contemporary luxury at the court and among the nobility, in contrast to the sad life of the average population. Some prose texts of Cai Yong were written on steles. He was famous for his excellent calligraphy that served as a model for later students learning to write Seal Script (*zhuanshu*) and Shancery Script. Cai Yong's collected writings were published as *Anthologies of Cai Yong* (*Cai Zhonglang ji*). They are lost, and only some fragments could be recovered as quotation in other books.
42 Fan, Ye. 1965. *Cai Yong zhuan* ("Biography of Cai Yong"), *Houhan shu* ("History of the later Han Dynasty"), Vol. 60, Zhonghua Book Company, 1965: 1990.
43 Song Qi (998–1061 A.D.), man of letters of the Song Dynasty. His posthumous title was Jingwen.

44 Hu, Zai. 1962. *Tiaoxi yuyin conghua* ("Series of Poetic Notes by the Recluse of the Brook Tiao"). Vol. 39. People's Literature Publishing House, 328.
45 Zhang, Shinan. 1981. *Youhuan jiwen* ("Records of You Huan"), Vol.3. Zhonghua Book Company, 28.
46 Ouyang, Xiu. 2001. *Xu siyin shi xu* ("Preface to Sequel Poems for *Missing Yingzhou*"). *Ouyang Xiu quanji* ("Complete Works of Ouyang Xiu"), Vol. 22, Zhonghua Book Company, 605.
47 Lu, You. *Ba Lingyan xiansheng shicao* ("Preface to Poems of Lingyang (Han Yu)"). *Weinan wenji* (Collective Works of Weinan). Vol. 27.
48 Lu, Zengxiang. 1985. *Baqiongshi Jinshi Buzheng* ("Supplements to Epigraphy in Eight Jade Chambers"),Vol. 108. Cultural Relics Press, 764.
49 Wang, Mingqing. 2001. *Hui Zhu lu* ("Swaying Deertail Whisk"), Vol. 3(2). Shanghai Bookstore Publishing House, 187.
50 Chen, Xiuming. *Dongpo shihua lu* (Commentaries on Su Dongpo's poems), Vol. 2. in *cong shu ji cheng chu bian*, Vol. 2574, 18.
51 Pan, Lang. 1989. *Xiao yao ci fu huang jing ti ji* (Peripatetic *ci* with inscription by Huang Jing). *Siyinzhai suoke ci* (*ci* works printed by Siyinzhai). Shanghai Chinese Classics Publishing House, 708.
52 Lu, Zengxiang. 1985. *Baqiongshi Jinshi Buzheng* ("Supplements to Epigraphy in Eight Jade Chambers"),Vol. 108. Cultural Relics Press, 93–113.
53 Wei, Tai. 1983. *Dongxuan bilu* ("Written Records at Dong Xuan"), Vol. 3, Zhonghua Book Company, 32.
54 Qin, Guan. 2000. *Yu Huangluzhi jian* ("Letters to Huang Luzhi"). Xu Peijun. *Huaihaiji qian zhu* (Collected works of Huaihai with annotations), Vol. 30, Shanghai Chinese Classics Publishing House, 1000.
55 Huang, Shan. *Yaochiyue ershou bing xu* (Two poems to the Tune *Yao Chi Yue*). *Yanshan Ji* (Works of Yanshan). *Siku quanshu* (Complete Library in Four Branches of Literature, Wenyuange edition), Vol. 1120, 211.
56 See: Su, Shi. *Yu Biancai chanshi* (To Chan Master Biancai) No. 4, *Yu Canliaozi* (To Canliaozi) No. 4, No. 16 and No. 21, *Yu Dajue chanshi* (To Chan Master Dajue) No. 3, *Yu Baoyue dashi* (To Master Baoyue) No. 3, in: Su, Shi. 1986. *Sushi wenji* ("A Collection of Su Shi's works"), Vol. 61. Zhonghua Book Company.
57 Zhang, Lei. 1990. *Du Zhongxingsong bei* ("On Reading *Zhongxing Song* (The Resurgence of Tang Dynasty)"). *Zhang Lei ji* ("Collections of Zhang Lei's works"), Vol. 13. Zhonghua Book Company, 233.
58 Hu, Zai. 1962. *Tiaoxi yuyin conghua* ("Series of Poetic Notes by the Recluse of the Brook Tiao"). Vol. 28. People's Literature Publishing House, 328.
59 Liu, Kezhuang. *Ba Lin Zhuxi, Ding Wu ben* ("Postcript to Lin Zhuxi, Ding Wu Ben"), *Houcun xiansheng da quanji* ("Complete Works of Liu Kezhuang"). Vol. 120.
60 Xu, Du. *Que shao bian* ("No More Sweeping to Greet Quests"). *Cong Shu Ji Cheng Chu Bian*, Vol. 2791, 147–148.
61 Miyan, whose Buddhist name is Wenhui, was a poet monk from Shandong in the early Northern Song Dynasty. He entered the monastery at a young age. He had a fondness for poetry and had a close relationship with the literary world.
62 Wen, Ying. 1984. *Xiangshan yelu* ("Records of Xiangshan"), Vol. 2. Zhonghua Book Company, 59.
63 Hu, Zai. 1962. *Tiaoxi yuyin conghua* ("Series of Poetic Notes by the Recluse of the Brook Tiao"). Vol. 37. People's Literature Publishing House, 247.
64 Ouyang, Xiu. 2001. *Xiangzhou Zhoujingtang ji* ("On Zhoujingtang in Xiangzhou"). *Ouyang Xiu quanji* ("Complete Works of Ouyang Xiu"), Vol. 40, Zhonghua Book Company, 586.
65 Su, Shunqin. 1961. *Wang Gong Zhi xingzhuang* ("Description of Wangzhi's image"). *Su Shunqin ji* ('Collections of Su Shunqin's Works'), Vol. 16. Zhonghua Book Company, 250.

66 Su, Shi. 1986. *Yuren ishou* ("Four Poems to Friends"). *Sushi wenji* ("A Collection of Su Shi's Works"), Vol. 60. Zhonghua Book Company, 1850.
67 Su, Shi. 1986. *Yu Yao Jun* ("To My Friend Yao"). *Sushi wenji* ("A Collection of Su Shi's Works"), Vol. 57. Zhonghua Book Company, 1734.
68 Lu, Zengxiang. 1985. *Baqiongshi Jinshi Buzheng* ("Supplements to Epigraphy in Eight Jade Chambers"), Vol. 108. Cultural Relics Press, 698.
69 Zhao, Mingcheng. 1985. *Jinshi Lu* ("Bronze and Stone Inscriptions"), Shanghai Lexicographic Publishing House, 1985: 241, 441.
70 Liu, Zihui. *Lin chi ge bing xu* ("Songs by the Pool and the Preface"), *Pingshan ji* ("A Collection of Pingshan's Works"), Vol. 10. *Siku quanshu* ("Complete Library in Four Branches of Literature", Wenyuange edition), Vol. 1134: 441.
71 Zhu, Yizun. *Shuicun qinqu xu* ("Preface to Music at Water Village"). *Pushu Ting ji* ("Collections at Pushu Pavilian") Vol. 40. *Sibu congkan* ("Four Series Books").
72 Fan, Zhongyan. *Fan Wenzheng gong ji* ("Collections of Fan Wenzheng"), Vol.2. *Sibu congkan* ("Four series books").
73 Su, Shi. 1986. *Huarui furen gongci ba* ("Postscript to Madamn Huarui's *ci* on Palace Life"). *Sushi wenji* ("A collection of Su Shi's works"), Vol. 5. Zhonghua Book Company, 2553.
74 Wu, Zeng. 1979. *Ai Daoshi Lao Canjun* ("The Dwarf Priest and Old Military Staff Officer"). *Neng Gai Zai Man Lu* (Notes of Neng Gai Studio). Shanghai Chinese Classics Publishing House, 308.
75 Tang, Guizhang. 1986. *Cixue Luncong* ("Studies on *ci* Works"). Shanghai Chinese Classics Publishing House, 1.
76 Li, Tao. 2008. *Xu Zizhi Tongjian chang bian* ("Sequel to *Comprehensive Mirror in Aid of Governance*"), Vol. 299, Zhonghua Book Company, (12): 7266.
77 Su Shi. *Zuiweng Ting ji shuhou ba* ("Postscript to Record of the Old Tippler's Pavilion"), *Sushi wenji* ("A collection of Su Shi's works"),Vol. 5. Zhonghua Book Company, 2549.
78 Ouyang, Xiu. 2001. *Gui tian lu* ("Resigning from Office and Returning Home"), Vol. 2. *Song Yuan biji xiaoshuo daguan* ("Grand View of Story-Telling Novels in Song and Yuan Dynasties"). Shanghai Chinese Classics Publishing House, 622.
79 Hu, Zai. 1962. *Tiaoxi yuyin conghua* ("Series of Poetic Notes by the Recluse of the Brook Tiao"). Vol. 58. People's Literature Publishing House, 398.
80 Yuan, Zhen. *Baishi changqing ji xu* ("Preface to Collections of Bai Juyi's works"). *Baishi changqing ji* ("Collections of Bai Juyi's Works"). *Sibu congkan* ("Four Series Books").
81 Shao, Bowen. 1983. *Shaoshi wenjian houlu* ("The Records of the Experience and Knowledge of Shao Bowen"), Vol. 18. Zhonghua Book Company, 142.
82 Hu, Zai. 1962. *Tiaoxi yuyin conghua* ("Series of Poetic Notes by the Recluse of the Brook Tiao"). Vol. 24. People's Literature Publishing House, 163.
83 Wu, Chuhou. 1985. *Qingxiang zaji* ("Miscellaneous Records of the Blue Box"), Vol. 8, Zhonghua Book Company, 87.
84 Huang, Sheng. 1986. *Zhongcing cihua* ("Poetic Talks at Glorious Age"). Zhonghua Book Company, 217.
85 Wu, Zeng. 1979. *Nenggai Zai manlu* (Notes of Neng Gai Studio). Shanghai Chinese Classics Publishing House, 306–307.
86 Hui, Hong. 2001. *Qinshaoyou zuo Dongpo biyu tibi* ("Qinshaoyou Inscribing Su Dongpo's Poems on the Walls"). *Lengzhai yehua* ("Night Talk in the Studio of Coldness"), Vol. 1. *Song Yuan biji xiaoshuo daguan* ("Grand View of Story-Telling Novels in Song and Yuan Dynasties"). Shanghai Chinese Classics Publishing House, 2166.
87 Wu, Chuhou. 1985. *Qingxiang zaji* ('Miscellaneous records of the blue box"), Vol. 6, Zhonghua Book Company, 60.

88 Hu, Zai. 1962. *Tiaoxi yuyin conghua* ("Series of Poetic Notes by the Recluse of the Brook Tiao"). Vol. 33. People's Literature Publishing House, 256.
89 Wu, Zeng. 1979. *Nenggai Zai manlu* ("Random Records of Nenggai Studio"). Shanghai Chinese Classics Publishing House, 478, 481, 494.
90 Hu, Zai. 1962. *Tiaoxi yuyin conghua* ("Series of Poetic Notes by the Recluse of the Brook Tiao"). Vol. 59. People's Literature Publishing House, 411.
91 Wen, Ying. 1984. *Xiangshan yelu* ("Records of Xiangshan"), Vol. 1. Zhonghua Book Company, 15.
92 Shao, Bowen. 1983. *Shaoshi wenjian houlu* (The records of the experience and knowledge of Shao Bowen), Vol. 14. Zhonghua Book Company, 107. Also in: Xu, Du. *Que shao bian* ("No More Sweeping to Greet Guests"). *Cong Shu Ji Cheng Chu Bian*, Vol. 2791, 162.
93 Zeng, Jili. 1983. *Tingzhai shihua* ("Talks on Poetry in Tingzhai"), Zhonghua Book Company, 296.
94 Ren, Yuan. 2003. *Shu Moya bei hou* ("Writings on the Back of Predipices"). Shangu shiji zhu ("Annotations on the Collection of Shangu's Poetry"), Vol. 20, Shanghai Chinese Classics Publishing House, 478.
95 Wu, Zeng. 1979. *Nenggai Zai manlu* ("Random Records of Nenggai Studio"), Vol. 16. Shanghai Chinese Classics Publishing House, 469.

2 The Spread of Poetry Anthologies in Song Dynasty

In contrast to that of the Tang Dynasty, the dissemination of literature during the Song Dynasty witnessed significant advancements and maturation. These strides were attributed to the utilization of printing technologies, which facilitated a more expedient and diverse means of transmission. Consequently, the Song Dynasty witnessed a more extensive repertoire of literary collections compared to its Tang Dynasty predecessor. As was documented in the "*Xian Cun Song Ren Zhu Shu Zong Lu*" ("A List of Existing Writings by People of Song Dynasty"),[1] the era saw the compilation of 97 comprehensive literary anthologies (*Zong ji*) and 743 collections of personal literary works (*Bie ji*)[2] by various individuals. Conversely, the "Publication Notes" of Wanman's *Literary Collections of the Tang Dynasty* recorded merely 108 anthologies of Tang poems, essays or a combination of poems and essays.[3] The number of surviving collections of the Tang Dynasty accounts for merely one-seventh of those of the Song Dynasty. Moreover, the Song Dynasty amassed an impressive compilation of 255 collections of *ci* works by specific authors and 13 collections of *ci* works by various authors, which the Tang poems were unable to attain. Consequently, the quantity of poetry preserved from the Song Dynasty significantly surpasses its Tang Dynasty counterpart by nearly a thousand works.

During the Song Dynasty, there were various media and methods used for the written communication of literature, including single-page documents and booklets. This chapter primarily focuses on the compilation and publication of individual collections of poems and prose, known as "collected works" or "anthologies", in the distribution of literary works during the Song Dynasty.

2.1 Compilers of Poetry Anthologies and Time of Compilation

Most of the collected works by Song writers were typically compiled by private individuals rather than through official governmental efforts, although a few exceptions are found in the form of officially commissioned collections. Official compilations of personal essays were often associated with influential political figures. For instance, it is known that the works by Wang Anshi (1021–1086) were once compiled under official supervision. In the eighth year of Zhenghe (1118), over 30 years after Wang's death, Emperor Huizong of the

DOI: 10.4324/9781032712512-3

Song Dynasty issued a decree appointing Prime Minister Xue Ang and three other officials to oversee the compilation of Wang Anshi's literary works.[4]

Regarding the compilation of these collections, it is worth noting that some were completed prior to the author's death, while the majority were compiled posthumously. Prominent writers often took the initiative to assemble their own collections during their lifetime. For instance, Xu Xuan (917–992 A.D.), a literary figure who lived during the transition from the Southern Tang Dynasty to the Song Dynasty, self-compiled a comprehensive 20-volume manuscript anthology including all his works.[5] Likewise, Yang Yi (974–1020 A.D.), an esteemed poet of the early Song Dynasty, curated his poems into the *New Collections of Wuyi* at the age of 34 in the fourth year of Jingde (1007 A.D.).[6] Su Zhe[7] (1039–1112 A.D.) also organized three collections, titled the *First Collection*, the *Second Collection* and the *Third Collection of Luancheng*, which were completed prior to his death. These collections of Su Zhe's works were not assembled by him until the first year of Zhenghe (1111 A.D.), preceding his demise. It was common for completed works to be compiled during the author's later years. For instance, the three collections of Su Zhe's "*Luancheng*" were not compiled until the first year of Zhenghe (1111 A.D.), one year before his death. Huang Shu (1019–1058 A.D.), the father of Huang Tingjian, compiled his poems and prose into the "*Fa Tan Ji*" ("Collection of Sandalwood Felling") five years prior to his passing.[8] Similarly, the collected works of Wang Yucheng (954–1001 A.D.) were edited by the author himself during his later years.[9]

Most anthologies in the Song Dynasty, however, were compiled by the author's descendants, disciples or other relatives and acquaintances, and some were even compiled and published tens or hundreds of years later. For example, "*Xia Wenzhuang Ji*" ("A Collection of Xia Wenzhuang's Works") by Xia Song (985–1051 A.D.), written in the early Song Dynasty, was not compiled until the tenth year (1140 A.D.) of the Shaoxing reign in the Southern Song Dynasty when Xia Song's grandson in Ezhou commissioned the compilation and printing of the anthology.[10] The anthology of Zu Wuze (1011–1085 A.D.) was also compiled by the author's great-grandson Zu Xing in the third year of Shaoxi reign in the Southern Song Dynasty (1192 A.D.), more than 100 years after the author's death.[11] "*Jing Yusheng Wen Ji*" ("The Anthology of Jing Yusheng"), the collection of literary works of Chao Yuezhi (1059–1129 A.D.), was compiled by the grandson Chao Zijian in the second year of Shaoxing reign (1132 A.D.), and by the third year of the Qiandao reign (1167 A.D.), it was printed and widely spread.[12]

2.2 Selection of Poetic Works and Editing of Anthologies

During the Song Dynasty, authors took great care in compiling their own anthologies by selecting only the most important works for inclusion. Conversely, anthologies compiled by the relatives of authors after their own passing served the purpose of preserving a comprehensive body of work. A notable example is Ouyang Xiu (1007–1072 A.D.), who meticulously arranged his own works in

"*Ju Shi Ji*" ("Anthology of Ju Shi") during his later years. It was recorded that he would spend several days deliberating over whether or not to include a particular piece.[13] Cheng Ju (1078–1144 A.D.), a renowned Chinese poet of the Song Dynasty, followed a similar practice in the compilation of his collected works. He even went so far as to discard certain pieces by burning them in fires.[14] These examples highlight the careful and cautious approach of Song scholars when compiling their personal collections.

Writers in the Song Dynasty established their own criteria for selecting and excluding works for their anthologies. For example, Li Gou (1009–1059 A.D.) of the Northern Song Dynasty compiled his collected works in adherence to the principle of eliminating redundancy, thereby discounting superfluous and ornate language.[15] Similarly, Qin Guan[16] (1049–1100 A.D.) exercised careful judgement by excluding expressions that were crude and illogical during his early years when compiling "*Huaihai Xian Ju Ji*" ("A Collection of Huaihai's Works").[17]

Certain poets took the proactive measure of burning their unsatisfactory writings before compiling anthologies, thus avoiding future problems. Huang Tingjian (1045–1105 A.D.), a renowned poet of the Northern Song Dynasty, exemplified this practice by burning two-thirds of his extensive early works, leaving only a handful of works. As a result, he named the remaining works the "*Jiao Wei Ji*" ("Embers"). With growing confidence in the enduring value of his anthology, Huang subsequently renamed it "*Bi Zhou Ji*" ("*Broken Broom Anthology*"). Despite his intention to revise and rectify the collection in his later years, only 380 pieces underwent this process before his passing. Nevertheless, the extant poems attributed to Huang today number in the thousands.[18] Chen Shidao (1053–1102 A.D.) maintained a highly selective approach to poetry creation throughout his lifetime. He would burn works that did not meet his standards, leaving only one-tenth of his original output.[19] He Zhu (1052–1125 A.D.) shared a similar practice of periodically reviewing his previous works. If he found any pieces that he deemed nonsensical or unsatisfactory, he would discard them by burning them in the stove. This practice of burning once-satisfying poems occurred on many occasions.[20] Yang Wanli (1127–1206 A.D.) of the Southern Song Dynasty initially imitated the Jiangxi School of Poetry[21] in his early literary creations. However, later on, he grew dissatisfied with his earlier works and decided to burn them all. He wrote, "Over a thousand poems I wrote in my youthhood were burned in July of the year Renwu (1162 AD) during the Shaoxing reign. These poems were mostly written in the style of Jiangxi School of Poetry".[22]

2.3 Layout and Scope of Poetry Anthologies: also on Division and Combination of *ci* Collection and Literary Collection

There are three primary ways of laying out literary anthologies in the Song Dynasty: arrangement by genre, chronological order or geographical regions. The majority of collections are organized by genre. An example of this is *The Anthology of Wen Guo Wen Zheng Sima Gong*, a block-printed edition published in the second year of the Shaoxing reign (1132 A.D.) during the Southern Song Dynasty. This anthology is compiled according to various categories, including *fu* works, poems, memorials to the throne, comments on drafting posthumous titles, regulations, imperial edicts, memorials, letters, orders, notes, biographies, inscriptions, proverbs, chants, discussions on origin, narratives, farewell articles, encyclicals, lyrics, comments, discussions, inquiries, commentaries attached to historical biographies, deliberations, questioning of Mencius' articles, philosophical works, inscriptions, monuments and rituals, etc. *The Anthology of Wen Guo Wen Zheng Gong* from *The Sibu Congkan* is a photographic reproduction of this work. By examining the classification of anthologies compiled in the Song Dynasty, we can gain insights into the stylistic concepts and literary ideals of the people during this period.

Certain anthologies adopt a chronological arrangement. An example is "*Shuixin Wen Ji*" ("A Collection of Shuixin's Works"), a collection of works of Ye Shi (1150–1223 A.D.) of the Southern Song Dynasty, which was edited by Ye's disciple Zhao Ruqian and is known as a chronological edition. This approach is illustrated with the following words: "If the book is arranged according to the chronological order, possibly the narrations and descriptions are true to the fact".[23] Some anthologies employ both style and time for organizational guidelines. For instance, "*Ouyang Wenzhong Gong Ji*" ("Collected works of Ouyang Xiu"), a block-printed edition compiled by Zhou Bida during the Qingyuan period, is divided into volumes based on the literary genre. Within these volumes, literary works are arranged in chronological order, with the year of creation presented in each work's catalogue entry. Anthologies of poetry by Li Gang (1083–1140 A.D.) and Lü Benzhong (1084–1145 A.D.) follow a chronological order. Such chronicles of works hold significant value in the study of the authors' lives and creative processes.

Some anthologies are organized according to the poet's place of residence or office. Each collection of poetry corresponds to a specific location of work or official position. For instance, whenever Yang Wanli assumed a new role as an official in a different area, he would compile a set of poems that covered his tenure in that specific position. Additionally, he would include a prelude to the anthology, providing insights into his creative process and background. This type of geographical arrangement serves as a form of chronicling. While the exact creation date of each poem may not be certain, the years and locations of their composition can be determined. For example, the *Jingxi Anthology* by Yang Wanli is a compilation of his poems written in 1174 during his time as the governor of Changzhou. The "Four Hundred Poems" within the "*Nan Hai Ji*" ("Anthology of South China Sea") was written between 1180 and 1182 when Yang was managing tea-salt affairs in Guangdong. By studying these collected works, we can gain insights into the time and place of Yang Wanli's poetic creations.

The scope of the collected works during this period is quite extensive, encompassing a wide range of writings. Almost all types of works are included, such as official documents, private letters, practical texts for folk exchanges, and even engagement invitations. However, there is one notable exception: the absence of *ci* works in the collected works compiled in the Northern Song Dynasty. This reflects the dismissive attitude of Northern Song literati towards the *ci* genre. They perceived writing *ci* as a mere pastime rather than a serious literary endeavour, leading them not to value it highly and discard it easily after completion, thus excluding it from their own collected works. During the early Southern Song Dynasty, Hu Yin remarked that *ci* works were considered inferior to folk arts, and thus they significantly lagged behind *Quli*[24] in terms of literary standing. As a result, scholars with a bolder poetic style paid less attention to *ci* and disposed of it casually, viewing it as nothing more than a writing game.[25] During the Northern Song Dynasty, the inclusion of *ci* works in collections was primarily driven by the high social demand for them and the general affection people had for the genre. Despite its somewhat marginalized status within the literary landscape of the time, there was a recognition of the widespread popularity and significance of *ci* works. Therefore, people took it upon themselves to include *ci* works in independent collections and ensure their inclusion in literary registers. In essence, *ci* works occupied a somewhat peripheral position within the s literary sphere of the Northern Song Dynasty and were referred to as "marginal literature".

During the Southern Song Dynasty, the concept of *ci* underwent significant changes. Its literary status experienced a gradual improvement, and the value of the *ci* works came to be recognized. *ci* emerged as a distinct genre of literature and began to be included in selected collections of poetry. However, most of *ci* collections were published independently.

There were two methods employed in compiling *ci* anthologies during this period. One approach treated *ci* with equal status to poetry, resulting in the inclusion of both in a single collection. *ci* works were either compiled into separate volumes or along with poems. For instance, in the 26th year (1156 A.D.) of the Shaoxing reign, Wu Hang compiled the "*Piao Ran Ji*" ("Collected works of Ouyang Che"), a collection of works by Ouyang Che (1097–1127), which included "87 ancient regulated verses, *ci* works and letters".[26] Similarly, Li Chuquan (?–1155), a poet of the Northern Song Dynasty, compiled his lifetime works – 5 narratives, 300 poems, 1,200 regulated verses, 200 essays and 100 long and short verses – into "*Song'an Ji*" ("A collection of works of Song'an").[27] In the third year (1167 A.D.) of the Qiandao reign, the works of Zhang Gang (1083–1166) were collected by his son Zhang Jian and printed as *Huayang Collection*, in which 34 *ci* poems were recorded in one volume together with other poetry and prose.[28] Furthermore, poets such as Zhang Xiaoxiang (1132–1169) and Liu Kezhuang (1181–1269) also compiled their *ci* works into individual collections of poetry and prose. Interestingly, some *ci* works from the Northern Song Dynasty, initially included in individual collections of poems, were actually edited and engraved during the Southern Song Dynasty rather than the Northern Song Dynasty itself. A notable example is three *ci* works of Sima Guang (1019–1086), which were not included at early times in the "*Zen Guang Sima Wen Gong Quan Ji*" ("Complete Works of Sima Wengong") until the publication of complete collections in the Shaoxing reign of the Southern Song Dynasty. Similarly, Huang Tingjian's *ci* works were not included in collections of his works until the ninth year of the Chunxi reign of the Southern Song Dynasty (1182 A.D.). These *ci* collections eventually gained worldwide recognition alongside their poetry.[29] The amalgamation of *ci* and poems can be seen as a validation of the "official" status of *ci*.

The other way was "to give *ci* a special treatment", with which *ci* works and poems were not compiled together into the same anthologies. Instead, *ci* works were compiled into separate ones, which were appended to the end of the anthologies, showing the difference between *ci* and traditional poems. For example, Zhao Ding's (1085–1147) "*Zhong Zhengde Wen Ji*" ("Collected Works of Zhong Zhengde"), published in the first year (1201 A.D.) of Jiatai reign in Chaozhou, "classified *ci* as a separate collection" and appended *ci* to the end of the collection.[30] The *ci* works of Chen Liang (1143–1193) were compiled into "*Wai Ji*" ("Extra Collections"), which was appended to the collection of poems and prose.[31] Ouyang Xiu's *ci* works in the Northern Song Dynasty were originally published independently instead of being included in the poetry and prose collections. In Qingyuan reign (1195–1200) of the Southern Song Dynasty, Zhou Bida compiled and printed "*Ouyang Wenzhong Gong Ji*" ("Collected works of Ouyang Xiu") where he included these *ci* collections in the anthologies. Owing to Zhou's effort, *ci* was finally appended to the end of the collection. That benefited the development of *ci* works. Later, Lu Ziyu, the son of Lu You (1125–1209), compiled and printed Lu You's collection of works in the same way so that *ci* was attached to the end of the collection. Its postscript goes as: "*ci* of *Yuefu* style should have been collected separately. To avoid that some works may be lost in the future, it is appropriate to learn the compilation of Ouyang Gongji published by Luling, to which *ci* works are attached".[32] Obviously, to some people in the Southern Song Dynasty, *ci* was still considered subordinate to poetry.

2.4 Publication of Anthologies and Commercialization of Literature

After the compilation of collected works, it seemed to be relatively flexible to have them printed and published in the Song Dynasty. Engraving books in the Song Dynasty required substantial funds.[33] There were approximately three methods employed for engraving and publishing collected works during this period: some families would compile the works themselves and then have them engraved and published; others would compile the works themselves and seek the assistance of government officials for engraving and publishing; while some would either compile the works themselves or commission a workshop to compile them before proceeding with the engraving.

When families undertook the printing of their own collections, their goal was not to generate profit but rather to disseminate the works and expand the reputation and influence of their family members. Once the collection was completed, they would proceed with the engraving process. For instance, Fan Chingda compiled his collection of works himself during his later years.[34] After his passing, his sons had it engraved at home. In the preface, the sons Fan Xin and Fan Zi wrote the following words:

> The collection consists of thirty volumes of poetry and prose. We sought a foreword from Yang Wanli, also known as Chengzhai, and invited Gong Yizheng, also known as Jiexiu, to review and revise it. Finally, it was engraved in our Shouli Hall.[35]

The cost of engraving books during the Song Dynasty was notably high. In the second year of the Jiing reign of the Southern Song Dynasty (1209), Chen Zhiqiang, a literary figure from Anzhou County, undertook the engraving of the collected works by the brothers Song Xiang (996–1066) and Song Qi (998–1061), which totalled over 800,000 words. Details of other miscellaneous expenses were not accounted for, but the labour cost alone amounted to 4,000 *guan*,[36] while the payment for the carving workers reached 120 *shi*.[37] It is estimated that publishing a collection of works containing 10,000 characters required 50 *guan* of money and 15 *shi* of grains, whereas a collection of approximately 100,000 characters necessitated 500 *guan* of money and 15 *shi* of grains. These were large sums for ordinary families, and thus some collected works failed to be engraved and published due to financial constraints. For instance, after the death of Hu Quan (1102–1180), his descendants compiled his collected works into *"Dan'an Ji"* ("Collected Works of Dan'an"), which is composed of 70 volumes, with the intention of engraving and disseminating them. However, their poverty prevented them from carrying out their plans. Nevertheless, with the help of concerned officials' sponsorship, the works were at last published.[38] The same circumstances applied to Li Liuqian (1123–1176), who had compiled a literary collection of works during his lifetime but could not publish it due to his family's financial difficulties. Consequently, it was not until 40 years after his death, in the seventh year of the Jiading reign of the Southern Song Dynasty (1214), that his son managed to have them published. In the postscript of the collection, Li Lianju, Li Liuqian's son, stated with the following words: "My father wrote numerous articles throughout his life, totaling over 100 volumes. His name shall live on forever, and he shall become immortal through these works. However, our family was too poor to have them published and promoted".[39]

Throughout the Song Dynasty, the majority of literary collections were compiled by individuals or their relatives and subsequently officially engraved and published. The reason lies in that most families lacked the financial means to undertake the expensive process of engraving books without external sponsorship. Official engraving projects relied on two main sources of funding: official donations and public funds.

Officials generously donated funds to engrave collections of works, including those from their own ancestors as well as those from local scholars and prominent figures. For instance, in the second year of the Shaoxi reign of the Southern Song Dynasty (1191), Zhang Bu, the governor of Zhichizhou Prefecture, personally financed the printing and publication of a collection titled "*Huayang Ji*" ("A Collection of Huayang's Works") by his ancestor Zhang Gang. Zhang Bu remarked, "I contributed funds to have this book engraved at the county school".[40] Similarly, in the first year of the Baoqing reign of the Southern Song Dynasty (1225), Zhao Dazhong, the magistrate of Chang County, used his modest salary to engrave and publish the "*Nanyang Ji*" ("A Collection of Nanyang's Works") of his sixth ancestor Zhao Xiang.[41]

Local governments frequently utilized public funds to print collections of renowned local figures. For example, in the fourth year of the Xuanhe reign of the Northern Song Dynasty (1122), the book-engraving institution of Jizhou Prefecture planned to engrave and publish 50 volumes of the "*Liuyi Jushi Ji*" ("Collected Works of Liuyi Jushi") by Ouyang Xiu. Chen Cheng, the governor of Zhizhou Prefecture, allocated funding for this project from the surplus of public expenditure.[42] Similarly, in the 13th year of the Chunxi reign of the Southern Song Dynasty (1186), Qin Yu, the governor of Anzhou Prefecture, utilized saved office expenses to engrave and print the "*Yunxi Ji*" ("Collected Works of Yunxi") by Zheng Xie (1022–1072), a renowned local scholar.[43]

Some collections of literary works were compiled by the authors or their relatives at the request of book workshops. These workshops would then handle the printing and publication of the works, similar to modern publishing houses seeking contributions from authors or their relatives. For instance, Chen Qi, a bookseller in Lin'an, the capital city of the Southern Song Dynasty, would actively approach authors for contributions. One such case involves Huang Wenlei, a poet of the Southern Song Dynasty, whose poetry collection "*Kanyun Xiaoji*" ("A collection of works by Kanyun") was included in the "*Jianghu Xiao Ji*" ("Poetry Anthology of Jianghu School")[44] at the request of Chen Qi. Huang Wenlei mentioned in the preface that Chen Qi, also known by his poetic name Yun Ju, approached him to invite contributions. Huang provided all his writings in stocks, including poems like "*Zhao Jun Qu*" (To Zhao Jun), to Chen Qi, who reviewed and revised the works.[45]

Similarly, the book workshop invited Li Zengbo (1198–1268) of the Southern Song Dynasty to have his collection of works engraved and printed in a convenient small format that could be stored in a headscarf box. This edition was known as the "*Jinsi Ben*" ("Books with the Size of Handkerchieves") at the time. In the sixth year of the Xianchun reign (1270), Li Shao, the son of Li Zengbo, mentioned in his "Ke Zhai Gao Ba" ("Postscript to *Collected Works of Kezhai*") that he discovered the small-sized books in the market, which could be conveniently brought to faraway places. Officials were then ordered to transcribe the works into regular script, ensuring their use by future generations.[46] However, the specific bookstore responsible for this edition remains unknown.

Towards the end of the Northern Song Dynasty, the works of the poet Tang Geng (1071–1121) gained popularity among students at the Imperial

Academy. As a result, bookstores in the capital approached his family for contributions and published them. In the fourth year of the Xuanhe reign (1122), Zheng Zong mentioned that once the scholars of the Imperial Academy had access to the poems, they would share them with each other. However, there were too many beloved works to be copied by hand individually, so the bookstores would have them engraved and published.[47] This bookstores are specialized in carving and selling books.

Some anthologies were personally bestowed by authors or editors to the bookstores to be engraved and printed, similar to the process by which authors at present submit their works to publishing houses. For instance, Xu Fei, during the Southern Song Dynasty (unknown–1249), submitted his poems to Chen Qi, requesting the latter to engrave and publish them as a collection. In the postscript of the "*Meiwu Gao*" ("Meiwu Manuscript"), Xu Fei wrote that during the spring of Jiachen, he compiled an anthology consisting of over 40 poems and sought out Chen Qi for the task of engraving and printing.[48] Subsequently, the "*Meiwu Gao*" ("Meiwu Manuscript") was included in the "*Jianghu Xiao Ji*" ("Poetry Anthology of Jianghu School") edited by Chen Qi.

In another example, when the capital was relocated to the south, Li Gongzu, a student of Sun Di, meticulously numbered, classified and annotated Sun Di's letters. He desired a bookstore to print and distribute these works to readers.[49]

Prior to being engraved by bookstores, anthologies had to undergo a process of selection, review and finalization. We may take Chen Qi, a renowned poet and publisher of the Southern Song Dynasty, for example. Before having the anthology of poems from the Jianghu School engraved, he would meticulously review the manuscripts. His works, such as "*Yun Ju Yi Ji*" ("Yun Ju Second Draft") and "*Yun Ju Yi Ji*" ("Posthumous Poem of Yun Ju"), have been passed down through generations. Chen Qi was not only skilled in writing poetry but also in the appreciation of poetry. Due to his esteemed aesthetic perspective within society, some poems were even written to praise him as the "Compass of Poems of Jianghu School".[50] His selection was conducted with great strictness. In the third year of the Baoyou reign (1255), Zhang Zhilong wrote in the preface of "*Xuelin Shanyu*" ("Revised Poems of Xuelin"):

> Ever since my childhood, I have had a fondness for composing poems. Over the course of forty years, I have accumulated a collection of poems, which have undergone several revisions. I sought the assistance of the venerable Chen Qi, who helped me select and edit these works. However, only one-tenth of the original poems were kept, each word condensed and filled with profound meaning. The resulting compilation is akin to a taut bow, fully drawn and poised for powerful execution. ... Thus, I requested Chen Qi to distill the collection further, resulting in a compilation entitled "*Xuelin Shanyu*" ("Revised poems of Xuelin"), intended as a guide for my son Geng Lao. The process of removal was not aimed at discarding the superfluous, but rather to focus more on the essence.[51]

After undergoing multiple rounds of editing and revising by Chen Qi, Zhang Zhilong's manuscript was reduced to just one-tenth of its original content. Instead of harbouring any resentment, Zhang Zhilong graciously requested Chen Qi to undertake a further selection process, highlighting the mutual trust and seriousness between them.[52]

During the Song Dynasty, both individual poems and collections of poetry could be printed and sold, indicating the emerging trend of "commercialization" of literature in the Song Dynasty. However, it is worth noting that not all writers fully understood the commercial value of their literary works at the time. The commercialization of literature in the Song Dynasty had a multifaceted impact on the development of literary culture.

Notes

1 Liu Ling, Shen Zhihong. *Xian Cun Song Ren Zhu Shu Zong Lu* (A List of Existing Writings by People of Song Dynasty), Bashu Publishing House, 1995: 5.
2 *Zongji* ("General Collection, Anthology") is a collection of various authors' poems and proses (distinct from *Bieji*, a collection of a particular author's literary works). In terms of content, an anthology could be either comprehensive or limited in selection. Chronically, an anthology can be a general collection spanning written history, or a general collection from one dynasty. In terms of the genre of collected works, it can be divided into collections of a specific genre and collections of various genres. The most representative anthology is *Selections of Refined Literature* compiled and edited jointly by Xiao Tong (501–531, Crown Prince Zhaoming of the Liang Dynasty during the Southern Dynasties) and his literary advisors. *Selections of Refined Literature* consists of more than 700 outstanding literary pieces of various genres from pre-Qin through the early Liang. It does not include any work that belongs to the categories of *jing* (Confucian classics), *shi* (history) or *zi* (thoughts of ancient scholars and schools) but does include a small number of prefaces, commentaries and eulogies from *shi*. *Selections of Refined Literature* reflects the literary trend of the time and exerted a far-reaching impact on the development of Chinese literature in the years to come. See: https://www.chinesethought.cn/EN/shuyu_show.aspx?shuyu_id=2326. *Bie ji* ("Individual Collection") refers to a collection of works by an individual author in contrast to an anthology which amalgamates the works of many writers. In the Western Han Dynasty, Liu Xin(?–23) composed Seven Categories, one of the categories being "The Catalogue of *Shi* and *Fu*", which collects the literary works of 66 writers, including Qu Yuan (340?–278? B.C.), Tang Le and Song Yu. Organized by author, "The Catalogue of *Shi* and *Fu*" was regarded as the beginning of individual collections. Many individual collections were compiled in the Eastern Han Dynasty, as exemplified by the 886 collections of writers from the Han through Wei and Jin to the Southern and Northern Dynasties, recorded in *The History of the Sui Dynasty*. Nearly every author had his own collection. Collections devoted to poetry were usually entitled collection of poems, while those concerned with prose or both poetry and prose were entitled collection of writings. An individual collection might be entitled after the author's name, pen name, posthumous title, birth place or residence. Containing all the major works of an author, an individual collection enables readers to learn about the author's aspirations and therefore provides a valuable source for the study of his ideas and literary achievements for later generations. See https://www.chinesethought.cn/EN/shuyu_show.aspx?shuyu_id=2233.

3 Wan, Man. 1980. *Tangji xulu* ("Literary Collections of the Tang Dynasty"). Zhonghua Book Company.
4 Yang, Zhongliang. *Xu Zizhi Tongjian changbian jishi benmo* ("Sequel to Comprehensive Mirror in Aid of Governance"), Vol. 134; Wei, Liaoweng. *Linchuan shi zhu xu* ("Preface to the Annotated Poems of Linchuan"). *Heshan Xiansheng daquan wenji* ("Complete collections of Heshan Xiansheng's works"), Vol. 51.
5 Zhu, Shangshu. 1999. *Songren bieji xulu* ("On Collections of Literary Works in Song Dynasty"). Zhonghua Book Company, 1–2.
6 Yang, Yi. Author's preface, *Wuyi xinji* (New Collections of Wuyi). *Siku quanshu* (Complete Library in Four Branches of Literature, Wenyuange edition), Vol. 1086, 354.
7 Su Zhe was a Chinese essayist, historian, poet and politician. He was highly honoured as a politician and essayist in the Song Dynasty, as were his father Su Xun and his elder brother Su Shi (Su Dongpo). All of them were among "The Eight Great Men of Letters of the Tang and Song Dynasties".
8 Zhu, Shangshu. 1999. *Songren bieji xulu* ("On Collections of Literary Works in Song Dynasty"). Zhonghua Book Company, 266.
9 Su, Song. In *Xiaochu waiji xu* of "Collection of Su Weigong's Works" (Vol. 66) there are the following words: "The manuscripts were collected and edited by the author himself in his later years. The collection, including thirty volumes, was titled *xiao chu*". *Siku quanshu* (Complete Library in Four Branches of Literature, Wenyuange edition), Vol.1092, 706.
10 Jiang, Miao. *Wenzhuang ji yuan xu* ("Original preface to *A Collection of Xia Wenzhuang's Works*"). *Wenzhuang ji* ("A Collection of Xia Wenzhuang's Works"), *Siku quanshu* (Complete Library in Four Branches of Literature, Wenyuange edition), Vol.1087, 48.
11 Zu, Xing. *Longxue wenji bing yuanliu shimo* ("A Collection of Longxue's Works, Its Origin and Compilation Process"). Longxue wenji ("A Collection of Longxue's Works"). *Siku quanshu* (Complete Library in Four Branches of Literature, Wenyuange edition), Vol. 1098, 882.
12 Chao, Yuezhi. Introduction to Chao Zijian. *Songshan wenji* ("A Collection of Songshan's Works"), Vol. 20. *Sibu congkan* ("Four Series Books").
13 Ma, Ruilin. 1985. *Wenxian tongkao: jingji kao* ("Comprehensive Textual Research of Historical Documents"), Vol. 61. East China Normal University Press, 1424.
14 Cheng, Yu. *Chenggong xingzhuang* ("A Description of Chenggong"). Cheng, Ju. *Beishan xiao ji* ("A Collection of Beishan"), Vol. 40. *Sibu congkan* ("Four Series Books").
15 Li, Gou. Author's preface. Yujiang ji ("A Collection of Yujiang's works"). *Siku quanshu* (Complete Library in Four Branches of Literature, Wenyuange edition), Vol.1095, 3.
16 Qin Guan (1049–1100) was a Chinese poet of the Song Dynasty. His courtesy name was Shaoyou, and his pseudonym Huaihai Jushi and Hangou Jushi. He was honoured as one of the "Four Great Disciples of Su Shi", along with Huang Tingjian, Zhang Lei and Chao Buzhi.
17 Qin, Guan. *Huaihai xianju ji xu* ("Preface to *A Collection of Huaihai's Works*"). *Huaihai ji qianzhu houji* ("Annotated Collection of Huaihai's works"), Vol. 6. Shanghai Chinese Classics, Vol. 2000, 1531.
18 Ye, Mengde. 1990. *Shilin bishu luhua* ("Records of Summer Resort in Stone Forest"), Vol. 2, Shanghai Bookstore Publishing House, 13.
19 Chao, Gongwu. *Zhaode Xiansheng junzhai dushu zhi* ("Records of Junzhai Xiansheng's Readings"). Vol. 4. *Sibu congkan* ("Four Series Books").
20 He, Zhu. Preface. *Qinghu yilao shiji* ("A Collection of Qinghu Elderly's poems"). *Siku quanshu* (Complete Library in Four Branches of Literature, Wenyuange edition), Vol. 1123, 197.

21 The Jiangxi School of Poetry was the first school of poetry and prose with a formal name in Chinese literary history. It took as its core tenets the notions of "turning a crude poem or essay into a literary gem" and "squeezing new life out of an old sponge", as proposed by Huang Tingjian (1045–1105), a Southern Song Dynasty poet from Jiangxi Province. Members of that school devoted themselves to writing poetry with themes about scholarly life. They championed a vigorously "thin and stiff" style, stressed drawing on the skillful wording or remarkable ideas of their predecessors and paid close attention to the techniques of writing to ensure that each word used in poetic composition can be traced to its origin. Huang's notions differed from Tang Dynasty poets' pursuit of impromptu inspiration, elegant subtlety of inspiring imagery as well as vim and vigour in poetic creation. The Jiangxi School's influence spread across the poetic community of the Southern Song Dynasty, affecting even early modern-day poetic creation. See https://www.china sethought.cn/EN/shuyu_show.aspx?shuyu_id=4450.
22 Yang, Wanli. *Chengzhai jianghu ji xu* ("Preface to *Collections of Chengzhai's Works*"). *Chengzhai ji* ("Collections of Chengzhai's works"), Vol.80. *Sibu congkan* ("Four Series Books").
23 Zhao, Rudang. 1961. *Shuixin wenji xu* ("Preface to a Collection of Shuixin's Works"). *Yeshi ji* ("A Collection of Yeshi's Works"). Zhonghua Book Company, 1.
24 *Quli* (rites of minor etiquette norms), is a part of the Book of Rites (*Li Ji*), one of the Five Classics of the Confucian canon which describes the social forms, administration and ceremonial rites of the Zhou Dynasty.
25 Hu, Yin. 1993. *Xiang Xianglin Jiubianji hou xu* ("Postscript to Xiang Xianglin's A Collection of ci Works with Wines by the Side"). *Feiran ji* ("A Collection of Huyin's Works"), Vol. 19. 403.
26 Wu, Hang. *Ouyang Xiu zhuan ji xu* ("Preface to *A Collection of Ouyang Xiu's Works*"). *Ouyangxiu zhuan ji* ("A collection of Ouyang Xiu's works"). *Siku quanshu* (Complete Library in Four Branches of Literature, Wenyuange edition), Vol. 1136, 335.
27 Li, Chuquan. *Song'an Ji zhuanshou zixu* ("Preface to *A Collection of Works of Song'an*"). *Siku quanshu* (Complete Library in Four Branches of Literature, Wenyuange edition), Vol. 1135, 580.
28 Zhang, Jian. *Huayang Ji ba* ("Postscript of *A Collection of Huayang's Works*") Zhang Gang. *Huayang Ji* ("A collection of Huayang's works"). *Sibu congkan* ("Four Series Books").
29 Zhu, Shangshu. 1999. *Songren bieji xulu* ("On Collections of Literary Works in Song Dynasty"). Zhonghua Book Company, 504.
30 Zhou, Bida. *Zhong Zhengde wenji xu* ("Preface to *Collected Works of Zhong Zhengde*"). *Wenzhong ji* ("A Collection of Wenzhong's Works"),Vol. 54. *Siku quanshu* (Complete Library in Four Branches of Literature, Wenyuange edition), Vol. 1147, 574. Also, Chen Zhensun stated in *A Collection of Dequan Jushi's Works* (*Dequan Jushi ji*) in (*Zhizhai shulu jieti*), Vol. 20, "The complete collection is titled '*Collected Works of Zhong Zhengde*'. The poet's grandson, Zhao Mi, collected and published his poems with *ci* works of *Yuefu* style as appendix". (Shanghai Chinese Classics Publishing House, 1987: 596.)
31 Chen Zhensun, included 40 volumes of "A Collection of Longchuan's Works" (*Longchuan ji*) and four volumes of "Extra Collections" (*Waiji*) into Vol. 18 of "Zhizhai's Collected Books" (*Zhizhai shulu jieti*). He also commented, "The 'Extra Collections' are all composed of long and short lines, lacking in craftsmanship yet filled with self-conceit, assuming that the profound meaning is present in them" (Shanghai Chinese Classics Publishing House, 1987: 548).
32 Lu, Ziyu. *Kan Weinan wenji ba* ("Postscript to *A Collection Weinan's Works*"). Weinan wenji ("A Collection Weinan's Works"). *Sibu congkan* ("Four Series Books").

33 The publication industry and related cultural activities in China during the Southern Song period reached a prosperous state. In that age, all three publishing sectors operated by government, private collectors and grassroots were well developed. The technology of wood block printing provided the key technical vehicle for such a development.
34 Yang Wanli. *Shihu ji xu* ("Preface to *A Collection of Shihu Jushi's Poems*"). *Shihu Jushi shiji* ("A Collection of Shihu Jushi's Poems"). *Sibu congkan* ("Four Series Books").
35 Fan, Xin and Fan, Zi. *Shihu ji ba* ("Postscript to *A Collection of Shihu Jushi's Poems*"). *Shihu Jushi shiji* ("A Collection of Shihu Jushi's Poems"). *Sibu congkan* ("Four Series Books").
36 Chen, Ziqiang. *Yuanxian ji xu* ("Preface to *A Collection of Yuanxian's Works*"). Song, Xiang. Yuanxian ji ("A Collection of Yuanxian's Works"). *Siku quanshu* (Complete Library in Four Branches of Literature, Wenyuange edition), Vol. 1087, 402. *Guan*, unit of currency in ancient China, which equals a string of 1,000 copper cash.
37 *Shi*, also called *dan*, the basic unit of weight in ancient China. The *shi* was created by Emperor Qin Shihuang, who became the first emperor of China in 221 B.C. and who is celebrated for his unification of regulations fixing the basic units. He fixed the *shi* at about 60 kg (132 pounds). The modern *shi* is equivalent to 71.68 kg (157.89 pounds).
38 Yang, Wanli. Dan'an Xiansheng wenji xu ("Preface to *Collected Works of Dan'an*"). *Chengzhai ji* ("Collections of Chengzhai's Works"), Vol. 82. *Sibu congkan* ("Four Series Books").
39 Li, Liuqian. *Danzhai ji* ("A Collection of Danzhai's Works"). *Siku quanshu* (Complete Library in Four Branches of Literature, Wenyuange edition), Vol. 1133, 762.
40 Hong, Mai. *Huayang laoren wenji xu* ("Preface of *A Collection of Huayang's Works*"). Zhang Gang. *Huayang Ji* ("A Collection of Huayang's Works"). *Sibu congkan* ("Four Series Books").
41 Zhao, Dazhong. *Hou ba* ("Postscripts"). Zhao, Xiang. *Nanyang Ji* ("A Collection of Nanyang's Works"), *Siku quanshu* (Complete Library in Four Branches of Literature, Wenyuange edition), Vol. 1086, 347. Zhao Xiang (959–993), a famous scholar in the Northern Song Dynasty, whose ancestral home is in Nanyang at that time.
42 Zhu, Shangshu. 1999. *Songren bieji xulu* ("On Collections of Literary Works in Song Dynasty"), Vol. 4. Zhonghua Book Company, 170.
43 Qin, Yu. *Yunxi Ji xu* ("Preface to *Collected Works of Yunxi*"). Zheng, Xie. *Yunxi Ji* ("Collected Works of Yunxi"). *Siku quanshu* (Complete Library in Four Branches of Literature, Wenyuange edition), Vol. 1097, 111.
44 The Jianghu School of Poetry was a poetic school that emerged in the late Southern Song Dynasty. It was thus named after the collection of poems titled "Jianghu Ji" published by the bookseller Chen Qi. At that time, Chen Qi maintained friendly relations with the itinerant poets, and thus sold books such as *"Jianghu Ji"*, *"Xu Ji"* and *"Hou Ji"*. Because of the similarities in poetic style among the poems in *"Jianghu Ji"*, this school came to be known as the "Jianghu School of Poetry". Most of the poets included in *"Jianghu Ji"* were either commoners or low-ranking officials, with humble identities, proudly embracing the ethos of the itinerant lifestyle. These *Jianghu* poets frequently expressed their admiration for seclusion and disdain for official careers, often criticizing the problems of the time and satirizing the government, expressing their desire to remain separate from the ruling class. Notable figures among the *Jianghu* poets include Dai Fugu and Liu Kezhuang. Many poets of the Jianghu School of Poetry identified themselves with the *Jianghu* (itinerant) lifestyle. Some works of the Jianghu School of Poetry provide profound

reflections on Southern Song society. These poems depict landscapes, recount events, and express the authors' patriotic sentiments, venting their discontent towards the court, denouncing the misdeeds of the powerful, and depicting the suffering caused by warfare on the people.

45 Huang, Wenlei. *Kanyun Xiaoji juanshou* ("Preface to *Kanyun Xiaoji*"). *Jianghu Xiaoji* ("Poetry Anthology of Jianghu School"), Vol. 50. *Siku quanshu* (Complete Library in Four Branches of Literature, Wenyuange edition), Vol. 1357, 3765.
46 Lu, Xinyuan. 1990. *Bisonglou cangshu zhi* ("Records of Collections of Books in Bisong Tower"). Zhonghua Books Company, 1012.
47 Tang, Geng. *Meishan Tang xiansheng wenji* ("Collected Works of Tang Geng from Meishan"). *Sibu congkan* ("Four Series Books").
48 Xu, Fei. *Meiwu gao juanshou* ("Preface to *Meiwu Manuscript*"). "*Jianghu Xiao Ji*" ("Poetry Anthology of Jianghu School"), Vol. 77. *Siku quanshu* (Complete Library in Four Branches of Literature, Wenyuange edition), Vol.1357, 608.
49 Cai, Jianhou. *Li Xueshi xin zhu Sun Shangshu neijian chidu xu* ("Preface to *Sun Di's Letters with Annotations by Li Gongzu*"). *Song Sun Zhongyi neijian chidu bianzhu* ("Sun Di's Letters with Annotations by Li Gongzu"). *Changzhou xianzhe yishu* ("Works of Great Sages from Changzhou").
50 Ye, Yin. *Zeng Chen Yunju* ("To Chen Yunju"). "*Jianghu Xiao Ji*" ("Poetry Anthology of Jianghu School"), Vol. 40. *Siku quanshu* (Complete Library in Four Branches of Literature, Wenyuange edition), Vol. 1357, 322.
51 Zhang, Zhilong. *Xuelin shanyu* ("Revised Poems of Xuelin"). *Nansong qunxian liushi jia xiaoji* ("The Minor Collections of 60 Distinguished Figures of the Southern Song Dynasty"), Shanghai Gushu Liutongchu, 1922.
52 Yao, Fushen.1990. *Zhongguo bianji shi* ("A History of Chinese Editing"). Fudan University Press. 167.

3 The Spread of Wall-Inscribed Poems in Song Dynasty

Wall inscriptions, a truly primitive form of "print" media, refer to the practice of writing texts or drawings on the walls of temples, post stations, houses, bridges and other architectural structures to disseminate information, express opinions and showcase literary, calligraphic and painting works.

Wall inscriptions with written characters appeared as early as the Warring States period (475–221 B.C.). In Wang Yi's "*Chuci Zhang Ju Xu*" ("Preface to *Annotations on the Odes of Chu*"),[1]

> It is said that Qu Yuan (about 340–278 BC) once saw paintings on the walls of the ancestral temples of the former king of the Chu state (1030–223 BC) and royal officials, depicting the deities who ruled over the heaven, earth, mountains, and rivers, as well as the actions of ancient sage rulers and wise kings. The paintings were magnificent and beautiful, with strange and magical images. After touring around, he felt tired and had a rest under the mural, looking up at the depicted patterns. Then he wrote on the wall.[2]

During the reign of Emperor Guangwu of the Eastern Han Dynasty, wall inscriptions had become a means of disseminating official documents and decrees. The book *Fengsu Tongyi* (Annotation of Customs) records that since the revival of Emperor Guangwu, proclamations and decrees were inscribed on the walls of villages and temples.[3]

The combination of the two Chinese characters "题壁" (ti bi) is believed to have originated from Xiao Gang (503–551), Emperor Jianwen of the Liang Dynasty.

> In the beginning, Xiao Gang wrote a preface while being imprisoned, in which he wrote: "There was a righteous man named Xiao Shizuan from the Liang Dynasty. He remained consistent in sticking to morality and justice throughout his life, regardless of whether it was amidst storms and darkness or the incessant crowing of roosters. He kept clear conscience even in places where no one could see, let alone in public. He had

DOI: 10.4324/9781032712512-4

encountered numerous hardships and been reduced to this point. It seems destined by fate and there is no way out?"[4]

Since the middle Tang Dynasty, the trend of inscribing on walls became more and more popular. By the time of the Song Dynasty (960–1279), it had become a daily and widespread form of mass communication.

Wall inscriptions in the Song Dynasty bear some resemblance to the current internet. Although this primitive form of communication may be no match for the modern electronic internet in terms of its dissemination function, the former does share some similarities with the latter in terms of information dissemination. Let's make a rough analogy between the past and the present to illustrate the popularity and characteristics of wall inscriptions in the Song Dynasty.

3.1 The Convenience of "Posting"

From the perspective of information dissemination, the current internet possesses four major characteristics: openness, freedom of expression, immediacy and cost-free access. Openness refers to the fact that information on the internet, whether it is on government websites or personal pages, is publicly accessible for anyone to visit, browse, download and search. Freedom of expression means that individuals can freely publish information and express their opinions online without being restricted by time and space, without having to undergo various forms of censorship as required for publishing articles in newspapers or magazines (excluding illegal content, of course). Among all mass media today, it is perhaps only with the internet do ordinary people enjoy the right to publish information, personal opinions and works freely. Immediacy means that people can instantly upload the information, opinions or works they want to share on the internet for others to promptly browse and read. Cost-free access refers to the fact that the publication and downloading of general information, opinions and works on the internet are free of charge.

Wall inscriptions in the Song Dynasty also had these four characteristics.

Let's start with openness. In the Song Dynasty, wall inscriptions were generally written on open walls in places where people gathered frequently, such as temples, post stations, public and private buildings and bridges, to allow passers-by to view and browse. At that time, the imperial court often announced edicts and government decrees through wall inscriptions, with explicit instructions to inscribe them on the walls that were situated in "key places" and "important roads". For example, the "Decree on Banning Alcohol Production in Liangchuan issued in the seventh year (982 A.D.) of the Taiping Xingguo Period stated,

> All states are hereby commanded to produce only silk brocade, damask, and silk fabric from now on, and cease production of all other textiles. Upon receiving this decree, each region is required to whitewash the walls along important roads and display the proclamation by affixing the decree.[5]

The "Decree on Prohibiting Cross-Regional Lawsuits" issued in January of the second year (964 A.D.) of the Qiande reign also explicitly stipulated,

> All states are still required to whitewash the walls along important roads and display the proclamation by affixing the decree.[6]

Similar requirements were also stated in other decrees, which explicitly specify,

> The annual rent and tax payment system, as the same as occupational licensing system, is required to be displayed on the walls along important roads.[7]
>
> Walls at key locations in various places is still be painted and proclamations will be posted to show to the public.[8]
>
> The states and counties are still ordered to paint the walls at key locations to display proclamations.[9]
>
> There are still judicial cases that need to be resolved and made known to the people nationwide. They should be published in papers or displayed on the walls of official temples for people to abide by.[10]

The so-called key places and main roads refer to the buildings along the road that are easily visible and known to the public. The content of the decree is naturally required to be open to the public and also to be followed and implemented.

From these decrees, we can also understand that in the Song Dynasty, it was a common practice to first paint the wall white and then write on it with ink to make it eye-catching and easy to recognize. The term *"fen bi"* (to paint the walls) mentioned in the decrees refers to the practice of whitewashing the wall with lime water[11] and then writing the decrees on the white wall. This method of dissemination is still used in many rural areas in China today, where local governments write relevant regulations, orders, and notices on walls that are easily visible to the public, ensuring that the masses are informed.

As for personal wall inscriptions, just like posting online nowadays, they are certainly open to the public. Not only are we not afraid of others seeing them, but also we hope that more people will see them. Let's see an example:

> During the Tian Sheng period (1023–1032), a woman with the surname Lu accompanied her father to Hanzhou (now within Sichuan province) for the official position of a county magistrate. After the term of service ended, the father and daughter began their long journey back to the capital. They rested at the Nixi Inn (also located within Sichuan province), where lady Lu wrote a poem on the wall. The preface of the poem roughly states: "When she climbed mountains and faced waters, she never forgot to sing. When she left her hometown, her heart was filled with longing.

She wrote a part of her composition '*Phoenix Perching on Plane Tree*' on the wall, hoping that future gentlemen would appreciate it and not underestimate her talent because she was a woman." The poem goes as: "The Sichuan road is shrouded in mist and blue sky. The emperor's capital is prosperous and wealthy, but the journey is so long, when will we arrive? Looking back at Jinchuan (now Jinzhou City in Liaoning province), she wiped away her tears. Her phoenix hairpin was slanted among her dense black hair, the hair accessory delicate and exquisite, the jade pendant making a tinkling sound. When the mountain mist encountered the cool jade pendant, the pearl ornaments condensed into droplets, falling as cold water. From then on, she wanted to add some changes to her makeup, shaping her eyebrows like distant mountains as a hidden expression of longing for distant loved ones".[12]

Obviously, this lady Lu inscribed on the wall in the hope that gentlemen passing by could read it but would not blame her for writing as a woman. In the Song Dynasty, it was not socially acceptable for women to publish their works, so Li Qingzhao, who openly published her poetry, often faced criticism and disdain from male literati and officers.[13]

If a post is deleted on the internet, it can be reposted. In the Song Dynasty, if an inscription on a wall was damaged or covered, the man who inscribed it could rewrite it. For example:

At Dayu Ridge, there is a Buddhist temple where visitors from afar inscribe on the walls. A woman wrote, "When I was young, I followed my father who held the position of magistrate in Yingzhou (now within Guangdong Province). Later, when the term of office was ended we returned home. My father knew that the Dayu Ridge was also known as *Meiling* (Plum Ridge), but then it stood barren without a single plum tree. Therefore, he bought thirty plum saplings and planted them on both sides of the ridge. At that she left a poem on the temple wall. Now, accompanying my husband to take his official post in Duanxi (also within Guangdong Province), I come to this temple again, only to find the poem covered and defaced. Therefore, I decide to rewrite the poem on its original place." The poem reads, "Today, I am in charge of administering justice, but I fail to see any plum trees on the *Meishan* (Plum Mountain). I buy and plant thirty trees with my salary, leaving their fragrance to bloom amidst the snow." As a result, kind-hearted people have planted numerous plum trees along the roadside.[14]

This anonymous woman, when she was young, accompanied her father to pass by the Da Yu Ridge (also known as Meiling), and her father bought thirty plum trees to plant along the road. She wrote a poem on the wall to commemorate the event. After growing up and getting married, she returned to the same temple with her husband, only to find that her original inscription had been covered. So, she rewrote her work on the same temple wall. Interestingly, her act of writing inspired many passers-by to plant plum blossoms along the road, turning Meiling into a true Plum Ridge.

Then let's talk about freedom of expression. Just as people today can freely post on the internet or write "blog" entries, the people of the Song Dynasty could freely inscribe on walls, expressing their thoughts and creating poetry. The wall inscriptions could be moral sayings or poetic works. In the early Southern Song Dynasty, Hu Zi (1110–1170) collected many moral sayings and aphorisms inscribed by others:

> I once saw someone inscribe two lines on the wall of an inn: "If one must seek satisfaction in life, when will he truly be satisfied? Only when one can attain a tranquil state of mind before growing old, can it be considered true leisure."[15]
>
> I once saw someone inscribe a line on the wall of the inn: "In the long journey ahead, do not inquire about success or failure. What is gained is what we deserve, and what is lost is what we don't deserve".[16]

The inscribers are not restricted by their identities. It is open to both men and women, regardless of their cultural background or social status. As long as one has the capacity to write and the desire to express, he is free to inscribe on the wall. When there is nowhere else to turn, one can pour out their emotions to the sky through writing on the wall:

> In the early days of the Jianyan era (1127–1130), a married woman inscribed on the wall of the *Jieguan Ting* ("Guests Reception Pavilion") at Huanglianbu with the following words: "I am from Poyang (now within Jiangxi Province). I'm skilled in needle works and also engaged in poetry and rituals. Unfortunately, my admirable father passed away due to a cold, and I have been wandering without a fixed home. The person I chose as my spouse is not suitable, and our relationship is incompatible. How can my emotions withstand such a blow? Yesterday, we sailed on the Dongting Lake, and the raging waves caused the boat to break, resulting in the death of my husband. Alas! Officials with integrity would not serve two emperors; neither would a woman serve two husbands. What should I do? I come to this guest pavilion with my little child, and feel the pains that time has brought me. Thus, I write this little piece of poem. Besides the heavens, who can really understand me?" The poem goes as the following: "The sight of the desolate scenery of my hometown disappointed me. I lament over my wandering and rootless existence, feeling empty for not having a place to return. My heart is filled with regret and resentment, yet there is no one to talk with. With sorrow in my eyes, I tell the pain within my heart to the Twilight Mountains".[17]

The woman from Poyang experienced a series of misfortunes, first losing her father and having to wander alone. Helplessly, she got married, only to find her husband turning into a water ghost overnight. With her husband dead and her child still young, how will she survive in the future? She is lonely and helpless, resorting to inscribing her inner pain on the wall to express her sadness.

The love hidden in one's heart, which is unable to be expressed to others, can also be anonymously inscribed on the wall and be silently conveyed. And if the beloved happens to see it, he will also understand the in-depth affection hidden within her heart:

> During the reign of Emperor Huizong of the Song Dynasty, someone inscribed on the wall of an inn set by the government in Shaanxi: "When we were young, my cousin and I, with the name Youqing, sat together at the same desk, sharing a common love for literature. Before I was fifteen years old, my cousin proposed a marriage with me. However, my parents thought that my cousin, without an official position, was not suitable for marriage. So they denied his proposal and married me to a military officer. One years later, he passed the imperial examination and became an officer in Tiao Fang (present Lintan of Gansu Province). When my husband commanded troops in Shaanxi, I coincidentally met with my cousin. He rode away on horseback without even glancing at me. Could it be that our past grievances were not yet resolved?" In response, I wrote "To the tune Lang Tao Sha" to express my emotions: "I gaze at the southern sky, my minds reaching the edge of the heavens, where clouds and rain vanish without a trace. An atmosphere of regret it seems to permeate everywhere, causing me to furrow my brows tightly. The lotus flowers, blooming late, have disappointed the early spring breeze. Sitting in an inn, I lament over our unpredictable and wandering lives, in which our reunions and separations happen in the blink of an eye. I see you vigorously whip your spirited horse, urging it to gallop away. You move farther and farther away under the falling sun, until I could no longer see you. My sleeves are wet with tears that were tinged red by the setting sun".[18]

"Youqing" may be the pseudonym for the woman. In her early years, she and her cousin were study partners and fell in love with each other, but they could not get married due to family opposition. Several years later, they unexpectedly encountered each other again. The cousin pretended not to see her. Instead, he whipped his horse and rode away while "Youqing" still held feelings of love. She then composed a poem and inscribed it on the wall, hoping that her cousin would see it in the future and understand her. The women's voices at the time, without the use of wall inscriptions, were generally unknown to the outside world if there were not any other medium of communication.

Nowadays, there is no barrier to publishing works online. People can share things on the internet as they want, allowing people to "appreciate extraordinary writings" together. The wall inscriptions during the Song Dynasty were similar to this. Regardless of the quality, one could freely inscribe and publish their works:

> You Zixi, a native of Longxi (now within Fujian Province), traveled to Jiangxi to participate in the imperial examination. He ascended a tavern and encountered a group of young people sitting together. Unaware that You Zixi was a man of letters, the young men drank to their heart's content. In the height of their merriment, they began inscribing poems on the wall, each displaying their arrogance and self-confidence, as if no one else mattered. You Zixi stood up and borrowed a pen to inscribe a poem, which drew ridicule from the young men. However, he swiftly wrote down his verses. The implication of the poem was so profound and exquisite that the young men quietly slipped away after reading it.[19]

The few young men in the tavern seemed to have only a rudimentary understanding of literature, yet they arrogantly inscribed poems on the wall as if no one else mattered. They intended to show off their skills, but unexpectedly, they encountered You Zixi, whose writing was profound and exquisite. Realizing that they were no match for him, they discreetly slipped away.

Although wall inscriptions allow the publication of works without distinguishing the level of proficiency or fame, the works of famous and influential figures are always more popular among the people. This is similar to how present blogs created by today's celebrities and influential figures receive attention and adoration from netizens. The story of *"Bi Sha Long Bi"* ("Emerald Green Gauze Veils the Walls") exemplifies this point most vividly:

> According to legend, Wei Ye once travelled with Prime Minister Cou Zhun[20] to visit a Buddhist temple in the Shaanfu and each left behind inscribed poems. When they revisited the temple later, they found that Kou Zhun's poems were protected by a blue gauze, while Wei Ye's poems were covered with a thick layer of dust, leaving the walls dim and gloomy. At that moment, a clever and witty girl who accompanied them used her sleeve to gently rub away the dust. Wei Ye slowly remarked, "If one could regularly use a red sleeve to brush away the dust, perhaps the work is better than the one covered with the blue gauze." Kou Zhun then burst into laughter at the words.[21]

Prime Minister Kou Zhun was a renowned scholar and high-ranking official, while Wei Ye was just a humble hermit. Therefore, when both of them inscribed poems on the walls of the Buddhist temple, they received vastly different treatment. Kou Zhun's inscriptions were protected by the monks with a blue gauze, while Wei Ye's inscriptions, left in the open air, were covered with dust.

Nowadays, many online portals employ various methods to increase click rates and attract celebrities and stars to open blogs on their platforms. Similarly, from the Five Dynasties to the Song Dynasty, temples would often brush their walls white and invite famous figures to inscribe poems as a means to increase their popularity.

For example, during the Five Dynasties, Yang Ningshi, a renowned calligrapher known for his unique style, resided in Luoyang (now within Henan province) and frequently visited temples. He enjoyed inscribing poems on the walls, leaving behind his distinctive brushwork. The walls of the temples were treasured and protected by the monks. Any areas that Yang Ningshi had not yet inscribed were meticulously whitewashed by the monks, eagerly awaiting his arrival to continue his writings. After arriving at the temple, Yang Ningshi

> saw the walls meticulously whitewashed, so he sat on the ground, scanning his surroundings with a seemingly mad gaze. He wielded his brush and ink, simultaneously reciting and writing, perfectly merging his brushwork with his state of mind. He continued to write until there was no empty space left on the walls, showing no signs of fatigue. The sight left the tourists in awe, marveling at his talent.[22]

During the Song Dynasty, there were often instances where monks would request famous poets of that time to inscribe poems on the walls. Mei Yaochen had a poem that stated, "An old monk swept the wall and, holding brush and inkstone, requested me to write a poem on the wall".[23] Su Zhe also had a poem that said, "A monk visits me, carrying a scroll of poetry, claiming it's just completed in the Pure Illumination Hall. I obtain a white wall to write the verses, regardless of the dust and stains on my clothes".[24] In his poems, Lu You also stated, "A monk begs for new poems to inscribe on the temple walls, while he helps me, half-drunken, down to the stairs". And, "A monk came to sweep the walls, requesting the calligraphy I create when intoxicated, while I, alone, leaned against the tower, with no one to share my inner sorrows".[25] Mei Yaochen, Su Shi, and Lu You were all renowned poets, and therefore the temple monks often invited them to inscribe poems on the walls.

There are two situations when it comes to inscribing poems on walls: one is that the author inscribes their own works, and the other is when someone else inscribes the completed work of the author. The latter is similar to today's online "reposting". When the author inscribes his own work, it is usually done simultaneously with the writing process, with the act of inscription and composition taking place concurrently. On the other hand, when someone else reposts the work on the wall, there is usually a time delay. Temple monks would invite renowned poets to inscribe poems on the walls. Some inscriptions are personally conducted by the poets themselves, equivalent to direct posting on the internet today, while others are done by asking someone else to inscribe the work of the poet, similar to "reposting".

Speaking of immediacy, there were three main forms of media for mass communication of literary works in the Song Dynasty: wall inscriptions, stone carvings, and engraved prints (including engraved printing of single works and collections of works for sale). In terms of speed of dissemination, wall inscriptions were the most efficient. For stone carvings, firstly, natural stone slabs needed to be polished and processed into stone tablets, then skilled craftsmen would carve the characters in the stone tablets and, finally, carvings would be printed for texts. On the whole, it would take a considerable amount of time for the task. Engraved prints also go through processes such as plate making, typesetting and printing, which also took a considerable amount of time. Only with wall inscriptions did authors not need any intermediate steps and could directly write relevant information, opinions or literary works on the wall in real time. Just like posting on the internet today, they could write and upload at the same time. The completion of writing is the beginning of dissemination.

For example, when Su Shi, after a long time of exile, returned from Hainan to the north, he passed through Dayu Ridge and received care and hospitality from an old man in a village inn. Su Shi, deeply moved, immediately wrote a poem on the wall of the inn:

> When Su Dongpo (Su Shi) turned back from the south, he arrived at Dayu Ridge and took a rest in a small village in the wilderness. An old man asked one of Su Dongpo's attendants, "Who is this honorable officer?" The attendant replied, "He is the Minister Su Dongpo." The old man said, "Is he the famous Su Zizhan?" The attendant replied, "Yes, he is." Then the old man approached Su Dongpo, bowed and said, "I heard that many people tried to harm you, but today you are back to the north safely. It's a blessing from heaven for good men like you." Su Dongpo smiled and showed his thanks. Then he wrote a poem on the wall of the inn: "My bones have grown old, my beard has turned white, and my heart is full of disappointment. The green pines I planted lined on both sides of the road. I come across an old man who lived at the top of Dayu Ridge and ask him, 'How many people exiled to the south, have come back to the north?'"[26]

During a lively gathering at a tavern in Hangzhou, the Southern Song poet Chen Renjie was deeply moved by the fact that the prosperous lives in Lin'an had eroded the heroic spirit of men at that time. In the heat of the moment, he immediately picked up his brush and inscribed a poem titled "To the Tune *Qin Yuan Chun*" on the wall to express his disappointment. The opening lines of the poem go as follows:

> I once ascended a tall building with my friends during our leisure time and called for wine. Not only could we clearly see the scenery of Zhongfu (today's Purple Mountain in Nanjing province) and Stone City, but also the calm and tranquil Huai River, which seemed to be within reach. I also travelled north to Huai Mountain by passing through Qi An, Dongting Lake, and Baling County. I climbed up Yueyang Tower and enjoyed the magnificent scenery of Jingzhou. The relics of Sun Quan and Liu Bei

filled me with much longing, and overall the mountains, rivers and vegetation are satisfactory for me. When I arrived in the capital city, I stepped up Fengle Tower to view the scenery of West Lake. After reciting the enchanting verses of my friends from the southeast, "people of the southeast are graceful and charming, and men are mostly womanly", I sighed for a long time. After getting drunken, I vigorously wielded my brush on the eastern wall, expressing the frustration in my heart. It was the late autumn of the fourth year of Jiaxi in the reign of Emperor Lizong.[27]

(1237–1240)

At about the same time as Chen Renjie, there was a talented man named Ao Taosun. One day, at the Three Yuan Tower in Hangzhou, Ao Taosun inscribed a satirical poem on the wall, mocking Prime Minister Han Tuizhou. Before he finished the poem, he was discovered by secret agents, and the constables were ordered to arrest him. Fortunately, he was highly alert and quickly disguised himself as a hotel waiter, narrowly avoiding capture as he brushed past the constables. He ultimately escaped from the arrest:

At the beginning of the Qingyuan era, after Han Tuozhou imprisoned and executed Zhao Ruyu, Ao Taosun, a student of the Imperial Academy, wrote a poem on the walls of Sanyuan Tower: "With the left hand, he rotates the Qian hexagram; with the right hand, he turns the Kun hexagram.[28] How can the officials incite and spread rumors? The wolf's den has no place for the loyal Ji Dan,[29] while the fish's belly still mourns the eternal suffering of Qu Yuan. Even in death, one knows the debt owed by the officials, and the loyalty of the lonely soul will be recorded in history. If in the realm of the afterlife, you encounter the loyal Han Zhongxian, there is no need to speak of Han Tuozhou, the descendant of his family.[30]" Before the ink of the poem dried, someone removed the wall panel and reported the incident to the officials. Ao Taosun quickly realized the danger and hastily dressed himself with the attire of a waiter. Carrying a set of warm wine utensils, he went downstairs. He unexpectedly bumped into the officials who came to arrest him. The official asked, "Is Ao Taosun upstairs?" Ao Taosun calmly replied, "He is drunken upstairs." While the officials went upstairs, he had already escaped. He secretly returned to the region of Fujian. Later, Ao Taosun passed the highest imperial examination.[31]

This example is enough to demonstrate the immediacy and rapidity of the spreading of wall-inscribed poems.

In today's era of instant communication through the internet, platforms like MSN and QQ chat allow visitors to leave messages when the other person is not available. In the Song Dynasty, wall inscriptions also served as a means of leaving messages. When a visitor couldn't meet the person they were looking for, they would leave a poem on the wall to indicate their presence.[32]

For example, Wang Anshi once paid a visit to an esteemed scholar but failed to meet him. He then inscribed on the wall, "Around the wall corner, several sprays of plum florets are in full blow. The effloresce in solitude, braving the frigid weather. Manifestly, they are a far cry from snow. For they clandestinely diffuse their inherent aroma hither".[33]

In instant messaging, when a guest leaves a message, the host usually responds promptly. This interactive approach can also be found in the wall inscriptions of the Song Dynasty. Zhang Lei and Chao Buzhi, two of the "Four Great Disciples of Su Shi", once visited Chen Shidao together. However, Chen was not at home at the time, so Zhang and Chao "inscribed on the wall" and left. When Chen returned and saw the inscriptions on the wall, he immediately composed a poem in response to express his gratitude:

> I left from *Baishe*[34] and *Shuanglin*,[35] and the two of you arrived in glorious cart. When the door is opened, birds and sparrows are scattered. When the wall is brushed, dust falls down from the wall. I'm not afraid of the trouble of cleaning the house but of the fact that I have no bosom friends to drink with so that I have to carry all the wine back. Achievements and honors are entrusted to all of you, and the path lies in the distant realm of *Penglai*.[36]

Here's another example that is quite interesting:

> Yu Chou, whose courtesy name is *Jilun* and pseudonym name *Chizhai*, is a poet from my hometown. Mr. Zhangquan greatly appreciates his works. One day, he wrote a letter and asked Yu Chou to visit Han Zhongzhi. Yu Chou waited at his door for a long time. When the person in charge came out, Yu Chou asked about the delay. But even after a long time, there was no response. So Yu Chou wrote two poems on the wall. One of them read, "I've been waiting to be received for a long time, sitting there like a withered plant. The servant came forward and asked why I came. The integrity of scholars has long been eroded, and people are easily suspicious. I have no worries about my own life, so why should I go on waiting with patience?" The other one goes as, "Your name has long been heard, and your progress in etiquette is pleasing. Some ancient people disdained teaching but demanded greater efforts. The eight high-ranking officials of the *Shangshu Sheng* are esteemed, and the lamp of the Ministry of Personnel symbolizes authority. You astonish the literary world, just like the great poet Jia Langxian (Jia Dao)." After writing these poems, Yu Chou gave a sweeping jerk with sleeves and left. Han Zhongzhi read the poems and sent someone to chase after Yu Chou, but Yu would not return.[37]

The poet Yu Chou, recommended by Mr. Zhangquan (Zhao Fan), went to visit the esteemed scholar Han Zhongzhi (with pen name Jianquan). Han kept him waiting for a long time without coming out to meet him. Instead, he only sent a servant to inquire about his identity. Frustrated, Yu Chou wrote two poems with anger on the wall before leaving. This is similar to the case that when someone is "invisible" on QQ and doesn't show up when visitors call out, the visitors have no choice but to leave a message and depart.

Then let's talk about cost-free access. It was free for people to inscribe poems on walls during the Song Dynasty. The act of inscribing poems on walls, as well as the act of appreciating these inscriptions, was an integral part of the cultural life of people in the Song Dynasty. It had become a customary practice, so public walls, especially those of temples and post stations, were painted white in advance for passers-by to inscribe the poems.

If it was a private wall, it seemed to be a different matter. Of course, we don't mean to say that there was a fee for inscribing on private walls. But at least the writer needed to obtain the permission and approval of the homeowner; otherwise, it may have led to disputes. Liu Ban's *"Zhongshan Shihua"* ("Lu Ban's Commentary of Poetry") records a story like this:

> There was a man who called himself old Li, claiming to be open-minded and fond of writing poetry. Wherever he went, he would inscribe poems on walls, but he was not skilled in writing. One time, without the homeowner's permission, he inscribed a poem on a freshly painted white wall, greatly angering the homeowner. The homeowner reported him to the authorities and had him arrested. Eventually, the authorities mediated the situation and released him after he purchased some lime to repaint the wall.[38]

If it were a famous poet like Su Shi who inscribed the poem, the homeowner probably wouldn't be "annoyed and angry" but rather would feel honoured. It seems that during that time, inscribing on public buildings was free and unrestricted, while inscribing on private walls was "conditional". At least in terms of the content, the inscription or calligraphy should not be offensive to others.

3.2 Daily Browsing

During the Song Dynasty, literati would always observe the inscriptions of works on walls whenever they arrived at a new place, much like people in modern cities today who browse news information or videos online. Nowadays, going online has become a daily lifestyle. Inscribing on walls and appreciating wall inscriptions were an important part of the daily life of literati in the Song Dynasty.

"To first seek out wall inscriptions when dismounting from the horses, and to casually take note of village names when going out",[39] these two lines in "To the Tune *Huan Xi Sha*", written by the Song Dynasty poet Zhou Bangyan, concretely illustrate the habit of people in the Song Dynasty: they would firstly observe inscriptions when they arrive at a new place. However, he is not the only one to mention this. Chen Shidao also wrote in his poetry,

"Passing through the red doors, I traverse the paths among the flowers, observing all the wall inscriptions from years past".[40] The poet Lu You also wrote, "On the left side of the road, I suddenly encounter an inn where I once lived, then leisurely I read the inscriptions left on the walls".[41] Zhu Xi once wrote the poem titled "Two Poems on Observing Inscriptions on the Walls of Hu's Guesthouse at Mei Xi".[42] In Jiang Kui's poem "To the Tune *Ruan Lang Gui*", there is also the line "leisurely observing the inscriptions on the walls with you".[43]

After a tiring journey at an inn or guesthouse, one can leisurely observe the inscriptions on the walls, not only to pass the time and relax but also to learn about the well-being of relatives and friends. If one comes across inscriptions left by relatives or friends, it naturally evokes a sense of familiarity and comfort within. Zhou Hui has also discussed this situation:

> At the postal inn or guesthouse, when one temporarily sets aside his travelling bags during the midday meal and evening rest, he would observe the inscriptions on the walls. Sometimes, he may come across writings of his relatives or friends that depict the hardships of the journey, and find some worthy pieces to collect.[44]

Let's provide two specific examples of "to first seek out wall inscriptions when dismounting from the horses":

> Once, Yan Shu (with style name Yuanxian) went to Hangzhou. On his way, he stayed overnight at the Daming Temple in Yangzhou. There were many poems inscribed on the temple walls. Yan Shu walked slowly, with his eyes half open. He asked his attendant to read the poems aloud. However, he cautioned the attendant not to mention the authors' names or official positions. Very few poems were recited in their entirety due to the poor quality. At that moment, the attendant recited another poem, which read, "The song 'To Water Melody' composed by Emperor Yangdi of Sui Dynasty once had a perfect melody. The emperor, who once listened to this melancholic composition, has already lost his empire, and only the remnants of those abandoned ponds bear witness to its past glory. The grand royal processions that once graced Yangzhou have faded into memory, and all that remains is the continuous croaking of frogs. The desolate scene is beyond words, with only the setting sun in the west casting its light upon the crumbling city of Yangzhou." Hearing it, Yan Shu asked who the author was. Learning that it was written by Wang Qi, a county sheriff in Jiangdu, Yan Shu immediately invited him to dine together. After the meal, they walked by the pond. It was already the late spring, and petals of flowers fell one by one. Yan Shu said, "Whenever I compose a good line of poem, I write it on the wall so that others can come up with the following lines. However, for some lines like 'Deeply I sigh for the fallen flowers in vain', I haven't yet found the suitable following line to match it even after a year's effort."

Wang immediately responded, "Vaguely I seem to know the swallows come again." Yan appreciated him greatly and recommended him for an official position in the court.

When returning to Nanhua Bamboo Pavilion from the southern valley, Huang Tingjian instructed his attendant to recite the inscriptions on the wall, specifically cautioning him not to mention the author's title or name. After a while, the attendant recited a quatrain: "There is no need for monks from the mountains to welcome me. In this world, there is no place that is more serene than this bamboo grove. I lie alone, propping my chin with one hand, stealthily observing the formation and dissipation of clouds." Upon hearing this poem, Huang Tingjian praised him highly and then looked at the author's name, saying, "Indeed, it is my student Ge Minxiu's work".[45]

Yan Shu passed by the Daming Temple in Yangzhou. He walked slowly with his eyes half-closed. He asked his attendant to read the inscriptions on the temple walls. After hearing several poems, he found that none of them satisfied him except for one that he particularly appreciated. He asked the attendant who the author was, and the attendant replied that based on the signature, it was written by Wang Qi, the officer of Jiangdu. On his way back to the south, Huang Tingjian also had his attendant recite the inscriptions on the walls. After listening, he guessed that it must have been written by his student, Ge Minxiu. Upon checking the signature, he was correct.

Let's take a look at a record from Chen Yanxiao's *Gengxi Poetic Talks*:

At every inn and lodging I visited all the way, I would have a look at inscriptions on the walls, and there were often remarkable ones. I saw a quatrain hand-written by Li Bing (with the courtesy name Zhongnan) in the walls of a lodging in Lin'an, which read, "Before Mount Taiyi lies my home, filled with old memories of books. In the spring city, I am captivated by wine and reluctant to leave. Though growing old, I live amidst endless peach blossoms." There was also a quatrain written on the walls of the Water Division Inn in Chong'an County of Jianzhou, which read, "In southern Jiangnan (regions south of the Yangtze River), the sound of cicadas is already heard in March. As wheat ripens and plum turns yellow, the silkworm cocoons is ready for harvest. I imagine my old hometown in the misty rain, where a slight chill still lingers, and the heaven is embroidered with flowers." Additionally, there was a quatrain written by Lü Shuqian (also named Lü Daqiu) on the walls of the Yuruquan Inn in Danyang County, Zhenjiang, which read, "Riding out in late spring, I find the sentimental willows fluttering as snowflakes in the sky. The heart of a wandering traveller really suffers during the long night, when finding a lodging for rest I'd better find where the sound of cuckoos cannot reach my ears."[46] All the three poems were good ones, but none of them told the names of the authors.[47]

From the previous two accounts of "cautioned the attendant not to mention the authors' names or official positions" and this narration of "none of them told the names of the authors", it can be seen that when people of the Song Dynasty inscribed on walls, some signed their names while others did not. This is similar to posting online today, where some are "real-name" and others are anonymous.

The dissemination of wall inscriptions does have its limitations. Firstly, as a medium of communication, walls are fixed and stationary, unable to be moved. Therefore, recipients can only view the inscriptions by personally visiting the "site" and cannot directly view them from different places at the same time (except for the case that they are copied and forwarded). The spatial breadth of reception is thus limited. In this regard, the functionality of walls is clearly inferior to that of stone carvings or engraved prints, which can be circulated and exchanged like commodities in the market. Thus, wall inscriptions cannot directly enter the realm of circulation. Secondly, walls are directly exposed to the outside, and the inscriptions would easily fade. Indoor walls may have a relatively longer preservation time, but outdoor walls are subject to sun and rain, making it difficult to preserve the inscriptions for a long time. Thirdly, walls themselves are prone to collapse. It is for these reasons that literati and officials in the Song Dynasty attached importance to collecting and preserving the written texts and poetic works inscribed on walls. As Liu Changshi stated,

> In my travels, I found some poems inscribed on wall are quite good one. Once I recorded a poem called "To the Tune *Sheng Zha Zi*," which was exceptionally excellent. It goes as the following: "My brows, reflected in the mirror, are furrowed with gloom. The melancholy in my heart makes it impossible for me to play the musical instrument *qin*. The cold dew moistens the silver railing illuminated by the autumn moonlight, while wisps of rising incense accompany a cold screen. The clouds have departed, and the moon is full again. I see migrating wild geese, but no letter has arrived. Standing alone under the parasol tree for a long time, I, holding a phoenix-shaped hairpin for divination, hope that the beloved will return soon." This poem was written by Wei Zijing.
>
> During the Shaoxing period (from 1131 to 1162 AD), Kang Boke (Kang Yuzhi) visited the Huili Temple when he passed by Linjiang. He inscribed two poems on the wall of the Songfeng Pavilion. Unfortunately, his poems have been erased, so I record them here for remembrance. The first one goes as: "In late spring, the earth is wrapped in green, and catkins of willow along the road flutter in the air. Birds chirp continuously saying that spring is leaving. Fallen flowers cover the ground, while those who went out to view the flowers are slowly returning." The second one goes: "Dense clouds remain at dawn on the river, and I take the moss-covered path with a slender walking stick. The chill of spring has already passed, but where does it come from again today?"[48]

The phrase "record them here for remembrance" means that Liu Changshi intentionally collected and recorded these poems to promote their circulation and ensure their longevity. Hong Mai's "*Rongzhai Suibi* (Spontaneous essays of the Studio of Forbearance)" has similar records:

> Thirty miles north of Yingzhou, there is a temple called Jinshan Temple. I once paid a visit there and read two quatrains inscribed on the back wall of the Dharma Hall. The monk told me, "These were written by Mrs. Zhao, the wife of Yu Si, the military officer of Guangzhou." The verses were extraordinary, and the calligraphy and painting were four inches in size, vigorous as that Xue Ji. Several years later, when I passed by again, the monks were gone and the wall was in ruins. However, I could still recall the verses and decided to record them here as a commemoration. One of the poems read, "Do not raise the leather armguard adorned with an eagle with a call. Which general has the ambition to exterminate the Xiongnu (Huns)? Over the years, everything has turned to ashes. Only the eyes that gaze at the mountains will not wither." The other poem read, "Going out for food in a bustling and noisy world, I am unable to reach the deep forest and springs. When the mood arises, there are still the worn-out shoes, leading me to the mountains in the southeast." These poems seem to be written by Yu Sizhi.[49]

Hong Mai visited Jinshan Temple in Yingzhou in his early years and saw two poems inscribed on the wall, which were written by Yu Sizhi and his wife, Mrs. Zhao. Several years later, when he passed by again, the wall had collapsed and the poems were lost. Based on his recollection, he recorded them in his book "*Rongzhai Suibi*" ("Spontaneous Essays of the Studio of Forbearance").

The wall inscriptions that we know of today were mostly collected and compiled by people of that time and recorded in relevant discussions on poetry and prose, as well as in historical notes. This is how they have been passed down to us.

3.3 Cumulative Nature of "Follow-Up Posting"

In today's internet era, there are posters, readers, and even "follow-up posters". After the original poster makes a post, others join in by expressing their opinions and comments. Interestingly, this phenomenon of "follow-up posting" can also be observed in the wall inscriptions during the Song Dynasty as the following:

> Zhang Tangqing was the Number One Scholar in the imperial examination. One day he attended a gathering at Xingguo Temple. He inscribed a poem on the wall, saying, "With one leap, I am enlisted on the Winners List; after ten years study, I am to be a high-rank official." Someone added two more lines after these: "You'd better have a look at Yao Ye and Liang Gu,[50] who simply served as the low-rank central government

official." Later, Zhang Tangqing indeed only achieved the low rank as a local officer in the capital.[51]

In the first year of Jingyou's reign under Emperor Renzong, Zhang Tangqing achieved the top score in the imperial examination and became the champion. He was extremely proud and inscribed on a wall, saying, "With one leap, I am enlisted on the Winners List; after ten years study, I am to be a high-rank official". His peers were displeased with his arrogance. They told him not to be so proud. "Haven't you seen that the champions of the Song Dynasty, Yao Ye and Liang Gu, who served simply as court officials? Perhaps you won't achieve much either". As was expected, the outcome was not what he had hoped.

If the inscription on the wall involved matters related to women's lives, there would be a much larger number of comments from the "followers", possibly accumulating to hundreds. As was recorded in Shen Kuo's *Mengxi bitan* ("Brush talks from Dream Brook", Volume 24):

> In the Shangxi Inn in Xinzhou (present the boundary area among Siping, Changchun and Sognyuan in Jilin Province), a woman wrote hundreds of words on the wall. She described that she came from a noble family of scholars, and her parents had married her to the son of Lusheng, a third-class official. Just three days after her giving birth, Lu Sheng, driven by his own pursuit of money, forced her to follow him on the road. She died at Shangxi. When she was dying, she wrote these words on the wall, describing in details the sufferings of the persecution, and complaining that her parents were so far away from her that she has nowhere to tell her sufferings. Her words were so sorrowful but eloquent that no passer-by would read without being moved by her pains. She was hastily buried at the foot of the hill behind the inn. Passers-by were angry about it and more than a hundred poems were composed to mourn her. Some people collected them into a collection of "Deer Slave Poetry," in which there are many good pieces. Lusheng was a domestic servant of the Xia Song's family. Despising his greed and cruelty, people call him "A Deer Slave".[52]
> (In Chinese, the surname "Lu" means "deer")

The story tells of a woman who, just three days after her giving birth, was forced by her father-in-law, who was in a hurry to assume his official duties, on the road. After enduring immense suffering, she died in Shangxi, Xinzhou. Before her death, she sorrowfully inscribed her sufferings on the wall of the inn. Passers-by who read it were deeply moved and outraged, leaving comments and composing poems to show sympathy with the woman's misfortune and condemn her husband for his cruelty. Furthermore, people conducted a thorough investigation and eventually discovered that Lusheng was actually a domestic servant of Xia Song (posthumously known as Xia Wenzhuang), a prime minister during the reign of Emperor Renzong. The poems inscribed on the wall numbered over a hundred. Some well-intentioned people compiled them into a book called *Deer Slave Poetry*. Unfortunately, they have not been preserved.

A woman's suffering naturally evokes sympathy from people. Even if the woman simply writes about the loneliness of her journey, it can still arouse people's interest to leave comments and compose poems. As was recorded in Volume 10 of Zhou Hui's "*Qing Bo Za Zhi*" ("Miscellaneous Records of Qingbo"):

> I once read a poem on the wall of an inn along the road in Changshan: "After a long journey, I arrived at the inn. The cold wind howls through the broken window. The lamp flickers, casting the shadow of a lonely person." It was signed by "Miss Zhang Huiqing." When I returned to the inn some time later, I found that the wall of the inn was already covered with verses. There was an inn between Qu Zhou and Xin Zhou which was called Shanxi ("three streams"), as the water nearby came from three streams resembling the character "彡" (*shan*). Bao Niang composed a poem: "The inn by the streams is originally named *shan*. The misty lights fill the emerald haze. Knowing that tonight is beautiful, our inn seems to be one in the beautiful Jiangnan." Later, Jiang Zhiqi (with the courtesy name Yingshu, a famous poet and politician in Northern Song Dynasty) jokingly echoed with the following poem: "Walking on the desolate path all day, I come across the miasmic mist. Bao Niang's verses are truly wonderful, and tonight we may stay in Jiangnan together." Yingshu didn't actually intend to engage in poetic exchange with the woman's verse. He simply read the poem during his journey back north and felt a pleasant mood in the tiresome journey. As a response, he composed a poem with the same rhyme to express his joy.[53]

On the way to Changshan, Zhou Hui came across a poem inscribed on a wall, signed by "Miss Zhang Huiqing". When he returned some time later, he found numerous verses left as echoing ones which covered the whole wall. At the Shanxi Inn between Qu Zhou and Xin Zhou, there was a poem by Bao Niang and an echoing one by Jiang Zhiqi, who had served as a Grand Preceptor during the Huizong reign. The renowned poet Xin Qiji also wrote echoing verses in reply to women's inscribed poems. In his *ci* work "Eyes Brimming with Tears: to the Tune *Jian Zi Mu Lan Hua*", the preface reads:

> On the way to Changsha, I came across a woman's inscription on a wall, the content of which seemed to contain a great deal of regret. So I wrote this lyric trying to figure out what she had in mind.[54]

In today's online forums, some comments are made in response to the original post, while others express differing opinions on the comments. This phenomenon can also be observed in the wall inscriptions during the Song Dynasty. One person might initially inscribe a message, and then other people would make comments on the original inscription. Subsequently, another person might disagree with the previous comments and leave a different post. The most typical example of this can be seen in the comments on the inscriptions of Kou Zhun and Ding Wei, two politicians and poets in the Northern Song Dynasty:

> Ganquan Temple ("Sweet Spring Temple") in Dingzhou is located beside the official road. The spring water in the temple was exceptionally sweet and suitable for rinsing and tasting. Travellers generally could not help stopping here. When Kou Zhun (with the courtesy name Pingzhong) was banished from the court and exiled to the south, he wrote a poem on the eastern railing of the temple, which read, "Passing by here, I gaze at the imperial palace in the north, with a strong sense of melancholy". Not long after, Ding Wei, the man who persecuted Kou Zhun before was also exiled to the south. On his way, he also passed by the temple. Seeing the lines written by Kou Zhun, Ding Wei felt ashamed and wrote the following words on the western railing, "I come here to taste the spring water, pay my respects to the Buddha, and then leave".

Subsequently, more and more people began to write poetic works, which filled all the walls. Among them, Fan Fang, the Pacification Commissioner of Hubei, wrote a poem as follows:

> Kou Zhun (*Ping Zhong*) paused his carriage to taste the spring water, while Ding Wei hurried to the south after paying respect to the Buddha. Standing beneath the grand hall of temple, they looked towards the hot and remote south, which made the monks around think little of fame and gain.

This poem was widely circulated among the people. However, some people were dissatisfied with it, believing that this poem inappropriately treats Kou Zhun and Ding Wei as equals without distinguishing their merits and flaws. Kou Zhun was known for his "integrity" and was "not someone who sought favor and glory". Cui Yi, a deputy minister of the Ministry of Justice, also wrote a poem that read,

> As the two ministers were on the way to the south, they arrived the temple and wrote poems here. The Ganquan spring cannot wash off their sadness and regrets, leaving the space to judge their failure.

Some people believe that this poem is "fairly unreasonable" because Kou Zhun was not exiled due to his own fault but rather for upholding justice. How can we talk about his "failure"? Consequently, several poems were written to voice his grievances.[55]

From the previous examples, we can see that inscribing on walls is not only an act of literary dissemination but also closely related to literary creation. The author of the inscription is both a creator and a transmitter. The act of inscribing by the primary author stimulates the creative desire of the recipient, becoming a driving force for their own creation and thus transforming them into a new author. This is the normal interaction between the dissemination and creation of inscriptions. In the poetry of the Song Dynasty, we often come across titles such as the following:

> *Two Poems Based on Wang Anshi's Works on the Walls of the Western Taiyi Palace (by Huang Tingjian)*[56]
> *A Poem Created after Reading the Two Little Poems by Su Zaiting, a Junior Official in the Guanyin Temple (by Lu You)*[57]
> *Two Quatrains Composed on the Wall, Painted with Swallows, of the Buddhist Abbot's Room of Qinglian Temple in the North of the City (by Lu You)*[58]
> *Echoing to Zhang Anguo's Poem on the Walls While Visiting Yinshan Temple: To the Tune Shui Diao Ge Tou (by Wang Zhi)*[59]

Wang Anshi wrote two poems on the walls of West Taiyi Palace, which aroused the interest of Huang Tingjian. Huang then wrote two more poems in response to the walls. Seeing two poems by his friend Su Zaiting on the walls of Guanyin Temple, Lu You could not resist the urge to compose two more poems in the same style. Similarly, at Qinglian Temple, there were numerous poems inscribed by passers-by on the paintings of swallows on the walls, which also sparked Lu You's interest. Lastly, when Wang Zhi passed by Yinshan Temple, he came across the wall inscriptions by his old friend Zhang Xiaoxiang (with the courtesy name Anguo) and couldn't help but feel a wave of sadness, which prompted him to write a poem in response.

The abundance of wall inscriptions from the Song Dynasty indicates that the interaction between inscribing and creating poems on walls was often a dynamic and continuous process. It was not only a two-way interaction but also a multi-directional interplay. The first author's inscription on the wall sparked the creative desire of the second author, which in turn attracted the attention of the third author, and so on and so forth, thus forming a cycle of creation, dissemination, reception, creation, dissemination and reception, etc. This forms a cyclic and interconnected system of creation and dissemination that is unique to wall inscriptions. It is not present in other forms of dissemination, such as block printing and stone carving.

The texts produced by block printing and stone rubbing can also inspire the recipients to create new works. However, due to the indirect and one-way nature of dissemination and reception in these two forms of texts, the created texts could not be simultaneously displayed in the same space as wall inscriptions. The newly created works and old works cannot be interconnected and presented together, thus failing to form an "effect field" with mutual influence. Just like the examples of *Deer Slave Poetry* mentioned earlier, the unfortunate fate of the wife aroused sympathy from numerous passers-by, leading them to express their emotions on the wall with poems. The collective "effect field" of shared emotions among the passers-by further stimulates sympathy towards the woman and arouses anger towards the unscrupulous husband. This collective "effect field" has a much greater impact on people compared to the influence of one isolated individual on another. Similar examples can be found, such as in the preface of Liu Jiangsun's poem "To the tune *Qin Yuan Chun*" during the late Song and early Yuan Dynasty, which reads:

> Qingjiang Bridge is a big bridge located about ten miles from Zhangshu Town. On the bridge there were two poems with titles "To the Tune *Qin Yuan Chun*" and "To the Tune *Man Ting Fang*" written by Wuwen Weng ("unknown old man"), which described the plundering of women during the invasion of the southern regions by the Yuan army. At the end of the poems there were phrases such as "the wronged sister" and "the grandma full of hatred", which sound vulgar. Later, Lady Yang, a woman from Luo Chuan, wrote two more poems. In the prelude to the poems, the author said that she was born in the Yang's family while she was married to the Luo's family. In the late spring of the Bingzi year (1276), when the Yuan army conquered the capital city Lin'an, the Southern Song Dynasty was overthrown. Mrs. Yang, to flee from calamity, took a boat at Fuweng Pavilion (a pavilion in memory of the poet Huang Tingjian who is also named Fu Weng). They were chased after by pursuers and had to hide in the mountains, but ultimately could not escape from being chased and robbed. After three days of travel, they passed by this bridge and saw the two poems by Wuwen Weng. Feeling that their own suffering had not been recognized, they wrote echoing poems on the wall. They wrote, "Do not assume that those who juggle with words are not from good families." Although these poems may be vulgar, they expressed personal emotions and touched upon the issue of corrupt officials who brought harm to the country. They further wrote, "I will go back and, like a young girl, no longer paint and powder my face." and "Who should be blamed for the faults?" These are all reminiscences of past events, which are really miserable. This reminded people of the wars between the North (the Yuan Dynasty) and the South (the Song Dynasty). Should this be the case, what limitations (of sufferings) are there in the world? They often felt pain in their hearts and, upon accidentally coming across these poems, wrote poems as echoing ones to express their emotions. Although the language may be plain, their sadness is fully conveyed.[60]

Liu Jiangsun said that Wuwen Weng first wrote two poems on Qingjiang Bridge, "To the Tune Qin Yuan Chun" and "To the Tune Man Ting Fang", which described the suffering of women he encountered while fleeing from chaos. Later, Lady Yang from Luo Chuan responded with two more poems, portraying even more tragic events and expressing deeper sorrow. After reading the wall inscriptions, Liu Jiangsun was filled with a thousand regrets and decided to write another poem on the wall. By placing the wall inscriptions of these three persons together, the impact on passers-by would be even greater. It is believed that there would be many more wall inscriptions after Liu Jiangsun, expressing the family tragedies and emotional wounds caused by the wars. However, there is a lack of further records.

Some poets, however, would write their own poems on walls, and years later, when revisiting the same place, they would marvel at the changes in life and of the world and write other poems on the same wall again. For example, Wu Wenying wrote a poem with the title "Passing Lady Li's Late Makeup Pavilion, Seeing the Old Inscriptions on the Wall, and Writing Another One: To the Tune *Yong Yu Le*". In the poem, there are the following lines,

> Since Pei Jingzhong[61] left here, Cui Hui's lovesickness became so severe that she died of depression, leaving behind her lingering regrets. Friends who came here with Pei Jingzhong urged him to write another poem for Cui Hui as a tribute to mourn her. Upon careful inspection, Pei Jingzhong found that the poem he wrote before on the wall of the Late Makeup Pavilion was as fresh as ever, untouched and protected better than that covered with a veil of emerald green gauze.[62]

This indicates that Wu Wenying had once inscribed wall poems together with Lady Li, his beloved, in Lady Li's Late Makeup Pavilion. Years later, when he passed by the pavilion again, Lady Li (as "Cui Hui" in the poem) had already passed away. The scene brought back the past memories, and he decided to write another poem. Similarly, when Wang Yucheng was exiled to Shangzhou, he once resided in the Miaogao Buddhist Temple, where he discovered that his own cursive script of a poem upon the emperor's order years ago was inscribed on the wall. He was greatly surprised. "Recalling past events", he "composed another poem".[63]

Therefore, wall inscriptions served not only as a means of communication but also as a catalyst for poetic creation. They would inspire recipients to create and give birth to new works.

3.4 Rapidity of Communication Effect

As a popular means of communication, wall inscription has a remarkable social impact, at least in discovering talents, reflecting demands and promoting advertisements.

Firstly, it performed the function of discovery and promotion of talents. "Throughout history, talented people are mostly lonesome". For those with talent, gaining recognition from influential figures "may come by something with luck, but not by searching for it". Hence, Han Yu lamented, "It is always said that swift horses are usually found but not the same as 'Bo Le' (the person who has good judgments to spot 'Long Distance Running Horse')" ("Miscellaneous Essays"). Talented individuals often lack the appropriate channels to make their abilities known and recognized by society. Wall inscriptions, however, provide an effective means of discovering and promoting talent.

The authors of wall inscriptions have the opportunity to fully showcase their talents and personalities, and they may even gain recognition from social elites and literary giants. Once they receive praise and recognition from these influential figures, they can immediately become renowned in their time and may even achieve great success in their careers. Wang Qi, a provincial judge in the early Northern Song Dynasty, is a typical example. His wall-inscribed poem at the Daming Temple earned the appreciation of Prime Minister Yan Shu, which led to his promotion to a higher position. Similarly, Liu Jisun gained the approval and appreciation of Wang Anshi through a piece of wall-inscribed poem, which brought him not only fame but also promotion in his official career.

> Initially, Liu Jisun was appointed as the Wine Supervisor in Raozhou, while Wang Anshi was the Judge-prosecutor in the Jiangdong region at the time. One day, Wang had an inspection visit to Raozhou. While dealing with wine affairs, Wang Anshi arrived at the hall and saw a poem inscribed on a folding screen. The poem read, "The twittering swallows perching upon the beam, when I'm totally free, what will disturb my dream? Though tell, others can't understand the thoughts of mine. I'd enjoy Zhishan, the fine scene, with stick and wine."[64] Wang Anshi greatly appreciated this poem and asked who the author was. Learning that it was Liu Jisun's work, Wang Anshi immediately summoned Jisun for a conversation. He highly praised Liu Jisun's talent, and then left with sighs of admiration unceasingly instead of further discussion of official affairs. When he reached his official residence, there were groups of students from the county holding a petition outside requesting the appointment of an official to manage educational affairs. Wang Anshi decided to appoint Liu Jisun, who was in charge of wine affairs before, to handle educational matters. The entire county was shocked by this decision, and Liu Jisun's name became renowned as a result.[65]

Another man named Lu Bing also received Wang Anshi's appreciation for his wall-inscribed poem. He was "recommended to the court", and within a few years, promoted to the position of a ministerial-level official.[66]

The monk Hui Quan from Suzhou gained fame by writing a poem on the wall of the temple, which was appreciated by Su Dongpo. Su Dongpo himself composed an echoing poem in response, which increased Hui Quan's reputation.[67] Similarly, a monk named Ke Zun became well-known because Su Dongpo appreciated his poem on the wall.[68]

If someone were lucky enough to receive the emperor's recognition, it would be a remarkable and auspicious event that would lead to his prosperous official career.

The Spread of Wall-Inscribed Poems in Song Dynasty   79

    Wang Qinruo (with posthumous name Wenmu), before passing the imperial examination, lived in poverty and worked as assistant to the ranking officials. At that time, the prince Zhang Sheng (posthumous name of Emperor Zhenzong of Song Dynasty) took the position of prefect in Kaifeng at the time. One evening, he happened to pass by Wang Qinruo's residence. The attendants had not expected that the prince would come, so they hurriedly grabbed a paper screen to shield against the wind. The prince glanced at the screen and saw a couplet on it: "A dragon, carrying the evening mist, leaves its cave-like abode; A geese, dragging the autumn colors, comes to Hengyang." The prince greatly appreciated the couplet and asked, "These words are graceful and noble. Who is the author?" The attendants replied, "It was written by Wang Qinruo." Zhang Sheng immediately summoned Wang Qinruo. Upon meeting Wang, he was captivated by his talent and personality. Afterwards, Zhang Sheng placed his trust in Wang Qinruo and promoted him as the Prime Minister. This fortuitous encounter laid the foundation for Wang Qinruo's remarkable political career.[69]

In his early years, Wang Qinruo was destitute and had to rely on others for support. By a stroke of luck, a couplet poem he inscribed on a folding screen was seen by the prince (later known as Emperor Zhenzong), who greatly appreciated the lines. Subsequently, when the prince ascended to the throne, Wang Qinruo gained immense trust and eventually rose to the position of prime minister.

    Secondly, wall inscriptions served as the medium for conveying demands and receiving responses. In ancient China, communication among people was not smooth, making it difficult for social issues to be promptly addressed. As a result, some people utilized wall inscriptions to express their demands, and the effect was quite remarkable. For instance, there was an official from Sichuan who had been waiting in the capital city for a job appointment for three to four years. In desperation, he wrote a poem on the wall of his rented house, expressing his frustration with the prolonged delay of his appointment. The wall-inscribed poem quickly spread throughout the capital. Hearing of it, the imperial court promptly arranged a new position for the man. Satisfied with the outcome, he "filled the vacancy with satisfaction".[70]

    Sometimes, when the authorities acted inappropriately, and the public had complaints, people would have wall inscriptions as the medium to express their dissatisfaction, which ultimately might lead to resolutions. For instance, during the Jiajing period of the Southern Song Dynasty, the government of Lin'an Prefecture sold official wine at the Sanxian Hall (the Hall of Three Sages), which was dedicated to the memory of Bai Juyi, Lin Bu and Su Shi. This sales behaviour sparked dissatisfaction among the public. A student from the Imperial Academy wrote a poem on the wall, which read, "He Jing (the posthumous name of Lin Bu), Su dongpo and Bai Juyi, are all men of integrity. Now, let's not dwell on the past, but use the money from selling wine to address official matters". Learning of this, the prefect felt ashamed and voluntarily ceased the sales of wine.[71]

In the early Song Dynasty, the salaries of government officials were very low. Some individuals wrote poems on walls to express their dissatisfaction. When the royal court learned about this, they increased their salaries.

> In the ancient system, officials in the Sanban Fengzhi (low-rank military officials) were paid a monthly salary of seven hundred *wen* and half a *catty* of meat. During the Xiangfu period, to show his dissatisfaction someone wrote a poem in the inns, which read, "The plight of the Sanban Fengzhi is truly pitiful, and their low and impoverished status is evident at a glance. With the meager salary of seven hundred *wen*, when will they live prosperous lives? With the half *catty* of meat, when will they become plump and strong?" Upon hearing this, the imperial court remarked, "How can we expect integrity and honesty under such circumstances?" Consequently, they decided to increase the monthly salary.[72]

Similar to the internet today, wall-inscribed poems served as a reflection of public opinions. Facing pressure from the public, the court had no choice but to alter certain policies and practices to meet the demands of various social classes.

Thirdly, wall inscriptions could enhance the endorsement and sales promotion of businesses. Advertising is an important function of modern media. Internet today performs such functions, and so do wall inscriptions in ancient times. Wall inscriptions were a means of mass communication, allowing businesses to spread their messages and increase their visibility among passers-by. If famous poets or scholars inscribed their poems on the walls of businesses, they would attract more attention and enhance the marketing and circulation of the products.

For example, in the early Song Dynasty, the Taoist Zhang Bai possessed extraordinary abilities. He would often visit the Cui family's tavern in Wuling to have a drink. Whenever he arrived, the tavern would become crowded in every part, thus having a flourishing business. Then the tavern would never charge him for his drinks. Grateful for the hospitality of the tavern owner, Zhang Bai inscribed a poem on the wall, which read,

> The Cui family's wine by the Wuling River, should have come from the heaven instead of the world. The Taoist from the south, after drinking a *dou* of wine, would lie down at the entrance of a deep cave amidst the white clouds.

From then on, the number of people visiting the tavern to drink doubled – "the customers multiplied".[73] Similarly, in the early Song Dynasty, there was a famous scholar named Xu Dong from Suzhou who had a fondness for alcohol. He once obtained wine on credit from a wine shop and was unable to repay the debt. In response, he composed a poem about wine. The poem, consisting of hundreds of words, attracted crowds of people who came to appreciate it. The wine shop made profits several times over those of the past[74] and thus waived Xu Dong's debt for the wine.

In October of the third year of the Chunhua period, the peony flowers at the Taiping Xingguo Temple bloomed magnificently, displaying vibrant shades of red and purple as if it were springtime. People flocked to enjoy the flowers, and even the monks' residences were crowded with spectators. Seizing the opportunity for self-promotion, an old prostitute made an advertisement for herself. She inscribed a poem on the temple wall, which read,

> I once took advantage of the east wind to watch it several times. Blooming peonies summon people from all over the city to come and appreciate. People eagerly cherish the remaining traces of brilliance, wishing to borrow this small springtime from Amitabha Buddha.

Subsequently, this old prostitute gained popularity again, and her establishment became bustling with visitors.[75]

The social impact of wall-inscribed poems extends beyond what has been discussed here. With the continuous discovery and exploration of relevant materials, additional effects and functions will be further recognized and understood.

From the descriptions in this chapter, we learn that wall-inscribed poems were a popular cultural phenomenon in the Song Dynasty. Inscribing and viewing these poems were part of the daily lives of literati and officials during that time. The act of inscribing poems on walls in the Song Dynasty was analogous to posting online today, exhibiting four key characteristics: openness, freedom, immediacy and non-commercial nature. It also had three main effects: talent discovery, reflecting societal demands and advertising and promotion. Similar to how people today post and comment on online forums, there were often echoing poems to the inscribed ones in the Song Dynasty. The dissemination and creation of these inscribed poems formed a closely intertwined and interactive relationship. After making a chance connection between anciently inscribed poems on walls and the modern electronic network, the author could not help but make a comparison between the two with great interest, hoping to gain a full understanding of the state of wall-inscribed poems in the Song Dynasty. This chapter provides a compilation of historical materials and an analysis of the phenomenon, and a more in-depth theoretical interpretation awaits future research.

Notes

1 *Chuci* (Odes of Chu) was a poetic genre first attributed to Qu Yuan (340?–278? B.C.). It later became the title for the first anthology of poetry depicting the culture in south China. *Chuci* was so named because it made use of Chu (now Hunan and Hubei provinces) dialect, accent and local special genres to describe the unique

landscape, history and folklore of the State of Chu. The term *Chuci* first appeared in the early Western Han Dynasty, and later Liu Xiang (77?–6 B.C.) compiled a literary collection including 16 pieces written by Qu Yuan, Song Yu, Huainan Xiaoshan (a group of authors of the Western Han Dynasty), Dongfang Shuo (154–93 B.C.), Yan Ji, Wang Bao and Liu Xiang. When Wang Yi later compiled *Annotations on the Odes of Chu*, he added a work of his own to the collection, making it an anthology of 17 works. Through its distinctive genre and unique cultural elements, *Chuci* reflected the special culture of the Chu region in southern China. As a genre, *Chuci* is characterized by profound emotions, wild imagination and rich allusions to the remote historical mythology from the dawn of Chinese history. It demonstrates an innovative and distinctive literary genre and spirit, standing with *The Book of Songs* as twin literary pinnacles. Later generations called this genre *Chuci* Style or Sao Style (Flowery Style) and its research *Chuci* studies.

2 Hong, Xingzu. 1983. *Tian wen* ("Questions to Heaven"). *Chuci buzhu* ("Supplemental Annotations to the Songs of Chu"), Vol. 3. Zhonghua Book Company, 85.
3 Li, Fang. 1960. *Taiping yulan* ("Taiping Imperial Encyclopedia"), Vol. 593. Zhonghua Book Company, 2670.
4 Yao, Silian. 1973. *Liang shu* ("History of Liang Dynasty"), Vol. 4. Zhonghua Book Company, 108.
5 Anonymous. 1962. *Song da zhaoling ji* ("Collection of Imperial Edicts of Northern Song Dynasty"), Vol. 183. Zhonghua Book Company, 664.
6 Anonymous. 1962. *Song da zhaoling ji* ("Collection of Imperial Edicts of Northern Song Dynasty"), Vol. 198, Zhonghua Book Company, 729.
7 Anonymous. 1962. *Zhaoyu Kaifeng liumin zhao* ("Decree to Summon and Instruct Kaifeng Refugees"). *Song da zhaoling ji* ("Collection of Imperial Edicts of Northern Song Dynasty"), Vol. 185. Zhonghua Book Company, 675.
8 Anonymous. 1962. *Jinzhi shanggong qianbo bude charao juren zhao* ("Decree on Prohibiting Disturbance of Residents by Demanding Money and Goods for Tribute"). *Song da zhaoling ji* ("Collection of Imperial Edicts of Northern Song Dynasty"), Vol. 198. Zhonghua Book Company, 730.
9 Anonymous. 1962. *Eryue zhi jiuyue jin bulie zhao* ("Decree on Prohibiting Hunting and Fishing from February to September"). *Song da zhaoling ji* ("Collection of Imperial Edicts of Northern Song Dynasty"), Vol. 198. Zhonghua Book Company, 731.
10 Anonymous. 1962. *Shanglü xisui jiaoyi bude shang qi suan zhao* ("Decree on Prohibiting Small-Scale Transactions of Merchants and Travelers from Calculating Their Profits"). *Song da zhaoling ji* ("Collection of Imperial Edicts of Northern Song Dynasty"), Vol. 198. Zhonghua Book Company, 733.
11 According to the records in "History of the Song Dynasty", Vol. 366, in the biography of Liu Qi, it is mentioned,

> When Liu Qi was in Yangzhou, he ordered all the houses outside the city to be burned, and the city walls were whitewashed with lime. Inscriptions on the walls read: "Wanyan Liang died here." Due to the suspicion of the Jin rulers, he was disliked, and he then resided in Guishan.
>
> (Zhonghua Book Company, 1977: 11408)

Based on this example, the term "fenbi" refers to the whitewashing of walls using lime. In many parts of southern China today, the practice of whitewashing walls with lime water is still referred to as "fenbi". Sometimes, "fenbi" not only involves the use of lime but also the use of talcum powder to enhance smoothness. In the book "Guihǎi Yuhéng Zhi" by Fan Chengda, it is mentioned,

> Talcum powder is produced in the affiliated villages of Guilin and in the Yao caves. There are two types: white and black, with similar properties. When first

extracted, it is like loose mud but hardens when exposed to the wind. It is also known as "cold stone." Local people use lime to plaster the walls, and before they dry, they polish them with talcum powder, making them shiny like jade.
(From: *Fan Chengda biji liuzhong* ("Six types of fan Chengda's notes")
Zhonghua Book Company, 2002: 90)

12 Peng, Cheng. 2002. *Moke huixi* ("Idle Talks from a Writer"), Vol. 4. Zhonghua Book Company, 322. Also see *Juanyou zalu* ("Random Records in the Tiresome Journey"). *Songchao shishi lei yuan* ("Categorized Garden of Historical Facts of the Song Dynasty"), Vol. 39. Shanghai Chinese Classics Publishing House, 1981: 504.)
13 In Shen Kuo's work "*Mengxi bitan* ("Brush Talks from Dream Brook", Vol. 14)", there are following statements, "Ouyang Wenzhong (Ouyang Xiu) once said, 'By observing the wall inscriptions left by people, one can judge their literary abilities'".

In the home of a scholar in Piling County, there was a young girl surnamed Li, who was only sixteen years old but quite talented in poetry. Many people in the Wu region admired her. She wrote a poem titled "Picking Up a Torn Coin", which goes: "A half-moon hiding in the dust, faintly revealing the Kaiyuan characters. Imagining the clarity before it was broken, it captures all the injustices in the world." She also wrote a poem titled "Playing the Zither", which goes: "In the past, I laughed at Zhuo Wenjun, never expecting to fall into the same predicament. Today, before even playing a note, my heart is already in turmoil. This heart was never under my control." Although she showed great sentiment, it was deemed unsuitable for a woman.
(From: *Yuankan Mengxi bitan* ("Brush talks from Dream Brook"),
Cultural Relics Publishing House, 1975, (14): 14–15)

According to Ouyang Xiu, although the poems written by Li were excellent, he believed that poetry writing was not a woman's proper role, and it was deemed "unsuitable". For further reference, please see Eleanor Goodman's article "The Burden of a Talented Woman: Ideas in Li Qingzhao's 'On Poetry' and Early Critiques of Her" in the journal "Changjiang Academic", 2009(2).
14 Peng, Cheng. 2002. *Moke huixi* ("Idle Talks from a Writer"), Vol. 4. Zhonghua Book Company, 323.
15 Hu, Zai. 1962. *Tiaoxi yuyin conghua* ("Series of Poetic Notes by the Recluse of the Brook Tiao"), Vol. 1. People's Literature Publishing House, 267.
16 Hu, Zai. 1962. *Tiaoxi yuyin conghua* ("Series of Poetic Notes by the Recluse of the Brook Tiao"), Vol. 54. People's Literature Publishing House, 367.
17 Zhou, Yinghe. 1990. *Jingding Jiankang zhi* ("History of Jiankang in Jingding Years"), Vol. 50. *Song Yuan fangzhi congkan* ("Collected Chronicles of the Song and Yuan Dynasties"). Zhonghua Book Company, 2173.
18 Wu, Zeng. 1979. *Nenggai Zai manlu* ("Random Records of Nenggai Studio"), Vol. 16. Shanghai Chinese Classics Publishing House, 478–479.
19 Wei, Qingzhi. 1978. *Shiren yu xie* ("Collection of Poets' Precious Remarks"), Vol. 21. Shanghai Chinese Classics Publishing House, 484.
20 Kou Zhun, a Northern Song politician and poet, was a much-praised official in ancient China's Northern Song Dynasty. He was the chancellor from 1004 to 1006 during Emperor Zhenzong's reign.
21 Wu, Chuhou. 1985. *Qingxiang zaji* ("Miscellaneous Records of the Blue Box"), Vol. 6, Zhonghua Book Company, 60–61.
22 Zhang, Qixian. 2003. *Luoyang jinshen jiuwen ji* ("Accounts of Hearsay from Luoyang"), Vol. 1. *Quansong biji* ("Notes from the Song Dynasty"). Daxiang Publishing House, 151. Ruan Yue's "*Shihua zonggui*" ("Compilation of Notes on Classical Poetry", Vol. 4) also records:

Yang Shaoqing's style is talented and self-confident, but since it is not widely used, he often pretends to be crazy and sloppy. While visiting temples and observing the serene beauty of water and bamboo, he would forget to return and fill the walls with his inscriptions. The monks and Daoists cherished and kept the inscriptions, making sure the walls were clean and waiting for his next brush strokes. Visitors praised and admired them. Therefore, the second son of Wang Ciji, Fengying, inscribed below: "Shaoqing's genuine inscriptions fill the abode of the monks, fearing that even Zhong Wang cannot compare. To repay the kindness of the venerable monk, this book shall have no other inscriptions after it." An Hongjian inscribed: "Duanxi stone inkstone, Xuancheng tube, Wangwu pine smoke, purple rabbit hair brush. To obtain the old letters of the lonely Shaoqing, there is nothing else as precious in the world".

(People's Literature Publishing House, 1987: 41)

23 Mei, Yaochen. 1991. *Song Shihou gui Nanyang hui tian dafeng sui su Gaoyangshan si mingri tong zhi Jiangdian* ("Seeing Off Shihou Who Returns to Nanyang and Encountering a Great Wind, I Stay Overnight at Gaoyangshan Temple to Visit Jiangdian Together"). *Quan Song shi* ("Complete Poetry Works of Song Dynasty"),Vol. 5, Peking University Press, 2795.
24 Su, Zhe. 1990. *Xiuzhou seng benying Jingzhao Tang* ("Jingzhao Hall of Monk Benying in Xiuzhou". *Luancheng ji* ("Collections of Luancheng"), Vol. 3, Zhonghua Book Company, 46.
25 Lu, You. 1976. *Xishu yanji* ("On Tea Table", Part 2), *You jinshan* ("Visit to Nearby Mountains"). *Lu You ji* ("Collected Works of Lu You") Vol. 71, Vol. 41. Zhonghua Book Company, 1682, 1043.
26 Zeng, Minxing. 1986. *Duxing zazhi* ("Miscellaneous Records of a Man Awaking Alone"), Vol. 2. Shanghai Chinese Classics Publishing House, 16–17.
27 Tang, Guizhang. 1965. *Quan Song ci* ("Complete *ci* Works of Song Dynasty"). Zhonghua Book Company, 3079.
28 Qian and Kun, either as trigrams or hexagrams, stand for Heaven and Earth, *yin* and *yang*.
29 Ji Dan, or Zhou Gong (the Duke of Zhou), surnamed Ji and named Dan, was the fourth son of King Wen of Zhou, Ji Chang, and the younger brother of King Wu of Zhou, Ji Fa, who twice assisted King Wu of Zhou in his eastern conquest of King Zhou and made rites and music. He was called the Duke of Zhou because he had his cemetery in Zhou and his title was Shang Gong. The Duke of Zhou was an outstanding politician, military man, thinker and educator at the beginning of the Western Zhou Dynasty, and is revered as a "Yuan sage" and a pioneer of Confucianism. The achievements of the Duke of Zhou in his life are summarized in the Shangshu-Da Zhuan as follows: "In one year, he saved the chaos, in two years, he grasped Yin, in three years, he trampled on Am, in four years, he built Houwei, in five years, he set up Cheng Zhou, in six years, he made rituals and music, and in seven years, he gave his administration to King Cheng". The Duke of Zhou, in his seven years of regency, proposed various aspects with fundamental rules and regulations, improved the patriarchal system, the feudal system, the law of succession of the first-born son and the well field system. The most important feature of these systems was that they integrated family and state, politics and ethics, with the patriarchal bloodline as the bond, which had a great influence on Chinese feudal society and laid the foundation for the 800-year rule of the Zhou Dynasty. See https://historytopic.com/377.html.
30 Qian, Shuoyou. 1990. *Xianchun Lin'an zhi* ("Record of Lin'an during Xianchun Era"), Vol. 93. *Song Yuan fangzhi congkan* ("Collected Chronicles of the Song and Yuan Dynasties"). Zhonghua Book Company, 4215–4216. Han Zhongxian (Han Qi) is a great politician and poet in the Song Dynasty, while his great grandson Han

Tuozhou (1152–1207) is considered as a treacherous court officer for his for his opposition to *daoxue* (the Song Neo-Confucianist movement), which was banned on his order during the years 1195–1199.

31 Qian, Shuoyou. 1990. *Xianchun Lin'an zhi* ("Record of Lin'an during Xianchun Era"), Vol. 93. *Song Yuan fangzhi congkan* ("Collected Chronicles of the Song and Yuan Dynasties"). Zhonghua Book Company, 4215–4216.

32 Hui Hong's "*Lengzhai yehua*"("Night Talk in the Studio of Coldness", Vol. 1) mentions the practice of leaving inscriptions on walls by visiting guests, which is said to have originated from Su Shi:

> Previous visitors who were not received did not write on the walls, but Dongpo would write, and he refused to write on plaques. It was his special practice to write on walls only. Before the arrival of the guest, he would clean the ink bamboo.
> (Zhonghua Book Company, 1988: 12)

However, this might not be entirely accurate. As early as the Tang Dynasty, there were instances of visitors leaving inscriptions on walls after being unable to meet the person they intended to visit. For example, Li Shangyin wrote in his poem "Leaving a Farewell at the Unmet Visitor's Estate": "You, you, do not spare the small window of spring, leaving to become a tall qiu tree's galloping horse. Leaning casually on the embroidered curtain, blown by willow catkins, in the deep courtyard when the sun is high, there is no one" (Ye, Congqi. 1985. *Li Shangyin shiji shuzhu* ("Annotations on Li Shangyin's Poetry Collection"). People's Literature Publishing House, 410.)

33 Hui, Hong. 1988. *Lengzhai yehua* ("Night Talk in the Studio of Coldness"), Vol. 5. 41. The translation is adapted from Huang Long's version. See Huang, Long. 2005. English Translation of Chinese Poems on Flowers. Nanjing Publishing House, 129.

34 *Baishe*, geographical name, present eastern Luoyang. It was originally Taoist Dong Dong Weilin's residence. Later, the term is used for the hermit's residence.

35 *Shuanglin*, the place where Sakyamuni, the founder of Buddhism, attained the state of "nirvana", which will enable him to escape this world and its constant sufferings – the fruit of human delusion and desire. The term in the poem refers to the Buddhist temples.

36 Luo, Dajing.1983. *Helin yulu* ("Crane Forest, Jade Dew"), Vol. 6. Zhonghua Book Company, 334. Penglai here refers to *Mishu Sheng* (Secretarial Department), where Zhang Lei and Chao Buzhi served as government officials.

37 Zhang, Shinan. 1981. *Youhuan jiwen* ("Records of You Huan"), Vol. 1. Zhonghua Book Company, 5–6.

38 *Lidai shihua ben* ("Comments on Poetry across Dynasties"). Zhonghua Book Company, 1981: 286–287. Also in: *Songchao shishi lei yuan* ("Categorized Garden of Historical Facts of the Song Dynasty"), Vol. 65. Shanghai Chinese Classics Publishing House, 1981: 866.

39 Tang, Guizhang. 1965. *Quan Song ci* ("Complete *ci* Works of Song Dynasty"). Zhonghua Book Company, 615.

40 Chen, Shidao. *Deng Fenghuang shan huai Zizhan* ("Climbing the Phoenix Mountain, I Reflect on Zi Zhan"). *Quan Song shi* ("Complete Poetry Works of Song Dynasty"), Vol. 19, Peking University Press, 12665.

41 Lu, You. 1976. *Ke huai* ("A Wanderer's Feelings"). *Lu You ji* ("Collected Works of Lu You"), Vol. 60. Zhonghua Book Company, 1450.

42 Zhu, Xi. 2002. *Hui'an xiansheng zhu wengong wenji* ("Collected Works of Huian Zhu Wengong"), Vol. 5. Zhuzi quanshu ("Complete Works of Zhu Xi"). Shanghai Chinese Classics Publishing House, Anhui Education Press, (12): 389.

43 Tang, Guizhang.1965. *Quan Song ci* ("Complete *ci* Works of Song Dynasty"). Zhonghua Book Company, 2171.

44 Zhou, Hui. 1994. *Qingbo zazhi* ("Miscellaneous Records of Qingbo"),Vol. 10. Liu, Yongxiang. *Qingbo zazhi jiaozhu ben* ("*Miscellaneous Records of Qingbo* with Annotations"). Zhonghua Book Company, 443.
45 All of the above references can be found in: Wu, Zeng. 1979. *Nenggai Zai manlu* ("Random Records of Nenggai Studio"), Vol. 11. Shanghai Chinese Classics Publishing House, 305–307.
46 The cuckoo always sings towards the north. Its calls are even more frequent during June and July, unceasing day and night. The sound it produces is extremely mournful, resembling the Chinese phrase "*bu ru gui qu*" ("it's better to return"). That's why it is also known as "*zi gui*" ("Caller of Return").
47 Chen, Yanxiao. 1983. *Gengxi shihua* ("Gengxi Poetic Talks"), Vol. 2. *Lidai shihua xubian* ("Supplementary Comments on Poetry across Dynastics"), Zhonghua Book Company, 191.
48 Liu, Changshi. 1986. *Lupu biji* ("Notes at Lupu"), Vol. 10, Zhonghua Book Company, 79–80, 74.
49 Hong, Mai. 1978. *Rongzhai suibi* ("Spontaneous Essays of the Studio of Forbearance"), Vol. 13. Shanghai Chinese Classics Publishing House, 165–166.
50 Yao Ye was the top scorer in the imperial examination in the first year of the Jingyou era, while Liang Gu achieved the same in the following year. Both of them rose to the position of court officials in the capital (lower-rank officials) before their deaths.
51 Shen, Kuo.1975. *Mengxi bitan* ("Brush Talks from Dream Brook"), Vol. 23. Cultural Relics Publishing House, 5. Also: Vol. 23. 5. Also: *Shihua zonggui* ("Compilation of Notes on Classical Poetry"), Vol. 34. People's Literature Publishing House, 1987: 333.
52 Shen, Kuo.1975. *Mengxi bitan* ("Brush Talks from Dream Brook"), Vol. 24. Cultural Relics Publishing House, 16–17.
53 Liu, Yongxiang. 1994. *Qingbo zazhi jiaozhu ben* ("*Miscellaneous Records of Qingbo* with Annotations"). Zhonghua Book Company, 443.
54 Deng, Guangming. 1978. *Jiaxuan ci biannian jianzhu* ("Notes to *Chronicle Collection of Jiaxuan's Works with Annotations*"). Shanghai Chinese Classics Publishing House, 65.
55 This passage can be found in Wang Dechen's "Zhu Shi" ("*History of a Flywhisk*", Vol. 2) in: *Quansong biji* ("Notes from the Song Dynasty"). Daxiang Publishing House, 47. It is also mentioned in Ruan Yue's "*Gujin shihua*" ("Remarks on Poetry in the Ancient and Contemporary Times") in "*Shihua zonggui*" ("Compilation of Notes on Classical Poetry", Vol. 17. People's Literature Publishing House,1987: 200) and in Huang Che's "*Gongxi shihua*" ("Huang Che's Commentary on Poetry", Vol. 9. People's Literature Publishing House, 1986: 151–152.)
56 Fu, Xuancong et al. 1991. *Quan Song shi* ("Complete Poetry Works of Song Dynasty"), Vol. 17. Peking University Press, 11345.
57 Lu, You. 1976. *Lu You ji* ("Collected Works of Lu You"), Vol. 7. Zhonghua Book Company, 182.
58 Lu, You. 1976. *Lu You ji* ("Collected Works of Lu You"), Vol. 8. Zhonghua Book Company, 227.
59 Tang, Guizhang. 1965. *Quan Song ci* ("Complete *ci* Works of Song Dynasty"). Zhonghua Book Company, 1645.
60 Tang, Guizhang. 1965. *Quan Song ci* ("Complete *ci* Works of Song Dynasty"). Zhonghua Book Company, 3529.
61 In "Song of Cui Hui", Yuan Zhen narrates the story of Cui Hui: Cui Hui was a courtesan in Hezhong Prefecture. By chance, she fell in love with an official named Pei Jingzhong who had temporarily come to Puzhou for official business. The two of them were deeply in love and spent several months in blissful harmony. However, when Pei Jingzhong's duties were completed, they were reluctantly forced to part.

After Pei Jingzhong left, Cui Hui became melancholic and fell ill due to her longing for her beloved. Coincidentally, there was a talented painter named Qiu Xia. Cui Hui asked Qiu Xia to paint her portrait and sent it to Pei Jingzhong, saying, "If ever I am no longer as beautiful as the person portrayed in this painting, I will die for the sake of my beloved". Sadly, not long afterwards, Cui Hui fell seriously ill and passed away.

62 Tang, Guizhang. 1965. *Quan Song ci* ("Complete *ci* Works of Song Dynasty"). Zhonghua Book Company, 3529. For the phrase "a veil of emerald green gauze", see the story of *"Bi Sha Long Bi"* ("Emerald Green Gauze Veils the Walls") in 1.3 of Chapter 1.
63 Fu, Xuancong, et al. 1991. *Quan Song shi* ("Complete Poetry Works of Song Dynasty"), Vol. 2. Peking University Press, 709.
64 Zhang, Mengjing. 1995. *Zhongguo gudian ming shi beisong 100 pian* ("Translation of Selected One Hundred Classic Ancient Chinese Poems for Recitation"). Beiyue Literature and Art Publishing House, 196.
65 Hu, Zai. 1962. *Tiaoxi yuyin conghua* ("Series of Poetic Notes by the Recluse of the Brook Tiao"). Vol. 3. People's Literature Publishing House, 264. Zhou Hui's *Qingbo zazhi* ("Miscellaneous Records of Qingbo", Vol. 8) also mentions this event, with slightly different wording:

> When Liu Jisun was the Wine Supervisor of Raozhou, he wrote a poem on the wall of the government office that read, "The twittering swallows perching upon the beam, when I'm totally free, what will disturb my dream? Though tell, others can't understand the thoughts of mine. I'd enjoy Zhishan, the fine scene, with stick and wine." At the time, Wang Anshi served as the Judge-prosecutor and once read the poem. Wang greatly appreciated it, and then issued an order to have it taught in the local schools. Later, Ye Shilin specifically recorded this in his *"Shi Hua"*. Zhishan is the name of a temple nearby the Raozhou city. However, in the later Chiyang edition, "Zhishan" (sweet and fragrant hill) was mistakenly changed to "Qianshan" (front hill), losing the implication of the entire poem. This can also show the lack of correct understanding of the teachers at the time.
> (Liu, Yongxiang. *Qingbo zazhi jiaozhu ben* ("*Miscellaneous Records of Qingbo* with Annotations"). Zhonghua Book Company, 336–337)

In addition, Ruan Yue's *"Shihua zonggui"* ("Compilation of Notes on Classical Poetry", Vol. 3) also mentions this event, "When Liu Jisun served as the Wine Supervisor of Raozhou, he wrote a poem on the wall of the Zhishan Temple, which read, 'Several sounds of swallows perching upon the beam, disturbed my dream when I was free. Though tell, others wouldn't believe what I say. I'd enjoy Zhishan, the fine scene, with stick and wine.' Wang Anshi served as the local officer at the time. When he read the poem, he appreciated it very much and ordered to have it taught in the local schools" (People's Literature Publishing House, 1987: 30). The fact that various books mentioned this incident shows that it was widely known and enjoyed by people.

66 Zhang Biaochen's *"Shanhu Gou Shihua"* ("Poetical Jottings on the Coral Crook").

> Lu Bing, the Left Minister, once served as a county official in Jiangnan. He wrote a poem in his temporary residence that said. ... Wang Anshi read it and praised it, recommending him at court. Within a few years, he was promoted to a higher position.... Alas! A scholar may have only a few words or lines of writing, but can encounter such fortune.
> (*Lidai shihua* ("Comments on Poetry across Dynasties". Zhonghua Book Company, 1981: 463)

67 Ruan Yue's "*Shihua zonggui*" ("Compilation of Notes on Classical Poetry", Vol. 44):

> The monk Hui Quan from Dong Wu pretended to be a madman, but his poetry was clear and elegant. He once wrote on the wall of a mountain temple by the lake, "As the setting sun and cold cicadas chirp, I return alone to the temple in the forest. The firewood door is not yet closed, and the crescent moon follows my footsteps. I only hear the sound of barking dogs, and I continue on the path through the clear vines." When Dongpo saw it, he composed a response, "Only the sound of bells outside the mist, the temple within the mist unseen. The secluded person's journey is not yet complete, and the dew wets the vast straw sandals. Only the mountain peak moon should be there, illuminating the nights, night after night." Hui Quan became famous for this poem.
> (People's Literature Publishing House, 1987: 281)

> It is also mentioned in Hui Hong's "*Lengzhai yehua*" ("Night Talk in the Studio of Coldness", Vol. 6, Zhonghua Book Company, 1988: 50) and Hu Zai's "*Tiaoxi yuyin conghua* ('Series of Poetic Notes by the Recluse of the Brook Tiao'). Vol. 57", quoted from "*Lengzhai yehua* ('Night Talk in the Studio of Coldness')" (People's Literature Publishing House, 1962: 391).

68 Ruan Yue's "*Shihua zonggui*" ("Compilation of Notes on Classical Poetry", Vol. 20): "Su Dongpo said that when he passed by the hot spring, he found a poem written on the wall that read, 'Only when all sentient beings are washed pure without flaws, would I get cold and flow with other water.' He asked who the author was, and got the reply 'Ke Zun'. Then Su Dongpo jokingly wrote a quatrain in reply, 'The stone dragon (i.e. water well) has a mouth but no roots. Where does the flowing spring in the nature come from? If you believe that all sentient beings are originally pure, where can this warm spring be found?' Ke Zun became famous because of this" (People's Literature Publishing House, 1987: 227).

69 Hu, Zai. 1962. *Tiaoxi yuyin conghua* ("Series of Poetic Notes by the Recluse of the Brook Tiao"). *Gaozhai Shihua* ("Poetic Notes in Elegant Study"), Vol. 25. People's Literature Publishing House, 171–172.

70 In Zhang Duanyi's "*Gui Er ji*" ("A Miscellany of Zhang Duanyi's Writings", Vol. 2), there are following words:

> There was an official in the capital who came from Sichuan to request for official appointment for three or four years. He wrote a poem on the wall of a rented building that said, "In the morning, I watch the Buddha trapped in a shell of mother-of-pearl leaves; at night, I worship the stars and offer them to heaven. When called back, I hear kind words, and would be gald to be appointed official of the third or fourth rank." This poem spread throughout the capital city, and as a result, he was granted with appointment and left the capital.
> (*Song Yuan biji xiaoshuo daguan* ("Grand View of Story-Telling Novels in Song and Yuan Dynasties"). Shanghai Chinese Classics Publishing House, 2001: 4309)

71 Luo, Dajing. 1983. *Helin yulu* ("Crane Forest, Jade Dew"), Vol. 5. Zhonghua Book Company, 207. In Li You's "*Gu Hang Za Ji*"("Miscellany of Ancient Hangzhou"), there is a slightly different version: "In the Bingxu year of Baoqing period, Yuan Qiao sold wine in the Sanxian Hall by the West Lake. Someone wrote a poem on the wall, 'He Jing, Su dongpo and Bai Juyi, are all men of integrity. But now, their faces are covered in dust, yet they have to borrow money for wine from Yuan Qiao'" (*Shuo Fu* ("Collections of all Good Writings", Vol. 57). *Shuo Fu san zhong* ("Three Types of *Collections of All Good writings*"), Vol. 5. Shanghai Chinese Classic Publishing House, 1988: 2192.

72 Shen, Kuo.1975. *Mengxi bitan* ("Brush Talks from Dream Brook"), Vol. 23. Cultural Relics Publishing House, 7–8. It is also mentioned in Peng Cheng's *Moke huixi* ("Idle Talks from a Writer"), Vol. 1, Zhonghua Book Company, 2002: 285.
73 Zhang, Shizheng. 2002. *Kuo yi zhi* ("Collection of Fantasy Tales"), Vol. 6. *Xuxiu siku quanshu* ("Continuation of *Complete Library in Four Branches of Literature*"), Shanghai Chinese Classic Publishing House, 543.
74 Fan, Chengda. 1999. *Wu Jun zhi* ("Records oF Wu Jun"), Vol. 25. Jiangsu Chinese Classic Publishing House, 368.
75 Yuan, Juo. 2001. *Fengchuang xiaodu* ("Small Tablets by the Maple Window"), Vol. 1. *Song Yuan biji xiaoshuo daguan* ("Grand View of Story-Telling Novels in Song and Yuan Dynasties"). Shanghai Chinese Classics Publishing House, 2001: 4759–4760.

4 The Spread of Poems by Singing and Dancing Girls in Song Dynasty

The dissemination methods of *ci* works in the Song Dynasty are mainly divided into two types: oral transmission and written transmission. Oral singing includes the performance of "professional" or "specialized" personnel and spontaneous random singing by amateur enthusiasts. This chapter mainly explores the singing of "professional" singers – namely, singing and dancing girls in the Song Dynasty and their influence on *ci* works in the Song Dynasty.

4.1 Main Participants of Singing

Before the Song Dynasty, both men and women could be famous singers. Wang Zhuo's "*Biji man zhi* ('Commentary from *Biji* Lane on *ci* works', Vol. 1)" lists the names of dozens of male and female singers from the Warring States period (475–221 B.C.) to the Tang Dynasty (618–907 A.D.). Among them, there were 15 male singers, such as Li Guinian and Mi Jiarong, and 19 female singers, such as Nian Nu, Zhang Haohao, Sheng Xiaocong and Fan Su. People in the Song Dynasty paid special attention to female singing, as Wang Zhuo explicitly stated:

> In ancient times, singers could gain reputation regardless of gender as long as one could sing well. … Nowadays, female singers are highly valued while their singing abilities are no longer so important. The lyrics created by scholars and officials are also elegant and graceful, with absolute artistic charm. During the Zhenghe period, Li Fangshu (Li Zhi, one of Su Shi's "Six Outstanding Disciples"), while passing through Yangdi, met an elderly man who was good at singing. Li Fangshu jokingly composed the "*Pinling*" song: "A good singer must be a beautiful woman with jade-like skin, red lips, and white teeth. Her trilling voice could convey emotions, and her voice are fair-sounding like threaded pearls. Although the old man was good at singing, he had white hair and a beard. With such appearance, how could he be compared to the beautiful singing girl Nian Nu?" Although Li Fangshu appreciates the singing in his front, the female voice is more soft and gentle. The lyrics are like

DOI: 10.4324/9781032712512-5

pearls strung together, which makes people intoxicated without deep thoughts.[1]

From Li Fangshu's lyrics and Wang Zhuo's disgruntled tone, it can be seen that people in the Song Dynasty prioritize female voices over male ones. In *ci* works in the Song Dynasty, almost all described the singing of females. For example:

> The *Yu Ren* (beauty) sings softly, urging the music to play.[2]
> In the last song of *Qin E* (singing girl) last song, every note drifts into the clouds.[3]
> The *Cui Mei* (beauty) sings another song, and the entire city of Wei is moved by it.[4]

The references to "Yu Ren", "Qin E" and "Cui Mei" in the text are all female singers.

People in the Song Dynasty particularly valued female singing because the environment for singing was mainly in male-dominated places such as taverns, brothels, banquets and gatherings where the majority of the attendants were men. Female singers not only had nice voices but also had attractive appearances that pleased male attendants. They could entertain the ears and please the eyes. Therefore, people in the Song Dynasty valued female singing but neglected male singing. Yang Zemin, a poet of the Southern Song Dynasty, once commented on the "emphasis on female singing" at the time:

> The world is full of hardships, and human emotions would can change in an instant. Only a beautiful appearance, emotional singing, and charming smile remain constant. With a new song in mind, the girl leans close to me and sing softly, her embroidered shoes tapping gently.[5]

The man has experienced the turmoil of officialdom and has seen through the fickleness of the world. Drinking wine and enjoying the singing of various singers, he would feel relaxed and comfortable. The poem "Peach Grove Revisited" by Guan Jian also shows the satisfaction and relaxation that men feel after listening to music: "With flowing hair and slight dance, the singing girl takes advantage. The oriole's chirping and the green willows make one drowsy. How many past sorrows and new resentments, all vanish with a drunken stupor".[6] The "past sorrows and new resentments" completely disappear in the light singing and graceful dancing. The reason why the "female voice" became the dominant force in the field of *ci* works in the Song Dynasty and music at that time was due to the aesthetic pursuit of society.

However, in the Song Dynasty, the dominance of the "female voice" did not mean that there were no male singers, but male singers were not as numerous or prominent as female girls. "The elderly man who is good at singing" mentioned by Wangzhuo is certainly one of them. Another singer named Yuan Tao, in the later period of the Northern Song Dynasty, once sang Su Shi's

"To the Tune *Shui Diao Ge Tou*" in Jinshan, Zhenjiang, which made Su Shi so happy that he danced to it.[7] He Cong, to whom Feng Quhua of the Southern Song Dynasty dedicated the poem "A Gift to Jinjiang Singer He Cong, to the Tune *Qin Yuan Chun*", was also a male singer.[8] From the line "the predecessors' outstanding skills didn't fail to be handed down" in the poem, it can be seen that He Cong's "predecessors" were also talented singers. Dai Biaoyuan, a singer from the end of the Song Dynasty and the beginning of the Yuan Dynasty, once wrote a song called "In Memory of the Previous Singers", which depicted a male singer of the late Song Dynasty in the style of Li Guinian, a singer in the Tang Dynasty: "Peonies and red beans bloom in the spring, and sandalwood boards and vermilion silk scrolls. With white hair, he drinks in Jiangnan, but no one knows he is another Li Guinian".[9]

During the Song Dynasty, the majority of female singers were "professional" or "specialized" singing and dancing girls. The practice of singing at home among people in the Song Dynasty resulted in a large number of singing and dancing girls during that period. The government at various levels had official singing and dancing girls (also known as registered girls, camp girls, county girls, official servants, etc.),[10] while wealthy families kept household girls (also known as family concubines, attendants, etc.); brothels and wine shops had "commercial" private girls.

At the beginning of the Song Dynasty, in order to win over the literati, Emperor Taizu (927–976) openly encouraged his ministers to "employ singers and dancers, and drink and enjoy themselves".[11] With the emperor's open call, the literati naturally responded actively, and they would spare no effort to hire singing and dancing girls for pleasure. During the reign of Emperor Renzong (1010–1063), a palace maid once said, "In the households of the two central government offices, there are always singers and dancers. If an official has successful career, he would employ even more".[12] This was common for officials in the *Zhongshu Sheng* (Imperial Secretariat), the Privy Council and the Imperial Academy, as well as other high-ranking officials. Occasionally, there were a few ministers who did not want to buy girls and concubines, but the emperor even paid to force them to do so. For example, during the reign of Emperor Zhenzong, the Prime Minister Wang Dan (957–1017) was known for being frugal. Once, during a casual conversation with the emperor, it was revealed that Wang Dan did not have any concubines in his house. As a result, the emperor "bestowed him with three thousand taels of silver" and sent someone to "urge and force" him to buy concubines. At first, Wang Dan was not happy about it. But since he couldn't go against the emperor's wishes, he had to reluctantly accept the order. Unexpectedly, once Wang Dan had concubines, he became extremely indulgent with them.[13] Although this is an extreme and individual example, it gives us a glimpse into the custom of keeping concubines and hiring girls during the Song Dynasty.

If the minister did not buy singing and dancing girls, the emperor would force him to do so. If the husband does not take concubines, his wife would actively buy for him. For example, when Wang Anshi was in charge of the imperial examination, his wife, Mrs. Wu, spent "900,000" *qian* (or 900 *guan*) without Wang Anshi's permission to buy him a concubine. When Sima Guang was appointed as the local magistrate of Taiyuan Prefecture, due to the lack of children after marriage, his wife took the initiative to "buy a concubine for him".[14] Unexpectedly, Wang Anshi and Sima Guang both sent their concubines back without gratitude. These two examples further demonstrate that women in the Song Dynasty fully agreed that their husbands could keep singing and dancing girls at home or take concubines.

It was common practice for people in the Song Dynasty to keep singing and dancing girls so that it became a virtue for a few people not to do so. In the Song Dynasty, if there were no singing and dancing girls in the family of the dead when writing epitaphs, people would emphasize their not having singing and dancing girls or not having an appetite for singing and dancing girls.[15] Having no singing and dancing girls in the family was a merit, which shows how common it was to keep singing and dancing girls at home in the Song Dynasty.

During the Song Dynasty, many poets had concubines and singing and dancing girls in their households. For example, in the home of Ouyang Xiu, there were often "young maids playing the strings and serving wine", together with eight or nine maidservants. Mei Yaochen once wrote a poem as follows, "There are eight or nine beauties in his house, whose hair like that of the raven. With vermilion lips and fair jade-like skin, they are merely around thirteen years old".[16] Even at the age of 85, Zhang Xian still kept singing and dancing girls and had a fondness for concubines. Su Shi once jokingly wrote the following lines: "When the poet passes away one day, his beauties are still very young; thought presently when the master returns, the singing and dancing girls are busy welcoming him".[17] Even Fan Zhongyan, who had a desire to "be the first to worry about the troubles across the land, and the last to enjoy universal happiness", also kept girls at home. When he was an official in Poyang, he took a fancy to a young girl. But she was too young for him to bring back. After he left his position, he couldn't forget the girl, so he wrote a letter to his friend Wei Jie. Later, Wei Jie bought the girl and sent her to Fan Zhongyan, which brought him peace of mind.[18] Su Shi also had many girls at home. Lü Benzhong once said, "Su Dongpo had several singing and dancing girls. Every time when he entertained guests with wine, he would say, 'There are several well-dressed girls waiting to serve. If you like, they will perform for you'".[19] Chao Buzhi also kept girls. Even after he was exiled, he brought his concubines and singing and dancing girls with him to his destination. When he passed through Xuzhou on his way to Yushan, he visited Chen Shidao and "set up a feast, where a young maiden danced to the music '*Liangzhou*'".[20]

During the Southern Song Dynasty, Fan Chengda had many girls in his house. In his later years, he lived in Shihu, Suzhou. Once, the poet Jiang Kui visited him and was invited to compose two songs, "Secret Fragrance" and "Scattered Shadows", to which Fan Chengda had his two girls perform. He greatly appreciated the performance and bestowed the talented girl Xiao Hong to Jiang Kui as a reward. From then on, Jiang Kui would often compose music and play the flute, to which Xiao Hong would sing and dance. This has become a famous story in the world of poetry.[21] Zhou Bida, Fan Chengda's friend, who had served as a political advisor, also bought girls. He once wrote to Fan Chengda: "I recently acquired Dong Bisheng at Zhejiang, and a girl who is quite skilled in singing and dancing. At first, I wanted to entertain guests with them, but within two years both of them passed away. Since then, I have no desire to acquire another".[22] The national hero Wen Tianxiang was known for his love of luxury and had many entertainers in his household. It was not until the fall of the Song Dynasty that he regretted his extravagance and donated all his wealth to fund the military troops in an attempt to resist the Yuan Dynasty and restore the country.[23]

People in the Song Dynasty were not satisfied with having one or two concubines. Sometimes, they had as many as dozens or even hundreds of girls. Firstly, we may look at the number of girls raised in the official family: Han Qi, the prime minister of Emperor Renzong's reign, had "more than 20 singing and dancing girls".[24] Han Jiang, the prime minister of Emperor Shenzong's reign, had over ten singing and dancing girls.[25] During the reign of Emperor Huizong, Prime Minister Wang Yi had "dozens of concubines, all of whom are extremely beautiful".[26] Cai Jing and Tong Guan have at least 20 singing and dancing girls.[27] Lü Yihao, the prime minister of Emperor Gaozong of the Southern Song Dynasty, had more than ten concubines.[28] Zhang Yuan, deputy director of Jiangdong in Shaoxing, had about 20 singing and dancing girls.[29] In the middle of the Southern Song Dynasty, there were hundreds of female singers from the aristocratic lyricist Zhang Xuan's family. Zhou Mi once recorded the grand occasion of holding a peony-appreciating meeting and singing peony lyrics at home:

> When the guests gathered, they sat in an empty hall, with nothing but silence. Suddenly, someone asked the servants, "Has the incense been lit?" They replied, "Yes." Then the curtains were rolled up, and a rare fragrance filled the room. A group of singing and dancing girls arrived with food, drink, and stringed and woodwind musical instruments. Ten girls, dressed in white with peony accessories, performed music and served drinks. After the singing and dancing, they left and the curtains were laid down again. The guests chatted happily. After a long time, the incense was lit again. Then other ten girls came out with changed clothes and accessories. Generally, the girls wear purple clothes when holding white flowers, wear light yellow clothes when holding purple flowers, and wear red clothes when holding yellow flowers. In this way, for ten rounds of drinks, the clothes and flowers were changed ten times in total. And the songs they sang were all about the peony. When the wine was finished, hundreds of musicians and singers escorted the guests out, with candlelight and incense all around. The guests felt as if they were in a fairyland.[30]

The scene and atmosphere were just like a modern large-scale party with songs and dances.

Generally, wealthy households would keep more than ten singing and dancing girls. During the Northern Song Dynasty, when Shi Manqing lived in Caihe, his neighbour was a mentally weak but "wealthy" young man who had "a group of girls" numbering more than ten in his house.[31] One wealthy man whom Su Shi had drunk with also had "more than ten maidservants with skills and talents".[32]

Fang Yinglong, a famous scholar of the Southern Song Dynasty, was originally a common person without official ranks. He once "bought dozens of singing and dancing girls to entertain guests with music, singing and dancing. When he was depressed, he missed his hometown and wrote poetry after getting drunk, and the singing of the girls was very charming".[33] From this, we can see that the custom of keeping singing and dancing girls was prevalent among people in the Song Dynasty. Liu Yong's *ci* work "To the Tune *Wang Hai Chao*" described Hangzhou as a city "with quite a lot singing and dancing girls filling the grand houses". In fact, the phenomena that "singing and dancing girls filling the grand houses" not only existed in Hangzhou but all over the country.[34] Wang Anshi's *ci* work "Meditation on the Past of Linling, to the Tune *Guizhi Xiang*" lamented over the prosperity of the Six Dynasties. Comparatively, it seems that the pursuit of people in the Song Dynasty for prosperity is no less than that of their predecessors.

During the Song Dynasty, a private household might have several girls or as many as several dozen or even hundreds. So how many registered official girls were there in the local governments? According to records, there were probably several dozen or even hundreds of registered singing and dancing girls in a provincial government.

Shi Rong's "*Shangu waiji shi zhu*" ("Annotations to Huang Shangu's extra poems", Vol. 13) has the following line: "There are no officials to ridicule, and there are twenty-four female *pipa* players". The annotation reads, "There is a poem before that says, 'there should not be twenty-four *pipa* players.' This refers to the number of official girls who play the *pipa* in Luling Prefecture (now Jizhou, Jiangxi Province)". This means that there were only twenty-four officially registered girls who played the *pipa* in Luling Prefecture. If we add in other girls who played other instruments such as the *qin*, *zheng* and flutes, then the total number of singing and dancing girls in the prefecture would be close to one hundred. The record in Volume 9 of "*Jingkang Yao Lu* ('Essential records of the Jingkang Era')" confirms our speculation: when Mao You became the governor of Hangzhou in the first year of the Jingkang era, he said, "How can there be less than one hundred officially registered singing and dancing girls in the prefecture?" So he "commanded the local officials to supervise the singing and dancing girls".[35] Mao You believed that a prefecture like Hangzhou should have more than 100 official girls. It seems that the number of official singing and dancing girls in other prefectures should be around one hundred as well. Every time there was a holy festival (the emperor's birthday) in a prefecture, the girls would perform large-scale dancing with the performers arranged in the shape of the Chinese pictographic characters "天下太平" (peace in the world).[36] It would be difficult to arrange such characters with only tens or hundreds of girls. During the Yuanfeng period of the Northern Song Dynasty, there were a total of 293 prefectures and armies and 1,235 counties in the whole country.[37] If each prefecture had dozens of singing and dancing girls and each county had several singing and dancing girls, then there were at least tens of thousands of officially registered singing and dancing girls in the Song Dynasty! With so many singing and dancing girls, how many new poems and *ci* works were needed to meet their needs?

During the Song Dynasty, officially registered and household singing and dancing girls generally had a "professional" division of labour. Each person was responsible for the specific performance of playing musical instruments and singing. The royal family of Pingyuan Commandery in the Southern Song Dynasty had "places for all singers to learn singing skills", and "there were Butou or heads for various groups of performers of blowing, dancing, and singing". The performers of *Sheng* (a reed pipe wind instrument in China) alone counted for more than 20.[38] Some of them have their own unique skills. The preface to the poem "To the Tune *Huan Xi Sha*" by Zhao Lingqian of the Northern Song Dynasty stated, "Liu Pingshu had 8 singing and dancing girls, each with unique skills. He asked me for *ci* works as gifts to him. The girls had unique feet, and unique skills in singing, in playing *qin*, and in dancing". "Unique feet" refers to the physical "uniqueness" that the girls' feet were extremely small with the practice of foot-binding.[39] "Unique skills in singing, in playing *qin*, and in dancing" all refer to the "uniqueness" of their performing skills.

In terms of the performance of musical instruments, there are several common divisions of labour: those responsible for playing the flute, playing the *qin*,[40] playing the *pipa*,[41] and playing the *guzheng*.[42]

Girls who play the flute are called "flute girls" or "flute maids". For example, in Su Shi's "*Ziyu's Family Banquet*", there is the following line that reads, "I poured a glass of wine and toasted with Meng Guang, and order the players of flute to play the music of *Yinzhou* and *Liangzhou*". The annotation reads, "In Ziyu's family there are flute girls".[43] In Huang Tingjian's poem, there is an annotation that reads, "The flute player in Wang Jinqing's family is named Zhaohua".[44] In Fang Shao's description, Yang Pan, an officer and poet in the Song Dynasty, was also fond of performances of singing and dancing girls. "Every time when he accompanies his relatives and friends, he would take a boat ride in the moonlight, with two flute maids performing to add to the fun. He took so much pleasure in it that he leisurely forget to return".[45] There are many girls and concubines in Xin Qiji's house, including flute maids. Once, the doctor cured Xin Qiji's illness. To show gratitude to the doctor, Xin Qiji presented a flute maid named Zhengzheng to the doctor and wrote a piece of *ci* work, "To the Tune *Hao Shi Jin*".[46]

The girls who played the *qin* are called "*qin* girls". For example, Chen Zao once wrote the poem "Two Poems for *qin* Girls",⁴⁷ and Liu Qingfu wrote the *ci* work "A Playful Work to *qin* Girls in Shayi: To the Tune *Jin Ju Dui Fu Rong*".⁴⁸

Those who played the *pipa* are called "*pipa* girls". Han Wei once wrote the poems "Echoing Again with the *pipa* Girls in Yang Zhimei's Family" and "Echoing Again with Yaofu's Desire to Borrow a *pipa* Girl".⁴⁹ In Ye Mengde's "Record of Summer Resort in Stone Forest" (Vol. 2), there are the following words: "Fan Deru was fond of the *pipa* music. In his later years, he suffered from insomnia. There were two maids in the house who was good at playing the *pipa* and *guzheng*. Every time before he went to bed, he would let the two play together until he fell asleep. Only after that could they leave".⁵⁰

The girls who played the *guzheng* are called "*guzheng* girls". Hong Peng of the Northern Song Dynasty once wrote a poem titled "A Playful Poem to the Little *guzheng* Girl",⁵¹ and Dong Sigao of the Southern Song Dynasty wrote the poem "A Gift for *guzheng* Girls at Night Banquet".⁵²

The terms "flute girls", "*qin* girls", "*guzheng* girls" and "*pipa* girls" simply indicate these girls' outstanding skills in certain areas and do not mean that they could only play the one specific type of musical instrument. At banquets, sometimes they would not only play the musical instruments but also sing lyrics.

4.2 Performance Settings

In the Song Dynasty, singing and dancing girls mainly performed in entertainment environments such as public and private banquets, hotels, teahouses, song halls and brothels.

The so-called "official banquets" refer to banquets hosted by government officials. In official banquets of the Song Dynasty, girls played music and sang lyrics to liven up the atmosphere. As Ye Mengde wrote in his "*Shilin Yanyu*" ('Random Thoughts in Stone Forest', Vol. 5): "At the public banquet, after each round of drinking, the actors or actresses must sing '*Zui Jiu*' (Drink-urging) before the music starts. This is a Tang Dynasty practice for toasting".⁵³ One of the "job responsibilities" of officially registered girls was to play music and sing lyrics at official banquets.

It was an officially recognized practice to have girls play music and sing lyrics during official banquets. It was forbidden to have such practice for non-official occasions. The court often ordered the officials to refrain from having girls for banquets for non-official events. For example, on the day of Guichou in January of the first year of Yuanfeng (1078), it was decreed that officials were not allowed to have girls for non-official banquets, and this was requested by Lü Gongyu, the governor of Yongxingjun.⁵⁴ In the 13th year of the Shaoxing years (1143), it was decreed that no girls were allowed for banquets unless it was hosted by the principal or deputy chief officer or it was an official event and permission was granted. Those who violated this decree or were related to the violation would be severely punished.⁵⁵ In the 26th year of Shaoxing (1156), it was decreed that county officials were allowed to have girls for official banquets on holidays but not for other occasions. Unauthorized use of girls would be reported to the court by the supervising officials, and the censorate would be constantly on the alert.[56]

These prohibitions reveal two phenomena from the opposite side: firstly, the use of singing and dancing girls for official banquets and holiday banquets in the Song Dynasty was customary, reasonable and legal. In the early Song Dynasty, there was a poem by Wei Ye that read, "It is only at feasts on official business, will they arrange singing and dancing girls".[57] Yin Zhu stated that in his official career, he worked diligently day and night and did not invite singing and dancing girls except for official banquets.[58] It is not that it was not permitted to invite singing and dancing girls for official banquets, but singing and dancing girls were necessary for official banquets. Lü Zuqian of the Southern Song Dynasty also warned in his "Family Norms: Official Proverbs" that "one should not go to a brothel or a banquet until the holiday every ten days off".[59] Someone once asked Zhu Xi if "entertainment with singing and dancing girls" could be held. Zhu Xi replied, "Nowadays, it is held all over the country and the states. Why can not we hold it at home? It depends on the host's consideration". Zhu Xi was the most self-righteous neo-Confucianism scholar, and even he himself admitted that "it is held all over the country and the state",[60] and his own family can also invite singing and dancing girls for entertainment. This indicates that such entertainment was very common at that time. Secondly, it is very common for local government officials at various levels to have singing and dancing girls' entertainment for banquets. Sometimes, for "official banquets", the singing and dancing girls were arranged, while sometimes, for those non-official or holiday banquets, the girls were also arranged.[61] That's why the royal court repeatedly imposed a ban on the use of girls for "non-official banquets".

The rule that it was forbidden to arrange officially registered singing and dancing girls for non-official banquets was regulated for all the officials in service. The private banquets of literati and ordinary officials were not limited in arranging the girls. They can either arrange singing and dancing girls at home or rent officially registered singing and dancing girls to accompany and sing lyrics. For example, in the Southern Song Dynasty, Chen Zao once "borrowed singing and dancing girls from the local prefecture to accompany guests", and the girls "sang for guests' drinks".[62] Xie Ximeng invited Chen Liang to a banquet in Taizhou and also "borrowed the singing and dancing girls from the local prefecture for the banquet at the East Lake".[63] When Su Shi of the Northern Song Dynasty was exiled to Huangzhou, he also "drank with accompany of singing and dancing girls' performance".[64] At that time, Su Shi was exiled here and was not a vassal of Huangzhou. He would naturally rent the singing and dancing girls temporarily for drinks. It can be seen that borrowing or renting officially registered singing and dancing girls to accompany drinks was a very popular phenomenon during the Song Dynasty.

During the Song Dynasty, official banquets were very frequent. When Su Shi was a judge in Hangzhou, he was invited to banquets day and night, but he had a limited drinking capacity for liquor and was exhausted from handling the invitations. He even helplessly described Hangzhou as the "hell of food and wine".[65] This kind of "hell of food and wine" probably existed everywhere in the country. For example, an officially registered singing and dancing girl in Yizhen once said, "As a member of the music department, guests come to Yizhen like clouds, and banquets are held all the time. It is impossible to find a moment of rest".[66] Yizhen refers to the present Zhenzhou, where official banquets were numerous and frequent, so much so that the girls in the music department were busy every day and had scarce free time.

During the Song Dynasty, wherever officials went, they were accustomed to having singing and dancing girls serve them. Once they arrived in a remote and poor county where there were no such girls, they would feel a strong sense of loss. For example, when Wang Yucheng was demoted to Shangzhou, he complained, "This mountainous city is so poor and there are no singing girls and music here. How would it comfort the troubled minds of men of letters?"[67] Zhang Lei also expressed similar feelings by saying, "In poor counties, one must be careful with the cost of wine. The customs are backward and there is no entertainment with singing and dancing girls".[68] It can be seen that entertainment with singing and dancing girls had become an important part of the lives of literati and officials. Once they lost it, their lives became less enjoyable.

The aforementioned is the common practice of entertainment with singing and dancing girls at official banquets. Let's take a look at some specific cases to see the performance of singing and dancing girls at official banquets:

> When Qian Weiyan, a Northern Song official, was stationed in Luoyang, he would order the registered singing and dancing girls to dance in socks only (i.e., without shoes) on the mat (*sha*) while singing "To the Tune *Ta Sha Xing*" ("Walking on Mat").[69] Kou Zhun would always have singing and dancing performances at his banquets. "At the gatherings, there were often thirty or more guests, together with lively music. He was especially fond of the 'Zhezhi Dance', which, performed by twenty-four dancers, wouldn't come to an end until several cups of drinking later".[70] When Yang Wanli was a supervisor during the Southern Song Dynasty; he was invited to a banquet by a county magistrate. "Officially registered singing girls sang his *ci* work 'To the Tune *He Xin Lang*' for wine". In the work, there are the following lines, "When will Yang Wanli's cloud sail arrive?" Yang Wanli immediately replied, "Yang Wanli arrived yesterday". The girl accidentally sang out Yang Wanli's name in the lyrics, which was taboo and made the county magistrate embarrassed.[71]

For the official banquets held by the local officials of states or counties, all the officially registered singing and dancing girls in the area were usually in attendance. When Su Shi was prefecture in Hangzhou, he held a banquet at the West Lake, and all the registered singing and dancing girls came.[72]

When Wu Zhongguang was the governor of Mianzhou in Sichuan, he invited his superiors to a banquet, and all the officially registered singing and dancing girls gathered together.[73] Some official banquets were very grand, with hundreds of girls in attendance. For example, in the third year of the Dazhong Xiangfu year (1010) of Emperor Zhenzong's reign, Li Yunze, the Peace Envoy of Hebei, held a banquet to entertain Kou Zhun. There were over 100 girls in attendance, which made even Kou Zhun, known for his extravagance, exclaim in great surprise.[74]

As for private banquets at home, singing and dancing girls were also indispensable. Yan Shu, the prime minister of the Northern Song Dynasty, was a typical example. He drank and feasted at home every day. For all the banquets, he had music and singing for accompaniment.[75] Xin Qiji also commanded the girls to sing his own *ci* works at the banquets he held.[76] Wang Zhuo of the Southern Song Dynasty said that in the 15th year (1145) of the Shaoxing period, he visited the Miaosheng Courtyard in Biji Lane, Chengdu, and stayed very close to his friends Wang Hexian and Zhang Qiwang. Every day, both Wang and Zhang had girls sing and dance to accompany their drinking. When Wang Zhuo returned from the banquets every day, he recorded the songs and stories sung by the girls in his guest room and traced their origins. With these, he compiled the book *Biji man zhi* ("Commentary from *Biji* Lane on *ci* Works"), which was the first large-scale work on poetry and *ci* works in the history of Northern and Southern Song Dynasties.[77]

In addition to the government offices and private residences where official or private banquets were held, commercial public places such as wine shops, brothels and inns were also sites for singing performances.

During the Song Dynasty, government-run wine shops and private wineshops or teahouses often employed singing and dancing girls to perform on stage to attract customers. For example, since the Xining New Policy was implemented during the reign of Emperor Shenzong of Northern Song, the government-run wine shops "ordered girls to stay in the shops and perform" to attract customers.[78] Yang Shi, a famous neo-Confucian philosopher during the transition period between the Northern and Southern Song Dynasties, was very dissatisfied with this and said, "The royal court tries to sell wine, and the officials in charge of them arrange music and girls to attract common people. This is the most harmful to education".[79] However, this trend did not change even at the end of the Southern Song Dynasty. Wu Zimu, a scholar of the late Song Dynasty, said,

> Since the Jingding period (1261–1264), many wine shops have made efforts to sell more wine, and there are many official and private singing and dancing girls in the shops. They select high-level girls who are graceful and beautiful, with rosy cheeks, cherry lips, delicate jade fingers, charming eyes, and melodious singing voices. When these girls sing or speak, their words are full of rhyme and charm, making people never get tired of hearing.[80]

According to the detailed record in *Wulin jiu shi* ("Former Events in Wulin (Hangzhou)"), each wine shop had "tens of officially registered singing and dancing girls, each with wine vessels worthy of a thousand taels of gold and silver for entertainment of guests". The names of these girls were written on "nameplates" in the shops. When guests entered the store, they would order by the nameplate.[81]

Private wine shops also gathered singing and dancing girls. At the end of the Song Dynasty, Wuhu County was a place where "singing and dancing girls gathered in wine shops, and fishermen and vendors traded in markets".[82] For wine shops in the capital city of Lin'an, there were "tens of private singing and dancing girls in each place. Dressed in fashionable clothes, with beautiful laughter, these girls were like white flowers competing for brilliance, jasmine overflowing in the summer with fragrant smells. They would attract customers by leaning against the railings".[83] Liu Guo, a famous poet of the Southern Song Dynasty, once wrote a poem titled "Wine Shop" to describe the scene of listening to songs in a wine shop:

> Going up to the Green Tower (brothel) at night, it seems as entering a deep but attractive cave. A thousand songs sung by the girls, mixed with dialects of customers from over the country. The girls' charming arms are white and delicate as lotus roots, and their costumes are colorful as yellow mandarins or shiny gold. Singing and reveling without restraint, they would no longer sing the songs of Yue.[84]

His other poem titled "At Completion of a Wine Shop in Nanjing and Preparing for Lights" also described that at the completion of a wine shop, customers flooded in with the sound of singing shaking the earth:

> All night long, the sound of music and singing hastens the end of the year, and the noise of the pipes and drums welcomes the return of spring. The people in the city splurge large amount of money, while we climb up to enjoy one cup.[85]

There were also girls in the teahouses who, "dressed in beautiful clothes, welcomed the guests by competitively showing their charm, singing and playing the strings day and night. Their performance pleased our eyes and hearts".[86]

In addition to those long-term resident girls, there were also some amateur girls who came to sing for some extra money. In the wine shops of the capital city Bianjing (present Kaifeng in Henan) in the Northern Song Dynasty, there was often the following scenery:

> Lower-class girls came without invitation. They sang and danced for the banquets, and were given some pennies in return and then sent back. They were called "*zha ke*" (local residents) or "*da jiu zuo*" (performing for small sum of money).[87]

In the wine shops of the capital city Lin'an in the Southern Song Dynasty, there was also the following scenery:

> Young girls came without invitation, who sang in a loud voice to seek a share of payment, hence the name "*ca zuo*" (temporary singing girls). There were also those who played the flutes, plucked the strings, played *xiqi* (a sort of musical instrument in the Song Dynasty), played the gongs and drums, sang the songs, and performed sideshows, hence the name "*gan chen*" (run for profit). ... The sound of music, singing and laughter continued throughout the night.[88]

In "*Yijian zhi* ('Talks on Oddities', Vol. 7)" written by Hong Mai, there are records about the "*da jiu zuo*" (performing for a small sum of money) by singing girls:

> Chen Dong, during the Jingkang period, drank at a wine shop in the capital, where there was a singer singing songs while seated on a bench. Chen Dong ignored her and stood alone by the railing. The girl sang the lyrics of "To the Tune *Wang Jiang Nan*" with a clear and melodious tone, to which Chen Dong could not help listening. When the song was ended, the girl got some money and went downstairs.[89]

In the Song-Yuan *hua-ben* novel *Jin Man Ji* (The Story of Golden Eel), there is also a description of Qingnu, the main character who was trapped in a hotel in Zhenjiang for poverty in the early Southern Song Dynasty. She had to go to the wine shops to sing and earn some money to live:

> Qingnu said, "I have some skills, and I can sing well. I'm not afraid to perform here. Why not buy a gong and go to various wine shops to perform, so that I can earn tens or hundreds of coins for living expenses?" Zhang Bin said, "You come from a good family. How can you do such things?" Qingnu replied, "I have no other choice. As long as you are safe, I will go to Lin'an to see my parents with you". From then on, Qingnu performed in the wine shops of Zhenjiang. ... Since she started performing, she earned several *guan* of money every day.[90]

Although this is a novelist's words, and maybe there are no real people involved. From Zhang Bin's words, it can be seen that singing in wine shops was a despised profession at the time.

During the festivals, some girls and performers would travel around, singing and performing along the streets. Wu Zimu once said,

> There are three to five musicians in the street, holding one or two young girls to dance and sing songs. They performed along the streets. On the day of the Lantern Festival, during the visits of Three Springs Garden,

and when visiting the lake to watch the tide, people would find them in the disreputable quarters of the city. But their payment was not much. They were called "desolate drums and boards".[91]

Brothels were the "headquarters" of private girls in the market. The famous figures there were mostly talented in singing and dancing. When entertaining guests, they would naturally sing lightly and dance gracefully. Zhang Bangji's "*Mozhuang Manlu* (Rambles from the Ink Cottage, Vol. 8)" contains a story about the famous girl Li Shishi in the capital city Bianjing, who was invited to a banquet:

> During the Zhenghe years, Bianjing was prosperous. The two girls Li Shishi and Cui Nianyue were most famous in the city at the time. Chao Chongzhi (with the courtesy name Shuyong) often invited them to banquets. More than ten years later, when he returned to the capital, the two were still there, and their reputation had spread throughout the country. Li Sheng came from a prestigious family. Chao Chongzhi, recalling the past days, wrote two poems and presented them to Jiang Zihi. One of them read, "As a young man, I drank and walked around the prosperous capital city, and paid a visit to the brothels. I watched the dance of *Ni Shang Yu Yi Qu*,[92] and listened to the song of the *Yu Shu Hou Ting Hua*.[93] The door was covered with pearl curtains, and the window was rolled up with cherry blossoms. The guests were half surprised and followed the flowing water. We scattered like stars and fell to the ends of the earth."[94]

In the poem "*Hong Chuang Ruan, Ji Shi*" (Red Window Complaints – Current Affairs) written by Wang Zhi of the Southern Song Dynasty, there is also the description of listening to songs with friends in a Hangzhou brothel during his youth:

> The curtain is not rolled up. The girls inside are hard to see. The ethereal singing voice follows the fragrance in the air. I remember listening to them several times with three or five friends in Hangzhou. They sang with unbleached silk fabric and white round fan. The evening breeze is cool, and the courtyard is full of shade of parasol trees. I wanted to paint her portrait, but I never had the chance to recognize her flower-like face.[95]

The reason why only the poet could hear the "ethereal singing voice" but could not see the "flower-like face" is that the girls usually had curtains to cover them. "The curtain is not rolled up", so "The girls inside are hard to see". The situation of girls singing behind curtains was often described in the poems of the Song Dynasty. For example, in Guo Xiangzheng's poem "Farewell to Wu Yuanqing, the Chief Officer, at the Age of 81", there are the following words: "The remaining flowers can still be enjoyed by the railing, and the singing of the little girls behind the curtain are often heard".[96] Ge Shengzhong's preface to the lyrics of "To the Tune *Huan Xi Sha*" also mentioned, "Ye Mengde and Ge Shengzhong, who were granted the *jinshi* degree in the same year. They had a singing girl play the *sheng* behind the curtain, then they each wrote a piece of poem".[97] The girls singing behind the curtains, partly hidden and partly visible, would arouse the audience's interest to have a see.

4.3 Selection of Lyrics

The lyrics sung by the girls at banquets, as well as the content of the lyrics, were generally determined by the host of the banquet.

If the host were the author, they generally had their own lyrics performed, which could both entertain the guests and show their own talent. For example, in the Song Dynasty, Kou Zhun once "composed a *yuefu* poem and had a little girl sing it" at an early spring banquet.[98] In the Northern Song Dynasty, Wu Gan had a maidservant named Hongmei (Red Plum Blossoms). Wu Gan once wrote a poem entitled *"zhe hong mei"* ("Folding Red Plum Blossoms"), which made the girl very proud. "His poem was very popular. At spring banquets, he always had the singing girls sing it".[99] At the end of the Northern Song Dynasty, Ye Mengde invited Ge Shengzhong, who obtained the *jinshi* degree in the imperial examination, with him in the same year to a banquet. Ye had his maidservant sing the *ci* works written by him.[100] In the Southern Song Dynasty, the poet Zhang Zi invited Lu You to a banquet and had his family maidservant Xin Tao "sing his *ci* works to accompany the wine".[101] Xin Qiji, on the other hand,

> would command the maidservants to sing his works at all the banquets. He was particularly fond of the work "To the Tune *He Xin Lang*". He would often recite the warning lines, "I think the green hills are very charming, and I expect the green hills would see me the same way." He also said, "I don't regret that I could not see the ancients, but I regret that the ancients could not see me a crazy man." Every time he when does so, he laughs and touches his belly. The guests around all praised him with one voice.[102]

From Xin Qiji's recitation of his warning lines and his behaviour of "laughs and touches his belly", it can be seen how satisfying it is to show off one's talent in front of the guests!

If there were poets among the guests, the host of the banquet sometimes would ask the girls to sing the guests' poems so that the guests would feel a sense of identity and honour, thus achieving the goal of mutual joy between the host and the guests. For example, during the Northern Song Dynasty, Jia Changchao garrisoned the Northern Capital (present Daming in Hebei), and Ouyang Xiu returned from the Liao Dynasty back to the Song Dynasty after he finished the diplomatic mission. Jia Changchao invited Ouyang Xiu to a banquet, and the girls sang Ouyang Xiu's poems during the meal. Ouyang Xiu was very pleased and drank a full cup for each song.[103] When Yan Shu was the prefect of Jingzhao, Zhang Xian (with the courtesy name Ziye) was the judge. Every time Zhang Xian visited, Yan Shu would ask his attendants to offer wine and sing Zhang's poems.[104] Li Bing (with the courtesy name Hanlao) wrote a famous poem on plum blossoms with the title "To the Tune *Han Gong Chun*" when he was young, which won universal praise. During the Zhenghe period, Prime Minister Wang Fu held a banquet to invite Li Bing, and many beautiful women from his family were present. When they sang "To the Tune *Han Gong Chun*" halfway through the drinks, Li was surprised and greatly delighted.[105] In the late Southern Song Dynasty, Yang Chun, the deputy prime minister, invited Chao Gongsu to a banquet and had the girls sing Chao's *ci* works for entertainment. Chao was very excited after listening and wrote a letter expressing his gratitude.[106]

Sometimes the host of a banquet wrote poems at the site and had girls sing them, or the girls asked the host to write poems on the spot. When Ouyang Xiu was exiled to Chuzhou, he held a banquet for someone who had passed the imperial examination in the same year as him and was appointed as a judge in Langzhou. Ouyang Xiu composed a farewell poem on the spot and had the girl sing it as a gift. "The song was sung for twenty years".[107] He accidentally wrote a masterpiece. Jiang Can of the early Southern Song Dynasty would improvise *ci* works whenever holding banquets for the guests. The girls, while singing, would hold cups and encourage more drinks. The poetic lines were elegant and fresh, not following the words of the predecessors. Such romantic stories were later written into Jiang's epitaph, showing that it was admirable at the time.[108] When Su Shi was prefect of Xuzhou, the Yellow River broke its banks. After Su Shi led the army and civilians to build the floodwall successfully, he held a banquet to celebrate the day of the Shangsi Festival (the third of lunar March). A girl said, "Since ancient times, there have been many songs for Shangsi Festival, but none has ever played an elegant tune after building a new floodwall. I hope to sing a song in front of the public". Su Shi improvised the poem "To the Tune *Man Jiang Hong*", and the girl sang it. The atmosphere was very lively.[109]

If guests could write poems, the host would usually ask them to write poems on the spot. For example, in Huang Renjie's preface to the poem "To the Tune *Man Jiang Hong*", there are the following words, "General Zhang, the secretary of the Grand Secretariat, held a banquet for guests at the city moat. They took a boat ride in the pool full of lotus fragrance, with beautiful scenery all around. The host asked the guests for poems, so they composed some".[110] At the banquet on the boat, guests swayed with the waves, enjoying the beautiful scenery, tasting fine wine and hearing songs and performances by girls. In such an atmosphere, even if the host did not ask for poems, literary figures would find it difficult to suppress their creative impulses. Sun Di's preface to the poem "To the Tune *Liu Shao Qing*" also describes a similar scene: "At the spring festival in Lin'an, we took a boat ride on the lake. When General Hu asked for poems, we composed some".[111]

Sometimes the singing girls took the initiative to ask for poems from the guests. This situation was frequently observed in Song poetry.[112] For example:

> Liu Pingshu had eight family maids who, each with exceptional skills, requested poems as gifts.[113]
> Among them, there was an official singing girl named Xiaoxiao who requested poems.[114]
> Zhao Zonglian exchanges her fan for poems, and I jokingly write this one. Zhao is very skilled at chess, calligraphy, tea-making, and playing the *qin*.[115]
> At Shi Fuzhi's banquet, the singer presented Yun Tou Incense as a gift and begged for poems.[116]
> When Zheng Deyu invited Yuan Yi to a banquet, I was also present. In my drunken state, the girls asked for poems, and I wrote this one for them.[117]
> Zhao Dequan met with a small group of colleagues and placed morningstar lily in red and yellow in front of the screen, and immediately asked for words.[118]
> In early summer, when trying new clothes, Wan Qing held a plain fan and asked for *ci* works, so I wrote this poem on the fan.[119]
> In the front, several girls asked for poems for their performance. Feeling inspired, I continued with the previous rhyme.[120]

Sometimes the host invited all the guests to compose poems together, not only for entertainment but also to have competition in their talent and show their creativity. At such times, the poets naturally had to use all their skills to stand out and show their talent. For example:

> During the Chunyou period, the prefect of Dan Yang repaired the Duojing Tower and held a grand banquet to celebrate its completion. Many famous people from all over the country were present. After the banquet, the host ordered the girls to ask the guests to compose poems. Li Yan (with the courtesy name Guangweng) was the first one to finish. Everyone was amazed and impressed by Li Yan's poem, so they no longer wrote their own. The poem reads...[121]

The author must have felt satisfied and pleasant when he received such a round of applause from everyone. The atmosphere must have been lively and joyful!

Singing and dancing by the girls were meant to please the guests and enliven the atmosphere. If the girls always sang old and boring songs, they would lack the force of attraction. Therefore, if the host or guests did not have any special arrangements or requests, the girls would try to sing new songs as much as possible. This is often mentioned in the *ci* works of the Song Dynasty:

The young talented men wrote new poems, and the beautiful women urged for more drinks.[122]

They casually tossed their hairpins around lying in someone else's arms, shedding tears while singing new lyrics.[123]

Don't cover the new lyrics with the waving sleeves.[124]

We enjoy new drinks happily together. To recite good verses, we need men of letters. After singing the new songs, we returned.[125]

Singing my new works, the girl covers her face and weeps.[126]

Don't frequently wave your hands to urge for new poems.[127]

Similar situations were also revealed in poems by poets of the Song Dynasty, "The girls sing new tunes, and the servants serve grinded tea".[128] The new works of poets were generally first spread by these beautiful and charming singing girls. Many of the new lyrics sung by the girls were composed on the spot for the guests, as introduced earlier, while others were obtained through other means.

4.4 Singing Styles

There are various ways of singing lyrics in the Song Dynasty. "*Chang Qu Men Hu*" ("The Guideline of Singing") in Tao Zongyi's "*Nancun chuo geng lu*" ("Nancun's Notes in the Intervals of Ploughing", Vol. 27) records nine different styles of singing, including "*Xiao Chang* (singing slowly with a castanets), *Cun Chang* (singing short songs), *Man Chang* (singing slow songs), *Tan Chang* (chanting Buddhism songs), *Bu Xu* (chanting Taoism songs), *Dao Qing* (Taoists' sermons), *Sa Lian* (uncertain), *Dai Fan* (uncertain) and *Piao Jiao* (chanting and shouting)".[129] The differences between these styles are not well understood today.

"*Xiao Chang*"[130] was the most common type of singing at the time, which mainly included singing *Xiao Ling* (short lyrics) or slow songs. Nai Deweng's "*Ducheng ji sheng* ('Famous Sages of the Capital')" states:

> In singing, "*Xiao Chang*" refers to singing slow songs with a castanet. It generally starts with a heavy tone and ends with a soft one, hence the saying "shallow sipping and low singing". It is coordinated with the forty major music and spinning dances.[131]

In essence, "*Xiao Chang*" refers to singing slow lyrics with a castanet, usually starting with a heavy tone and ending with a soft and gentle one, hence the saying "shallow sipping and low singing".[132] Wu Zimu's "*Meng Liang Lu*" ("Record of Millet Dream", Vol. 20) also states that "*Xiao Chang*" means singing short lyrics with a soft and tender voice.[133] Zhang Yan's "*Ci Yuan*" ("Source of ci Poetry", Vol. 3) also discusses "*Xiao Chang*", saying that it requires clear pronunciation, a clear and round voice and is best accompanied by a mute flute: "*Xiao Chang* must include a clear and round voice. With the accompaniment of a mute flute, the sound is very complete, which the *Xiao* (a vertical bamboo flute) cannot achieve".[134]

In the Song and Yuan Dynasties, "*Xiao Chang*", in most cases, referred to female singing. For example, in Meng Yuanlao's *Dongjing meng hua lu* ("Reminiscences of the Eastern Capital", Vol. 5), most of the performers who were skilled in "*Xiao Chang*" in the market in the late Northern Song Dynasty were women:

> Since the Chongguan period, in the market of the capital…the masters of Xiao Chang include the following: Li Shishi, Xu Poxi, Feng Yinu, Sun Sansi. These are really the most well-known performers![135]

From their names, we learn that Li Shishi, Xu Poxi, Feng Yinu and Sun San Si all seem to be women. In the book "Guixin Zashi" ("Miscellaneous Records of Guixin Years", Vol. 2) written by Zhou Mi, it is recorded that during the Qingyuan years, a woman with the surname He was "skilled in *Xiao Chang* and *Piao Chang* and could sing over five hundred songs. She was also adept at playing *Shuang Yun qin* (Double Rhyme Qin) and could play over fifty pieces".[136] These singers good at *Xiao Chang*, in today's terms, were famous female singers who sang popular songs at the time.

At that time, there also seemed to be men who were skilled in "*Xiao Chang*". In Zhou Mi's book *Wulin jiu shi* ("Former Events in Wulin (Hangzhou)", Vol. 6), in "Various Types of Performers", there is a list of those who specialize in *Xiao Chang*:

> *Xiao Chang*: Xiao Popo (from Grand Tutor Han's mansion), He Shou, Chen Weifan, Hua Yu Zhou, Lu Enxian (steward), Sheng Zhang, Zhou Yizhai, Wu Dushi, Ding Ba.[137]

He Shou, Lu Enxian, Wu Dushi and Ding Ba should be men from their names. Of course, the vast majority of those who sang "*Xiao Chang*" were female singers based on the descriptions in *ci* works of the Song Dynasty.

"*Xiao Chang*" is generally performed with castanets and cappella. As is described in Liu Yong's poem "To the Tune *Feng Qi Wu*", "The clear and melodious singing from behind the curtain enlivens the banquet outside. Although one can hear the lovely and novel singing, the beautiful faces of the singers cannot be seen. The rhythmic clapping of the castanets sounds like pearls falling on a jade platter, and the vibrating sound gradually sinks into the crystal-clear wine cup".[138] This tells that the girls sing behind the curtain while holding a red castanet. Similar descriptions can be found in Sima You's poem "To the Tune *Huang Jin Lü*", "Striking the castanet and singing a beautiful melody",[139] and in Zhao Fuyuan's poem "A Gift to Singing Girls, to the Tune *Zhe Gu Tian*", "she opens her cherry-like lips to sing songs, while using her slender hands like jade shoots to tap on the red castanet".[140]

The Spread of Poems by Singing and Dancing Girls in Song Dynasty 109

Sometimes the singing is accompanied by musical instruments. As is found in Huang Shang's poem "Winter Banquet, to the Tune *Yong Yu Le*", "With wind and string music, they proposed more toasts, while enjoying the singing of female singers with white teeth and beautiful faces".[141] In Li Guang's poem "Banquet at Qiongtai on Double Ninth Day, to the Tune *Nan Ge Zi*", there are the following lines, "The beautiful girl sings gently, and the wind and string instruments quicken her".[142] All the about describe the beautiful girls singing with low voices softly and gently with the accompaniment of wind string instruments. Peng Yuexun's *ci* work "To the Tune *Die Lian Hua*" even directly states the accompaniment with a *pipa*, and the girls play the instruments themselves while singing: "Outside the curtain, there is a clear singing voice; at the bottom of the curtain, there is accompanying music. The girl plays the *pipa* herself without the accompaniment of *sheng huang* (a reed pipe wind instrument)".[143]

Sometimes there is not just one instrument in accompaniment, but several instruments playing together or taking turns to play. Wu Wenying's poem "Returning to the Capital with Music" states, "Friends take boats on the lake, and musicians are arranged to play the *zheng, sheng, pipa,* and *fangxiang* in succession".[144] During this lake excursion, four musical instruments, namely *zheng, sheng, pipa,* and *fangxiang* (an ancient musical instrument, which is similar to bronze chime), were played in succession. Zhang Yuangan's poem "To the Tune *Rui Zhe Gu*" describes a singing girl accompanied by *fangxiang* and *qin*:[145]

> The young orioles are chirping and the tips of the sprouts are new. The double-pistil flowers are delicate as the girl's slender figure. She always pours a full cup of wine and persuades the guests for more drinks, and she is magnificently dressed. Full of tender affection, she looks backward with soft tapping. The sound of *fangxiang* and *qin* turns even more harmonious. The spring is about to come at the tips of the cardamom, and the Mt. Wu is waiting for the clouds because of deep affection.[146]

The first part describes the clear and crisp singing of the girl, her slender figure and her charming and affectionate nature. She is good at persuading guests and adjusting the atmosphere. The second part describes her playing the *fangxiang* while singing and constantly "flirting" with the guests. The guests were mesmerized and enchanted, as if drunken and infatuated.

During the "*Xiao Chang*" process, sometimes there are dancing activities. This can be seen from the following lines:

> I remember attending a banquet. We were welcomed with beautiful dances and clear songs, while the girls wore beautiful silk headbands.[147]
> The beauty sings clearly, and her dancing sleeves sway like snow.[148]
> Beautiful songs and dances surround the red stove.[149]

In dancing, her slender waist is tender as drifting snow, and her clear voice stops the clouds.[150]

Her clear songs and graceful dances are unparalleled.[151]

The "clear songs" and "clear voice" were put together with "dances", so the singing and dancing might be performed at the same time, or some girls sang songs while others danced. Hong Mai's "*Yijian zhi* ('Talks on Oddities')" described a banquet in which "more than ten maid servants were in service" and "they listed one the left or on the right, with some dancing and some singing".[152]

The easiest way for *Xiao Chang* is *Qing Chang* (unaccompanied singing), which is accompanied by neither musical instruments nor dance. Such unaccompanied singing is also described in poems of the Song Dynasty, such as "The singing girl Xiaoxing, with her tender voice, sings the lyrics of Jia Dao. Sumei, another singing girl, sings unaccompanied".[153] The so-called "sings unaccompanied" means singing without the accompaniment of musical instruments.

As to the number of people involved in the singing, there were solo singing and chorus singing at the time. The examples of "*Xiao Chang*" quoted earlier seem to be mostly solo singing. As for the chorus singing, it is also recorded. For example, when the Duojing Building in Zhenjiang was completed, Zhang Xiaoxiang composed a poem and "ordered the girls to sing it in chorus".[154] Chorus singing is also called "group singing". As quoted earlier, when Wang Fu, the prime minister of the Northern Song Dynasty, set up a banquet for Li Hanlao, tens of his maidservants "sang in groups" the poem "To the Tune *Han Gong Chun*". The preface of the poem "To the Tune *Dongpo Yin*" written by Yang Guanqing of the Southern Song Dynasty, records that in a dream, a young man "ordered the subordinates to call in tens of beautiful girls, who, standing around a square table, sang in groups with miserable voice".[155] What the girls sang in the dream was all written by Yang Guanqing. Although it is a dream, it is something possible in real life. In the late Southern Song Dynasty, Feng Zhiqia wrote a poem titled "To the Tune *Qing Yuan Chun*", in which there are the following lines: "What is most unforgettable, is that the song of Yangchun, was sung in groups in front of you". Jiang Jie also wrote the poem "Tao Cheng's Birthday, to the Tune *Da Sheng Le*", in which there are the following lines: "I heard they sing songs with regional characteristics, then sang slowly the words for birthdays, and sang lotus songs in groups".[156]

There were many singing and dancing girls in the royal court, so the lyrics in the palace were often sung in choruses. For example, in the first year of Jingding years (1260), the girls in the palace once sang the ci works of "Happiness, to the Tune *Sheng Sheng Man*" written by Chen Yu (also named Zang Yi):

> In August, the Crown Prince invited the Emperor and the Queen to the Qingji Pavilion to enjoy the fragrance of the hibiscus and sweet-scented osmanthus. Chen Paner, the head of the musical troupe, in order to liven up the atmosphere with some wine, held a castanet and sang a song.

The Spread of Poems by Singing and Dancing Girls in Song Dynasty 111

The song was "To the Tune *Sheng Sheng Man*", a famous work by the poet Li Qingzhao. However, immediately after the singing of the first line "I search and search", the Emperor said, "This work is too melancholic and gloomy, not suitable for such a setting". Then he said to the prince, "You may ask Chen Yu to write a lively version of 'To the Tune *Sheng Sheng Man*' on the spot in accordance with the current scenery". Chen Yu then knelt down and accepted the order. He finished the poem during the time of five drinks. Two rounds of wine later, dozens of people could recite it. The Emperor was so excited that, in addition to the official payment, he specially bestowed a hundred taels of silver. On April 9 of the next year, the Crown Prince ordered Chen Yu to write a poem "To the Tune *Bao Dinger*" for his birthday, and had all in the palace sing the song in chorus for celebration.[157]

If it were a palace banquet, such as a royal gathering in the morning or a royal festival, the scene would be grand with various instruments and performances, similar to today's large-scale cultural evening shows. Singing lyrics was only part of the programme. Meng Yuanlao's *Dongjing meng hua lu* (Reminiscences of the Eastern Capital, Vol. 9) described in detail the scene and process of court performance for the Tianning Festival (Emperor Huizong's birthday) during the Song Dynasty.[158] At that time, the birthday ceremony banquet and artistic performances were held together. The grand and spectacular scene was acclaimed as the acme of perfection. The performances ranged from singing slow songs to dances and dramas, from acrobatics and variety shows to sports competitions such as sumo wrestling and ball games.[159] Zhou Mi's *Wulin jiu shi* ("Former Events in Wulin (Hangzhou)", Vol. 1) also records the programme list of the palace banquets during the reign of Emperor Lizong. The programme list listed the names of the instruments, songs and performers one by one, similar to today's programme list for artistic performances. This performance for the celebration of Emperor Lizong's birthday was more of a pure music and dance concert, with occasional performances of puppets, variety shows and dramas in between. The entire performance was mainly composed of music and singing, such as singing the song "*Yanshou Chang*" ("For a Long Life").

4.5 The Effect of Singing

The performance of singing girls in the Song Dynasty had a profound influence on the development of *ci* works.

Firstly, the singing of girls expanded the artistic influence of *ci* works. In other words, it was through the singing of girls that the artistic charm of *ci* works was realized. As Wang Yan (also named *Shuangxi*) wrote in the preface to "*Shuangxi shi yu* ('A Collection of *ci* Works of Shuangxi')": "*ci* works are suitable for singing instead of for recitation. Except those who have rosy lips and ivory white teeth, none can full display their artistic charm". This shows that the unique artistic charm of *ci* works could be fully displayed only with the singing of girls. In the Song Dynasty, singing *ci* works were a form of audio-visual art with comprehensive entertainment effects. Especially when girls sang, there were not only physical performances but also beautiful music in accompaniment. The girls' beautiful appearance and charming demeanour have a visual impact, and their clear and delicate singing voices, coupled with the accompaniment of beautiful music, also have an auditory impact. The texts of *ci* works have a stronger appeal of language, so *ci* works at that time were a fusion of performative, musical and linguistic significance with an overall function of pleasing the eyes, ears and hearts. People of the Tang and Song Dynasties, when "listening" to *ci* works, had aesthetic feelings which were completely different from those of later generations when "reading" such works but were similar to the feelings of listening to popular songs today. Especially in the Song Dynasty, most of the recipients of *ci* works were groups of people who collectively enjoyed them in entertainment venues, such as public and private banquets, teahouses and taverns. There was a kind of emotional atmosphere that infected and stimulated each other between the performers and the audience and among the audience themselves, which had a particularly strong "sense of presence". In his poem "To the Tune *Fan Qing Tiao*", Zhang Xian wrote, "One beauty from Wu urged for more drinks, while another from Han sang tender songs. Both of them, with exquisite beauty, makes a world of spring on both sides". In his poem "To the Tune *Jian Zi Mu Lan Hua*", Ouyang Xiu wrote,

> The singing girl displayed her grace and composure as she sang. She gently rolled up her sleeves and, while tapping on the sandalwood board, began to sing. Her voice was sometimes clear and melodious, lingering and echoing among the intricately carved beams and painted rafters, persisting for a long time and even stirring up the faint dust. At other times, her voice was gentle and smooth, resembling a string of luminous pearls threaded together. The singing girl's lips were as rosy and luscious as ripe cherries, and her teeth gleamed like white jade. Her voice, ethereal and enchanting, seemed as if celestial beings in the heavens were expressing their innermost thoughts. Her magnificent singing captured the wandering clouds in the sky. All the guests at the banquet were enthralled and bewitched as if their hearts and souls were captivated.

Xiang Zikun also wrote the poem "To the Tune *Huan Xi Sha*" to express his feelings when listening to music, "After the song, the blue sky is scattered and the shadows are chaotic. In dancing, their red sleeves flutter like snowflakes. After a few times of seeing each other, their soul is overwhelmed with joy".[160] Whether for "a world of spring on both sides", "enthralled and bewitched as if their hearts and souls were captivated", or "overwhelmed with joy", they all express the artistic enjoyment of the audience at that time from different perspectives. The enjoyment in such an atmosphere cannot be approached by reading poetry or other literature alone. Therefore, in the Song Dynasty, *ci* works were more popular and loved by the urban population than poetry, and it became a dominant form of social and cultural entertainment consumption at that time.

The high entertainment value and wide popularity of *ci* works in the Song Dynasty inevitably stimulated and expanded the society's extensive demand for *ci* works. The annual and daily performances at public and private banquets alone required a large number of "new words" to meet the demand. The increasing popularity and widespread singing of *ci* works promoted the popularity of *ci* writers and brought them a high and broad social reputation. The expansion of social demand and the increase of *ci* writers' reputation also stimulated their enthusiasm for creation. The amount of *ci* works created by writers in the Song Dynasty is generally higher than that of writers in the Tang and Five Dynasties,[161] which is inseparable from the social demand at that time. The interaction between dissemination and creation promoted the creation and development of *ci*.

Secondly, the theme orientation and the formation of the style of *ci* works in the Song Dynasty are also restricted by the performance of the singing girls. People in the Song Dynasty highly valued female singing, and most of the performances by singing and dancing girls were held in entertainment sites and banquets or brothels, where the audience sought sensory stimulation. To adapt to the atmosphere of such performance and the identity of the performers, the subjects of the *ci* works must be suitable for expressing provocative and charming women and female sexuality. The poets of the Tang Dynasty and Five Dynasties and the so-called natural and popular poets of the Northern Song Dynasty, such as Liu Yong, Yan Shu, Ouyang Xiu, Qin Guan and Zhou Bangyan, wrote *ci* works that expressed female images and emotions. This was closely related to the consumption environment and audience. Modern Chinese scholar Xia Chengtao had long realized this point and once said that many of Wen Tingyun's *ci* works "were written for girls in the palace and wealthy families to sing. In order to suit the identities of these singers and listeners, the style of the works tended to be graceful and restrained".[162]

Women's voices are generally tender and soft. Wu Zimu wrote in his work "*Meng Liang Lu*" ('Record of Millet Dream', Vol. 20) with the following words, "In singing tender and slow songs, the singer must have a gentle and soft voice". When describing female singing of *ci* works in the Song Dynasty, people usually described their voices as down and soft, "In pronouncing words or singing songs, their voices are generally tender and soft".[163] "Their tones are soft and childish".[164] The tender and soft voice of the girls requires that the style of the *ci* work be graceful and charming so that the singing can be coordinated and the artistic effect of expressing emotions through voice can be achieved. Liu Jiangsun of the late Song Dynasty said, "Those who are fond of harmony and elegance in words, are not satisfied with those who attaches more importance to the expression of emotions; those works praised by men of letters, are not to be accepted by those are fond of music and rhythm".[165]

It also shows that the female voice requires "harmony and elegance". Yan Nan Zhi An, a Chinese opera and music theorist in Yuan Dynasty, said that "men do not sing tender and soft *ci* works, while women do not sing heroic songs".[166] It also shows that at that time, girls should sing feminine and soft songs instead of heroic and magnificent "heroic songs". After listening to soft and gentle *ci* works for a long time, people gradually developed specific "horizon of expectation" that *ci* works should be gentle and tender. Chen Shidao, in his "*Houshan shihua*" ("Houshan Poetic Talks"), stated that Su Dongpo's *ci* works were bold and unrestrained, and, "although they are the best in the world, they are not of the fundamental nature";[167] instead, only those soft and gentle *ci* works like Qin Guan's are really good ones. Wang Yan of the Southern Song Dynasty, in his preface to *Shuangxi shi yu* (A Collection of *ci* Works of Shuangxi), also stated, "The reason why *ci* works are also called *qu* (songs) is that songs should fully express the human emotions. Therefore only gentle and tender ones are good, and those heroic ones are not so valuable".[168] The establishment of the soft and gentle style of *ci* works in the Song Dynasty and the formation of the concept of the "fundamental nature" of *ci* works are closely related to the performance of female singing and dancing. It is precise because of this that Wang Zhuo, in his "*Biji man zhi*" ("Commentary from *Biji* Lane on *ci* Works"), stated that "modern people only value female voices", "and the *ci* works written by scholars or officials also emphasize gentleness and tenderness".

Notes

1. Yue, Zhen. 2000. *Biji man zhi jiaozheng* ("Revision to *Commentary from Biji Lane on ci Works*"). Bashu Publishing House, 26.
2. Li, Guang. *Nan ge zi: chong jiu ri yan qiongtai* ("Holding Banquet on Double Ninth Festival at Qiong Tai, to the Tune *Nan Ge Zi*"). Tang, Guizhang. 1965. *Quan Song ci* ("Complete *ci* Works of Song Dynasty"). Zhonghua Book Company, 785.
3. Li, Lü. *Man ting fang* ("To the Tune *Man Ting Fang*"). Tang, Guizhang.1965. *Quan Song ci* ("Complete *ci* Works of Song Dynasty"). Zhonghua Book Company, 1478.
4. Zeng, Dun. *Nian nu jiao:song huai cao Qian chu he* ("To Qian Chuhe in Huaicao: To the Tune *Nian Nu Jiao*"). Tang, Guizhang.1965. *Quan Song ci* ("Complete *ci* Works of Song Dynasty"). Zhonghua Book Company, 1174.
5. Tang, Guizhang.1965. *Quan Song ci* ("Complete *ci* Works of Song Dynasty"). Zhonghua Book Company, 3006.
6. Tang, Guizhang.1965. *Quan Song ci* ("Complete *ci* Works of Song Dynasty"). Zhonghua Book Company, 1570.
7. Cai, Ta. 1983. *Tieweishan congtan* ("Collective Writings on the Tieweishan Mountain"), Vol. 3. Zhonghua Book Company, 58. According to Yuan Yuan, also called Yuan Tao, is still alive in Jingkang. Vol. 1 of "Essential Records of the Jingkang Era" records that after the Jin soldiers captured Bianjing on the 12th day of the first lunar month in the first year of Jingkang (1126), Yuan Yu, Bianjing Li Shishi and other family fortunes were confiscated to serve the Jin people. The emperor wote, "Confiscation of the properties of Zhao Yuannu, Li Shishi, Wang Zhongduan and Zeng Zhiying, as well as Yuan Tao, Wu Zhen, Shi Yan, Jiang Yi, and Guo' mother" (*Siku quanshu* (Complete Library in Four Branches of Literature, Wenyuange edition), Vol. 329: 420.)

8   Tang, Guizhang. 1965. *Quan Song ci* ("Complete *ci* Works of Song Dynasty"). Zhonghua Book Company, 2657. Feng Quqia also mentions He Cong in the preface to another song "Shui Tiao Ge Tou": "Three days after the festival, you are invited to climb to the top of the North Mountain, drinking wine and looking into the distance, although the fun is different, but everyone is very happy. Therefore, he made this poem and gave it to He Jun, and the maid sang it to accompany the wine" (*Quan Song ci* ("Complete *ci* Works of Song Dynasty"). Zhonghua Book Company, 2658).
9   Dai, Biaoyuan. *Yanyuan dai xiansheng wenji* ("The Collected Works of Dai Biaouan"), Vol. 30. *Sibu congkan* ("Four Series Books"). Also in Tian, Rucheng. *Xihu youlan zhi yu* ("Book of tour in the West Lake", Vol. 11): "Dai Biaoyuan, originally from Fenghua, was a student at the Imperial Academy during the Song Dynasty. However, he chose not to serve under the Yuan Dynasty. His poem 'A Farewell Song to the Singer on the Lake' (*hushing zen gezhe*) reflects his longing for his homeland" (Shanghai Chinese Classics Publishing House, 1998: 166).
10 Wang, Shunu. 1988. *Zhongguo cangji shi* ("A History of Prostitutes in China"), Shanghai SDX Joint Publishing Company, 123–158; Li, Jianliang. 1999. *Tang Song ci yu Tang Song geji zhidu* ("*ci* works in Tang and Song Dynasties and Singing and Dancing Girls"). Hangzhou University Press. 30–45.
11 Sima, Guang. 1989. *Shuishui Jiwen* ("Records of Rumors from the Man of Su River"), Vol. 1, Zhonghua Book Company, 12.
12 Zhu, Bian. 2002. *Quwei jiuwen* ("Old Stories at the Winding Wei River"), Vol. 1. Zhonghua Book Company, 89.
13 Zhu, Xi. *Song mingchen yanxing lu* ("Records of Words and Deeds of Eminent Officials of Song Dynasty"), Vol. 1. Wang Dan zhuan (Biography of Wang Dan), Vol. 2. *Sibu congkan* ("Four Series Books").
14 Shao, Bowen. 1983. *Shaoshi wenjian houlu* ("The Records of the Experience and Knowledge of Shao Bowen"), Vol. 11. Zhonghua Book Company, 121–122. According to ancient times, the status of a family prostitute and a concubine were similar, so they were often mentioned together. For example, in "Old History of Tang Dynasty: Biography Yang Ping", it says, "He extensively recruited prostitutes and concubines in the side courtyard of Yongle". In "Old History of Tang Dynasty: Biography of Ding Gongzhuo", it says, "He had no interest in singing and dancing with prostitutes and concubines for his whole life". In "History of Song Dynasty: Biography of Wang Yan", it says, "When the public died in Shanxi, he had many prostitutes and concubines" (Zhonghua Book Company, 1977, (25): 8849). In "History of Song Dynasty: Biography of Han Xizai", it says, "He received many rewards and kept over 40 prostitutes and concubines, many of whom were skilled in music. He did not restrict their movements and allowed them to freely enter and exit the outer chambers, mingling with guests and students" (Vol. 40: 13866).
15 According to the Epitaph of Liang Gong, a great official of the right court, in Vol. 65 of Ji Lei Collection by Chao Bu: "He always used respectful language when speaking at home, kept himself clean, was diligent and thrifty, and had no interest in girls" (*Siku quanshu* (Complete Library in Four Branches of Literature, Wenyuange edition), Vol. 1118: 903). In Vol. 33 of *Hongqing Jushi ji* ("A Collections of Hongqing Jushi's Works") by Sun Di, in the epitaph of Zhang Gong, a former official of the left court and a direct member of the Dragon Pavilion: "There were no girls serving at home, and not a day went by without reading" (*Siku quanshu* (Complete Library in Four Branches of Literature, Wenyuange edition), Vol. 1135: 343). In Vol. 19 of Jie Zhai Collection by Yuan Xie, in the epitaph of Hu Fu Jun: "No girls were entertained, no leisure or enjoyment was sought, and no jokes were made" (*Siku quanshu* (Complete Library in Four Branches of Literature, Wenyuange edition), Vol. 1157: 264). In the supplement of Vol. 1 of Wu Du Wen Cui Xu Ji by Yang Shi, in the epitaph of Zhang Gong, a former official of the left court and a

direct member of the Dragon Pavilion: "He never loved girls or rare treasures, but only read countless books, constantly seeking improvement" (*Siku quanshu* (Complete Library in Four Branches of Literature, Wenyuange edition), Vol. 1386: 693).

16 Ge, Lifang. 1981. *Yunyu yangqiu* ("Well-Covered Commentary on Poetry"), Vol. 1. *Lidai shihua* ("Comments on Poetry across Dynasties"), Vol. 2. Zhonghua Book Company, 606.

17 Wang, Mao. 1987. *Yeke congshu* ("Comprehensive Writings of Wang Mao"), Vol. 29. Zhonghua Book Company, 332. Also in Zhao, Lingzhi. *Hou Qing lu* ("Records of Literary Delicacies"). *Song Yuan biji xiaoshuo daguan* ("Grand View of Story-Telling Novels in Song and Yuan Dynasties"), Vol. 2. Shanghai Chinese Classics Publishing House, 2001: 2088.

18 Wu, Zeng. 1979. *Nenggai Zai manlu* ("Random Records of Nenggai Studio"), Vol. 11. Shanghai Chinese Classics Publishing House, 307. Also in Yao, Kuan. 1993. *Xixi congyu* ("Commentary by Yao Kuang"), Zhonghua Book Company, 93.

19 Lü, Benzhong. 1988. *Xuanqu lu* ("A Collection of Jokes"). *Shuo Fu san zhong* ("Three Types of *Collections of All Good Writings*"). Shanghai Chinese Classics Publishing House, 1577. Also in "*Chao Yun shi bing yin* ('To Lady Chao Yun')", Su Shi himself said, "I had several concubines in my home, and they left one after another in the span of four or five years. The only one left was Chao Yun, who accompanied me when I moved south" (*Sushi shiji* ("A Collection of Sushi's Poems"), Vol. 34. Zhonghua Book Company, 1982: 2073). These "several concubines" refer to several girls.

20 Zhang, Bangji. 2002. *Mozhuang manlu* ("Rambles from the Ink Cottage"), Vol. 3. Zhonghua Book Company, 96.

21 Lu, Youren. *Yanbei zazhi* ("Rambles of Yanbei"), Vol. 2. *Siku quanshu* (Complete Library in Four Branches of Literature, Wenyuange edition), Vol. 86. 605.

22 Zhou, Bida. *Yu Fan Zhineng can zheng* ("On Fan Chengda's Participation of Political Affairs"). *Wenzhong ji* ("A Collection of Zhou Bida's Works"), Vol. 191. "*Siku quanshu* (Complete Library in Four Branches of Literature, Wenyuange edition), Vol. 1149.160.

23 Tuo, Tuo et al. 1977. *Wen Tianxiang zhuan* ("Biography of Wen Tianxiang"). *Song shi* ("History of the Song Dynasty"), Vol. 418. Zhonghua Book Company, (36): 12534.

24 Jiang, Shaoyu. 1981. *Songchao shishi lei yuan* ("Categorized Garden of Historical Facts of the Song Dynasty"), Vol. 8. Shanghai Chinese Classics Publishing House, 79.

25 Cai, Zhengsun.1982. *Shilin guangji* ("Compilation of Selected Poems and Poetic Theories"), Vol. 3. Zhonghua Book Company, 241.

26 Wang, Mingqing. 1991. *Yuzhao xin zhi* ("New Records of Jade Illumination"), Vol. 3. Shanghai Chinese Classics Publishing House, 44–45.

27 Li Tianmin's "*Nanzheng Lu Hui* ('Compilation of Records from the Southern Expedition')" records that on the 28th day of the first month of the second year of Jingkang, after the Northern Song Dynasty was destroyed, "Kaifeng Prefecture rewarded two generals, Cai Jing, Tong Guan and Wang Fu, with 24 songstresses each". Cui, Wenying. 1988. *Jingkang baishi jianzheng* ("Annotations on the *Records of the Jingkang Incident*"), Vol. 4. Zhonghua Book Company, 139.

28 Xiong, Ke. 1985. *Zhongxing xiaoji* ("Records of National Revitalization"), Vol. 18, Fujian People's Publishing House, 225.

29 In Vol. 1 of Hong Mai's "*Yijian zhi* ('Talks on Oddities')", there are following words: "Observing Envoy Zhang Yuan, was the Deputy General Manager of Jiangdong during the Shaoxing period, living in Jiankang. He would always go to the capital to buy beautiful concubines at a high price, and had 20 houses for them. He was strict in their education, and would punish even minor mistakes. Once,

when he had guests, the girls filled the room, and the singing and dancing were exquisite. They all drank and enjoyed themselves" (Zhonghua Book Company, 1981: 1391).
30 Zhou, Mi. 1983. *Qidong ye yu* ("Wild Talk from East of the State of Qi"), Vol. 20. Zhonghua Book Company, 374.
31 Shen, Kuo. 1975. *Mengxi bitan* ("Brush Talks from Dream Brook"), Vol. 9. Cultural Relics Publishing House, 12–14.
32 Ruan, Yue. 1987. *Shihua zonggui* ("Compilation of Notes on Classical Poetry"), Vol. 47, People's Literature Publishing House, 293.
33 Wang, Mai. *Puyang Fang Meishu muzhi ming* ("Inscription on the Tomb of Fang Meishu from Puyang"). *Quxuan ji* ("A Collection of Quxuan's works"), Vol. 11. *Siku quanshu* (Complete Library in Four Branches of Literature, Wenyuange edition), Vol. 1178: 593.
34 Zhong, Zhenzhen. *Hu Ying Luo Qi xinjie* ("A New Interpretation of 'Hu Ying Luo Qi'"). Journal of Zhejiang Normal University, 1983(1).
35 Anonymous. *Jingkang yao lu* ("Essential Records of the Jingkang Era"), Vol. 9. *Siku quanshu* (Complete Library in Four Branches of Literature, Wenyuange edition), Vol. 329: 591.
36 Zhou, Mi. 1983. *Qidong ye yu* ("Wild Talk from East of the State of Qi"), Vol. 10. Zhonghua Book Company, 189.
37 Wang Cun's *Yuanfeng jiuyu zhi* ("Treatise of the Nine Regions from the Yuanfeng Reign-Period (1078–1085)") states that at that time, there were "a total of 23 roads, 4 capital prefectures, ten secondary prefectures, 242 subordinate prefectures, 37 armies, 4 supervisory offices, and 1,235 counties" at the time (Zhonghua Book Company, 1984: 1). *Yuanfeng jiuyu zhi* ("Treatise of the Nine Regions from the Yuanfeng reign-period (1078–1085)") is an imperial geography from the Northern Song period (960–1126). It was compiled on imperial order by Wang Cun (1023–1101), Zeng Zhao (1047–1107) and Li Dechu.
38 Zhou, Mi. 1983. *Qidong ye yu* ("Wild Talk from East of the State of Qi"), Vol. 17. Zhonghua Book Company, 310.
39 Foot-binding was a practice first carried out on young girls in Tang Dynasty China to restrict their normal growth and make their feet as small as possible. Considered an attractive quality, the effects of foot-binding were painful and permanent. It was widely used as a method to distinguish girls of the upper class from everyone else and later as a way for the lower classes to improve their social prospects. The practice of foot-binding continued right up to the early 20th century. See https://www.worldhistory.org/Foot-Binding/.
40 *qin*, or *Guqin* (ancient *qin*), a seven-stringed plucked instrument in some ways similar to the zither.
41 *pipa*, a plucked string instrument with a fretted fingerboard; four-stringed Chinese lute.
42 *guzheng*, a 21- or 25-stringed plucked instrument in some ways similar to the zither.
43 Su, Shi. 1982. *Sushi shiji* ("A Collection of Sushi's Poems"), Vol. 11. Zhonghua Book Company, 540.
44 Shi, Rong. 2003. *Shangu waiji shi zhu* ("Annotations to Huang Shangu's Extra Poems"), Vol. 16. *Shangu shi ji zhu* ("Annotations on the Collection of Shangu's Poetry"), Vol. 2. Shanghai Chinese Classics Publishing House, 1015.
45 Fang, Shao. 1983. *Bo zhai bian* ("Historical Records by Fang Shao"), Vol. 7. Zhonghua Book Company, 42.
46 Zhou, Hui. *Qingbo zazhi* ("Miscellaneous Records of Qingbo"), Vol. 3. *Siku quanshu* (Complete Library in Four Branches of Literature, Wenyuange edition), Vol. 1039: 118.
47 Fu, Xuancong et al. 1991. *Quan Song shi* ("Complete Poetry Works of Song Dynasty"), Vol. 45. Peking University Press, 28255.

48 Tang, Guizhang. 1965. *Quan Song ci* ("Complete *ci* Works of Song Dynasty"). Zhonghua Book Company, 2699.
49 Fu, Xuancong et al. 1991. *Quan Song shi* ("Complete Poetry Works of Song Dynasty"), Vol. 8. Peking University Press, 5168, 5286.
50 Ye, Mengde. 1990. *Shilin bishu luhua* ("Records of Summer Resort in Stone Forest"), Vol. 2, Shanghai Bookstore Publishing House, 6.
51 Fu, Xuancong et al. 1991. *Quan Song shi* ("Complete Poetry Works of Song Dynasty"), Vol. 22. Peking University Press, 14466.
52 Fu, Xuancong et al. 1991. *Quan Song shi* ("Complete Poetry Works of Song Dynasty"), Vol. 68. Peking University Press, 42668.
53 Ye, Mengde. 1984. *Shilin yanyu* ("Random Thoughts in Stone Forest"), Vol. 5. Zhonghua Book Company, 68.
54 Li, Tao. 2008. *Xu Zizhi Tongjian chang bian* ("Sequel to *Comprehensive Mirror in Aid of Governance*"), Vol. 287. Zhonghua Book Company, (20): 7015.
55 Li, Xinchuan.1988. *Jianyan yilai xinian yaolu* ("Summar of Annual Events from the Jianyan Period"), Vol. 148. Zhonghua Book Company, 2391.
56 Li, Xinchuan.1988. *Jianyan yilai xinian yaolu* ("Summar of Annual Events from the Jianyan Period"), Vol. 172. Zhonghua Book Company, 2825.
57 Wei, Ye. *Shang Zhifu Li Dianyuan shi yun* ("Presented to Li Dianyuan the Magistrate"). *Dongguan ji* ("Collections of Dongguan"), Vol. 8. *Siku quanshu* (Complete Library in Four Branches of Literature, Wenyuange edition), Vol. 1087: 387.
58 Yin, Zhu. *Yu silu zhaotaosi mufu Li Fengtian Pei Yuanji zhongshu er shou* ("Two Poems Written to Li Fangtian and Pei Yuanji, Officials of the Four Routes Recruitment Office". *Henan ji* ("Collected works of Yin Zhu"), Vol. 9. *Siku quanshu* (Complete Library in Four Branches of Literature, Wenyuange edition), Vol. 1090: 43.
59 Lü, Zuqian. *Donglai ji* (Collected Works of Lü Zuqian),Vol. 6. *Siku quanshu* (Complete Library in Four Branches of Literature, Wenyuange edition), Vol. 1157: 264.
60 Li, Jingde. 1986. *Zhuzi yu lei* ("Collected Dialogues between Zhu Xi and His Disciples"), Vol. 92. Zhonghua Book Company, 2349.
61 There are many records of this type. For example, in the seventh year of the Xu Zizhi Tongjian Changbian Long Edition, in April of the second year of Zhenzong Dazhong Xiangfu, Ren Yin said,

> It is an imperial edict that all officials, both inside and outside, will not be dismissed from their posts unless they take a vacation. Wai Lang, an official in the capital of the time, and Su Wei, an official in Huzhou, knew that they were involved in the Xizai Yueyi Daochang Mountain, praying for rain and drinking together. When they returned at dusk and the boat was heavy, Liu Jineng, a judge, and Yue the girl were drowned, and the rest of them were only exempted.
> (Zhonghua Book Company, 1980 edition, Vol. 6, p. 1063)

In the same volume 498, in May of the first year of the Yuan Fu era, Jia Zi stated, "(L ü) Wen Qing was in Huainan yesterday and was not allowed to use girl's music for banquets in Qizhen, Chu, and Sizhou unless it was a holiday. He followed it. He was also appointed as a general and a supervisor, and was allowed to transfer officials from the governor to the governor. Although it was not a holiday, he was allowed to use girl's music, but he also followed it" (Zhonghua Book Company, 1993 edition, Vol. 33, p.11853). Li Xinchuan's *Jianyan yilai xinian yaolu* ("Summar of Annual Events from the Jianyan Period", Vol. 161) records his own death in June of the 20th year of Shaoxing, stating, "Wang Zhan of the Zhimi Pavilion knew that Langzhou had returned, begged for strict legal prohibitions, obeyed orders to

persuade farmers, and was not allowed to use girls to entertain guests" (Zhonghua Book Company, 1988 edition, p. 2615).
62. Chen, Zao. *Ji Huang Chang* ("Record of *Huang Chang*"). *Jianghu Changweng ji* ("A Collection of Chen Zao's Works"), Vol. 22. *Siku quanshu* (Complete Library in Four Branches of Literature, Wenyuange edition), Vol. 1166: 280.
63. Wu, Ziliang. *Huiweng an Tang Yuzheng* ("Huiweng's Commentary on Tang Yuzheng"). *Jingxi linxia outan* ("Random Talks in the Tree Shade at Jingxi"), Vol. 3. *Siku quanshu* (Complete Library in Four Branches of Literature, Wenyuange edition), Vol. 1481: 507.
64. Zhou, Hui. 1994. *Qingbo zazhi* ("Miscellaneous Records of Qingbo"), Vol. 5. Zhonghua Book Company, 197.
65. Zhu, Yu. 1989. *Pingzhou ketan* ("Records of My Journey by Zhu Yu"), Vol. 3. Shanghai Chinese Classics Publishing House, 60.
66. Hong, Mai. 1981. *Yijian zhi* ("Talks on Oddities"), Vol. 12. Zhonghua Book Company, 638.
67. Wang, Yucheng. *Dui xue shi Jia You* ("Showing Jia You in the Snow"). *Wang Huangzhou xiao xu ji* ("Collected Works of Wang Yucheng"), Vol. 12. *Sibu congkan* ("Four Series Books").
68. Zhang, Lei. 1990. *Xiao Bai Ti Er Shou* ("Two Poems in the Style of Bai Juyi"). *Zhang Lei ji* ("Collections of Zhang Lei's Works"), Vol. 24. Zhonghua Book Company, 431.
69. Wu, Zeng. 1979. *Nenggai Zai manlu* ("Random Records of Nenggai Studio"), Vol. 11. Shanghai Chinese Classics Publishing House, 328.
70. Ye, Mengde. 1984. *Shilin yanyu* ("Random Thoughts in Stone Forest"), Vol. 4. Zhonghua Book Company, 60.
71. Chen, Hui. *Xingdu ji shi* ("Records of Xingdu"). *Shuo Fu san zhong* ("Three Types of *Collections of All Good Writings*"), Vol. 5. Shanghai Chinese Classic Publishing House, 1988: 1403.
72. Hu, Zai. 1984. *Tiaoxi yuyin conghua* ("Series of Poetic Notes by the Recluse of the Brook Tiao"). Vol. 39. People's Literature Publishing House, 327.
73. Hong, Mai. 1981. *Yijian zhi* ("Talks on Oddities"), Vol. 12. Zhonghua Book Company, 1123.
74. Li, Tao. 2008. *Xu Zizhi Tongjian chang bian* ("Sequel to *Comprehensive Mirror in Aid of Governance*"), Vol. 73. Zhonghua Book Company, (12): 1669.
75. Ye, Mengde. 1990. *Shilin bishu luhua* ("Records of Summer Resort in Stone Forest"), Vol. 2, Shanghai Bookstore Publishing House, 9.
76. Yue, Ke. 1981. *Ting shi* ("History at Rectangle Table"), Vol. 3, Zhonghua Book Company, 38.
77. Yue, Zhen. 2000. *Biji man zhi jiaozheng* ("Revision to *Commentary from Biji Lane on ci works*"). Bashu Publishing House, 1.
78. Wang, Yong. 1981. *Yanyi Yimou lu* ("Records for Later Generations"), Vol. 3. Zhonghua Book Company, 23. Also Li, Jianliang. 1999. *Tang Song ci yu Tang Song geji zhidu* ("*ci* Works in Tang and Song Dynasties and Singing and Dancing Girls"). Hangzhou University Press, 38–39.
79. Yang, Shi. *Yu lu* ("Quotations"). *Guishan ji* ("A Collection of Guishan's Works"). *Siku quanshu* (Complete Library in Four Branches of Literature, Wenyuange edition). Vol. 1125: 202.
80. Wu, Zimu. 1982. *Meng liang lu* ("Records of Dreams of Glory"), Vol. 20. China Business Press, 178.
81. Zhou, Mi. 1982. *Wulin jiu shi* ("Former Events in Wulin (Hangzhou)"), Vol. 6. China Business Press, 119.
82. Wu, Longhan. *Bo Wuhu xian* ("Mooring in Wuhu County"). *Gumei yi gao* ("Manuscripts of Wu Longhan"), Vol. 2. *Siku quanshu* (Complete Library in Four Branches of Literature, Wenyuange edition), Vol. 1188: 849.

83　Zhou, Mi. 1982. *Wulin jiu shi* ("Former Events in Wulin (Hangzhou)"), Vol. 6. China Business Press, 119.
84　Liu, Guo. 1978. *Longzhou ji* ("A Collection of Longzhou's Works"), Vol. 7. Shanghai Chinese Classics Publishing House, 59.
85　Liu, Guo. 1978. *Longzhou ji* ("A Collection of Longzhou's Works"), Vol. 7. Shanghai Chinese Classics Publishing House, 42.
86　Zhou, Mi. 1982. *Wulin jiu shi* ("Former Events in Wulin (Hangzhou)"), Vol. 6. China Business Press, 120.
87　Meng, Yuanlao. 1982. *Dongjing meng hua lu* ("Reminiscences of the Eastern Capital"), Vol. 2. China Business Press, 17.
88　Zhou, Mi. 1982. *Wulin jiu shi* ("Former Events in Wulin (Hangzhou)"), Vol. 6. China Business Press, 119.
89　Hong, Mai. 1981. *Yijian zhi* ("Talks on Oddities"), Vol. 7. Zhonghua Book Company, 57.
90　Cheng, Yizhong. 2000. *Song Yuan xiaoshuo jia huaben ji* ("A Collection of Novels by Novelists in Song and Yuan Dynasties"). Shandong Qilu Press, 673, 677.
91　Wu, Zimu.1982. *Ji yue* ("Music of girls"). *Meng liang lu* ("Records of Dreams of Glory"), Vol. 20. China Business Press, 177.
92　"*Ni Shang Yu Yi Qu*" (Song of Rainbow Skirt and Coat of Feathers) is the name of famous dance in Tang Dynasty. Both Emperor Xuanzong, named Li Longji, and his concubine Yang Yuhuan had a deep love of music and dance. They married when Li was 56 years old and Yang was 22. The Rainbow Skirt and Feathered Coat was a romantic, enchanting dance personally choreographed by Li Longji for Yang Yuhuan. He combined emotional mortal love with the magical beauty of the fairy world, rendering a perfect blend of reality and fantasy. See http://archivesspace.mocanyc.org:8081/repositories/2/archival_objects/1108.
93　"*Yu Shu Hou Ting Hua*" (Flowers and Jade Trees in the Backyard) is a palace-style poem created by Chen Shubao, the last emperor of the Southern Chen Dynasty. The first two lines describe the splendid environment of the palace and the beautiful appearance of the ladies. The next two lines depict their captivating gestures, while the last two lines praise their delicate beauty and radiant charm. The theme of the entire poem is very simple: it praises the grace and beauty of the palace ladies. However, due to the poem's association with the downfall of the Chen Dynasty, it is generally regarded as a lament for a fallen nation.
94　Zhang, Bangji. 2002. *Mozhuang manlu* ("Rambles from the Ink Cottage"), Vol. 8. Zhonghua Book Company, 222.
95　Tang, Guizhang.1965. *Quan Song ci* ("Complete *ci* Works of Song Dynasty"). Zhonghua Book Company, 1648.
96　Guo, Xiangzheng. *Qingshan ji* ("A Collection of Qingshan"). Vol. 23. *Siku quanshu* (Complete Library in Four Branches of Literature, Wenyuange edition), Vol. 1116: 705.
97　Tang, Guizhang.1965. *Quan Song ci* ("Complete *ci* Works of Song Dynasty"). Zhonghua Book Company, 721.
98　Wen, Ying. 1984. *Xiangshan yelu* ("Records of Xiangshan"), Vol. 2. Zhonghua Book Company, 44.
99　Gong, Mingzhi. *Zhong Wu ji wen* ("Record of Things Heard in the Wu Region"), Vol. 1. *Siku quanshu* (Complete Library in Four Branches of Literature, Wenyuange edition), Vol. 589: 298.
100　Ge Shengzhong's preface to the *ci* work "To the Tune *Huan Xi Sha*" reads, "Ye Mengde and Ge Shengzhong, who were granted the *jinshi* degree in the same year, came out of the back hall and wrote two *ci* works to accompany the wine" (Tang, Guizhang.1965. *Quan Song ci* ("Complete *ci* Works of Song Dynasty"). Zhonghua Book Company, 720.)

101 Zhou, Mi. 1982. *Wulin jiu shi* ("Former Events in Wulin (Hangzhou)"), Vol. 2. China Business Press, 17.
102 Yue, Ke. 1981. *Ting shi* ("History at Rectangle Table"), Vol. 3. Zhonghua Book Company, 38.
103 Chen, Shidao. 1989. *Houshan tan cong* ("A Collection of Talks by Chen Shidao"), Vol. 3. Shanghai Chinese Classics Publishing House, 27.
104 Wang, Wei. *Daoshan qing hua* ("Daoshan Clear Talk"). *Siku quanshu* (Complete Library in Four Branches of Literature, Wenyuange edition), Vol. 1037: 656.
105 Wang, Mingqing. 1991. *Yuzhao xin zhi* ("New Records of Jade Illumination"), Vol. 3. Shanghai Chinese Classics Publishing House, 45.
106 In the third and fourth volumes of Chao Gongsu's *"Songshan ji"* ("Collected Works of Songshan"), he wrote about the banquet and expressed his gratitude to Yang Chun. Here, "Yang Canzheng" refers to Yang Chun because during the reigns of Emperor Gaozong and Emperor Xiaozong of the Southern Song Dynasty, the only deputy prime minister with the surname Yang was Yang Chun. Yang Chun served as a deputy prime minister in the 31st year of the Shaoxing period (1161) after serving as the minister of war.
107 Wen, Ying. 1984. *Xiangshan yelu* ("Records of Xiangshan"), Vol. 1. Zhonghua Book Company, 15.
108 Sun, Di. *Hongqing Jushi ji* ("A Collections of Hongqing Jushi's Works"), Vol. 37. *Siku quanshu* (Complete Library in Four Branches of Literature, Wenyuange edition), Vol. 1135: 396.
109 Yang, Shi. 1986. *Gujin ci hua* ("Commentaries on Past and Present *ci* Works"). *ci hua congbian* ("Series on *ci* Poetry"). Zhonghua Book Company, 29.
110 Tang, Guizhang. 1965. *Quan Song ci* ("Complete *ci* Works of Song Dynasty"). Zhonghua Book Company, 2018.
111 Tang, Guizhang.1965. *Quan Song ci* ("Complete *ci* Works of Song Dynasty"). Zhonghua Book Company, 1315.
112 Shen, Songqin. 2000. *Tang Song ci de shehui wenhuaxue yanjiu* ("A Study of the Social and Cultural History of *ci* Works in Tang and Song Dynasties"). Zhejiang University Press, 105–109.
113 Zhao, Lingshi. 1965. *Huan Xi Sha ci xu* ("Preface to *Huan Xi Sha*"). *Quan Song ci* ("Complete *ci* Works of Song Dynasty"). Zhonghua Book Company, 496.
114 Mao, Pang. 1965. *Yu Mei Ren ci xu* ("Preface to *Yu Mei Ren*"). *Quan Song ci* ("Complete *ci* Works of Song Dynasty"). Zhonghua Book Company, 688.
115 Xiang, Zikun. 1965. *Huan Xi Sha ci xu* ("Preface to *Huan Xi Sha*"). *Quan Song ci* ("Complete *ci* Works of Song Dynasty"). Zhonghua Book Company, 975.
116 Gao, Guanguo. 1965. *Sheng Cha Zi ci xu* ("Preface to *Sheng Cha Zi*"). *Quan Song ci* ("Complete *ci* Works of Song Dynasty"). Zhonghua Book Company, 2354.
117 Guan, Jian. 1965. *Taoyuan Yi Gu Ren ci xu* ("Preface to *Taoyuan Yi Gu Ren*"). *Quan Song ci* ("Complete *ci* Works of Song Dynasty"). Zhonghua Book Company, 1570.
118 Yao, Shuyao. 1965. *Nan Ge Zi ci xu* ("Preface to *Nan Ge Zi*"). *Quan Song ci* ("Complete *ci* Works of Song Dynasty"). Zhonghua Book Company, 1552.
119 Zhao, Changqing. 1965. *Zhe Gu Tian ci xu* ("Preface to *Zhe Gu Tian*"). *Quan Song ci* ("Complete *ci* Works of Song Dynasty"). Zhonghua Book Company, 1790.
120 Zhao, Changqing. 1965. *Chao Zhong Cuo ci xu* ("Preface to *Zhe Gu Tian*"). *Quan Song ci* ("Complete *ci* Works of Song Dynasty"). Zhonghua Book Company, 1796.
121 Zhou, Mi. 2000. *Haoran Zhai ya tan* ("Commentary on Poetry in the Haoranzhai Library"), Vol. 2. Liaoning Education Press, 39.
122 Ouyang, Xiu. 1965. *Yulou Chun* ("To the Tune *Yu Lou Chun*"). *Quan Song ci* ("Complete *ci* Works of Song Dynasty"). Zhonghua Book Company, 134.
123 Qin, Guan. 1965. *Yi Cong Hua* ("To the Tune *Yi Cong Hua*"). *Quan Song ci* ("Complete *ci* Works of Song Dynasty"). Zhonghua Book Company, 457.

124 Zhu, Dunru. 1965. *Lin Jiang Xian* ("To the Tune *Lin Jiang Xian*"). *Quan Song ci* ("Complete *ci* Works of Song Dynasty"). Zhonghua Book Company, 841.
125 Cao, Xun. *Qing Yu An* ("To the Tune *Qing Yu An*"). *Quan Song ci* ("Complete *ci* Works of Song Dynasty"). Zhonghua Book Company, 1226.
126 Cheng, Gai. 1965. *Zui Luo Po, Bie Shaocheng zhou su Huanglong* ("Farewell to Shaocheng and Staying Overnight at Huanglong, to the Tune *Zui Luo Po*"). *Quan Song ci* ("Complete *ci* Works of Song Dynasty"). Zhonghua Book Company, 1999.
127 Liu, Tiandi. 1965. *Feng Qi Wu, Wu Jiu Ji* ("Dancing with the Wine Girl, to the Tune *Feng Qi Wu*"). *Quan Song ci* ("Complete *ci* Works of Song Dynasty"). Zhonghua Book Company, 3562.
128 Zhang, Zhilong. 1965. *Li Meijian xue ye liu yin* (Li Meijing Stays for a Drink on a Snowy Night). Fu, Xuancong et al. 1998. *Quan Song shi* ("Complete Poetry Works of Song Dynasty"), Vol. 62. Peking University Press, 9086.
129 Tao, Zongyi. 1998. *Nancun chuo geng lu* ("Nancun's Notes in the Intervals of Ploughing"), Vol. 27. Liaoning Education Press, 20.
130 *Xiao Chang* sometimes refers to a type of artist. Xu Mengxin's "*San chao bei meng hui bian*" ("Collected Records of the Northern Alliance during Three Reigns", Vol. 78) records that in the second month of the Jingkang period, after the Jin army conquered the Song Dynasty, they took people of various levels to the north, inculding "twenty *Xiao Chang* singers, one hundred and fifty miscellaneous actors, and fifty spinning dancers".
131 Nai, Deweng. 1982. *Ducheng ji sheng* ("Famous Sages of the Capital"). China Business Press, 10.
132 Xie, Taofang. 1999. *Song ci bian, Song ci yanchang kao lue* ("Study of *ci* Works in Song Dynasty and Their Performance"). Shanghai Chinese Classics Publishing House, 340.
133 Wu, Zimu. 1982. *Ji yue* ("Music of Girls"). *Meng liang lu* ("Records of Dreams of Glory"), Vol. 20. China Business Press, 178.
134 Zhang, Yan. 1986. *ci yuan* ("Etymology"). *ci hua congbian* ("Series on *ci* Poetry"). Zhonghua Book Company, 256.
135 Meng, Yuanlao. 1982. *Dongjing meng hua lu* ("Reminiscences of the Eastern Capital"), Vol. 5. China Business Press, 31.
136 Zhou, Mi. 1988. *Guixin zashi* ("Miscellaneous Records of Guixin Years"). Zhonghua Book Company, 272.
137 Zhou, Mi. 1982. *Wulin jiu shi* ("Former Events in Wulin (Hangzhou)"), Vol. 6. China Business Press, 133.
138 Tang, Guizhang. 1965. *Quan Song ci* ("Complete *ci* Works of Song Dynasty"). Zhonghua Book Company, 24.
139 Tang, Guizhang. 1965. *Quan Song ci* ("Complete *ci* Works of Song Dynasty"). Zhonghua Book Company, 696.
140 Tang, Guizhang. 1965. *Quan Song ci* ("Complete *ci* Works of Song Dynasty"). Zhonghua Book Company, 2652.
141 Tang, Guizhang. 1965. *Quan Song ci* ("Complete *ci* Works of Song Dynasty"). Zhonghua Book Company, 375.
142 Tang, Guizhang. 1965. *Quan Song ci* ("Complete *ci* Works of Song Dynasty"). Zhonghua Book Company, 785.
143 Tang, Guizhang. 1965. *Quan Song ci* ("Complete *ci* Works of Song Dynasty"). Zhonghua Book Company, 3315.
144 Tang, Guizhang. 1965. *Quan Song ci* ("Complete *ci* Works of Song Dynasty"). Zhonghua Book Company, 2888.
145 *qin*, an ancient musical instrument with seven strings, which is similar to a zither.
146 Tang, Guizhang. 1965. *Quan Song ci* ("Complete *ci* Works of Song Dynasty"). Zhonghua Book Company, 1091. In Chinese there is a story of "Wu Shan Yun Yu" (Rain Clouds over Mt. Wu). Song Yu in his "*Fu* on the Gaotang Shrine" and

"*Fu* on the goddess" addressed the story vividly: When King Xiang of Chu and Song Yu were visiting the Terrace of Cloud Dreams, Song Yu said, "In the past, the King of Chu had visited this place. Feeling tired, he fell asleep. In their dream, a beautiful and enchanting woman appeared and introduced herself as a lady from Mt. Wu. She offered her own pillow and mat for King of Chu. Thrilled by the implicit message, the King was delighted and immediately engaged in a romantic affair with the lady from Mt. Wu. The lady told the King that if he wanted to find her again, he should come to Mt. Wu. In the morning, she would be like 'morning clouds', and in the evening, she would be like 'drizzling rain'. This is how the phrase 'Wu Shan Yun Yu' came into use, metaphorically describing passionate encounters between men and women".

147 Qin, Guan. 1965. *Meng Yangzhou* ("Dreaming of Yangzhou"). *Quan Song ci* ("Complete *ci* Works of Song Dynasty"). Zhonghua Book Company, 456.
148 Fu, Daxun. 1965. *Nian Nu Jiao* ("To the Tune *Nian Nu Jiao*"). *Quan Song ci* ("Complete *ci* Works of Song Dynasty"). Zhonghua Book Company, 1830.
149 Zhang, Lun. *Xi Jiang Yue* ("To the Tune *Xi Jiang Yue*"). *Quan Song ci* ("Complete *ci* Works of Song Dynasty"). Zhonghua Book Company, 1415.
150 Yuan, Quhua. 1965. *Si Jia Ke* ("To the Tune *Si Jia Ke*"). *Quan Song ci* ("Complete *ci* Works of Song Dynasty"). Zhonghua Book Company, 1505.
151 Guo, Yingxiang. 1965. *Huan Xi Sha, zeng Chen Xixi and Chen Lianlian* "To Chen Xixi and Chen Lianlian, to the Tune *Huan Xi Sha*". *Quan Song ci* ("Complete *ci* Works of Song Dynasty"). Zhonghua Book Company, 2226.
152 Hong, Mai. 1981. *Yijian zhi* ("Talks on Oddities"), Vol. 7. Zhonghua Book Company, 765.
153 Yan, Jidao. 1965. *Huan Xi Sha* ("To the Tune *Huan Xi Sha*"). *Quan Song ci* ("Complete *ci* Works of Song Dynasty"). Zhonghua Book Company, 240.
154 Zhou, Mi. 1988. *Guixin zashi xuji* ("Sequel to *Miscellaneous Records of Guixin Years*"). Zhonghua Book Company, 209.
155 Tang, Guizhang. 1965. *Quan Song ci* ("Complete *ci* Works of Song Dynasty"). Zhonghua Book Company, 1864.
156 Tang, Guizhang. 1965. *Quan Song ci* ("Complete *ci* Works of Song Dynasty"). Zhonghua Book Company, 2656, 3434.
157 Chen, Shichong. 1990. *Sui yin man lu* ("Random Records of Chen Shichong"), Vol. 2. Shanghai Bookstore Publishing House, 4.
158 Meng, Yuanlao. 1982. *Dongjing meng hua lu* ("Reminiscences of the Eastern Capital"), Vol. 9. China Business Press, 58–62.
159 Zhou, Mi. 1982. *Wulin jiu shi* ("Former Events in Wulin (Hangzhou)"), Vol. 1. China Business Press, 17–21.
160 Tang, Guizhang.1965. *Quan Song ci* ("Complete *ci* Works of Song Dynasty"). Zhonghua Book Company, 82, 124, 975.
161 Wang, Zhaopeng. 2000. *Song ci fanrong changsheng de lianghua biaozhi* ("The 'Quantitative' Symbol of the Prosperity of *ci* Works in Song Dynasty"). *Tang Song ci shi lun* ("On the History of *ci* in Tang and Song Dynasties"), Section 2, Chapter 2. People's Literature Publishing House, 104–106.
162 Xia, Chengtao. 1997. *Tang Song ci xinshang: bu tong feng ge de Wen Wei ci* ("Appreciating *ci* Works from Tang and Song Dynasties: Wen Tingyun and Wei Zhuang's *ci* Works with Different Styles"). *Xia Chengtao ji* ("A Collection of Xia Chengtao's Works"). Zhejiang Classics Publishing House, 623. Also in Huang, Wenji. 1995. *Song dai geji fansheng dui ci ti zhi yingxiang* ("The Impact of Singing and Dancing Girls in Song Dynasty on the Style of *ci*"). Papers of the First International Symposium on Song Dynasty Literature. Taiwan Liwen Publishing Group, 230–232.
163 Xie, Yi. 1965. *Yulou Chun* ("To the Tune *Yulou Chun*"). *Quan Song ci* ("Complete *ci* Works of Song Dynasty"). Zhonghua Book Company, 648.

164 Xiang, Ziyin. 1965. *Huan Xi Sha* ("To the Tune *Huan Xi Sha*"). *Quan Song ci* ("Complete *ci* Works of Song Dynasty"). Zhonghua Book Company, 977.
165 Liu, Jiangsun. *Xincheng Rao Keming ji ci xu* ("Preface to *A Collection of Rao Keming's ci Works in Xincheng*"). *Yangwu Zhai ji* ("Collections of Yangwuzhai Studio"), Vol. 9. *Siku quanshu* (Complete Library in Four Branches of Literature, Wenyuange edition), Vol. 1199, 84.
166 Tao, Zongyi. 1998. *Nancun chuo geng lu* ("Nancun's Notes in the Intervals of Ploughing"), Vol. 27. Liaoning Education Press, 321.
167 Chen, Shidao. 1982. *Houshan shihua* ("Houshan Poetic Talks"). *Lidai shihua* ("Comments on Poetry across Dynastics"). Zhonghua Book Company, 309.
168 Wang, Yan. 1989. *Shuangxi shi yu* ("A Collection of *ci* Works of Shuangxi"). *Siyin Zhai suo ke ci* ("Siyinzhai Studio's General Collection of ci Works"). Shanghai Chinese Classics Publishing House, 793.

5 The Remuneration for Writers in Song Dynasty

Remuneration for literary work is a reflection of the commercialization of literature. When it is pursued as a creative purpose, it can stimulate the writer's desire to create and promote literary production. When it serves as additional income for the writers as subsidies to the writer's livelihood, it can improve the writer's living conditions and subtly influence their creative mindset and style. Therefore, even in ancient Chinese society, remuneration directly or indirectly influenced the development of literature. There have been some articles discussing remuneration in ancient China, but they are often brief introductions or broad summaries, failing to provide detailed information on the specific circumstances and changes in remuneration during different dynasties. Based on extensive research of historical materials, this chapter intends to focus on the remuneration system in the Song Dynasty in order to gain a rough understanding of the process of commercialization of literature during that period.

The remuneration in the Song Dynasty, known as *"runbi"*, was also referred to as *"runhao"*, *"ruhao"* or *"ruren"*. The remuneration during that time was quite different from modern remuneration. In modern times, remuneration is generally paid by commercial publishing institutions to authors, with the purpose of purchasing the author's copyright for public dissemination of the works. However, in the Song Dynasty, remuneration was paid by specific individuals for their particular needs, and the subjective purpose of the payers was not to profit from the public dissemination of the works but rather to enjoy the specific value of the purchased poems or *ci* works.

In the Song Dynasty, remuneration, known as *"runbi"*, could be roughly divided into two categories: those obtained from drafting specific official documents and those obtained from writing poems or *ci* works at the request of others.

5.1 Remuneration for Drafting Official Documents

In the Song Dynasty, the "drafter officials" (*ci chen*, officials responsible for drafting official documents), such as imperial academicians and drafters responsible for secretarial matters, could get remuneration from their work.

DOI: 10.4324/9781032712512-6

The documents written by "drafter officials" were similar to appointment letters or commendation certificates nowadays.

The practice of court officials receiving remuneration for drafting official documents is generally believed to have originated in the Sui Dynasty (581–617 A.D.). In Volume 38 of the "Biography of Zheng Yi" in the "History of Sui Dynasty", there are following words said by Zheng Yi, "I don't get any money, then how can I pay you remuneration?"[1] The officials responsible for drafting official documents in the Tang and Five Dynasties also received remuneration for their work, but it may not have been a well-established rule. So sometimes the drafters were paid remuneration while sometimes they were not. When the remuneration was not paid, the drafters may have demanded it directly. During the Five Dynasties, Yin Wengui, a court official, once drafted documents for Li Decheng, the minister of public works. Not having received remuneration for a long time, Yin Wengui wrote poems to express his demand for remuneration directly, but "he was despised by the people at the time".[2] The fact that he was criticized and despised for demanding remuneration directly indicates that the practice of drafters demanding remuneration was not widely accepted at that time. However, by the time of the Song Dynasty, it had become a common phenomenon for drafters to demand remuneration.

In the Song Dynasty, the rule that drafters should be paid remuneration was established by Emperor Taizong and later became a "general practice" in the country. According to Su Qi's "*Ci xu hanlin zhi*" ("The Continued Records of Imperial Academicians"),

> Remuneration to drafters has been practised since the Sui and Tang dynasties. However, in recent years, military officials who have been promoted for new jurisdiction, or high-ranking officials who have taken up the new posts, mostly fail to pay remuneration to the drafters.

Emperor Taizong ordered that, though there were budget deficits, the remuneration should be regulated and supervised by the government institutes. Once the regulations were made, they were submitted to the emperor for review. From that point, there were no delays in the payment of remuneration. This rule became standard practice.[3] Ouyang Xiu's "*Gui Tian Lu*" ("Resigning from Office and Returning Home", Vol. 1) also records,

> In recent times, sometimes when Document Drafting Office ("*She Ren Yuan*"), an agency of the central government responsible for the preparation of all state documents, was commissioned to draft official documents, it couldn't get the remuneration on time. Then it would send attendants to pay a visit and urge for the payment, but sometimes those who should pay didn't do it. Such practice having been executed for long, both those urging for payment and those that should pay, became accustomed to it and would not find it strange.[4]

This indicates that during the reign of Emperor Renzong, sometimes, due remunerations were not paid on time. Then attendants would be sent to urge for the payment. Over time, both those who urged for payment and those who should pay were accustomed to such practice. This is different from the controversies about Yin Wengui's urging for remuneration during the Five Dynasties period.

However, not all the draftings would be paid with remunerations. Firstly, officials who were demoted or exiled did not need to pay any remuneration for drafting documents. This is easy to understand. After being demoted or having been reduced to lower ranks, the officials were already very unhappy. Offering remuneration to others would only add insult to injury. Secondly, lower-rank officials did not need to pay remuneration. According to the regulations at that time, usually officials of the fourth rank or above were eligible to pay remuneration. Being eligible to pay remuneration itself was a prestigious matter! As was recorded in *"Xu Zizhi Tongjian chang bian"* ("Sequel to *Comprehensive Mirror in Aid of Governance"*), "When princes, ministers, princesses, and consorts, as well as military commissioners were promoted or rewarded, they would pay remuneration to those drafters". "For the appointment to new posts for the civil officials such as '*Dai Zhi*' (Academician Awaiting Orders),[5] and the military officials such as '*Heng Hang Fu Shi*' (Deputy Commissioners of the Crosswise Ranks)[6] and '*Yao Jun Ci Shi*' (Governor of Remote Commandery),[7] or officials with higher ranks, remuneration was paid to the drafters".[8] Shen Kuo in his work *"Mengxi bitan* ('Brush talks from Dream Brook', Vol. 23')" also states,

> For official documents, remuneration was provided by officials of certain ranks such as *"Ji Shi Zhong"* (Supervising Secretary) and *"Jian Yi Da Fu"* ("Grand Master of Advisory"), or those with higher ranks. During Emperor Taizong's reign, the amount of money for remuneration was regulated, and an imperial decree was engraved on a stone tablet which was set in the Document Drafting Office (*"She Ren Yuan"*). Whenever an official was appointed to the new post, the document would be sent for supervision, and all the relevant people ranging from the principle official to the lowest-ranking attendants, would have an equal share for the remuneration. During the Yuanfeng period, the official system was changed, and all the officials were paid subsidies beyond salary, thus eliminating the need for remuneration.[9]

Shen Kuo stated that Emperor Taizong issued a decree commanding that drafters of official documents should be paid remuneration, and the decree was engraved on stone tablets in the Imperial Academy. This is consistent with Su Qi's narration in *"Ci Xu Han Lin Zhi"* (The Continued Records of Imperial Academicians)" that "the amount of money as remuneration was formerly regulated" at the time. Shen Kuo's account also indicates the following three points:

> Firstly, there were regulations for the amount of remuneration. Ouyang Xiu also described a similar situation by stating, "When Wang Yuanzhi was an Imperial Academician, he once drafted a document for Li Jiqian

of Xia Prefecture, who sent him the remuneration that was several times more than usual".[10] The phrase "several times more than usual" indicates that there was a standard for remuneration, but Li Jiqian's remuneration exceeded the usual amount by several times (he bestowed 50 horses as remuneration).[11]

Interestingly, the remuneration for drafters was determined according to the ranks of the appointed officials, and not all drafters were paid the same amount of money. As was recorded in "Cai Kuanfu Shi Hua" (Comments on Poetry of Cai Kuanfu),

> According to the old system, there were remunerations for all draftings, the amount of which was determined by the ranking of the newly-appointed officials. This means that when the officials' ranking varied, the remuneration to the drafters was also different. Therefore, they would have them gathered together and distribute them accordingly. This is why Yan Shu (with posthumous name Yuan Xian) wrote the line "the remuneration was equally distributed". If those who were supposed to pay failed to do so, they would be urged with letters to pay.

"During the Yuanfeng period, the system of remuneration was abolished. Now, only the engraved list of ranks and quantities of remuneration remain on the walls of the Imperial Academy".[12] This is consistent with Shen Kuo's account.

Then what is the specific number of remuneration for drafters? It is not recorded specifically in the literature. We may have a look at an example: During the reign of Emperor Shenzong, Imperial Academician Wang Gui wrote a decree for granting Princess Qing, and was given "100 taels of silver and 100 bolts of colored silk" as payment.[13] The remuneration for drafting may vary in different situations, but we can make a rough estimation that it may be a litter higher or lower than that of Wang Gui. In the Southern Song Dynasty, the remuneration to drafters was even higher. Those who drafted the official edicts for the appointment of empresses, crown princes and prime ministers could receive a remuneration of 100 or 200 taels of gold.

Secondly, the remuneration, whether in the form of money or goods, was initially received solely by the drafter. However, later on, it was equally distributed by officials of various ranks in the Imperial Academy or the Document Drafting Office ("*She Ren Yuan*"). The phrase "all the relevant people ranging from the principle official to the lowest-ranking attendants, would have an equal share for the remuneration" clearly shows this. Wang Gui also mentioned in his "*Mian Xueshi Yuan runbi zhazi* ('Memorial to the Throne on Waiving the Remuneration of Hanlin Academician')" that "according to the customs of the Imperial Academy, all the remuneration should be equally distributed among the in-service Academicians".[14] Wu Zeng of the Southern Song Dynasty specifically described how Yang

Wengong (Yang Yi) had the remuneration for his drafting imperial edicts equally distributed among his colleagues:

> Yang Wengong was exceptionally talented in literature and hence was favored by Emperor Zhenzong, and he served as a member of *Nei Wai Zhi* (Imperial Academician or Drafter). At that time, in drafting imperial edicts, none could be his rival. All the courtiers who were about to be granted new appointments, were willing to invite him to write the drafts. Therefore, his remuneration was the highest among all the drafters. At the time it was customary for the drafter to receive the remuneration exclusively. However, thinking that it would do harm to his integrity, Yang Wengong requested to share the remuneration equally with his colleagues. The emperor issued an edict for equal distribution of remuneration.[15]

This indicates that prior to Yang Wengong, the drafter would receive the remuneration alone. But ever since Yang Wengong, it became customary to share the remuneration equally among colleagues.

Thirdly, after the implementation of the New Official System in the Yuanfeng years, the policy of paying remuneration to drafters was temporarily abolished. The specific date of abolition was the 25th day of the third lunar month in the sixth year of Yuanfeng (1083).

> On that day, the Imperial Academy stated, "According to the long-standing tradition of our academy, when princes, ministers, princesses, and consorts, as well as military commissioners were promoted or rewarded, they would pay remuneration to those drafters. However, since the implementation of the new official system, there is increase in officials' salaries. Therefore, it is requested to abolish the practice of remuneration for drafters." *Zhongshu Sheng* (the Imperial Secretariat) also reported, "For the appointment to new posts for the civil officials such as '*Dai Zhi*' (Academician Awaiting Orders), and the military officials such as '*Heng Hang Fu Shi*' (Deputy Commissioners of the Crosswise Ranks) and '*Yao Jun Ci Shi*' (Governor of Remote Commandery), or officials with higher ranks, remuneration was paid to the drafters. It is requested to abolish this practice by accepting the advice of the Imperial Academy." Their requests were accepted and implemented.[16]

During the early years of the Southern Song Dynasty, the practice of remuneration to drafters was restored. In the spring of the 24th year (1154) of Shaoxing years, Supervisory Censor Wang Lun temporarily held the position of imperial academician. He drafted the decree for the promotion of Lady Liu from *Wanyi* (high-ranking imperial concubine) to even higher-ranking concubine. Emperor Gaozong "praised Wang Lun's excellent drafting, and awarded him the remuneration of nearly ten thousand strings of cash as well as a rare and precious inkstone".[17] The fact that a single piece of edict was awarded by "ten thousand strings of cash" during the Southern Song Dynasty indicates a significant increase in remuneration to drafters compared with the Northern Song Dynasty. However, it should be noted that this was a special favour granted by the emperor and was not a customary practice. It is unlikely that ordinary officials would have the financial capacity to provide such remuneration. In July of the 31st year (1161) of the Shaoxing period, Palace Censor Du Xinlao impeached Chancellor Zhou Linzhi of "frequently seeking remuneration for drafting in the Imperial Academy".[18] This indicates that during the Shaoxing period, not only Wang Lun but also other imperial academicians received remuneration for drafting. During the Longxing and Qiandao years during Emperor Xiaozong's reign, the quantity of money paid as remuneration to drafters was quite large. Zhou Bida, who once served as an imperial academician, said that after drafting the documents for imperial consorts, crown princes and prime ministers, "they would receive valuable gold items such as inkstone boxes, paper-weight, pen rack, paste boards, and water pots, weighing around two hundred taels. Once the drafts for appointment or removal the officials were finished, these items would be paid as rewards. This practice continued during the early years of the Longxing period. However, since the Qiandao period, only regular writing utensils such as writing brushes and inkstones were provided...generally a plaque made of one hundred taels of gold marked with manufacturer's names would be awarded as remuneration. The remuneration for imperial edicts setting the queens or crown princes would be twice the usual."[19] Before the Longxing period (1163–1164), the remuneration for drafting imperial edicts for the appointment of imperial consorts, the setting of crown princes, and the appointment of prime ministers were nearly 200 taels of gold. However, after the Qiandao period (1165–1173), the customary remuneration was reduced to one hundred taels of gold. In the case of drafting edicts for the enthronement of queens, the remuneration remained at 200 taels of gold.[20]

5.2 The Remuneration for Drafting Epitaphs and Other Poems and Proses

During the Song Dynasty, it was common to receive remuneration for drafting poems or prose at the invitation of others. This remuneration was paid by the inviters. From the imperial court to the folk, there were abundant examples of paying remuneration to drafters of poems or prose.

On the night of the Mid-Autumn Festival in the second year (1069) of the Xining period, Emperor Shenzong held a small-scale feast in the palace hall, in which he had a conversation on poetry with Imperial Academician Wang Qigong (Wang Gui). As the wine flowed and the atmosphere heated up, Emperor Shenzong instructed the palace concubines to request poems from Wang Gui. Wang Gui, according to each one's advantages, wrote poems in response one by one. His poems conveyed "fresh ideas of the time" and pleased everyone's heart. Emperor Shenzong was so delighted that he said,

"We cannot let this go without reward; we must provide remuneration for him". Subsequently, everyone took a flowery headdress made of beads from the heads and had them placed on Wang Gui's official hat as adornment. For those who couldn't be placed on Wang Gui's official hat, they put them in the sleeve of his official robes.[21] Although the payment was not money but goods, it was still considered as remuneration.

Though the act of paying such remuneration was not a common practice in the imperial court, it was a customary practice in the folk community. For example, Zhao Shijian, a member of the imperial family, commissioned Chen Shidao to compose a poem titled "Paying a Visit in a Large and Glorious Cart". Later, Zhao Shijian presented "ten bolts of fine silk" as remuneration to Chen Shidao.[22] Su Shi, at the invitation of Yao Chun of Suzhou, wrote the poem "Poem to Sanrui Hall" (*San Rui Tang Shi*). Yao paid him "eighty pots of eupatorium (*Huixiang*)" as remuneration.[23] Unwilling to accept anyone's remuneration, Su Shi entrusted others to return them.[24] The reason why Su Shi refused to accept the remuneration is not to be discussed here, but it indicates that during that time, when someone commissioned others to write poems, it was customary for them to pay remuneration. Fang Hui, a scholar of the late Song and early Yuan Dynasties, stated that whenever someone requested him to write a preface to the poems, he wouldn't start writing until he had received the remuneration, "For those mean fellows of the marketplace who seek poems, I demand five coins as remuneration. Only after the money has been presented to me would I casually write a few words".[25]

When it comes to being commissioned to write articles of other literary genres, there is also demand for remuneration. In Northern Song, there was an official in Bozhou who constructed a Buddhist temple, for which Mu Xiu was invited to compose a commemorative article. However, in the article, the name of the official was not mentioned. Then "the official gifted him 5 catties (or 2.5 kilograms) of silver", hoping that he would "have the name inscribed on stone tablets for immortal commemoration".[26] Five catties of silver as remuneration is a really high payment. However, despising the official who commissioned him, Mu Xiu neither wrote his name in the inscription nor accepted the remuneration. In the Northern Song Dynasty, the renowned scholar Li Gou once composed a commemorative article titled "Record of the Newly Constructed Monastery" for a monk. The monk presented him with "ten thousand cash as remuneration". Ten thousand cash, or ten strings of cash, was a low payment. Due to the meagreness of the payment, Li Guo's friends felt indignant on his behalf. They even wrote a poem as follows, "The bumpkin does not know the market quotations, and the drafter receives only ten thousand cash".[27] As to remuneration for various practical genres, the most generous one is to be found in drafting epitaphs. The main reason is that tomb epitaphs serve as a definitive record of a person's whole life, and Chinese people lay great emphasis on posthumous reputation and honour. Inscriptions that record and commend the virtues and accomplishments of the deceased on tombstones would ensure their enduring fame. Consequently, purchasing an epitaph is not only a way for the living to express their remembrance of the deceased, but more importantly, it serves to perpetuate the fame of the deceased to eternity and enhance the glory of the entire family. Therefore, the remuneration for epitaphs naturally tends to be more than usual.

The practice of paying remuneration for epitaph drafters dates back to the Tang Dynasty. By the Song Dynasty, just as the remuneration received by drafters of official documents, it became a customary practice. Sometimes some scholars who wrote epitaphs were unwilling to accept remuneration, and then even the emperor would intervene and persuade them to accept. For example, after Yang Yi wrote the inscriptions on the tablet by the side of the tomb, giving a biographical sketch of Quan Yi, the father of Ma Zhijie, the vice minister of military affairs, Yang Yi "refused to accept any remuneration". Ma Zhijie petitioned Emperor Zhenzong, saying, "I asked Yang Yi to write the epitaph for my late father. It is customary for drafters to receive remuneration. I humbly ask for your decree to command him to accept the remuneration". Hearing the words, Emperor Zhenzong issued a decree which read, "Minister Yang, you should not decline the remuneration".[28] This event occurred during the Northern Song Dynasty. Similar situations also took place during the Southern Song Dynasty. For instance, when Zhou Bida was invited by Han Yangu to write the inscriptions on the tablet for the tomb, giving a biographical sketch of the latter's father, Han Shizhong, Han Yangu presented "two hundred taels of gold as remuneration". However, Zhou Bida felt that it was not morally right and refused to accept it. He submitted a memorial titled "Request for Exemption of Remuneration" to Emperor Xiaozong. In reply, the emperor wrote, "Remuneration is necessary according to the established practice, so there is no need for exemption".[29] These were two disputes between ministers in the Northern and Southern Song Dynasties regarding the giving and declining of remuneration, both of which were ultimately decided by the emperors' decrees. This demonstrates that the practice of giving and accepting remuneration had indeed become a "national norm", and the emperors' decisions were based on the established customs. This was true not only among high-ranking officials but also among common people. During the Yuan You era of the Northern Song Dynasty, Zhao Tingzhi once said to Huang Tingjian, "In my hometown, remuneration is highly emphasized. Whenever an epitaph is completed, the host would send gifts to the drafter by carriage".[30]

The remuneration for drafting epitaphs during the Song Dynasty was quite generous. If the drafter of the epitaphs were high-ranking and esteemed ones, they would usually receive remunerations of several hundred taels of silver or several thousand bolts of silk. According to *"Shaoshi wenjian houlu"* (The records of the experience and knowledge of Shao Bowen), it is recorded that "when a high-ranking official passed away, a man of letters was commissioned to write the epitaph, for which he received five thousand bolts of silk as remuneration".[31] Indeed, those five thousand bolts of silk would require many carriages to carry. The "man of letters" in the text was none other than Ouyang

Xiu.³² Ouyang Xiu also once wrote the epitaph "The Monument to the Virtuous and Elderly Minister Wang Dan" for Prime Minister Wang Dan. Wang Dan's son, Wang Su (with the courtesy name Zhongyi), presented "ten sets of golden wine cups and two wine-pouring scoops as remuneration". Ouyang Xiu jokingly remarked that he needed a maidservant to hold the wine cups. Immediately, Wang Su sent someone to purchase two maidservants with a thousand silver coins and sent them to Ouyang Xiu. However, as a henpecked man, Ouyang Xiu ultimately only accepted the golden articles and declined the maidservants.³³ This remuneration, including both golden goods and maidservants, cost Wang Su several thousand strings of 1,000 cash. Wang Gui once wrote epitaphs for Gao Qiong (Prince Wei) and Gao Jixun (Prince Kang). The emperor granted him "five hundred taels of silver, five hundred bolts of silk each, a golden waist belt, and a set of clothing" as remuneration.³⁴ Fan Zuyu drafted the epitaph for Prince Wei and was paid "two hundred taels of silver and three hundred bolts of silk as remuneration".³⁵ During the Huizong reign, the renowned poet Zhou Bangyan drafted the epitaph for Minister Liu Bing's grandfather. Liu Bing "paid tens of catties of silver as remuneration".³⁶ At the end of the Song Dynasty and the beginning of the Yuan Dynasty, Zhao Mengfu asked Hu Jizhong to draft an epitaph for the minister of education, who paid "one hundred ingots of silver as remuneration".³⁷ Fifty taels of silver make one ingot, and 100 ingots amount to 500 taels of silver. From the number of these transactions, we can roughly understand the market price for drafting epitaphs in the Song Dynasty.

An epitaph draft could cost the host as much as several hundred taels of silver. How much did it mean at the time? Let's make some comparisons.

First, let's look at military expenditures. According to research, the average annual cost per soldier in imperial and regional armies in the Song Dynasty was approximately 50 strings of 1,000 cash.³⁸

Now let's look at the salaries of the literati and officials in the Song Dynasty. According to Wang Cong's "*Yanyi Yimou lu*" ("Records for Later Generations", Vol. 2), in the early Song Dynasty, the monthly salary of a county magistrate was less than ten strings of 1,000 cash, while the monthly salary of a deputy governor and county official next only to the magistrate was only three strings of 1,000 cash and 570 *wen* of money, two-thirds of which were used to pay for tea, salt and wine. After the third year of Emperor Zhenzong's Jingde era (1006), official salaries were increased slightly. The monthly salary for a county magistrate in Chijin County was 20 strings of 1,000 cash and a total of 7 *hu* (bushel, a dry measure used in former times) of rice and wheat. County officials of other ranks received salaries below 20 strings of 1,000 cash.³⁹ According to the "History of Song Dynasty: Official Positions and Salaries", the highest-ranking administrative officials in the Song Dynasty, such as the prime minister and the chancellor of the secretariat, received a monthly salary of 300 strings of 1,000 cash, together with 20 bolts of thin silk and 30 bolts of tough silk for spring and winter attire, and 100 taels of cotton for winter clothing.⁴⁰ In addition, according to Chen Qi's "Nansong Guan Ge Lu" (Records of

Imperial Archives in Southern Song Dynasty, Vol. 9), the chief secretariat of *Mishu Sheng* (Secretarial Department) in the Southern Song Dynasty received a monthly salary of 42 strings of 1,000 cash, along with ten *shi* of rice and wheat, an additional ten strings of 1,000 cash and 12 strings of 1,000 cash for kitchen expenses, totalling 64 strings of 1,000 cash (excluding rice and wheat). The chief scribe of *Mishu Sheng* received a monthly salary of 16 strings of 1,000 cash, along with 9 strings of 1,000 cash for kitchen expenses, totalling 25 strings of 1,000 cash.[41]

The remuneration presented to Fan Zuyu by Prince Wei's family, mentioned previously, was relatively small compared to the other examples discussed earlier. Anyhow, it still consisted of 200 taels of silver and 300 bolts of silk fabric. One tael of silver was equivalent to one string of 1,000 cash of money (although the price of silver in the Song Dynasty fluctuated, and sometimes one tael of silver was equivalent to one string of 1,000 cash and 200 *wen* or one string of 1,000 cash and 400 *wen*). Therefore, 200 taels of silver would be at least 200 strings of 1,000 cash. The remuneration to Fan Zuyu for his drafting of one epitaph was equivalent to the annual salary of a county magistrate after the Jingde era, approximately five months' salary of the chief secretariat of *Mishu Sheng* and ten months' salary of the chief scribe of *Mishu Sheng*. Chen Shidao, a renowned poet, once held the position of chief scribe, and his ten months' salary in total was equivalent to the remuneration to Fan Zuyu for his drafting of one epitaph. The remuneration to Wang Gui for his drafting of one epitaph was 500 taels of silver and 500 bolts of silk, which exceeded the monthly salary of a prime minister and was equivalent to the annual cost of ten imperial or regional soldiers. Obviously, the remuneration for drafting epitaphs in the Song Dynasty was indeed quite high.

After the epitaph was drafted, calligraphers would be invited to handwrite and engrave it on the tombstone. The calligrapher would also receive remuneration. Ouyang Xiu's friend, "Lu Jing, often wrote epitaph inscriptions for others and was paid much money as remuneration".[42] The remuneration was so high that sometimes a calligrapher who wrote a single piece of epitaph inscription on a tombstone could get out of poverty. For example, Xi Daguang, a man in the transition period between the Northern and Southern Song Dynasties, hired calligrapher Wu Fupeng to handwrite his mother's tombstone by "preparing six thousand strings of 1000 coins as remuneration". Someone said, "Wu Fupeng has got rid of poverty now".[43] Six thousand strings of 1,000 coins are equivalent to the salary of a prime minister for 20 months, so Wu Fupeng had indeed "got rid of poverty"! By handwriting a single epitaph, one can receive "six thousand strings of 1000 coins" as remuneration and get rid of poverty, so it is natural that he can make more money and become wealthy by that. In the early Southern Song Dynasty, Sun Di became prosperous because he often wrote epitaph inscriptions for others: "Sun Zhongyi often wrote epitaph inscriptions for others and became wealthy from the remuneration, which led to his family's prosperity".[44]

5.3 Selling Poetry and Prose for a Living

Due to the high profitability of drafting poetry and prose for others, it was common in the Song Dynasty for literati to make a living by selling their works or to supplement their household income through such sales.

In the capital city of Bianjing during the Northern Song Dynasty, there was a man named Zhang Shoushan who claimed, "For over thirty years in the city, I have made a living by selling seventeen-character poems".[45] Zhang Shoushan made a living in the capital city by selling poetry for 30 years, which indicates the popularity of and social demand for selling poetry at that time. If it were just an occasional sale of poetry, he would not have been able to sustain himself. Also, there was a woman named Cao Xiyun in the Northern Song Dynasty who frequently made money by "selling poems". As was recorded in "*Tongjiang Shihua*" ("Tongjiang Poetry Talks"),

> Cao Xiyun sold her poems in the capital city. Someone requested her to write a poem titled "New Moon", with the lines ending with three rhyming Chinese characters "*qiao*" (toll), "*shao*" (treetops) and "*jiao*" (together). Cao's poem goes as follows: "As the evening draws near, and the curfew drum begins to toll,[46] a crescent moon, in the western sky, hangs on the treetops. Whose newly polished bronze mirror is this? Its round lid is even smaller than the mirror itself. It, revealing one edge of the round mirror, is not tightly enclosed together".[47]

These poets who sold their works must have quick thinking and be able to immediately write the poems based on the specific demands of the buyers. In Yangzhou, there was also a poet named Lü Chuan who "sold poetry in the market, with some lines worth collecting". When Lü Huiqing was prefecture of Yangzhou, he often had poetic exchanges with Lü Chuan.[48] During the early Song Dynasty, there was a man named Xu Dong from Suzhou who sold poetry to repay his debts for wine:

> Xu Dong was renowned for his literary talent in Wu (the region around Suzhou), especially his profound understanding of the "Zuo Zhuan" (The Commentary of Zuo, a Chinese classic). He had a special fondness for alcohol and would often have drinks on credit from taverns. One day, he composed a song of several hundred words on the wall. Then the local people flocked to have a look. The tavern sold wine several times more than usual, and his debts were all exempted.[49]

During the Southern Song Dynasty, there were also some literati who made a living by selling their literary works. Wang Yan repeatedly said that he once sold his writings to make a living. In the preface to "Collected Works of Er Tang" in his collection "*Shuangxi lei gao*" ("Categorized Works of Shuangxi"), he stated, "When I was fourteen or fifteen years old, I learned to write like a *ju ren* (a successful candidate in the imperial examinations at the provincial level in ancient China)", and "later on, I made a living by selling my poetic works and playing the *qin*", In the preface to *"Nanchuang Za Zhu"* ("Miscellaneous Records of Nanchuang") of the same collection, he stated,

> I relied on the knowledge of the great scholars to luckily pass the imperial examination. When I was settled, I sold my poetic works to make up for the lack of income during the hot summer and cold winter. When I travelled, I carried my writings with me to make a living in various places.

His friend, Wang Zhiqing, also sold his writings to make a living. In the preface to *"Chusou Shiji"* in the same collection, there are the following words, "Wang Zhiqing, amidst the ups and downs of life, sold his poetic works and played the *qin* to make a living".[50] Wu Sili of the Southern Song Dynasty was also known for "selling his writings to support himself" and to provide for his elderly mother. Zhen Dexiu, the contemporary poet, praised him by saying, "That is why Wu Sili is respected as being virtuous".[51] In the late Song Dynasty, Zeng Ziliang, after the fall of the Song Dynasty, "retreated to the mountains and sold his writings to support himself".[52]

During the Song Dynasty, the sales of literary works were sometimes conducted in a manner similar to sales of commodities, with people setting up stalls and openly crying their writings for sale. Chen Zao of the Southern Song Dynasty wrote in his poem "To My Hometown Folks": "Leaving my broken home behind, I ventured to distant lands. Little did I expect my wealth to scatter away. I have no choice but set up stalls to sell my literary works".[53] Unfortunately, due to a lack of historical records, it is difficult for us to understand the prices of literary works at the market stalls. It can be assumed that the prices were not very high, at least much lower than the prices of epitaphs. Otherwise, these writers would have been building up the family fortunes rather than simply making a living.

Such forms of setting up stalls to sell literary works targeted individual customers, catering to their specific demands in order to obtain money or goods. This can be seen as another form of remuneration. However, unlike the previously mentioned commissions for poetry, where the host took the initiative, and the poets were relatively passive in their writing, in sales of literary works, the poets generally took a proactive approach by openly advertising their works.

In the study of literature in the Song Dynasty, or the ancient Chinese literature as a whole, we should not only examine the broader social, political and economic contexts but also focus on the individual circumstances of the writers, their sources of income and material living conditions. As one of the sources of income for Song Dynasty writers, remuneration should be studied from the perspectives of the policy system and its impact. The popularity of remuneration for commissioned poetry and the act of selling literary works as a means of livelihood indicate that the commercialization of literature had developed to a certain extent in the Song Dynasty. Further exploration is needed to understand other manifestations of literary commercialization and their impact on Song Dynasty literature.

Notes

1 Wei, Zheng. 2004. *Sui Shu* ("History of Sui Dynasty"), Vol. 38. Zhonghua Book Company, 757.
2 Ji, Yougong. 1987. *Tang shi ji shi* ("Collection of Criticism on Poets and Poetry of Tang Dynasty"), Vol. 68. Shanghai Chinese Classics Publishing House, 1017–1018.
3 Hong, Zun. 2003. *Han Yuan qun shu* ("Collection of Works on Hanlin Academy"), Vol. 9. Fu, Xuancong and Shi Chunde. *Han Xue san shu* ("Three Works on Hanlin Academy"). Liaoning Education Press, 72.
4 Ouyang, Xiu. 2001. *Gui tian lu* ("Resigning from Office and Returning Home"), Vol. 1. *Song Yuan biji xiaoshuo daguan* ("Grand View of Story-Telling Novels in Song and Yuan Dynasties"). Shanghai Chinese Classics Publishing House, 610.
5 *Dai Zhi*, or *Dai Zhao*, Academician Awaiting Orders, is a duty assignment for officials of literary talent holding substantive posts elsewhere in the central government since the Tang Dynasty. From the Song Dynasty on, it was a substantive post in the Imperial Academy.
6 *Heng Hang Shi* ("Commissioner of the Crosswise Ranks"), is an honorific designation of the man in charge of the highest-ranking military officers in court audience. *Duputy Heng Hang Shi* is assisstant *to Heng Hang Shi*.
7 Yao Jun, literally meaning "distant or remote Commandery", suggests posts over which the central government could exercise only limited control.
8 Li, Tao. 2004. *Xu Zizhi Tongjian chang bian* ("Sequel to *Comprehensive Mirror in Aid of Governance*"), Vol. 334. Zhonghua Book Company, 8040.
9 Shen, Kuo. 1975. *Mengxi bitan* ("Brush Talks from Dream Brook"), Cultural Relics Publishing House, 4.
10 Ouyang, Xiu. 2001. *Gui tian lu* ("Resigning from Office and Returning Home"), Vol. 1. *Song Yuan biji xiaoshuo daguan* ("Grand View of Story-Telling Novels in Song and Yuan Dynasties"). Shanghai Chinese Classics Publishing House, 610.
11 Sima, Guang. 1989. *Shuishui Jiwen* ("Records of Rumors from the Man of Su River"), Vol. 3, Zhonghua Book Company, 45.
12 Hu, Zai. 1962. *Tiaoxi yuyin conghua* ("Series of Poetic Notes by the Recluse of the Brook Tiao"). *Gaozhai Shihua* ("Poetic Notes in Elegant Study"), Vol. 35. People's Literature Publishing House, 272.
13 Wang, Gui. *Mian Xueshi Yuan runbi zhazi* ("Memorial to the Throne on Waiving the Remuneration of Hanlin Academician"). *Huayang Ji* ("A Collection of Huayang's Works"), Vol. 8. *Siku quanshu* (Complete Library in Four Branches of Literature, Wenyuange edition), Vol. 1093, 56.
14 Wang, Gui. *Huayang Ji* ("A Collection of Huayang's Works"), Vol. 8. *Siku quanshu* (Complete Library in Four Branches of Literature, Wenyuange edition), Vol. 1093, 56.
15 Wu, Zeng. 1979. *Nenggai Zai manlu* ("Random Records of Nenggai Studio"), Vol. 12. Shanghai Chinese Classics Publishing House, 364–365.
16 Li, Tao. 2004. *Xu Zizhi Tongjian chang bian* ("Sequel to *Comprehensive Mirror in Aid of Governance*"), Vol. 234, Zhonghua Book Company, 8040.
17 Zhou, Bida. *Yu Tang za ji* ("Miscellaneous Records of Yu Tang"), Vol. 2. *Siku quanshu* (Complete Library in Four Branches of Literature, Wenyuange edition), Vol. 595, 565.
18 Li, Xinchuan. 1988. *Jianyan yilai xinian yaolu* ("Summar of Annual Events from the Jianyan Period"), Vol. 191. Zhonghua Book Company, 3200.

19 Zhou, Bida. *Yu Tang za ji* ("Miscellaneous Records of Yu Tang"), Vol. 3. *Siku quanshu* (Complete Library in Four Branches of Literature, Wenyuange edition), Vol. 595, 569.
20 Zhou, Mi. 1982. *Wulin jiu shi* ("Former Events in Wulin (Hangzhou)"), Vol. 8. China Business Press, 159.
21 Qian, Shizhao. 1983. *Qian shi si zhi* ("The Qian Clan's Private Record of Events"). *Siku quanshu* (Complete Library in Four Branches of Literature, Wenyuange edition). *The Commercial Press (Tai Wan)*. Vol. 1036: 662.
22 Ruan, Yue. 1987. *Shihua zonggui* ("Compilation of Notes on Classical Poetry"), Vol. 19. People's Literature Publishing House, 213.
23 Su, Shi. 1986. Yu Tong zhanglao ("To Monastery Tong"). *Sushi wenji* ("A Collection of Su Shi's Works"), Vol. 61. Zhonghua Book Company, 1877.
24 Gong, Mingzhi. *Zhong Wu ji wen* ("Record of Things Heard in the Wu Region"), Vol. 2, *Song Yuan biji xiaoshuo daguan* ("Grand View of Story-Telling Novels in Song and Yuan Dynasties"), Vol. 3. Shanghai Chinese Classics Publishing House, 2843.
25 Zhou, Mi. 1988. *Guixin zashi* ("Miscellaneous Records of Guixin Years"), Vol. 1. Zhonghua Book Company, 252.
26 Su, Shunqin. 1961. *Aimu Xiansheng wen* ("Collected Works of Aimu"), Vol. 15. Zhonghua Book Company, 233–234.
27 Wu, Yu. 1983. *Guanlin shi hua* ("Poets' Anecdotes and Their Comments on Poetry"). *Lidai shihua xubian* ("Supplementary Comments on Poetry across Dynastics"), Vol. 1. Zhonghua Book Company, 132.
28 Shi, Wenying. 1984. *Xiangshan ye lu* ("Worldly Tales from Wenying"), Vol. 2. Zhonghua Book Company, 59.
29 Zhou, Bida. *Ci mian runbi zhazi* ("Memorial to the Throne on Waiving the Remuneration"). *Wenzhong ji* ("A Collection of Wenzhong's Works"), Vol. 123. *Siku quanshu* (Complete Library in Four Branches of Literature, Wenyuange edition), Vol. 1148: 363.
30 Wang, Mingqing. 2001. *Hui Zhu lu* ("Swaying Deertail Whisk"), Vol. 6. Shanghai Bookstore Publishing House, 123.
31 Shao, Bowen. 1983. *Shaoshi wenjian houlu* (The Records of the Experience and Knowledge of Shao Bowen), Vol. 22. Zhonghua Book Company, 171.
32 Fei, Gun. 1985. *Liangxi man zhi* ("Liangxi Miscellany"), Vol. 8. Shanghai Chinese Classics Publishing House, 95–96.
33 Zeng, Zao, *Gaozhai man lu* ("Random Notes from a Lofty Studio"). *Siku quanshu* (Complete Library in Four Branches of Literature, Wenyuange edition). Vol. 1038: 315.
34 Wang, Gui. *Mian zhuan Gao Wei Wang Kang Wang bei runbi zhazi* ("Memorial to the Throne on Waiving the Remuneration for Epitaphs for Prince of Wei Gao Qiong and Prince of Kang Gao Jixun"). *Huayang Ji* ("A Collection of Huayang's Works"), Vol. 8. *Siku quanshu* (Complete Library in Four Branches of Literature, Wenyuange edition), Vol. 1093, 56.
35 Fan, Zuyu. *Ci runbi zhazi* ("Memorial to the Throne on Waiving the Remuneration"). *Fan Taishi ji* ("Collected Works of Fan Taishi"), Vol. 26. *Siku quanshu* (Complete Library in Four Branches of Literature, Wenyuange edition), Vol. 1100: 305.
36 Zhuang, Chuo. 1983. *Jilei bian* ("Miscellaneous Writings of Zhuang Chuo"), Vol. 2. Zhonghua Book Company, 70.
37 Tao, Zongyi. 1998. *Nancun chuo geng lu* ("Nancun's Notes in the Intervals of Ploughing"), Vol. 4. Liaoning Education Press, 48.
38 Wang, Shengduo. 1995. *Liang Song caizheng shi* ("History of Finance in Northern and Southern Song Dynasties"). Zhonghua Book Company, 25.

39 Wang, Yong. 1981. *Yanyi Yimou lu* ("Records for Later Generations"). Zhonghua Book Company, 13.
40 Tuo, Tuo et al. 1977. *Song shi* ("History of the Song Dynasty"), Vol. 171. Zhonghua Book Company, (12): 4101.
41 Chen, Kui. 1998. *Nan Song guan ge lu* ("A History of Libraries in Southern Song Dynasty"), Vol. 9. Zhonghua Book Company, 147.
42 Kong, Pingzhong. *Tan Yuan* ("Tan-Yuan"), Vol. 2. *Siku quanshu* (Complete Library in Four Branches of Literature, Wenyuange edition), Vol. 1037: 136. Dong Geng's "Shu Lu" also mentioned, "Lu Jing, the Bachelor, was once reprimanded and impoverished, but Ouyang Wenzhong sympathized with his poverty. Whenever he worked on an epitaph inscription with someone, he would always ask Lu Zilu to write it, hoping to assist him with his skilled hand. As a result, Lu Zilu's reputation as a calligrapher flourished" (*Siku quanshu* (Complete Library in Four Branches of Literature, Wenyuange edition), Vol. 814, 303).
43 Zhang, Duanyi. 2001. *Gui Er ji* ("A Miscellany of Zhang Duanyi's Writings"). *Song Yuan biji xiaoshuo daguan* ("Grand View of Story-Telling Novels in Song and Yuan Dynasties"), Vol. 4. Shanghai Chinese Classics Publishing House, 2001: 4317.
44 Wang, Mingqing. 2001. *Hui Zhu lu* ("Swaying Deertail Whisk"), Vol. 11. Shanghai Bookstore Publishing House, 167.
45 Wang, Pizhi. 2001. *Shengshui yan tan lu* ("Fleeting Gossip by the River Sheng"), Vol. 10, *Song Yuan biji xiaoshuo daguan* ("Grand View of Story-Telling Novels in Song and Yuan Dynasties"), Vol. 2. Shanghai Chinese Classics Publishing House, 1307.
46 In ancient China, the morning was heralded by the ringing of bells and in the evening by the beating of drums.
47 Hu, Zai. 1962. *Tiaoxi yuyin conghua* ("Series of Poetic Notes by the Recluse of the Brook Tiao"). *Gaozhai Shihua* ("Poetic Notes in Elegant Study"), Vol. 25. People's Literature Publishing House, 168.
48 Ma, Chun. *Taozhu xin lu* ("A New Account from the Mount Taozhu"), Vol. 1. *Siku quanshu* (Complete Library in Four Branches of Literature, Wenyuange edition), Vol. 1047: 198.
49 Zhu, Changwen. *Wujun tujing xu ji* ("Continuation of Local Chronicles of Wu County"), Vol. 2. *Siku quanshu* (Complete Library in Four Branches of Literature, Wenyuange edition), Vol. 484: 46.
50 Wang, Yan. *Shuangxi lei gao* ("Categorized Works of Shuangxi"), Vol. 25. *Siku quanshu* (Complete Library in Four Branches of Literature, Wenyuange edition), Vol. 1155: 715, 718, 720.
51 Zhen, Dexiu, *Song Wu Sili xu* ("Preface Presented to Wu Sili"). *Xishan wen ji* ("Collected Works of Xishan"), Vol. 29. *Siku quanshu* (Complete Library in Four Branches of Literature, Wenyuange edition), Vol. 1174: 449.
52 Liu, Xun. *Zeng Pingshan xu Shui Yuncun shi* ("Preface to the Poems of Shui Yuncun by Zeng Pingshan"). *Yinju tong yi* ("Discussions while Living in Seclusion"), Vol. 15. *Siku quanshu* (Complete Library in Four Branches of Literature, Wenyuange edition), Vol. 866: 140.
53 Chen, Zao. *Lexuan ji* ("Collected Works of Lexuan"), Vol. 2. *Siku quanshu* (Complete Library in Four Branches of Literature, Wenyuange edition), Vol. 1152: 49. However, the term "setting up stalls to sell my literary works" mentioned here may be a figurative expression and may not necessarily mean actually opening a store to sell articles. Further research is needed to find supporting evidence.

6 Dissemination Effects of Obtaining Recognition from Prominent Figures

There are many phenomena in literary history that deserve special attention and explanation, yet they have not received the necessary recognition. For instance, it is worth making a thorough analysis of the terms "renowned writers" and "masterpieces" that have been widely used. What kind of person can be considered a renowned writer, and who determines their status? How did ancient writers become renowned and gain societal recognition? What qualifies the work as a masterpiece, and who first determines its status? What are the means and channels through which the works are recognized? What are the differences in their fates between renowned and non-renowned writers, as well as between masterpieces and non-masterpieces in literary history? What associations exist between renowned writers and masterpieces? Once someone becomes a renowned writer, do his works receive more attention and spread more widely? Are the works of non-renowned writers more likely to be neglected and eventually forgotten? What direct or indirect links exist between the dissemination of literary works and the fame of the authors? What are the roles of non-literary factors in the development and dissemination of literature? These questions involve both the dissemination and reception of literature and are relevant to their creation and development. In the past, we focused on the influence and impact of political, economic and cultural environments on the development of literature. However, there are still many aspects of literary development and dissemination that remain unclear, such as literary trends and operational methods within the literary world. This chapter cannot address all these questions but provides a preliminary exploration of the paths to fame for writers in the Song Dynasty.

6.1 Obtaining Recognition from Prominent Figures

In the Song Dynasty, there was no highly developed media as in modern times to create "celebrities" through packaging and media hype. However, how did Song writers gain fame and social recognition before becoming well-known?

Let's first look at the preface to the *ci* work "To the Tune *Qin Yuan Chun*" written by Chen Renjie, a *ci* writer of the Southern Song Dynasty:

Effects of Obtaining Recognition from Prominent Figures   141

> I believe that all ambitious poets, regardless of their talents and strengths, even if they are confident in their own abilities, still need the praise and recognition from contemporary celebrities so that they can gain widespread acceptance and their names would be passed down through generations. In the past, Liu Cha wasn't famous at first. However, after Han Yu appreciated and praised his two poems, "Snow Cart" and "Ice Pillar," he quickly became as renowned as the famous poets Zhang Ji and Meng Jiao. I once obtained a collection of Liu Cha's works, and found that while many of his other poems are not so impressive, the two have been cited widely until today because of Han Yu's praises. Today, there are many talented poets whose abilities surpass that of Liu Cha. However, there is no one who cherishes their talents and supports these younger generations as Han Yu. Talented people are not scarce, but there is no good judge of their talent. Reciting Huang Tingjian's poems, I cannot help but sigh and compose a poem in remembrance of ancient people. If I meet a kindred spirit in the future, I wouldn't mind exchanging ideas.[1]

The above is an expression of Chen Renjie's profound sentiments as expressed when he felt lonely and unaided. He mentioned the following two points: Firstly, for a literary figure at the time, even if he had self-confidence, he still needed the "praise and recognition" of contemporary celebrities so that he could stand out and gain broad social acceptance. Only then would his works be favoured by and disseminated among the people. He quoted the example of Liu Cha from the Tang Dynasty to illustrate this point. Liu Cha was not well-known at first, but when Han Yu appreciated and praised his poems "Snow Cart" and "Ice Pillar", he gained considerable fame in a short time. Soon he was on par with the already renowned poets Zhang Ji and Meng Jiao. However, when reading Liu Cha's other poems, one might feel a considerable gap between the famous ones and other works. Secondly, there were many talented pots at the time, but unfortunately, there was no generous patron like Han Yu, who had a sharp eye for discovering able men and tirelessly promoted the younger generations. Talented people were not scarce, but there was no good judge of their talent. Chen Renjie's two points could be summarized as the need for "praise and recognition" of celebrities if the literati wanted to gain fame.

The term *"yin ke"* refers to confirmation and approval. As was explained in Ye Mengde's *"Shilin Bishu Luhua"* ("Records of Summer Resort in Stone Forest", Vol. 1), the term means "confidence and mutual agreement resulting in *yin ke*".[2] Originally a Buddhist term, *"yin"* (seal) means to determine without doubt, indicating that when a disciple's cultivation reaches a certain level, the master acknowledges and silently approves the realm he has attained. In literary criticism, the term *"yin ke"* indicates that a person's literary creative level has been acknowledged and affirmed by others. In the eyes of people in the Song Dynasty, even if someone's literary creation reaches a high level and attains a significant artistic realm, he still needs the approval of his predecessors to gain self-affirmation and enhance his confidence. Han Ju, during the transition between the Northern Song and Southern Song Dynasties, said, "When composing poems, without a shadow of doubt one should gain the *yin ke* (approval) from the famous literati. This is why our predecessors were so eager to seek approvals".[3] Similarly, Zhou Bida of the Southern Song Dynasty also said,

> If a man of letters has great talent in his youth, and his poems and essays are already excellent, he still needs the evaluation and recognition of their predecessors. Only after that would he have confidence in his talent. It is similar to practicing meditation for Buddhists, where even if one gains insight, he still need the *yin ke* (recognition) of the great masters.[4]

In fact, in the Song Dynasty, the eager pursuit of praise and recognition from predecessors and celebrities aimed at not only establishing literary self-confidence but, more importantly, gaining fame rapidly.

6.2 Shortcut to Fame

During the Song Dynasty, gaining the praise and recognition of renowned literati was a shortcut to fame for men of letters. Once an unknown person obtained the praise and recognition of these celebrities, his fame would be immediately and greatly boosted.

Ouyang Xiu, a master of literary works in his generation, could make a man famous immediately in the whole country with his approval. Bi Zhongyou of the Northern Song Dynasty made the following comments,

> Ouyang Xiu's morality and literary creation were highly valued by three emperors and all the literati of the time, who respected him as the esteemed teacher. His disciples, once receiving his praise and recognition for certain phrases or works, would gain fame throughout the country.[5]

Some famous figures, such as Su Shi and his brothers and Zeng Gong, also benefited from Ouyang Xiu's support and guidance. Therefore, the "Biography of Ouyang Xiu" in the "History of the Song Dynasty" stated that with his appreciation and praise, many became renowned.

Wang Anshi, known for his extensive knowledge, was also considered a grand master of the time. Those who obtained his guidance considered it a great honour and their names would become renowned throughout the country.[6] For example, when Wei Xiang was at the age of 17, he presented his essay "Jie Zhu Fu" to Wang Anshi. The latter was greatly impressed by the work and exclaimed, "In my travels to Jiangnan and Wu Yue, I have found excellent writings only in you and Dong Gu." From then on, Wei Xiang became a renowned writer, and all his works were widely circulated among the men of letters.[7] Similarly, Liu Jisun, a talented poet, was not widely known in his early years. When he served as an inspector of liquor taxes in Raozhou, he happened to meet his superior, Wang Anshi, who came to inspect the liquor affairs. Wang Anshi read the short poem written by Liu Jisun on the screen and greatly praised it. Then he summoned Liu Jisun for a conversation for a long time and praised him. Without investigating the liquor affairs further, Wang Anshi departed in his carriage, and Liu Jisun became "known" ever since.[8] Although Wei Xiang and Liu Jisun had little influence in later generations and their surviving works were mostly ordinary without any distinguishing features, they gained temporary fame through the praise and recognition of the celebrity Wang Anshi.

There were even more literary figures who gained fame through the praise of Su Shi. The "Four Great Disciples of Su Shi" and "Six Gentlemen of the Su's Disciplines" were well-known ones already. Even for those ordinary men of letters, once they received Su Shi's praise and recommendation, they would attract the attention of the world as if they were wearing a dazzling halo. Xing Jushi (1068–1087 A.D.), a premature, short-lived poet of the Northern Song Dynasty, died an early death when he was only 20 years old. His fame was related to Su Shi's praise and recommendation. At the age of 14, he wrote the poem "*Ming Fei Yin*" (To Wang Zhaojun), which greatly impressed Su Shi and won his recognition. Then Xing Jushi became a renowned poet. After his death, Huang Tingjian mourned him in his poetry with the following lines, "A white jade was buried in yellow earth". Su Shi, Huang Tingjian, Chao Buzhi and other famous literati also wrote prefaces or postscripts for his posthumous collection, further enhancing his reputation.[9] During the transition period between the Northern Song and Southern Song Dynasties, the renowned recluse Su Xiang also gained fame through Su Shi's praise. Su Shi and Su Xiang's father, Su Jian, were old friends. When Su Shi read the poem "To the Tune *Qingjiang Tune*" written by Su Xiang, he was amazed and said, "If this piece were included in the anthology of Li Bai's poems, who would doubt its authenticity? It is great as Su Yangzhi's poem 'To the Tune *Qingjiang Tune*'".[10] As a result, Su Xiang became "known" in the whole country.[11]

During the Song Dynasty, not all men of letters had the honour and opportunity of receiving recognition and praise from literary giants like Ouyang Xiu, Wang Anshi and or Su Shi. However, even without the approval of the aforementioned "superstars", those who obtained the praise and recognition of other influential figures in the literary circles would also be well-known. For instance, Su Shen, a politician and writer from Jinjiang in the Northern Song Dynasty, served as a judge in local and central governments. Serving as a judge for a long period, he was not so well-known to the general people. After the death of his mother, he lived in Yang Zhou.

> In Yang Zhou, there was an official named Sheng Du who was conceited with his own literary works. However, once reading Su Shen's works, Sheng Du was greatly amazed and thought that his own works were much worse in comparison. From then on, Su Shen became a well-known figure.[12]

Similarly, Liu Yifeng (with the courtesy name Shaomei) from Puzhou in the early Southern Song Dynasty became known after his writings were praised by Feng Xie, the senior assistant to the minister, a high-ranking official.[13] Although Su Shen and Feng Xie were not literary giants, their praise and recommendation, due to their local fame or high political positions, propelled Su Shen and Liu Yifeng to the fore.

Because praise and recognition of eminent figures had an immediate impact on one's fame, this inspired the men of letters at the time to make every effort to obtain the famous ones' recognition for social acceptance. Liu Guo, in his early years, wrote the poem "Presented to Xin Jiaxuan" in which there are the following lines:

The scholar has no desire for a golden seal, or bravely leading an army of one hundred thousand soldiers to the battlefield. All he wants is the recognition from Xin Jiaxuan (Xin Qiji, a great poet) for his works. Then, like a spring breeze, his heroic spirit lingers even after death.[14]

If their long-term efforts failed to earn recognition, they would have a deep sense of loss. Someone even said, "Without the recognition and acceptance of famous literary figures or high-ranking officials, I feel like wearing clothes without warmth or being on short commons".[15] The yearning for the praise and recognition from renowned figures reached a desperate level.

6.3 The Communication Effect

For ordinary men of letters, the recognition from eminent figures fulfilled both their practical needs for fame and wealth and psychological needs for self-satisfaction. If they couldn't obtain it, they felt anxious and unsatisfied, as if lacking enough to wear and eat. However, once they received it, they felt extremely honoured and fulfilled. This is why scholars in the Song Dynasty were enthusiastic about forming alliances and passing on the title of "grand masters" from one generation to another, from Ouyang Xiu to Su Shi, from Su Shi to Huang Tingjian, and from Huang Tingjian to other members of the Jiangxi School of Poetry. The "grant masters" of these alliances positioned themselves as leaders, while the members willingly prostrate themselves under the masters' tutelage, driven by their personal considerations and needs. The members sought the recognition and support of the masters to enhance their own reputation and social recognition, while the masters needed more disciples to strengthen their own schools or groups and realize their literary and even political goals, thus promoting the development of literature in the desired direction. The collective effect and influence of a group far surpassed that of isolated individuals. The impact of the Four Great Disciples of Su Shi, who gathered under Su Shi's tutelage, was much greater than that when they fought alone. Li Zhi of the Ming Dynasty recognized this, saying that although Huang Tingjian, Qin Guan, Chao Buzhi and Zhang Lei were talented poets, their reputation and influence wouldn't be so fully established if they hadn't received the recognition of Su Shi.[16]

The reason the recognition of eminent figures was so important for making a name for a man of letters can be analysed from a psychological perspective: It is the result of people's admiration of the eminent ones. People admired celebrities and literary masters, and they had extraordinary trust in their words and actions. They would accept and identify with the eminent ones' evaluations of people and things without reservation. Therefore, once someone received recognition and appreciation from an eminent figure, he would naturally gain the favour and acceptance of the general people. Zhang Lei's words to Huang Tingjian serve as evidence, "The master Su Shi first praised your writings in Qiantang (Hangzhou). Those who admire him also have a high opinion of your works".[17] As scholars admired Su Shi, when Su Shi highly praised Huang Tingjian's writings, they also took delight in and sought after Huang's works, thus spreading his reputation and influence.

The effect of recognition by eminent figures in the literary world did not first show itself in the Tang and Song dynasties. As early as the Western Jin Dynasty, when Zuo Si's *ci* work "*San Du Fu*" ("To the Three Capital Cities") was first published, it was not accepted by the people and faced much criticism. However, once it received recognition and appreciation from the famous figure Huangfu Mi, "those who initially doubted now eagerly praised it".[18] The work was so popular afterwards in Luoyang that the paper became expensive in the city – the overwhelming popularity of the work caused a shortage of printing paper. The story demonstrates not only the tremendous impact of recognition from eminent figures on the fame of a man of letters but also the significant role it plays in the widespread dissemination of their works.

Notes

1 Tang, Guizhang. 1965. *Quan Song ci* ("Complete *ci* Works of Song Dynasty"). Zhonghua Book Company, 3077.
2 Ye, Mengde. 1990. *Shilin bishu luhua* ("Records of Summer Resort in Stone Forest"), Vol. 1, Shanghai Bookstore Publishing House, 13.
3 Wu, Zeng. 1979. *Nenggai Zai manlu* ("Random Records of Nenggai Studio"), Vol. 10. Shanghai Chinese Classics Publishing House, 282.
4 Zhou, Bida. *Ti Shangu yu Han Zicang tie* ("To Huang Tingjian and Han Zicang"). *Wenzhong ji* ("A Collection of Wenzhong's Works"), Vol. 19. *Siku quanshu* (Complete Library in Four Branches of Literature, Wenyuange edition), Vol. 1147: 194.
5 Bi, Zhongyou. *Ouyang Shupi zhuan* ("Biography of Ouyang Fei"). *Xitai ji* ("Collected Works of Bi Zhongyou"), Vol. 6. *Siku quanshu* (Complete Library in Four Branches of Literature, Wenyuange edition), Vol. 1122: 73.
6 Wang, Pizhi. 2001. *Shengshui yan tan lu* ("Fleeting Gossip by the River Sheng"), Vol. 10, *Song Yuan biji xiaoshuo daguan* ("Grand View of Story-Telling Novels in Song and Yuan Dynasties"), Vol. 2. Shanghai Chinese Classics Publishing House, 1307.
7 Lu, Xinyuan. 1991. *Wei Xiang zhuan* ("Biography of Wei Xiang"). Song Shi yi (Supplements to *History of Song Dynasty*), Vol. 26. Zhonghua Book Company, 274.

8 Ye, Mengde. 1981. *Shilin shihua* ("Poetic Talks in Stone Forest"), Vol. 2, *Lidai shihua* ("Comments on Poetry across Dynastics"), Vol. 1, Zhonghua Book Company, 433.
9 Chao, Gongwu. *Zhaode Xiansheng junzhai dushu zhi* ("Catalogue of the Magistrate Chao Gongwu's Library"), Vol. 4. *Sibu congkan* ("Four Series Books").
10 Hu, Zai. 1962. *Tiaoxi yuyin conghua* ("Series of Poetic Notes by the Recluse of the Brook Tiao"). *Gaozhai Shihua* ("Poetic Notes in Elegant Study"), Vol. 54. People's Literature Publishing House, 363.
11 Tuo, Tuo et al. 1977. *Yinyi zhuan* ("Records of Hermits"). *Song shi* ("History of the Song Dynasty"), Vol. 459. Zhonghua Book Company, (28): 13462.
12 Tuo, Tuo et al. 1977. *Su Shen zhuan* ("Biography of Su Shen"). *Song shi* ("History of the Song Dynasty"), Vol. 294. Zhonghua Book Company, (28): 9808.
13 Tuo, Tuo et al. 1977. *Liu Yifeng zhuan* ("Biography of Liu Yifeng"). *Song shi* ("History of the Song Dynasty"), Vol. 389. Zhonghua Book Company, (34): 11940.
14 Liu, Guo. 1978. *Longzhou ji* ("Collected Works of Longzhou"), Vol. 8. Shanghai Chinese Classics Publishing House, 68.
15 Chen, Qiqing. *Dai tong Wang Sheren shu* ("A Letter to Wang Sheren"). *Yun Chuang ji* ("Collected Works of Yun Chuang"), Vol. 5. *Siku quanshu* (Complete Library in Four Branches of Literature, Wenyuange edition), Vol. 1178: 46.
16 Li, Zhi. 1959. *Shu Su Wenzhonggong waiji hou* ("Postscript to *Supplementary Su Shi's Works*"). *Xu Fenshu* ("Sequel to *A Book to Burn*"), Vol. 2. Zhonghua Book Company, 68.
17 Zhang, Lei. 1990. *Yu Luzhi shu* ("Letters to Luzhi"). *Zhang Lei ji* ("Collections of Zhang Lei's Works"), Vol. 55. Zhonghua Book Company, 827.
18 Liu, Yiqing. 1984. *Shi shuo xin yu* ("New Account of Tales of the World", Literature, Vol. 4). Xu, Zhen'e. *Shi shuo xin yu jiao jian* ("Revision and Annotation on *New Account of Tales of the World*"). Zhonghua Book Company, 136.

7 Non-literary Factors for the Communication Effect of Literature

In ancient China, writers and poets had varying levels of fame and achievements, as is a normal phenomenon. However, behind this phenomenon, there are many factors worth contemplating and questioning. Is the fame directly proportional to the literary achievement? Can we say that writers with greater fame always had greater literary achievements, while those lesser-known ones always had lower achievements? It is perhaps not always the case. The fame and influence of ancient writers may have been influenced by other factors besides their literary achievements. There are likely "non-literary" factors at play. This chapter attempts to explore this issue with the examples of Li Qingzhao (1084–1155 A.D.) and Zhu Shuzhen (1135–1180 A.D.),[1] two female poets in the Song Dynasty.

7.1 The Fluctuating Fame of Li Qingzhao and Zhu Shuzhen in the Southern Song Dynasty

Li Qingzhao (with the courtesy name Yi'an Ju Shi) and Zhu Shuzhen, both talented women of the Song Dynasty, were excellent at writing poems and *ci* works. However, their fame in their lifetimes differed significantly. Li Qingzhao enjoyed widespread popularity during her lifetime. Wang Zhuo, the contemporary poet of hers, remarked as follows,

> She already gained a reputation for poetry in her childhood with her extraordinary talent, and was even on par with her predecessors. Among the literati, few could match her. If compared with women of the current era, she should be considered the No. 1 *ci* poet of the time.[2]

Zhu Bian praised that she "is good at writing, particularly at composing the poems".[3] Hu Zai remarked, "In recent times, there are some women who are good at writing poems, such as Li Yi'an who has written many excellent ones".[4] Li Qingzhao had even more fame after her death, earning admiration from numerous men of letters. As was written in "*Cai Fu Lu*" ("Records of Talented Women"), "Li Qingzhao was skilled in calligraphy, painting, and *ci* poetry, with a remarkable talent for ornate language. Even to this day, whenever scholars read the preface to the '*Jin Shi Lu*'" ("Critical Studies of Metal and Stone Inscriptions"), their minds are enlightened and inspired. They marvel at the extraordinary achievements of this elderly woman. Truly remarkable! Truly remarkable![5]

However, Zhu Shuzhen was unknown and buried in oblivion during the 150 years of the Southern Song Dynasty. She was not known to the public during her lifetime, and even after her death, few people mentioned or praised her. Had it not been for Wei Zhonggong, who happened to hear someone reciting her poetry when he was in an inn in Hangzhou and collected and compiled her works into the "*Duan Chang Ji*" ("Anthology of Heartbroken Poems") out of sympathy with her miserable life, it was likely that future generations would have little knowledge of Zhu Shuzhen. It was worth noting that when Wei Zhonggong compiled the anthology, it was in the ninth year (1182) of Chunxi years during the reign of Emperor Xiao Zong. However, in Zhang Duanyi's commentary on female writers during the Chunxi years, there was no mention of Zhu Shuzhen, "During the Chunxi years, there were simply two women who were well-matched with Li Qingzhao in literary achievements, namely Lady Bao from Qing'an and Lady Fang from Xiuzhai".[6] The great scholar Zhu Xi, who lived around the same time as (slightly later) Zhu Shuzhen, also mentioned Li Qingzhao and Lady Wei when evaluating women's literary accomplishments in the dynasty, with Zhu Shuzhen completely neglected, "In this dynasty, women who were excellent in literary works are only Li Qingzhao and Lady Wei".[7] This shows that Zhu Shuzhen's name was little known among the literati.

However, among the poets of the Southern Song Dynasty, Li Qingzhao was often mentioned, with some poetic works echoing her *ci* works or imitating her style. Zhu Dunru, who lived at about the same time as Li Qingzhao, wrote the *ci* work "*Que Qiao Xian: He Li Yi'an Jin Yu Chi Lian*" ("Echoing with Li Qingzhao's Poem 'Goldfish and Lotus', to the Tune of *Que Qiao Xian*"); Xin Qiji, who lived slightly later, wrote the *ci* work "*Chou Nu Er: Bo Shan Dao Zhong Xiao Li Yi'an Ti*" ("Imitating Li Qingzhao's Style in Boshan, to the Tune *Chou Nu Er*"); Hou Zhi wrote the *ci* work "*Yan'er Mei: Xiao Yi'an Ti*" ("Imitating Li Qingzhao's Style, to the Tune *Yan'er Mei*"). Towards the end of the Southern Song Dynasty, Liu Chenweng also imitated Li Qingzhao's *ci* work "To the Tune *Yong Yu Le*" and described himself as follows,

> Since the Shangyuan Festival of the Yihai year, I have been reciting Li Qingzhao's *ci* work "To the Tune *Yong Yu Le*", and it always brings tears to my eyes. Now, three years later, every time when I hear this poem, I cannot help but feel unbearable. Following its rhythm, I also assume the self-reference of Li Qingzhao. Although my wording falls short, my sorrow and suffering surpass it.[8]

However, in comparison, no *ci* composer ever mentioned Zhu Shuzhen at the time.

Commentaries on poems and *ci* works, historical records and unofficial historical notes of the Southern Song Dynasty frequently mentioned Li Qingzhao by discussing her *ci* works or evaluating her poems, but few had a mention of Zhu Shuzhen. For example, Zhao Yanwei wrote,

> Li Qingzhao, who names herself as Yi'an Ju Shi, is the wife of Zhao Mingcheng (with courtesy name Defu) and the daughter of Li Gefei (with courtesy name Wenshu). With her extraordinary talent and poetic thoughts, whenever she finishes new works, people copy and spread them immediately. Her *ci* works, winning universal praise, are widely praised and have been published.[9]

Chen Yu remarked, "Li Qingzhao is skilled in composing poems. Hence, the phrase 'flourishing leaves and withering flowers' in the poem of 'To the Tune *Ru Meng Ling*' is widely acclaimed throughout the country".[10] Zhou Hui commented, "As a woman, she composed such excellent works. One who doesn't possess profound thoughts wouldn't possibly write such works".[11] In the eyes of the people of the Southern Song Dynasty, Li Qingzhao was the epitome of a female writer. People usually had her as an example of a talented woman. For example, there was the following comparison,

> Lady Hu is the wife of the Ministy Huang You and the daughter of the Minister Ke Yuan Gong. She is endowed with intelligence and a good memory. She reads various classics extensively and can recite most of them. She can write good poems and ci works, which are also admirable. She is particularly skilled in playing the chess, Chinese qin, calligraphy and painting, so she names herself as Hui Zhai Ju Shi. People of the time regarded her as parallel to Li Qingzhao.[12]

In the preface to the "*Duan Chang Ji*" ("Anthology of Heartbroken Poems"), Wei Zhonggong praised women who were adept at "elegant words and beautiful sentences", with specific mention of Li Qingzhao, "in recent times, Li Qingzhao stands out prominently".[13] On the other hand, Zhu Shuzhen was mentioned at all.

The literary anthologies compiled in the Southern Song Dynasty also did not include Zhu Shuzhen's works. Whether in Zeng Zao's "*Yue Fu Ya Ci*" ("Refined *ci* Works"), compiled in the early Southern Song Dynasty, or in the anonymous compiler's "*Cao Tang Shi Yu*" ("Anthology of Thatched Cottage Poems"), Huang Sheng's "*Hua'an Ci Xuan*" ("Selection of *ci* Works of Hua'an") and Zhao Wenli's "*Yang Chun Bai Xue*" ("White Snow in Early Spring") compiled in the middle and late Southern Song Dynasty, Li Qingzhao's poems were included. Among them, the anthology "*Yue Fu Ya Ci*" ("Refined *ci* Works") alone included 23 *ci* works of Li Qingzhao. However, not a single piece of work by Zhu Shuzhen was included in these anthologies.

In the public and private catalogues of the Song Dynasty, there was also no record of an anthology or catalogue of Zhu Shuzhen's literary works,[14] indicating that *"Duan Chang Ji"* ("Anthology of Heartbroken Poems"), the collection of her works compiled by Wei Zhonggong, had very limited circulation range during the Southern Song Dynasty. On the other hand, there are various versions of Li Qingzhao's collected poems and *ci* works from the Southern Song Dynasty, such as the 12-volume *"Li Yi'an Ji"* ("Collection of Li Qingzhao's Works"), the seven-volume *"Yi'an Jushi Wen Ji"* ("Anthology of Li Qingzhao"), the 6-volume *"Yi'an ci"* ("Li Qingzhao's *ci* Works") and the *"Shuyu Ji"* of 1-volume, 3-volume and 5-volume editions.[15] The multiple versions of her works indicate that Li Qingzhao had a high level of fame and was widely popular among readers during the Southern Song Dynasty. Generally speaking, the number of versions of the poets' works in circulation is often proportional to their level of fame and influence. The higher the poet's reputation, the more the readers desire and demand for reading, hence more versions in circulation.

7.2 The Fluctuating Fame of Li Qingzhao and Zhu Shuzhen, Along with Their Family and Literary Background

From the perspective of contemporary people, although Zhu Shuzhen's achievements in poetry may be slightly inferior to Li Qingzhao's, there is no immeasurably vast difference between the two. If we consider Li Qingzhao as a first-class female poet, then Zhu Shuzhen can be regarded as a second-class poet at least. However, in the Southern Song Dynasty, Li Qingzhao had first-rate influence and reputation that matched her talent, while Zhu Shuzhen's influence and fame were even inferior to that of the lowest-ranking poets. Even the relatively obscure poets like Lady Bao from Qing'an and Lady Fang from Xiuzhai, whose works were not passed to later generations, drew the attention of Zhang Duanyi, while Zhu Shuzhen, who had over three hundred surviving poems, did not receive any comments in the Song Dynasty except those from Wei Zhonggong. This is truly puzzling and perplexing. The reasons behind this cannot be fully explained solely based on their literary achievements. So, what other factors were at play in determining the varying levels of fame between these two female poets?

Li Qingzhao gained fame at a young age, which was undoubtedly related to her family background. Her father, Li Gefei, was a prominent figure in the literary world of the Song Dynasty. Liu Kezhuang of the Southern Song Dynasty described his writings as "elegant and flavorful, surpassing those of Chao Buzhi and Qin Guan".[16] Han Hu went as far as saying that his writings "ranks only second to Sima Qian".[17] Although both Liu Kezhuang's and Han Hu's words might be overly flattering and not so reliable, they indicate the high praise people held for Li Gefei at the time. As the daughter of such a well-known figure, Li Qingzhao naturally benefited from the "halo effect" of her famous father, making it easier for her to attract people's attention. Whenever Li Qingzhao was mentioned in relevant records of the Song Dynasty, she was usually introduced as Li Gefei's daughter. For example, Li Xinchuan introduced, "Li Qingzhao, the daughter of Li Gefei, is good at composing *ci* works and calls herself Yi'an Ju Shi".[18] When Chen Zhensun introduced Li Qingzhao in the preface to the collection "*Shu Yu Ji*", he described her as "the daughter of the famous scholar Li Gefei, who was married to Zhao Mingcheng".[19] Similarly, in Zhao Yanwei's "*Yunlu Man Chao*" ("Loose Notes of the Cloud-Covered Foothill"), Li Qingzhao is introduced with the following words, "Li Qingzhao, who names herself as Yi'an Ju Shi, is the wife of Zhao Mingcheng (with courtesy name Defu) and the daughter of Li Gefei (with courtesy name Wenshu)".[20] In the "Song Shi-Yi Wen Zhi" ("History of the Song Dynasty, Records of Arts and Literature"), the author of the collection "*Yi'an Jushi Wen Ji*" ("Anthology of Li Qingzhao") was directly termed as "Li Gefei's daughter", without even mention of Li Qingzhao's personal name. If this is the case in written records, it is even more obvious in daily life. Therefore, Li Qingzhao's fame in her lifetime undoubtedly was related to her father's.

Certainly, in the introduction of women in ancient classics, it was common to describe her as someone's daughter or someone's wife. Women's identities were always attached to their fathers or husbands. This was a customary practice in ancient China and a notable indication that women lacked independent social status. However, regardless of the social status of women, they could only rely on the social positions of their natal or marital families for social recognition. In terms of fame for ancient Chinese women, those who had a better family to rely on were more advantageous than those who did not.

Li Qingzhao's husband's family was also prestigious. Her husband, Zhao Mingcheng, was a renowned epigrapher who studied calligraphy and stone inscriptions at that time. Her father-in-law, Zhao Tingzhi, even held the position of prime minister. The fact that the daughter-in-law of the prime minister was good at composing poems would naturally arouse people's interest. When introducing Zhao Mingcheng or the Zhao couple, people of the Song Dynasty usually highlighted the status of Zhao Tingzhi, the prime minister. For example, Hong Shi introduced Zhao Mingcheng as "the son of Zhao Tingzhi, the Prime Minister".[21] In "*Zhi Zhai Shu Lu Jie Ti*" ("Commented Library Catalogue of the Zhizhai Studio"), Zhao Mingcheng is introduced as "the son of the Prime Minister Zhao Tingzhi, and his wife is the Yi'an Ju Shi with the surname Li".[22] In the "History of the Song Dynasty, Biography of Li Gefei", it was narrated that Li Qingzhao "was particularly acclaimed for her poetry and *ci* works, and she got married with Zhao Mingcheng, the son of Zhao Tingzhi".[23] The prime minister was, of course, an eminent figure, and his daughter-in-law naturally gained more attention from the people. Moreover, Li Qingzhao had a somewhat rebellious spirit and even wrote a poem with the lines "Being roasted, hands could be hot enough, yet one's heart might still be cold" to satirize her father-in-law, the in-position prime minister! These words and actions attracted even more attention to Li Qingzhao, the daughter-in-law of the prime minister.

Relevant to the family background is Li Qingzhao's literary background. Her father, Li Gefei, was an important figure in the core circle of the literary world in the later period of the Northern Song Dynasty. Li Gefei was tutored by Su Shi, and he was one of the Four Disciples of Su Shi in the Later Period.[24] He had a close relationship with the well-known Four Great Disciples of Su Shi. With the father's connection with the literati, Li Qingzhao had the privilege of not only receiving guidance from the disciples of Su Shi but also being praised and recommended by them. According to the records in Zhu Bian's *"Feng Yue Tang Shi Hua"* ("Poems on the Past Romance"), Chao Buzhi praised Li Qingzhao "in front of many literati", and Zhang Lei also "praised her poetry".[25] In the Song Dynasty, people highly valued the praise and recognition of the literary masters. A single sentence of praise or recommendation from a literary giant was enough to make one famous. By the later period of the Northern Song Dynasty, Chao Buzhi and Zhang Lei had become great masters in the literary world. Their praise of Li Qingzhao was undoubtedly influential and sufficient to make her famous throughout the country. With the combination of various factors and the "celebrity effect", it was inevitable for Li Qingzhao to become well-known.

Li Qingzhao also had a relatively wide social communication circle. Those who had interactions with Zhao Mingcheng likely had contact or acquaintance with her. Even from Li Qingzhao's own works, it can be seen that she communicated with many high-ranking officials, such as Han Xiaozhou, a senior official of the Privy Council, Hu Songnian, the Minister of Works, and Qi Chongli, an academician of the Imperial Academy. According to Yue Ke's record in *"Bao Zhen Zhai Fa Shu Zan"* ("Calligraphies of *Bao Zhen Zhai*"), Li Qingzhao communicated with Mi Youren, the son of the famous calligrapher Mi Fu. It was also possible that she had an acquaintance with the renowned poet Zhu Dunru, as was shown in Zhu Dunru's *ci* work *"Que Qiao Xian: He Li Yi'an Jin Yu Chi Lian"* ("Echoing with Li Qingzhao's Poem 'Goldfish and Lotus', to the Tune of *Que Qiao Xian*"). These prominent figures in the political and literary circles may not have explicitly introduced Li Qingzhao wherever they went, but they would well possibly mention her on appropriate occasions. This would positively contribute to her fame in the literati's circle.

Zhu Shuzhen was far less fortunate than Li Qingzhao. She lacked all the privileges that Li Qingzhao had. Her natal family was not prestigious, and her husband's family was not a well-known one. Whether her father was an official or a common civilian was unknown, and so were the surname and given name of her husband. She had no support from political figures, social elites, or literary giants who would actively praise and recommend her, and she had no opportunity to meet these renowned and influential figures herself. Her poetry reflects a very small world of social communication and her simple interpersonal communication with others. From the titles of her poems, we can only find three women: Lady Wei, Lady Xie and Lady Wu. It was well possible that these three ladies didn't come from high-ranking noble families. Zhu Shuzhen indeed spent her time in an isolated and confined world in which she wrote her literary works! As a lonely individual without others' help, Zhu Shuzhen was destined to write in obscurity, with her works rising or falling on their own. She did not dare to have the hope for posthumous fame. In her poem "To the Tune *Jian Zi Mu Lan Hua*", she described herself as "walking alone, sitting alone, singing alone, playing alone and sleeping alone". This is a vivid description of both her spiritual world and her real life. Zhu Shuzhen's solitary and secluded life and living environment limited her communication with literati and officials, making it difficult for her talent and works to enter mainstream society and the upper literary circles.

With the case analysis of Li Qingzhao and Zhu Shuzhen, we may find that, in addition to their literary achievements, the fame of ancient writers was closely related to their family background, literary background, relationships with tutors and friends, interpersonal connections and social and political status. The degree of a writer's popularity also interacted with the dissemination of their works. Readers' choices of reading works were often directly or indirectly influenced by the writers' fame, and the scope and range of a work's dissemination affected its fame. The wider the dissemination of the work, the higher the writer's fame and the greater their influence.

7.3 Extensive Dissemination of Zhu Shuzhen's Poetry in the Ming Dynasty and Zhu Shuzhen's Equal Popularity with Li Qingzhao

Since the Yuan Dynasty, with the increasingly widespread dissemination of Zhu Shuzhen's works, the people gradually knew this female poet. Particularly since the Ming Dynasty, Zhu Shuzhen's fame and influence expanded significantly, so much so that she could stand shoulder to shoulder with Li Qingzhao. Finally, these two talented women of the Song Dynasty enjoyed equal popularity.

Zhu Shuzhen's poetry collection, "*Duan Chang Ji*" ("Anthology of Heartbroken Poems"), was already popular during the Yuan Dynasty. The exact time of its initial publication in the Yuan Dynasty is unclear. However, there are records in the period that mentioned Zhu Shuzhen's poetry anthology. The "Great Collection of Lineages, Newly Arranged by Rhyme and Expanded with Historical Events" (*Shi Zu Da Quan*), compiled by an anonymous author, stated, "There is an anthology of Zhu Shuzhen's poems".[26] Although it did not provide specific details about the title or version, it indicates that people of that time already knew about Zhu Shuzhen's poetry collection. Furthermore, the poetry collection of Zhu Shuzhen, published during the Yuan Dynasty, was reported to have been passed down to the early 20th century. Kuang Zhouyi's "Notes of Canyingwu" (*Canyingwu Sui Bi*) recorded,

> The Fan family's library at Tianyi Pavilion in Yinxian County, has been preserved for three hundred years since the Ming Dynasty without any loss of books. However, this spring, thousands of books were stolen and sold at bookstores in Shanghai at a low price. Among the books on sale, there are not many from the Song and Yuan dynasties (I only saw the

Song edition of *"Ouyang Wenzhong Gong Ji"* ("Collected Works of Ouyang Xiu") and the Yuan edition of *"Zhu Shuzhen Shi Ji"* ("Collected Poems of Zhu Shuzhen")). The majority of the books are meticulously copied editions from the early Ming Dynasty, which account for about eighty to ninety percent. For example, there are historical books *"Shi Lu"* ("Veritable Records") that records Emperor Taizu and Emperor Chengzu of the Ming Dynasty, etc. Most of books are rarely seen before. In a short time, a ship merchant and bookstore owner named Jin Songqing obtained the books. The prices of the books skyrocketed because he refused to sell them individually, leaving no books in the market. Later, a descendant of the Fan family filed a lawsuit in Shanghai, and the judge ordered an immediate investigation. However, shortly afterward, the two parties of the lawsuit reached an accommodation. Then the books were securely sent abroad, with no chance of returning to the country. What a great pity![27]

From this account by Kuang Zhouyi, we can learn at least two points: Firstly, the Tianyi Pavilion originally housed the "Yuan edition of '*Zhu Shuzhen Shi Ji*' ('Collected Poems of Zhu Shuzhen')". The juxtaposition of Song and Yuan editions with "meticulously copied editions from the early Ming Dynasty" suggests that the "Yuan edition of '*Zhu Shuzhen Shi Ji*' ('Collected Poems of Zhu Shuzhen')" should be a printed edition rather than a handwritten copy. Even if it were a copy, it would undoubtedly be a copy of the Yuan Dynasty. Secondly, this "Yuan edition of '*Zhu Shuzhen Shi Ji*' ('Collected Poems of Zhu Shuzhen')" has already found its way to the eastern country of Japan, while its specific whereabouts are unknown. The fact that the "Yuan edition of '*Zhu Shuzhen Shi Ji*' ('Collected Poems of Zhu Shuzhen')" was preserved at least indicates that the collection was published during the Yuan Dynasty.

During the early years of the Ming Dynasty, there were also surviving copies of *"Zhu Shuzhen Shi Ji"* ("Collected Poems of Zhu Shuzhen"). In Yang Shiqi's *"Wenyuange Shu Mu"* ("Catalogue of the Wenyuange Library"), there are the following records, "One volume of *Zhu Shuzhen Shi Ji*, missing; one volume of *Zhu Shuzhen Shi Ji*, missing".[28] The catalogue *"Wenyuange Shu Mu"* ("Catalogue of the Wenyuange Library") was compiled by Yang Shiqi in the sixth year of the Zhengtong years (1441). It listed the books from the government store of books that were transported from Nanjing to the Wenyuange in Beijing in the 19th year of the Yongle reign (1421).[29] This indicates that the *"Zhu Shuzhen Shi Ji"* ("Collected Poems of Zhu Shuzhen") had been stored in the secret library since the nineteenth year of Emperor Yongle's reign, but it was lost during the Zhengtong years. This edition might be the Yuan edition or at least a printed edition from the early Ming Dynasty.

There are surviving Ming editions of *"Duan Chang Ji"* ("Anthology of Heartbroken Poems") of Zhu Shuzhen, which were printed in the early Ming Dynasty. The National Central Library in Taipei houses a Ming edition with annotations by Zheng Yuanzuo titled "Newly Annotated Zhu Shuzhen's

'*Duan Chang Ji*' ('Anthology of Heartbroken Poems')". It consists of ten volumes of the main collection and eight volumes of additional collections, with a postscript by Mao Guangsheng, a scholar from a later period.[30] The National Library of China in Beijing also holds an early Ming edition called the "Newly Annotated Zhu Shuzhen's '*Duan Chang Ji*' ('Anthology of Heartbroken Poems')" consisting of eight volumes of the main collection and eight volumes of additional poems.[31] These two editions from the early Ming period have the same title but are slightly different in content and format. The Taipei edition contains a total of 18 volumes, with half a page containing 10 lines and each line consisting of 18 characters, while the Beijing edition consists of 16 volumes, with half a page containing 10 lines and each line consisting of 20 characters. It is evident that they are not the same version, indicating that there were at least two different printed editions during the early Ming Dynasty.

Afterward, the number of block-printed Ming editions gradually increased. The National Library of China stores another printed Ming edition called the "Newly Annotated Zhu Shuzhen's '*Duan Chang Ji*'", consisting of ten volumes of the first collection. According to the Ming scholar Gao Ru's "*Baichuan Shu Zhi*" ("Baichuan's Library Catalogue"), "The '*Duan Chang Ji*' consists of ten volumes. It was composed by the woman named Zhu Shuzhen, with annotations by Zheng Yuanzuo of Qiantang".[32] The title of this version is different from the one currently held by the National Library of China, indicating that it was another printed edition. Zhu Shuzhen's "*Duan Chang ci*" also had surviving manuscript editions. Among them, there was a handwritten copy of the Ming edition of "*Song Yuan Ming Jia Ci*" (in Beijing University Library), a copy of the late Ming edition called "*Shi Ci Za Zu*" in Mao Jin's Jiguge Library, and a Qing edition titled "*Jiguge Weike Ci*" from Zhisheng Daozhai. These editions were copied from the Ming edition.

The classic works from the Ming Dynasty often mentioned "*Duan Chang Ji*" ("Anthology of Heartbroken Poems"). Tian Rucheng, in his "*Xihu Youlan Zhi Yu*" ("Book of Tour in the West Lake"), narrated,

> Zhu Shuzhen, a native of Qiantang, was clever and witty at a young age. She was good in her studies and was adept at writing poems which were elegant and charmful. In her youth, her uneducated parents arranged her marriage with a vulgar family, and her husband proved to be a vile person, making the household environment unpleasant. Zhu Shuzhen felt frustrated and unable to realize her aspirations. She wrote many poems of sorrow and resentment. She wanted to place her emotion on someone who really understood her but failed. At last, she died of grief and sadness. Her parents collected her writings and burned them according to the Buddhism manner. The works that have been passed down today are only a small fraction of her entire works. Wang Tangzuo of Lin'an wrote a biography for her, and Wei Zhonggong (with courtesy name Duanli) of Wanling compiled her poems into an anthology titled "*Duan Chang Ji*" ("Anthology of Heartbroken Poems").[33]

This record by Tian Rucheng was largely excerpted from Wei Zhonggong's preface to the *"Duan Chang Ji"* ("Anthology of Heartbroken Poems"). He should have seen the block-printed popular version *"Duan Chang Ji"* ("Anthology of Heartbroken Poems") during that time. Jiang Yikui and Xu Boling, two scholars in the Ming Dynasty, introduced the life experience of Zhu Shuzhen and, respectively, stated, "Wei Duanli of Wanling collected and compiled her poems in an anthology titled '*Duan Chang Ji*' ('Anthology of Heartbroken Poems')'",[34] and "she left '*Duan Chang Ji*' in ten volumes, which has been passed down to the present day".[35]

Zhang Xingzhong, a man in the Song Dynasty, wrote a poem *"Ti Duan Chang Ji"* ("To *Anthology of Heartbroken Poems*"), in which he remarked,

> This woman is talented but lacks the female virtue. She is good at writing astonishing works, so what? In marriage she wouldn't live a life of ease and happiness, while with wine cups she has a lot of poetic emotions. She feels sorrowful in the face of the beautiful flowers and spring gardens, and laments over the lonely windows on moonlit nights. Men should not envy her literary talents, because women in the Song dynasty don't need to read.[36]

Although Zhang Xingzhong had disguised criticism towards Zhu Shuzhen, he must have read her *"Duan Chang Ji"* so that he could not help but write this poem to express his false viewpoint.

In the novels of the Ming Dynasty, there was also mention of *"Duan Chang Ji"* ("Anthology of Heartbroken Poems"). For example, in the third chapter of *"San Ke Pai'an Jing Qi"* ("Three Collections of Striking the Table in Amazement"), there are the following words,

> Old Xie's daughter, Fangqing, with a naturally free-spirited character, had learned many skills. She once said, "Su Xiaomei (Su Shi's younger sister who is also a talented poet) doesn't have my beauty, and even the famous beauty Xi Shi of the Yue State doesn't have my talent." On the table, there was a book *"Duan Chang Ji"* ("Anthology of Heartbroken Poems") by Zhu Shuzhen. After reading it, she sighed and remarked, "Such a talented and beautiful woman has to be married with an ordinary person. It is indeed detestable! It would be better if she were paired with her lover as Wen Jun and Xiangru,[37] whose fame would have been passed down through the ages!"[38]

Even in popular novels, possibly there was a copy of Zhu Shuzhen's *"Duan Chang Ji"* on the desk of the main characters. It can be imagined that *"Duan Chang Ji"* ("Anthology of Heartbroken Poems") must have been widely circulated at that time, and the general public was familiar with the book. This explains why the novelists included the poetic collection in their works.

Due to the wide dissemination of *"Duan Chang Ji"* ("Anthology of Heartbroken Poems"), Zhu Shuzhen became a prominent figure in historical and cultural circles during the Ming Dynasty. There were even avid fans who traced her former residence in Hangzhou. Tian Rucheng stated, "The Dawa Lane in Hangzhou, which links with Baokang Lane to the north, is where the female poet Zhu Shuzhen of the Yuan Dynasty lived".[39] Although Tian Rucheng made a minor mistake by mentioning Zhu Shuzhen as a poet from the Yuan Dynasty, he must have some evidence to make the judgement on Zhu Shuzhen's former residence.

Some well-intentioned people even turned Zhu Shuzhen's story into novels. In the Ming Dynasty, Zhou Ji, in the novel titled "*Yue Xia Lao Cuo Pei Ben Shu Qian Yuan*" ("The Matchmaker Wrongly Arranged the Marriage: A Predestined Misfortune") in Volume 16 of "*Xihu Er Ji*" ("The Second Volume of Stories in the West Lake"), told the story of Zhu Shuzhen. The story depicts how Zhu Shuzhen was deceived by her uncle "Pi Qiqiu" ("Leather Balloon") and was married to the extremely ugly "Jin Monster", the son of a grocery store owner. Eventually, Zhu Shuzhen died in despair. Let's take a look at two excerpts from the novel:

It is said that Zhu Shuzhen was a native of Qiantang during the Song Dynasty. Her parents were of humble backgrounds and were only concerned with the basic necessities of life. They had no knowledge of "poetic books." However, Zhu Shuzhen was naturally intelligent and clever, and enjoyed reading and literacy from the age of ten.

After Shuzhen's death, Pi Qiqiu also died in a short time. It was rumored that he was captured and taken away by Zhu Shuzhen's spirit, serving as a warning to those matchmakers who deceive others. The foolish parents believed the words of the monk and immediately cremated Shuzhen's body three days before the Qingming Festival. It was a common practice in Hangzhou for lower-class families to cremate their deceased and scatter the ashes under the Broken Bridge in the West Lake. It is detestable to see such a huge pack of white bones! What's more, it was lamentable that Zhu Shuzhen's remains and her literary works in her life were all burned, and only one percent of her writings have been passed down to this day. What a pity! Later, Wang Tangzuo wrote her biography, and Wei Duanli compiled her poems into a collection titled "*Duan Chang Ji*" ("Anthology of Heartbroken Poems"), which was published and widely acclaimed. Her name then became renowned, and people sighed at her tragic fate. Even today, there is a popular saying in Hangzhou, "The grievance of Dawa Lane reaches the heaven," with reference to this story.[40]

The novel quoted local slang from Hangzhou, stating that Zhu Shuzhen lived in Dawa Lane in her lifetime, which was consistent with Tian Rucheng's words. The novel also mentioned that after the "*Duan Chang Ji*" ("Anthology of Heartbroken Poems") was published, "Her name then became renowned, and people sighed at her tragic fate". Though we cannot fully believe what the novelist said, it must be a fact that Zhu Shuzhen was a well-known figure among all the people in the Ming Dynasty.

Zhu Shuzhen had already enjoyed equal fame with Li Qingzhao during the Yuan and Ming dynasties. Yang Weizhen of the Yuan Dynasty once said,

> Among women who read books and write literary works, Ban Zhao[41] (also named Cao Dagu, or Venerable Madame Cao) of the Eastern Han Dynasty who was widely praised in the history. In recent times, Li Qingzhao and Zhu Shuzhen showed their literary talents through poems and *ci* works, each moving people in their own ways.[42]

In the writings of Ming authors, when discussing talented women of that era, they often compared them to Li Qingzhao and Zhu Shuzhen. For instance, Xu Xian stated,

> Zhu Jingan, a remarkable woman in Haichang, was the wife of the official Zhou Ruhang. She was born into a prestigious family. With extensive knowledge and talents, she was good at writing poems, which earned her a prominent reputation during the Chenghua and Hongzhi years. Her poems in the style of Yuefu poetry and her *ci* works exuded the elegance of the ancient people without any hint of womanish flavor. Her poetry collection, titled "Jing'an Ji," was treasured within her home. Throughout her life, she upheld the merits of a virtuous woman, maintaining purity akin to ice and chastity akin to jade. She was no less admirable when compared to virtuous women such as Zhu Shuzhen and Li Qingzhao.[43]

As was recorded in "Ming History: Biographies of Paragon of Chastity",

> Jiang Liefu was the wife of Jiang Shijin from Danyang. ... Initially, her brothers noticed her literary talents and would often compare her to Li Qingzhao and Zhu Shuzhen. She frowned with dissatisfaction and said, "Li Yian married twice, whereas Zhu Shuzhen was unsatisfied with her husband. Despite their literary talents, they had no moral integrity".[44]

Although Jiang Liefu despised Li and Zhu, the fact that the man of the time compared her to the two indicated that she must be well familiar with Li Qingzhao and Zhu Shuzhen. Gu Qiyuan of the Ming Dynasty, when commenting on the mother of Zhao Ding, a poet of the Song Dynasty, also compared her to Li Qingzhao and Zhu Shuzhen,

> The mother, like two virtuous women Ban Zhao (Cao Dajia) and Song Xuanwen,[45] and others, was also a talented individual but did not obtain great fame. This was not that his literary works were not outstanding, but that she disdained acclaim for fame in the literary world as Li Qingzhao and Zhu Shuzhen. It's truly a great pity![46]

From the above words, we can see that Li Qingzhao and Zhu Shuzhen were already well-known figures at the time. In discussing poetry, the author of "*Yaoshantang Wai Ji*" ("Records at Yaoshantang Studio") also placed Zhu Shuzhen and Li Qingzhao in the same breath:

> Meng Shuqing once commented on Zhu Shuzhen's poetry by saying, "Poetry should have a unique style and profound meaning. The poems of monks should be devoid of worldly atmosphere, and women's poetry should be devoid of rouge and powder. Although Zhu Sheng (Zhu Shuzhen) has some traces of worldliness, she was still worth mentioning when compared to Li Qingzhao".[47]

In popular novels of the Ming Dynasty, outstanding female characters were often portrayed, with Li Qingzhao and Zhu Shuzhen as examples. For example, in "*Lianfang Lou Ji*" ("Tower of Two Beauties") of Qu You's "*Jiandeng Xinhua*" ("New Discussions of Jiandeng"), the sisters Xue Lanying and Xue Huiying, two girls in Wu County were both intelligent and beautiful and skilled in poetry and prose. "Their fame spread far and wide. People compared them to virtuous women such as Ban Zhao and Cai Wenji. They say the two sisters surpass even Li Qingzhao and Zhu Shuzhen".[48] In the story "Li Gongzuo's Clever Interpretation of a Dream, Xie Xiaoe's Wise Capture of Thieves on a Ship" from "*Pai An Jing Qi*" ("Striking the Table in Amazement"), when discussing women skilled in literature, the author also mentioned "the likes of Li Qingzhao and Zhu Shuzhen".[49] In the story "*Suxiaomei San Nan Xinlang* ('Lady Su Bewilders the Groom Three Times')" from Volume 11 of "*Xing Shi Heng Yan*" ("Lasting Words to Awaken the World"), there are the following words, "Among the remarkable women of the Song Dynasty, there were many, with Li Qingzhao and Zhu Shuzhen included. Both of them were accomplished in the women's literary world with brilliant talents".[50]

> In the story "*Saxuetang Qiao Jie Liang Yuan*" ("Happy Wedding in Saxuetang Hall") from Volume 27 of "*Xihu Er Ji*" ("The Second Volume of Stories in the West Lake"), the female protagonist Jia Pingping was described as "skilled in composing poems and melodies with exquisite styles. She is comparable with Li Qingzhao and Zhu Shuzhen".[51] In the story "*Li Xiuqing Yi Jie Huang Zhen*" ("Li Xiuqing Forms a Righteous Alliance with Huang Zhen") from Volume 28 of "*Gu Jin Xiao Shuo*" ("Stories Old and New"), there is a list of ancient women with "great knowledge and talent," including "Ban Zhao (Cao Dajia), Ban Jieyu, Su Ruolan, Shen Manyuan, Li Qingzhao and Zhu Shuzhen, etc."[52]

Ming Dynasty popular novels frequently mentioned Li Qingzhao and Zhu Shuzhen, which clearly indicated the reputation of these two individuals in the minds of the general public during that time. It was comparable to the high level of fame enjoyed by certain well-known figures in today's entertainment culture, such as certain "sisters" and "super girls" seen online or on various media platforms.

Zhu Shuzhen gained fame and became a figure of interest for both literati and the general public in the Ming Dynasty. Apart from her talent and poetic achievements, there were also other non-literary factors at play – namely, the sympathy for her unfortunate fate as a talented woman. For the common people, it was not necessarily her skill in poetry that captivated them but rather her ill-fated marriage and tragic destiny. As was stated in the novel "*Yue Xia Lao Cuo Pei Ben Shu Qian Yuan*" ("The Matchmaker Wrongly Arranged the Marriage: A Predestined Misfortune"),

> Throughout history, it is said that "the beauty often has an unfortunate life". This "beauty" does not simply mean physical appearance such as autumn water-limpid eyes, vermilion lips, lotus-like face, snow-white skin, and exquisite beauty, which is too limited in range. How can it be compared to the term "*jia ren*" (excellent woman)? That "excellent woman" possesses a deep understanding of the Five Classics and various historical texts, excels in composing music and poetry, and rivals Li Bai and Du Fu. She stands out among her peers, displaying the aura of mountains and rivers. Occasionally, she deviates from favoring men to favoring women. Yet, she is not merely a scholarly talent adorned with hairpins and accessories, nor a literary genius wearing a headpiece. If we speak of misfortune befalling the beautiful, it is of little consequence. But now, if the "excellent woman" is met with misfortune, how can one not weep and shed tears?

Zhu Shuzhen truly is the embodiment of the unfortunate "excellent woman". That was why "everyone laments her ill-fated destiny". People's curiosity, sympathy, and longing for a happy marriage find suitable expression and release through the tragic fate of Zhu Shuzhen. In the third chapter of the novel "*San Ke Pai'an Jing Qi*" ("Three Collections of Striking the Table in Amazement"), Xie Fangqing read Zhu Shuzhen's "*Duan Chang Ji*" ("Anthology of Heartbroken Poems") and sighed, "Such a talented and beautiful woman has to be married with an ordinary person. It is indeed detestable!" In the story "*Suxiaomei San Nan Xinlang* ('Lady Su Bewilders the Groom Three Times')" form "*Xing Shi Heng Yan*" ("Lasting Words to Awaken the World"), the author also commented that Zhu Shuzhen was "a female literary genius, and a talent in the realm of literature". "As to her marriage, she should have had an intelligent and wise man as her husband. However, the matchmaker made a mistake. She had to be the wife of a man without virtue or talent". That was why she was pitied and lamented. Even the officials for the *Siku Quanshu* (Complete Library in Four Branches) in the Qing Dynasty believed that the reason why Zhu Shuzhen's "*Duan Chang Ji*" ("Anthology of Heartbroken Poems") received so much attention was that "People had sympathy for her tragic life. Therefore her works has been passed down to later generations".[53]

It is necessary to point out that in the Ming Dynasty, Li Qingzhao and Zhu Shuzhen did not simply receive affirmation, praise and sympathy; they also faced criticism and reproach. This reflected the conflict between the orthodox ethical values and the secular perceptions of women in the Ming Dynasty. As mentioned earlier, Jiang Liefu expressed dissatisfaction with Li Qingzhao's remarriage and Zhu Shuzhen's unsatisfaction with her husband. Although from today's perspective, Jiang Liefu herself was a victim of feudal chaste ideals, her disdain for Zhu and Li reflects the ethical views and value judgements of orthodox women in the Ming Dynasty.

Male literati were particularly critical of Zhu Shuzhen and Li Qingzhao. As previously mentioned, Zhang Xingzhong, in his work "*Ti Duan Chang Ji*" ("To *Anthology of Heartbroken Poems*"), commented that Zhu Shuzhen "lacks the female virtue". Xu Boling, in "*Yin Jing Juan*" ("Notes of Yin Jing"), also compared the merits and flaws of Zhu Shuzhen and Li Qingzhao:

> Zhu Shuzhen's poetic lines, such as "The bamboo casts its elegant shadow on the quiet window in the gentle breeze, while birds in pairs are chirping joyfully under the falling sun. In this early summer when cherry blossoms fade and willow catkins have flown away, the hot weather makes one feel tired and lethargic, and the daylight begins to stretch into long hours", was widely spread in the world. She once composed "Historical Poem" that read, "The selection of historical materials by historians is actually highly subjective, and future generations have been misled by those historical books. They believe that the so-called 'kingly endeavor' and 'hegemonic endeavor' are merely different interpretations of the same motives. In fact, whether it is a kingly endeavor or a hegemonic endeavor, it is not easy to succeed." This was not a poem an ordinary woman could compose. At that time, Li Qingzhao, known as the Yi'an Jushi, the wife of Zhao Mingcheng, was particularly outstanding in writing poems and *ci* works and was highly praised by the literati. Her lines "The red flowers should languish and the green leaves must grow" and "You'll see a thinner face than yellow flower", have been passed down through the ages. Moreover, her lines of "Favorite willows there, coquettish flowers here" were also appreciated in lyrical discussions. Zhu Xi (with the courtesy name Hui'an) said, "Among contemporary women capable of literary works, there are simply Li Qingzhao and Lady Wei." Li Qingzhao has a poem "On History" that reads, "The two Hans were the true dynastic lineage, the New Reign was like a blister. That is why Courtier Ji Kang, to his dying day disparaged the Yin and Zhou." Ji Kang opposes the revolutionary ways to usurp the throne, with a hint of Wang Mang who seized the throne. Can such lines be written by a woman? Therefore, it seemed that Zhu Shuzhen did not quite match up with Li Qingzhao.

Then Liu Boling criticized the two of them for lacking moral integrity and virtue:

> While Li Qingzhao lost her moral integrity in her later years by getting married with Zhang Yuzhou and was given to philandering by the man. She once wrote a letter to Imperial Academician Qi Chongli, in which there are lines, "To my dismay, I realized that at an advanced age, when the sun hung in the mulberry and elm, I had married a worthless shyster of a man." On the other hand, Zhu Shuzhen complained about her miserable life, stating that she "would like to write a volume of sorrowful tears and send it to the unfortunate person at the South Tower". Despite their talent, they lack moral virtue of women.[54]

Ye Sheng was even more scathing in his critique of Li Qingzhao:

> Li Yian's *ci* work "To the tune *Wuling Chun*" goes as, "When the winds stop, the ground is fragrant, the flowers all are down, as the day wears on I'm too lazy to comb my hair. The objects are right, the people wrong, everything is over now! About to speak, tears first flow. I've heard spring is still lovely at Twin Streams, I'd like to go boating in a light skiff. But I fear the little grasshopper boats they have, could not carry such a freight of sorrow."[55] Studying these words and their meanings, I wonder if they were written after her preface to the "*Jin Shi Lu*" ("Critical Studies of Metal and Stone Inscriptions")? Or were they composed after another visit to Zhang Ruzhou? Unfortunately, Li Gefei had such a daughter, and Zhang Mingcheng had such a wife! Her literary works can really be called bad omens, leaving a thousand years of ridicule.[56]

Lang Ying also expressed his disapproval of Li Qingzhao's remarriage:

> Zhao Mingcheng, with the courtesy name Defu, was the son of Zhao Tingzhi (with the posthumous name Xiangong). He wrote a series of books called "*Jin Shi Lu*" ("Critical Studies of Metal and Stone Inscriptions") which consisted of one thousand volumes. His wife, Li Qingzhao, was an outstanding literary figure, as well as a scholar in the study of ancient artifacts. Her language was mostly elegant and refined. "*Shu Yu Ji*", the collection of her poetic works, has been spread through the ages. All the books revealed their shared ideals, their harmonious relationship and their deep love for each other. After reading her narration of "*Jin Shi Lu*", I find it is evident. However, I do not understand why she was willing to get married with Zhang Ruzhou. Alas! What great difference between Li Qingzhao and the virtuous woman Cai Yan![57]

Li Qingzhao's poetry and writings that were transmitted during the Southern Song Dynasty were mostly lost during the Yuan Dynasty. In the Ming Dynasty, there were few collections of her literary works in circulation.[58] Is this relevant to people's dissatisfaction with her in the Ming Dynasty?

As for the changes in fame and status of Li Qingzhao and Zhu Shuzhen since the Qing Dynasty, they will be discussed in the future.

Notes

1. Zhu Shuzhen (1135–1180), also known as Youqi Jushi, was a renowned female *ci* poet of the Southern Song Dynasty and one of the most prolific female writers whose works have survived from the Tang and Song Dynasties. She was born in Haining, Zhejiang. From a young age, she displayed keen intelligence and a love for reading. But throughout her life, she suffered from unrequited love. Her husband was a low-ranking official. Due to their mismatched interests, they didn't have a harmonious relationship with each other, leading to her early death due to depression in life. It is said that after Zhu Shuzhen passed away, her parents burned most of her manuscripts. The surviving collections attributed to her include "*Duan Chang Shi Ji*" ("Anthology of Heartbroken Poems") and "*Duan Chang ci*" ("Heartbroken Anthology of ci Works"), which are the remnants left after the burning.
2. Wang, Zhuo. 1988. *Biji man zhi* ("Commentary from *Biji* Lane on *ci* Works"), Vol. 2. Shanghai Chinese Classics Publishing House, 64.
3. Zhu, Bian. *Fengyue Tang shi hua* ("Poems on the Past Romance"), Vol. 1. *Siku quanshu* (Complete Library in Four Branches of Literature, Wenyuange edition), Vol. 1479: 21.
4. Hu, Zai. 1962. *Tiaoxi yuyin conghua* ("Series of Poetic Notes by the Recluse of the Brook Tiao"). *Gaozhai Shihua* ("Poetic Notes in Elegant Study"), Vol. 60. People's Literature Publishing House, 416.
5. Zhang, Chou. *Qinghe shuhua fang* ("Qinghe Studio's Collection of Paintings and Calligraphies"), Vol. 9. *Siku quanshu* (Complete Library in Four Branches of Literature, Wenyuange edition), Vol. 8 17: 347.
6. Zhang, Duanyi. 1936. *Gui Er ji* ("A Miscellany of Zhang Duanyi's Writings"). *Congshu jicheng chubian* ("First Anthology of Books from Collectanea"). The Commercial Press, Vol. 2783: 60.
7. Li, Jingde. 1986. *Zhuzi yu lei* ("Collected Dialogues between Zhu Xi and His Disciples"), Vol. 140. Zhonghua Book Company, 3332.
8. Liu, Chenweng. 1998. *Xuxi ci* ("A Collection of *ci* Works of Liu Chenweng"). Shanghai Chinese Classics Publishing House, 345.
9. Zhao, Yanwei.1996. *Yunlu man chao* ("Loose Notes of the Cloud-Covered Foothill"), Vol. 14. Zhonghua Book Company, 245.
10. Chen, Yu. *Cang Yi hua yu* ("Commentary of Chen Yu'), Vol. 2. *Siku quanshu* (Complete Library in Four Branches of Literature, Wenyuange edition), Vol. 865: 554.
11. Zhou, Hui. 1994. *Qingbo zazhi* ("Miscellaneous Records of Qingbo"),Vol. 8. Zhonghua Book Company, 332.
12. Zhou, Mi. 1983. *Qidong ye yu* ("Wild Talk from East of the State of Qi"), Vol. 10. Zhonghua Book Company, 183.
13. Zhu, Shuzhen. 1985. *Zhu Shuzhen ji zhu* ("Collection of Zhu Shuzhen's Works with Annotations"). Zhejiang Classics Publishing House, 1.
14. In "Catalogue of Anthology of Heartbroken Poems" (*Duan Chang ci tiyao*) of "Catalogue of the Complete Library of the Four Branches of Literature" (*Siku quanshu zongmu*, Vol. 199), there are the following words: "The '*Duan Chang ji*' ('Anthology of Heartbroken Poems') consists of ten volumes,' and 'Only one volume of 'Commented Library Catalogue of the Zhizhai Studio' (*Shulu jieti*) was

left, but it has not been widely circulated for a long time" (Zhonghua Book Company, 1965: 1821).
15 As was mentioned in the "Catalogue of the Magistrate's Library" ("*Junzhai dushu zhi*", Vol. 4), "Li Qingzhao was the daughter of Li Gefei, the Right Prime Minister. She was first married to Zhao Mingcheng and gained literary fame. When her father was dismissed from office, her father-in-law Zhao Tingzhi (with courtesy name Zhengfu) was appointed as right prime minister during the Huizong period. Li Qingzhao composed a poem to show her satire to her father-in-law, 'Being roasted, hands could be hot enough, yet one's heart might still be cold.' However, as a woman without moral integrity, she later got married with Zhang Ruzhou and failed to maintain her virtue to the end. She lived a wandering life and passed away in her later years".
16 Liu, Kezhuang. 1983. *Houcun shi hua* ("Houcun's Comments on Poetry"), Vol. 3. Zhonghua Book Company, 122.
17 Han, Biao. *Jianquan ri ji* ("Diary of Jianquan"), Vol. 2, *Congshu jicheng chubian* ("First Anthology of Books from Collectanea"). The Commercial Press, 1936, Vol. 2983: 30.
18 Li, Xinchuan.1988. *Jianyan yilai xinian yaolu* ("Summar of Annual Events from the Jianyan Period"), Vol. 158. Zhonghua Book Company, 1003.
19 Chen, Zhensun. 1987. *Shu Yu ji* ("A Collection of Jade Grugling"). *Zhizhai shulu jieti* ("Commented Library Catalogue of the Zhizhai Studio"), Vol. 21, Shanghai Chinese Classics Publishing House, 621.
20 Zhao, Yanwei.1996. *Yunlu man chao* ("Loose Notes of the Cloud-Covered Foothill"), Vol. 14. Zhonghua Book Company, 245.
21 Hong, Shi. *Li shi* ("Investigation of Stele Inscription"), Vol. 26. *Siku quanshu* (Complete Library in Four Branches of Literature, Wenyuange edition), Vol. 681: 750.
22 Chen, Zhensun. 1987. *Zhizhai shulu jieti* ("Commented Library Catalogue of the Zhizhai Studio"), Vol. 8, Shanghai Chinese Classics Publishing House, 233.
23 Tuo, Tuo et al. 1977. *Li Gefei zhuan* ("Biography of Li Gefei"). *Song shi* ("History of the Song Dynasty"), Vol. 444. Zhonghua Book Company, 13122.
24 In Volume 1 of Han Biao's "Diary of Jianquan" (*Jianquan ri ji*), there are the following words: "Liao Zhengyi (with courtesy name Minglue), Li Gefei (with courtesy name Wenshu), Li Xi (with courtesy name Yingzhong), and Dong Rong (with courtesy name Wuzi), were collectively known as the Four Disciples of Su Shi in the Later Period". *Congshu jicheng chubian* ("First Anthology of Books from Collectanea"). The Commercial Press, 1936, Vol. 2983: 9.
25 Liu, Kezhuang. 1983. *Houcun shi hua* ("Houcun's Comments on Poetry"), Vol. 3. Zhonghua Book Company, 123.
26 Anonymous. *Shizu da quan* ("Great Collection of Lineages Newly Arranged by Rhyme Expanded with Historical Events"), Vol. 3. *Siku quanshu* (Complete Library in Four Branches of Literature, Wenyuange edition), Vol. 952: 125.
27 Kuang, Zhouyi. 1979. *Canyingwu Suibi* ("Notes of Canyingwu"). *Zhongguo jindai shiliao congkan* ("Catena of Modern Chinese Historical Data"), Vol. 64. Taipei Wenhai Publishing House, 1979, Vol. 635: 201.
28 Yang, Shiqi. 1994. *Wenyuange shumu* ("Catalogue of Wenyuange Library"), Vol. 10. *Mingdai shumu tiba congkan* ("Catalogue of Bibliography Inscriptions and Postscripts of Ming Dynasty"). Bibliography and Literature Publishing House, 113.
29 Yon, Rong. 1965. *Wenyuange shumu tiyao* ("Annotated Catalogue of Wenyuange Library"). *Siku quanshu zongmu* ("Catalogue of the Complete Library in the Four Branches of Literature"), Vol. 85. Zhonghua Book Company, 731.
30 See *"Guoli zhongyang tushuguan" shanben xuba jilu: ji bu* ("Prefaces and Postscripts of Rare Books in the National Central Library"). "National Central Library".

1994: 594; *Biaodian shan ben tiba jilu: ji bu* ("Prefaces and Postscripts of Rare Books with Punctuation Marks"). "National Central Library", 1992:552; *"Guojia tushuguan" shanben shuzhi chugao* ("Initial Draft of Catalogue of Rare Books in the National Library"), "National Library (Taiwan)", 1999: 435.

31 Zhu, Shangshu. 1999. *Songren bieji xulu* ("On Collections of Literary Works in Song Dynasty"). Zhonghua Book Company, 949.

32 Gao, Ru. 1994. *Baichuan shu zhi* ("Baichuan's Library Catalogue"), Vol. 14. *Mingdai shumu tiba congkan* ("Prefaces and Postscripts to Library Catalogue of Ming Dynasty"). Bibliography and Literature Publishing House, 1318.

33 Tian, Rucheng. 1998. *Xihu youlan zhi yu* ("More Notes about the West Lake"), Vol. 16. Shanghai Chinese Classics Publishing House, 253.

34 Jiang, Yikui. 1995. *Yaoshantang wai ji* ("Records at Yaoshantang Studio"), Vol. 54. *Siku quanshu cunmu congshu* ("Catalogue of the Complete Library in Four Branches of Literature"), Vol. 148. Shandong Qilu Press, 92.

35 Xu, Boling. *Yin Jing Juan* ("Notes of Yin Jing"), Vol. 14. *Siku quanshu* (Complete Library in Four Branches of Literature, Wenyuange edition), Vol. 867: 172.

36 Tian, Rucheng.1998. *Xihu youlan zhi yu* ("More Notes about the West Lake"), Vol. 16. Shanghai Chinese Classics Publishing House, 253.

37 Zhuo Wenjun (175 B.C.–121 B.C.) was born in Linqiong, Sichuan, during the Western Han Dynasty. She was the daughter of a wealthy man named Zhuo Wangsun and was recognized as one of the Four Talented Women in ancient China. Zhuo Wenjun was born in a wealthy family, and she was known for her beauty, her expertise in music and her skill in playing the *qin*. At a young age, she was engaged to the son of an official family. They got married when she was 16, but soon after the wedding, her husband passed away, leaving her to live alone. Later, at a family banquet, she fell in love with Sima Xiangru, her true love. Sima Xiangru, a famous writer, was invited to the Zhuos for a gathering. He sang *"Feng Qiu Huang"* (a male phoenix is pursuing a female phoenix) and played his *qin* while delivering his admiration to Zhuo. Hearing the beautiful music, Zhuo peeked through the door crack and was deeply attracted by Sima's charm and talent. Consequently, they eloped together. After Sima Xiangru became an official, he thoughts about their relationship and considered abandoning Zhuo Wenjun. In response, she wrote a poem called "The Resentment of a Neglected Wife". When Sima Xiangru read it, he was filled with shame and regret and abandoned his selfish thoughts. They reconciled and resumed their relationship as before.

38 Zhou, Xueting (Mengjue Daoren). 1990. *Sanke pai'an jingqi* ("Three Collections of Striking the Table in Amazement"), Vol. 3. *Guben xiaoshuo jicheng* ("A Collection of Ancient Fictions"). Shanghai Chinese Classics Publishing House, 80.

39 Tian, Rucheng. 1980. *Xihu youlan zhi yu* ("More Notes about the West Lake"), Vol. 13. Shanghai Chinese Classics Publishing House, 187.

40 Zhou, Ji. 2000. *Xihu er ji* ("The Second Volume of Stories in the West Lake"), Vol. 16. *Guben jinhui xiaoshuo wenku* ("Forbidden and Destroyed Novels in Ancient China"). China Drama Press, 147, 153–154. Also in Chen, Shuji. 1985. *Duan Charg ji xunhuan ping yuelao*. *Xihu shi yi* ("Neglected Stories in the West Lake"), Vol. 34. Zhejiang Classics Publishing House, 511, 523.

41 Ban Zhao (45–116 A.D.) was a poet and writer, and the first known female Chinese historian. Born into a family of imperial scholars around 45 A.D., she was educated by her mother. By the age of 14, she was married to a local resident, Cao Shishu, but following his death a few years later, she moved with her children to the capital to live with her brother, Ban Gu, who had taken over the authorship of the *Book of Han* after the death of their father, the famous historian Ban Biao. In 92, Ban Gu was executed because of his involvement in palace intrigues, and in 97, the emperor called Ban Zhao to take over his work and complete the *Book of Han*. She also

tutored Deng Sui, who became regent when her infant son ascended to the throne in 106, and frequently relied on Zhao for guidance. Ban Zhao is clearly known to have authored a long poem, *Dongzheng fu* ("Travelling Eastward"); fragments of three short poems, including "Ode to the Sparrow"; two memorials, "Petition to Queen Deng" and "Petition to Find a Substitute for My Brother Ban Chao" (letters to the throne); and *Nujie* (Precepts for My Daughters), a manual of instructions for her daughters who were about to be married. *Nujie* remains an eloquent commentary on the situation of women in Confucian China. See https://www.newworlden cyclopedia.org/entry/Ban_Zhao.

42 Yang, Weizhen. *Dongweizi ji* ("Collected Works of Yang Weizhen"), Vol. 7. *Siku quanshu* (Complete Library in Four Branches of Literature, Wenyuange edition), Vol. 1221: 445.

43 Xu, Xian. 1936. *Xiyuan za ji* ("Miscellanea of Xiyuan"), Vol. 2. *Congshu jicheng chubian* ("First Anthology of Books from Collectanea"). The Commercial Press, Vol. 2914: 175–176.

44 Zhang, Tingyu et al. 1974. *Lie nü zhuan* ("The Biographies of Exemplary Women"). *Ming shi* ("History of Ming Dynasty"), Vol. 302. Zhonghua Book Company, 7723.

45 Song Xuanwen (Madam Song), the mother of Wei Cheng who served as the minister of ceremonies, was a wise woman. During the reign of Fu Jian in the former Qin Dynasty, there was a lot of chaos in the world, resulting in a decline in ritual and music. The Zhou Dynasty's rituals and annotations were no longer taught by knowledgeable scholars. Later, it was discovered that the mother of Wei Cheng was a wise woman. She passed on her father's knowledge to Wei Cheng. Despite living in turbulent times, she did not forget what her father had taught. Even in her old age of over 80, Madam Song had clear eyes and sharp hearing. Therefore, a lecture hall was established in her home, where she instructed 120 students. They listened to her lectures behind a red veil and referred to her as Lady Xuanwen or Song Xuanwen. The King Fu Jian even sent her ten maids to serve her. Since Lady Xuanwen started explaining the Zhou rituals, the study of Zhou rituals became widely popular throughout the country.

46 Gu, Qiyuan. 1987. *Zhaomu shou jing* ("Zhao's Mother Teaching a Lesson"). *Kezhuo zhuiyu* ("Wordy Notes for Guests") Vol. 5. Zhonghua Book Company, 154.

47 Jiang, Yikui. 1995. *Yaoshantang wai ji* ("Records at Yaoshantang Studio"), Vol. 93. *Siku quanshu cunmu congshu* ("Catalogue of the Complete Library in Four Branches of Literature"), Vol. 148. Shandong Qilu Press, 436.

48 Qu, You. 1981. *Lianfanglou ji* ("Tower of Two Beauties"). *Jian deng xin hua* ("New Discussions of Jiandeng"), Vol. 1. Shanghai Chinese Classics Publishing House, 29. Also in Feng, Menglong (Zhanzhan Waishi). 1986. *Xueshi er fang* ("Two Beauties of Xue's Family"). *Qing shi* ("Love Stories"), Vol. 3. Shenyang Chunfeng Literature and Art Publishing House, 75–76.

49 Ling, Mengchu. 1985. *Pai'an jing qi* ("Striking the Table in Amazement"), Vol. 19. Shanghai Chinese Classics Publishing House, 785.

50 Feng, Menglong. 1981. *Xing shi heng yan* ("Lasting Words to Awaken the World"), Vol. 11. People's Literature Publishing House, 217. Also in *Suxiaomei san nan xinlang* ("Lady Su Bewilders the Groom Three Times"). *Jingu qi guan* ("Strange Sights Ancient and Modern"), Vol. 17. People's Literature Publishing House, 1979: 326.

51 Zhou, Ji. 2000. *Xihu er ji* ("The Second Volume of Stories in the West Lake"), Vol. 27. *Guben jinhui xiaoshuo wenku* ("Forbidden and Destroyed Novels in Ancient China"). China Drama Press, 248.

52 Feng, Menglong. 1981. *Li Xiuqing Yi Jie Huang Zhen Nü* ("Li Xiuqing Forms a Righteous Alliance with Huang Zhen"), *Gu Jin Xiao Shuo* ("Stories Old and New"). People's Literature Publishing House, 416.

53 Yong, Rong. *Duan Chang ci tiyao* ("Catalogue of Anthology of Heartbroken Poems"), *Siku Quanshu Zongmu* ("Catalogue of the Complete Library of the Four Branches of Literature", Vol. 174): "'Anthology of Heartbroken Poems' is a two-volume work written by Zhu Shuzhen of the Song Dynasty. Zhu Shuzhen, a woman from Qiantang, called herself 'Youqi Jushi' (Reclusive Dweller). She married an ordinary man but died of her depressive life. Wei Duanli from Wanling compiled her poems into the 'Anthology of Heartbroken Poems' which was this particular edition. Her poetry was shallow and weak, still influenced by the customs of the women's quarters. People had sympathy for her tragic life. Therefore her works has been passed down to later generations" (Zhonghua Book Company, 1965: 1542–1543).
54 Xu, Boling. *Yin Jing Juan* ("Notes of Yin Jing"), Vol. 14. *Siku quanshu* (Complete Library in Four Branches of Literature, Wenyuange edition), Vol. 867: 172.
55 Egan, Ronald. 2019. *The Works of Li Qingzhao*, Boston and Berlin: De Gruyter, 153.
56 Ye, Sheng. 1980. *Shuidong riji* ("Miscellaneous Notes by Ye Sheng"), Vol. 21. Zhonghua Book Company, 214.
57 Lang, Ying. *Li Yi'an* ("Li Qingzhao"). *Qi xiu lei gao* ("Notes on Seven Categories"), Vol. 17. Shanghai Bookstore Publishing House, 174.
58 Collections of Li Qingzhao's works published in the Ming Dynasty that were passed down to later generations was scarce, with only a single volume of "Shuyu Ci" preserved. It is the edition stored by Mao Jin in his Ji Guge library in the late Ming period, containing 17 poems, which are far from the original Li's poetry. Yang Shen, a poet and official in the Ming Dynasty, mentioned in Volume 2 of "*Ci Pin*" that Li Qingzhao's works were compiled into the anthology titled "Shuyu Ji", which couldn't be found at the time. Even the knowledgeable Yang Shen was unable to find it, indicating that the circulation of the "Shuyu Ji" during the Ming Dynasty was extremely limited.

8 The Communication of Poetry through Paintings and Songs

Painting is not only an artistic creation but also a medium of dissemination. When poets inscribe their verses on a painting, the work becomes a unique vehicle for the spread of poetry. Conversely, when painters depict poetic themes in their artwork, the paintings serve as a medium for the cross-media dissemination of poetry. Similarly, singing is both an art form and a means of transmission. The integration of *ci* works into musical performances during the Song Dynasty was well-known, and it was also known that during the Tang Dynasty, the poems could be sung out. In fact, not only could *ci* works of the Tang and Song Dynasties be sung during the time, but they could also be adapted into musical compositions in later periods. It is worth noting that not only poetry but also prose and essays could be transformed into musical songs.[1] The dissemination of poetry through painting and song possesses a unique artistic charm and influential effect. Wang Wei's "Seeing Off Yuan'er on His Mission to Anxi" not only experienced dissemination through paintings but also gained popularity through repeated singing. Therefore, this chapter takes it as a case study to explore the avenues of poetry transmission through painting and song.

8.1 Spread of "Seeing Off Yuan'er on His Mission to Anxi" with Paintings

As a classic work of Tang poetry, Wang Wei's "Seeing Off Yuan'er on His Mission to Anxi" was not only adapted into a popular song called "Three Farewells of Yang Guan (*Yang Guan San Die*)" by musicians but also depicted by painters, giving rise to a series of "Yangguan" paintings. This demonstrated its significance in the history of poetry dissemination. In this section, we will focus on Li Gonglin's "Yangguan" painting from the Northern Song Dynasty and explore the characteristics and impact of the visual dissemination of Wang Wei's "*Song Yuan Er Shi An Xi*" ("Seeing Off Yuan'er on His Mission to Anxi").

DOI: 10.4324/9781032712512-9

8.1.1 Six Versions of "Yangguan Paintings" in the Song Dynasty

During the Song Dynasty, there were six versions of the "Yangguan" painting, all inspired by Wang Wei's poem "Seeing Off Yuan'er on His Mission to Anxi". The earliest and most influential version was created by the renowned Northern Song painter Li Gonglin, also known as Bigu. During the Yuanfeng reign of Emperor Shenzong, Anfen Sou was appointed to the Xixia Prefecture, and Li Gonglin painted the "Yangguan" based on the poetic theme of Wang Wei's poem, accompanied by a poem dedicated to Anfen Sou. The poem is titled "A Small Poem and Painting Scroll Presented to Anfen Sou, Who Is Departing for Xixia Prefecture in the Same Year", and it goes as follows:

> The painting depicted the sorrowful departure from the banquet, truly unable to bear the separation in the spring of Wei City. The willow trees of Wei City cease to annoy with their green hue, as one heads westward through Yangguan, meeting an old acquaintance.[2]

The poetic sentiment of Li Gonglin was also derived from Wang Wei's "Seeing Off Yuan'er on His Mission to Anxi". Although it did not lack a sense of sorrow in parting, it consoled his friend of the same year, advising him not to dwell on the separation. It contrasted with the melancholy of Wang Wei's original poem, saying, "Heading west through Yangguan, there are old friends", exhibiting a sense of transcendence and broad-mindedness, reminiscent of Wang Bo's lines, "Hai Nei Cun Zhi Ji, Tian Ya Ruo Bi Lin" (If you have a friend afar who knows your heart, distance cannot keep you two apart).

The exact time of Li Gonglin's creation of the "Yangguan Painting" was not recorded in the literary works of the Song Dynasty. "*Jinshi Cuibian*" (Selected Rubbings of Ancient Inscriptions) of Wang Chang in the Qing Dynasty, based on Zhang Shunmin's work "Jingzhao Anfen Sou's Journey to Lintao Prefecture", provided evidence that the "Yangguan Painting" was created in the fifth year of Yuanfeng (1082):

> The term "Lintao Prefecture" refers to General Gao Zunyu's military command center. According to the records in "Chronicles of Song Poetry," Zhang Shunmin was a poet who wrote two quatrains on his way back from the Western Expedition. Later, Su Dongpo wrote a postscript, stating that Shunmin was knowledgeable about the Western Expedition and composed these two quatrains on his way back from Gao Zunyu's camp. According to the records of Emperor Shenzong of the Song Dynasty, Gao Zunyu was appointed as the Frontier Marshal of Huanqing in the fourth year of Yuanfeng. At that time, Shunmin would have been in his military command center. In the first month of the fifth year of Yuanfeng, Gao Zunyu was demoted to the position of Deputy Envoy of Yuanzhou. Shunmin returned with him, which suggested that this poem was written when Shunmin returned from the military command center.

According to the "Biography of Zunyu," Gao Zunyu was initially appointed as the pacifier of Tongyuan Army. At that time, Wang Shao restored control over the Tao-Long region and captured Hezhou. The so-called "Lintao Prefecture" probably referred to Wang Shao's military command center. Anfen Sou, Yun Sou, and Boshi were in Gao Zunyu's military command center, preparing to go to the court, which was why this painting and poem came into existence. The significance of viewing the "Yangguan Picture," Shunmin's poetry, and the book "*Guo Qu Lai Ci*" all seem to carry a sense of farewell, possibly due to Gao Zunyu's demotion and return. ... Boshi created the painting and poem, but we currently have no way of verifying Boshi's poem. The stele lacks the date and the name of the stone carver. Based on research, this poem was likely written around the fifth year of Yuanfeng, so it was included here.[3]

According to Su Shi's postscript, as well as the entries for Emperor Shenzong and Gao Zunyu in *History of Song*, Wang Chang concluded that in 1081, Zhang Shunmin served as a staff member to Gao Zunyu, the frontier marshal of Huanqing. In January of the following year, he returned due to Gao Zunyu's demotion. This claim was supported by Li Tao's "Sequel to *Comprehensive Mirror in Aid of Governance*". Wang Chang further believed that Zhang Shunmin's poem and Li Gonglin's painting were both created in January of 1082, when "the camp was about to return". At that time, Anfen Sou, Li Boshi and Zhang Shunmin were together in Gao Zunyu's camp, preparing to proceed to Wang Shao's camp. However, there are no historical records to prove whether Li Gonglin was in Gao Zunyu's camp. Based on the title of Li Gonglin's poem, it can be inferred that he saw off Anfen Sou to Xihe Prefecture, indicating that he may have been in the inland region bidding farewell to the An family on their journey to the border rather than personally escorting them to another camp at the border. As for Anfen Sou, specific details about him were unknown, except that he and Li Gonglin were both successful candidates in the imperial examination of the same year. According to Huang Tingjian's "Collected Works of Huang Xiansheng from Yuzhang", Anfen Sou hailed from Yong Province and had a collection of several volumes of books by Yan Lugu. In Li Tao's "Sequel to *Comprehensive Mirror in Aid of Governance*", it was mentioned that there was a person named An Ding in Gao Zunyu's camp:

> In the tenth month of the fourth year of the Yuanfeng era, the Jingyuan army had already captured the narrow pass of Moqiqi and continued to advance to Shangyi Mouth. There were two roads here, one leading north through the Daidai Ridge and another northwest through the Mingsha River. The generals wanted to choose the route through Daidai Ridge, but Liu Changzuo said, "When we left Hanzhong, we transported a month's worth of food. It has been eighteen days now, and we have not yet reached Lingzhou. What will we do if we don't receive further supplies? I've heard that there are stored grains in Mingsha, referred to as

the Imperial Granary by the Xia people. We can take them for consumption. Although Lingzhou is a bit further, it's nothing to worry about." After arriving at Mingsha, they found a cellar with a million catties of rice. As a token, they loaded the rice and continued to hasten towards Lingzhou. On the day of Renwu, the army arrived at the city gates. At this time, the Huanqing army had not arrived, and the city gates were still open. The vanguard troops rushed in. Gao Zunyu dispatched Li Lin and An Ding with a letter, saying, "I have sent Wang Yongchang into the city to surrender. Do not kill him." After a while, the city gates closed, and the guards inside strengthened their defense.[4]

It was unknown whether this An Ding was the same as Anfen Sou. If An Ding was indeed Anfen Sou, then Anfen Sou entered Gao Zunyu's camp before October of the fourth year of Yuanfeng. Li Gonglin's poetry and painting should have been created during the time when Anfen Sou joined Gao Zunyu's camp, which was around the fourth year of Yuanfeng or slightly earlier. Of course, this was just speculation. Considering Wang Chang's research, the upper limit for the creation of Li Gonglin's "Yangguan Tu" painting and poem was between the fourth and fifth years of Emperor Shenzong's Yuanfeng reign (1081–1082) and no later than the second year of Emperor Zhezong's Yuanyou reign (1087). This was because in the second year of Yuanyou, Huang Tingjian had already written a poem titled "*Ti Yangguan Tu*" ("To the painting of *Yangguan Pass*").[5] In summary, Li Gonglin's "*Yangguan Tu*" was created around the fifth year of Yuanfeng (1082).

Apart from Li Gonglin's "Yangguan Painting", there were at least two other versions of "Yangguan Painting" during the later period of the Northern Song Dynasty. One of them was created by Xie Yunwen, a friend of Chao Yuezhi. Chao Yuezhi wrote a poem titled "*Xie Yunwen Chengyi 'Yangguan Tu'*" (In Praise of Xie Yunwen's "*Yangguan Tu*"):

> In a place of refuge, I unexpectedly encountered an old friend, whose temperament and demeanor were remarkable. While his poetry recitation seemed plain and tasteless, his paintings were filled with emotions.[6]

According to Chao Yuezhi's poetic interpretation, Xie Yunwen's "Yangguan Painting" was also painted in accordance with Wang Wei's poem "Seeing Off Yuan'er on His Mission to Anxi". Little was known about Xie Yunwen except that he had interactions with Chao Yuezhi. In Chao Yuezhi's collection, there were also poems titled "Xie Yunwen's Narcissus" and "Xie Yunwen's Shepherd's Purse Dumplings".[7] Chao Yuezhi (1059–1129), with the courtesy name Yidao, was from Juye, Jizhou (now part of Shandong). He passed the imperial examination in the fifth year of Emperor Shen Zong's Yuanfeng era. During Emperor Qin Zong's Jingkang period, he served as an official in the Ministry of Rites. He retired in the early years of the Jianyan era. Xie Yunwen and Chao Yuezhi were both figures of the late Northern Song Dynasty.

Another "Yangguan Painting" was written by Xiu Shi. Han Ju wrote a poem titled "Inscription on Xiu Shi's Yangguan Painting", which goes as follows:

> Amidst the wind and rain, the road desolate, weary travelers and imprisoned officials are filled with tears. Why do Taoist priests always meddle in such affairs, seemingly devoid of thoughts of departure or return?[8]

Xiu Sh's identity was unknown. Han Ju (1080–1135), with the courtesy name Zicang, was from Xianjingjian (present-day Renshou, Sichuan). In the second year (1112) of Zhendi, during the reign of Emperor Huizong, he was granted the status of a *jinshi* (successful candidate in the imperial examination). At the beginning of the Jingkang era, he served as a middle-level official in the Imperial Academy. Xiu Shi, who lived during the same period as Han Ju, was also a figure of the transition period of Northern and Southern Song dynasties. No other historical records on the paintings of Xie Yunwen and Xiu Shi's "Yangguan" have been found.

In the Southern Song Dynasty, there were three other famous versions of the "Yangguan Paintings" created by three renowned artists: the monk Fan Long, Liu Songnian and Li Song. The "Yangguan" painting by the monk Fan Long has been passed down to the Ming Dynasty, and it was recorded in Volume 1, Upper Section of Zhang Chou's "Qinghe Shuhua Fang".[9] The "Yangguan" painting by Liu Songnian still existed in the Ming Dynasty. Wang Keyu's "*Shanhu Wang*" included the following record: "Liu Songnian's 'Yangguan' painting, 'West Lake' painting, 'Yiqiao Journey' painting, 'Zhaojun Leaving the Frontier' painting, 'Nine Elders' painting, each in three scrolls; 'Silk Worms in the Palace' painting, in two scrolls; landscape and figure paintings, each in one scroll".[10]

Li Song's "Yangguan" painting was also passed down to the Ming Dynasty and was collected by Lu Shen. In Lu Shen's "Postscript to the Yangguan Painting", he stated,

> The right assistant of the Prince of Tang wrote a poem, which has been praised by people as the "Three Farewells of Yang Guan (*Yang Guan San Die*)". The tune has been preserved but the repetition method has been abandoned. When I was in the capital, I discussed this issue with Wang Yangming and Du Nanhao. Some people believed that each line can be repeated three times, while others believed that only the concluding line of the song can be repeated three times. There was still no consensus on this matter, and different records vary. There may have been musical notation at that time, but it was now impossible to verify. Some people believed that each line constitutes a separate song, and each song was repeated three times, with two characters subtracted each time until it was repeated three times, thus forming a three-line song. These words were beautifully expressed and convey a sense of parting. This view had

its merits, but it was unknown if it aligned with the original lyrics. The painting was from my collection, an old copy by Li Song, made under the instruction of Si Zhaizi. The Western scenery was pleasant and contemplative, suitable for appreciation, not just for craftsmanship. Therefore, I have recorded this poem on the left side, along with these explanations, for Si Zhaizi's review.[11]

The "Yangguan Painting" preserved by Lu Shen was an "old version" by Li Song. Lu Shen's friend, Si Zhaizi, instructed the painters to copy the "old version" to widen its circulation. Lu Shen discussed the "Yangguan Painting" together with the "Three Farewells of Yang Guan (*Yang Guan San Die*)", and it can be confirmed that the "Yangguan Painting" was also created in accordance with the poetic sentiment of "Seeing Off Yuan'er on His Mission to Anxi".

The monk Fan Long, Liu Songnian and Li Song were all renowned painters of the Southern Song Dynasty. Xia Wenyan's "*Tu Hui Bao Jian*", Volume 4, records the following:

The monk Fan Long, with the courtesy name Maozong and the sobriquet Wuzhu, was a native of Wuxing (present-day Jiaxing, Zhejiang). He excelled in portraying figures and landscapes and was a student of Li Bosheng. Emperor Gaozong greatly admired his paintings and would often inscribe them with comments. However, his artistic style and charm were considered inferior to that of Longmian (the renowned Daoist painter).[12] Fanlong was a disciple of the renowned ci poet Ye Mengde and resided on Bianshan for a long time. As a result, his paintings were diverse and rich. During the evaluation of paintings at the Deshou Palace, it was acknowledged that Fanlong was the authentic disciple of Longmian.

Liu Songnian, a native of Qiantang, resided near the Qingbo Gate and was commonly known as "Hidden Gate Liu". He was a student of the Chunxi Painting Academy and received special treatment from Shaoxi Nian. His mentor was Zhang Dunli. He excelled in painting figures and landscapes, creating works that were vivid and exquisite, surpassing the fame of his master. During the reign of Emperor Ningzong, his work "Farming and Weaving" was highly praised and awarded a golden belt. He was considered a gem within the painting academy.

Li Song, also a native of Qiantang, started as a carpenter in his youth and had some knowledge of ropes and ink. He later became the adopted son of Li Congxun. He excelled in painting figures and Daoist themes and was able to comprehend Li Congxun's intentions. He was particularly skilled in boundary paintings. He received favorable treatment in the painting academies of the Guang, Ning, and Li dynasties.[13]

Li Gonglin's "Yangguan Painting" not only captured the poetic atmosphere of Wang Wei's verses but also specifically inscribed Wang Wei's original poem on the painting. Zhou Mi of the Southern Song Dynasty mentioned in Volume 2 of his book "*Yun Yan Guo Yan Lu*":

> Li Boshi executed a meticulous portrayal of the 'Yangguan Painting' and it was later inscribed with a poetic postscript by Xue Shaopeng. The poem also included the verse by Minister Wang.[14]

By drawing inspiration from Wang Wei and incorporating the original poem, the synergy between poetry and painting was achieved. Coupled with the aura of Li Gonglin's reputation, the "Yangguan Painting" naturally accelerated the dissemination of the "Yangguan Tune". During the Northern Song Dynasty, Xie Qiao remarked, "Mo Jie's verses possess wisdom, while Longmian's works can express mystical imagery. Their excellent writings and artworks are masterpieces. The verses written on the small sheets of paper are like vivid images". Xie Qiao: "Jian An Mo Le Yuan Guan Li Boshi's Painting 'Yangguan Landscape'".[15] Whether Li Song, Liu Songnian and others also inscribed Wang Wei's poem on their "Yangguan Painting" paintings remains unknown.

8.1.2 Characteristics of Literary Communication with Paintings

Communication with paintings has two major characteristics: mobility and visual appeal.

In our impression, the text in a picture is unique, and the mobility of visual communication seems to be limited. Indeed, the original artwork by the author is unique, but it can be copied and printed. A picture often has a draft version and a final version. After the original artwork is circulated, there will be copies, handwritten versions, imitations, printed versions, stone-carved rubbings and so on. For one picture, there are often multiple versions.

The painting of *Yangguan Pass* by Li Gonglin[16] has both a draft version and a final version. Huang Tingjian had seen both the draft and final versions of the painting. In Volume 29 of Huang's "Chronicles by Huang Tingjian" (*Shangu Nianpu*), there are the following records:

> In the first year of Chongning (1102), Master Li wrote a postscript to the poem in which there are the following lines: "In the earlier years of Yuanyou era, I wrote this poem as a dedication to painting of *Yangguan Pass* by Boshi" (Li Gonglin). In the fifth month of the first year of Chongning, I saw the draft version of this painting at Zhao Shengshu's house, which was especially exquisite compared to the final version. Zhao Shengshu was Boshi's son-in-law. At that time, we were both staying on a boat near the Dagguan Terrace of Grand Yuncang.

Huang Tingjian first saw the final version of the painting *Yangguan Pass* in the second year of Yuanyou (1087) and wrote a poem titled "Inscription on the Painting of *Yangguan Pass*". In the first year of Chongning (1102), when he visited Zhao Shengshu, the son-in-law of Li Gonglin, he saw the draft version of the painting. As a result, he wrote another postscript as above. In Huang Tingjian's view, the draft version of the painting was even more "exquisite compared to the final version".

Li Gonglin's painting *Yangguan Pass* has various surviving versions. There are authentic works and copies, as well as rubbings. Volume 7 of the "*Xuanhe huapu*" ("Painting Manual of Xuanhe Era")[17] records that there are a total of 107 paintings by Li Gonglin in the imperial court, including the painting "*Yangguan Pass*". This particular painting is believed to be an authentic artwork. However, whether it is a draft version or a final version cannot be determined yet.

As to the stone-carved rubbings, Volume 138 of Wang Chang's "*Jinshi Cuibian*" (Selected Rubbings of Ancient Inscriptions) records the stone carving of Li Gonglin's painting *Yangguan Pass*:

> The stone tablet is horizontal, with two paintings. The total height is 3 Chinese feet and 8.5 inches (around 1.28 meters), and the width is 2 feet and 3 inches (around 0.77 meters). It is divided into two sections, with paintings in the lower section. The upper section features a poem written on the painting "Yangguan Pass", consisting of 48 lines with 8 characters per line. It also has a partial inscription of the Tao Yuanming's poem '*Gui Qu Lai Ci*' (Returning Home), leaving a total of 22 lines with 7 characters per line, but the latter half is missing. It is written in regular script.[18]

Although there is no specific date mentioned for this stone carving, it at least indicates the existence of a stone-carved version of the painting "Yangguan Pass".

Paintings have a commodity nature, which means they can be circulated instead of being owned by one collector. The collection of paintings is different from that of books in general. When a reader buys a book, he does so for reading. Except for rare editions, the book generally does not re-enter the circulation sphere. However, the paintings, after being owned by a collector for a certain period of time, can still be circulated and traded again. According to existing documentation, Li Gonglin's painting "*Yangguan Pass*" was continuously circulated and collected by several collectors. It was first acquired by Lin Dan in the third year of the Yuanyou era of Emperor Zhezong (1088), and Su Shi wrote a poem to record the event of Lin Dan's reception of the "*Yangguan Pass*". Later, the painting fell into the hands of Xie Qie, a famous poet of the Jiangxi School, as was recorded in his poem. In the mid-Southern Song Dynasty, Wang Jilu also collected the painting. By the end of the Southern Song Dynasty, the painting passed through the hands of Zhao Lanpo[19] and came into the possession of Hao Qingchen.

During the Yuan Dynasty, the painting "*Yangguan Pass*" was owned by Zhang Keyu in Jinan, but it is uncertain whether it was the same copy as the one owned by Hao Qingchen. In the Ming Dynasty, the painting owned by

Hao Qingchen was acquired by the Lu's family of Chenhu in Jiangsu. As was recorded in Zhang Chou's "*Qinghe Shuhua Fang*" ("Qinghe Studio's Collection of Paintings and Calligraphies"),

> Li Gonglin drew a monochrome painting entitled "*Yangguan Pass*". Its lines are as fine as a strand of hair, and it exudes a vibrant and lively aura. There are poems written by close acquaintances, including a poem inscription by Xue Shaopeng, and seals such as those of the "*San Feng Hou Ren*" (Descendants of the Three Phoenixes). Additionally, there are two other seals: one reads "*Zhongshu Eryi*" (only loyalty and forgiveness), while the other reads "*Guanxi Cangfu*" (a humble villager from Guanxi). The owners of these seals are unknown. This painting was originally owned by Zhao Lanpo and later came into the possession of Hao Qingchen, as documented in Zhoumi's "*Yunyan Guoyan Lu*" (Records of Clouds and Mist Passing before One's Eyes). Presently, it is in the possession of the Lu's family of Chenhu, who obtained it from Quanqing (Lu Quanqing, an esteemed connoisseur of antiquities, amassed a collection of thousands of masterpieces in calligraphy and painting. Alas! It was truly magnificent). My house is located to the east of Chenhu, therefore I visited and appreciated the painting for numerous times.[20]

After that, the whereabouts of the painting "*Yangguan Pass*" became unknown. It is also unknown whether the painting still exists in the world.

Paintings, as works of art, also possess an aesthetic quality for enjoyment. The paintings of renowned artists have a stronger artistic appeal; thus, when collectors acquire a painting, they often invite others to appreciate it together. Unlike the private and solitary reading of poetry and literature by individuals, paintings, especially the famous ones, are often enjoyed and appreciated by a group of people who gather together, much like listening to songs in groups. This is the collective characteristic of painting communication. The communicative effect of collective appreciation is more powerful than that of individual appreciation. Through collective appreciation, people can share their opinions and inspire each other, engaging in discussions and critiques on the artistic value of the artwork, which aids in the appreciation and assessment of the original painting. This aligns with the saying in the book *Mencius* that goes, "To enjoy alone, and to enjoy with others, which is more enjoyable?"

In the late Northern Song Dynasty, when Xie Ke obtained the painting "*Yangguan Pass*", he invited friends to appreciate it together. He wrote a poem to describe the gathering. In the poem, there is a line "passing it to appreciating guests", which tells of the gathering of various guests to have a view at the painting. Each guest was requested to compose a poem with the various rhyme schemes, with one person for each rhyme pattern. Therefore, there must have been at least ten guests gathering to view the painting together.

8.1.3 Effect of Literary Communication with Paintings

The effect of using paintings for poems can be summarized by two main aspects: proliferation and derivation.

Proliferation refers to the fact that when artists communicate poetry through paintings, they don't simply depict the literal meaning of the poem. Instead, they incorporate their own life experiences and values, infusing their unique understanding and emotions about life, society and nature into their artwork. This process enhances and expands the emotional and conceptual meaning of the original poem. The transformation from poetry to visual art is a form of reinterpretation or recreation. It represents a cultural enrichment, as the visual text creates new meaning on top of the original poetic text. For example, let's examine how Li Gonglin's painting "*Yangguan Pass*" enriched the content of Wang Wei's poetry. Unfortunately, the original painting by Li Gonglin is no longer available, making it impossible to analyse its specific content. However, we are fortunate to have Zhang Shunmin's contemporaneous work, which provides a detailed description of the content depicted in the "*Yangguan Pass*":

> In ancient times, people would send farewell gifts accompanied by words. My friend Li Gonglin, however, not only sent his regards but also conveyed his sentiments through his paintings. He depicted the boundless emotions of the *Yangguan Pass*, presenting them as a gift to those setting off on the journey to Anxi. Using the pure white paper from Chengxin Hall, as radiant as silver, his brushstrokes were delicate and clear, expressing a carefree and elegant spirit. In a small pavilion, there was a farewell feast with songs and dances. While underneath, there was a bustling crowd of carriages and horses. By the stream, an old angler silently fished, and on the bridge, two travelers carrying firewood unexpectedly crossed paths. The falcon was unleashed, following the hunting dog, and a towering donkey, with its ears perked up, supported a lone cart. On the streets of Chang'an, there were many bold and chivalrous figures, especially during the lively spring months. The clean rain at dawn dampens the light dust, and the colors of willows revive all green around the guest lodge. I urge you now to drink some more cups of wine: once you go west out on westward journey there will be no old friends. With great enthusiasm, a song was sung, but it was left unfinished, as the performer's back was drenched with tears, staining their silk handkerchief. At the end of the revelry, the young servants bid farewell to their loved ones, filled with a determined spirit. Children clung to the robes of the departing guest, while elderly people shed tears, and passers-by on the road all felt a pang of sorrow. Only the old angler by the stream, quietly casting his fishing line, seemed untouched by it all, in his own world of tranquility. How difficult it is for Li Jun to create this painting, for it carries profound meaning in depicting the fisherman and woodcutter. It illustrates the idea of parting in the mortal world, unaffected by fame and fortune.

The magnificent halls of Honglian Mansion are filled with extraordinary talents, and their home is adorned with lush greenery from the southern mountains. The resplendent vermilion gates stand proudly in the bustling streets, while the murmuring flowing water surrounds pavilions and terraces. In front of the veranda, rare and peculiar rocks can be seen, and along the paths, towering pine trees planted by one's own hands. In the tranquil gardens, birds engage in conversation, and swallows startle and dart back in through the corridor windows. May I ask where the master is now? Is he recently stationed at the Anxi Prefecture? The songs and dances have aged him, his hair now turned white. Though his achievements are yet to be established, old age urges him on. I am no longer young and energetic, and where are the experienced horse riders? Having already divined the purchase of land beneath the Ji Ridge, I now gaze upon the construction of a dwelling by the banks of the Ying River. I rely on you to convey a message to Wang Wei, to paint a picture of Tao Yuanmin's journey of departing and returning.[21]

According to Zhang Shunmin's account, Li Gonglin used the white paper from Chengxin Hall for his painting. From the lines "The clean rain at dawn dampens the light dust, and the colors of willows revive all green around the guest lodge. I urge you now to drink some more cups of wine: once you go west out on westward journey there will be no old friends", it can be seen that the painting "*Yangguan Pass*" also depicts the farewell scene described in Wang Wei's original poem.[22] However, the farewell scene and characters in the painting are much more elaborate and complex compared to Wang Wei's poem.

Wang Wei's original poem only features the host bidding farewell and the departing friend, while in the painting, there are not just two characters but two groups of people. One group consists of the farewell party in a small pavilion, including attendants and horses of the host and guests. The other group includes an old angler by the water and two pedestrians carrying firewood on a bridge, followed by a hunting dog and a donkey pulling a single-wheel cart. In the painting, there are many people bidding farewell, including attendants and singing and dancing girls accompanying the host, as well as children, elderly people and servant boys who came to see off the departing guest. There are also passers-by on both sides of the road, swiftly moving like "figurants" in a play or a film.

Wang Wei's original poem primarily focuses on the temporary scene of raising a cup to urge the departing guest during the farewell banquet. However, the painting presents a continuous sequence of scenes, depicting the pre-departure festivities with music and dance, the bustling presence of horses and carriages, the toasting and mingling of the host and guest during the farewell, the tearful singing by the performers, the weeping of young and old as they part ways, the poignant reactions of passers-by along the road, and the serene and unaffected demeanour of the angler by the stream which remains blissfully unaware of it all.

The two groups of characters in the painting create a contrasting effect while the scenes undergo changes, transforming the atmosphere from warmth to melancholy.

If we were to talk about the characters and scenes related to the departure and farewell between the hosts and the guests, ordinary readers might imagine and anticipate them. However, the fisherman and woodcutter depicted in the painting go far beyond the imagination and expectations of the average reader. Wang Wei's original poem did not involve any other characters beyond the host and the guest, yet the painting "*Yangguan Pass*" ingeniously added a group of seemingly unrelated fishermen and woodcutters. What is the intention behind this? Zhang Shunmin has already understood it, hinting at the "profound meaning" of depicting the fishermen and woodcutters.

The "profound meaning" of Li Gonglin's painting is perhaps that most people endure the pain of separation and taste the bitterness of farewell in their journeys for the sake of fame and fortune. To avoid suffering from such separations, one should be content with a simple life and refrain from pursuing fame and fortune, just like the fishermen and woodcutters. This greatly develops and enriches the ideological connotation of Wang Wei's original poem.

Li Gonglin's painting "*Yangguan Pass*" has been highly praised by later generations for its unique theme beyond the expectations of all. Su Shi, for instance, described the painting as "marvelously extraordinary" in his writings *Xuanhe huapu* ("Painting Manual of Xuanhe Era") also has comments on it:

> Li Gonglin prioritizes the theme and then arranges the embellishments and decorations. The refinement and delicacy of his brushwork can be studied by ordinary craftsmen, but when it comes to simplicity and ease, they can never come close. He deeply grasped the poetic style of Du Fu and applied it to his painting. Just as Du Fu's poem "Ballads of Binding a Chicken" (*Fu Ji Xing*) does not focus on the gains and losses of the chicken and worms, but on the moment when "I fix my eyes on the cold river, leaning against a tower in the hills."[23] Li Gonglin's painting of Tao Yuanmin's poem "Returning Home", does not focus on the fields, pine and chrysanthemums of the pastoral setting, but on the riverside where he contemplates the clear stream. In Du Fu's poem "A Song on How My Thatched Roof Was Ruined by the Autumn Wind", the poet was not concerned about the worn-out quilt or the leaky house, but held the desires that "If only I could get a great mansion of a million rooms, broadly covering the poor scholars of all the world, all with joyous expressions."[24] In Li Gonglin's "*Yangguan Pass*", the painter captures the common human emotions of sorrow for departure, but places a fisherman by the water's edge who sits absorbed in his own thoughts, detached from the sorrow and joy. Various other instances also follow this approach, and one can only grasp it upon his own viewing.[25]

Wang Shizhen (1634–1712), a scholar of the Qing Dynasty, made comments on Li Gonglin's painting in his work "Continuation of the Silkworm Tail" (*Chan Wei Xu Wen*) to illustrate the technique of poetry:

> Li Gonglin's painting '*Yangguan Pass*' does not aim at depicting the carriages and horses of Wei City, but rather sets a fisherman on the riverbank. The fisherman sits by the side of the river, ignoring the sorrow and joy around him. This is the essence of poetry.[26]

Shifting from poetry to painting is not merely a conversion of medium but a form of cultural proliferation. For a piece of poem, a painting that depicts its poetic essence signifies the addition of a new and meaningful text, achieving cultural proliferation. Wang Wei's poem "Seeing Off Yuan'er on His Mission to Anxi" (*Song Yuaner Shi Anxi*)" had six different pictorial versions during the Song Dynasty, resulting in six instances of cultural proliferation.

The derivative nature of painting communication refers to the fact that new literary works, such as poems, can be derived from the process of painting communication. This is closely related to the collective viewing of paintings. As mentioned previously, after collectors obtained a painting, they often invited friends, relatives and famous literati to appreciate it. If the appreciators happen to be poets or writers, their encounter with the painting can evoke poetic inspiration, leading them to compose poems or postscripts. This creates an interactive cycle of communication, reception and creation, forming a chain for the formation of poetry, painting and poetry. For example, during the Northern Song Dynasty, after Lin Cizhong collected Li Gonglin's paintings of "*Yangguan Pass*" and "*Returning Home*", he invited Su Shi to appreciate them. Su Shi, after appreciating the paintings, happily composed two poems on them. So did Su Zhe and Huang tingjian. After Xie Ke obtained the painting "*Yangguan Pass*", he invited over ten friends to appreciate and write poems together. Apart from quoting poems of his friends, Xie Ke also wrote "Two Poems on Appreciating Li Gonglin's Paintings": "Sitting opposite to the paintings, I sorrow over partings, tears mingling with the morning rain. The willow branches by the road stay year after year, witnessing countless travelers who never return". "Spring grass and ripples are embodied with endless sadness; the verdant willow is most captivating. Li Gonglin himself harbors the sorrow of leaving home, when he faces the hazy rain of Yangguan".[27]

In the Southern Song Dynasty, when Wang Jilu obtained the painting "Yangguan Pass", he invited Lou Yue, a renowned literati of the time, to write poems. Lou Yue immediately composed two poems with the same title "On Wang Jilu's Collection of Li Gonglin's 'Yangguan Pass'". The first one reads as follows: "With a departing toast, my tears pour forth for you; I ask about your journey, in haste with your luggage. There is no need to seek old tunes; within the painting, there is a heart-wrenching sound". The second one reads as, "The painting portrays ancient partings at Yangguan; the desolate and sparse willow reveals an inconsolable sorrow. Travelers cast glances and sigh, at those who shed tears of departure, but the fisherman beneath the willow remains oblivious". The lines "travelers cast glances and sigh, at those who shed tears of departure, but the fisherman beneath the willow remains oblivious" can be echoed by Zhang Shunmin's lines: "passers-by on the road all felt a pang of sorrow. Only the old angler by the stream, quietly casting his fishing line, seemed untouched by it all, in his own world of tranquility".

When the poets appreciate the paintings, some are inspired afterwards and voluntarily write poems on the paintings, while others compose poems in response to the request of the collectors. For example, Wang Anshi composed a poem with the following lines:

> Throughout the ages, there have been countless painters, too numerous to count. Although the Huichong emerged late, he is the one who truly captures my heart. In the scorching weather of June, when I encountered his painting, I felt as if I were transported to a small islet by the water, instantly feeling refreshed.[28]

This poem was written in response to the request of Wang's younger brother, Chun Fu, to write a poem on the painting of Huichong, a famous poet, painter and monk at the time.

When a painting is adorned with poems by distinguished literati, it becomes a new text that combines poetry, calligraphy, and painting together, enhancing the harmony among the three art forms. The act of renowned literati composing poems signifies their recognition and approval, while the influence of these literati further enhances the value of the artwork. The paintings gain value through the poems, and the poems gain popularity through the paintings. There is a mutually beneficial relationship between poets, painters and collectors, resulting in a win-win situation. Hence, painters and collectors often invite esteemed poets to compose poems for their paintings, and poets and renowned people are also delighted to do that.

Since Li Gonglin painted the "Yangguan Pass", 13 poets composed 20 poems in the Song Dynasty and 11 poets composed 12 poems that described the "Yangguan Painting" in the Jin, Yuan and Ming Dynasties. Among them, there are two poems by Su Song, two by Su Shi, two by Su Zhe, two by Huang Tingjian, three by Xie Ke, one by Wang Zhuo, two by Lou Yue, two by Yuan Wangyun and one by Ma Zuchang. All 15 poems were explicitly dedicated to Li Gonglin's painting "Yangguan Pass". These poems constituted a splendid landscape in the literary circle of the Song Dynasty.

From Wang Wei's poem "Seeing Off Yuan'er on His Mission to Anxi" to the painting "Yangguan Pass" and then to the poems of "Yangguan Pass", they form the interaction between poems and paintings, including poetic creation, dissemination, reception and re-creation. The dissemination of Wang Wei's poem "Seeing Off Yuan'er on His Mission to Anxi" gave rise to Li Gonglin's painting "Yangguan Pass". Li Gonglin's painting not only brought about the imitation and continuation of five other painters but also ignited the creative enthusiasm of other poets, providing new opportunities for creation. As a result, more than 20 poets from the Song, Jin, Yuan, and Ming Dynasties, including Su Shi, Su Zhe, Huang Tingjian and Yang Shen, composed over 30 poems dedicated to "Yangguan Pass".

Without Wang Wei's poem "Seeing Off Yuan'er on His Mission to Anxi", there would not have been the painting "Yangguan Pass". Without the painting "Yangguan Pass", there would not have been dozens of poems dedicated to the painting by Su Shi, Huang Tingjian and others. "Seeing Off Yuan'er on His Mission to Anxi" is not only a piece of poem that can be repeatedly read and disseminated but also a proliferating and regenerative resource. Just as one blooming flower attracts hundreds of others; one poem led to the creation of six paintings and over 30 poems. The painting "Yangpass Pass" serves not only as a medium for disseminating "Seeing Off Yuan'er on His Mission to Anxi" but also as an incubator for the creation of poems dedicated to paintings. Like the poem "Seeing Off Yuan'er on His Mission to Anxi", the painting "Yangguan Pass" is not only an artistic product but also a perennial source of poetic creation.

8.2 Spread of "Seeing Off Yuan'er on His Mission to Anxi" with Songs

Dissemination of literature through artistic media, such as music and painting, is a common phenomenon in the history of Chinese literary and artistic communication. Once a poem is sung in music or portrayed in a painting, it often accelerates and expands its influence, becoming a popular and classic piece of work. In this section, we will use Wang Wei's poem "Seeing Off Yuan'er on His Mission to Anxi" as a case study to analyse the dissemination of poetry through music.

After being set to music, "Seeing Off Yuan'er on His Mission to Anxi" (*Song Yuan Er Shi An Xi*) was also named "A Farewell Song at Weicheng"(*Wei Cheng Qu*), "A Farewell Song at Yangguan Pass" (*Yang Guan Qu*) or "Three Farewells of Yang Guan" (*Yang Guan San Die*). The first question that comes to our mind is when was "Seeing Off Yuan'er on His Mission to Anxi" sung as "A Farewell Song at Weicheng"? When did it become a popular song? When did it become a classic song? After the rise of *ci* works in the Song Dynasty and operas in the Yuan Dynasty, was this old song still sung by people? In the Ming and Qing Dynasties, were "Three Farewells of Yang Guan" still circulated among the people? How did its mode of transmission change? The next question is how many different ways are there to sing "Three Farewells of Yang Guan"?

8.2.1 Being Sung in the Flourishing Tang Dynasty

It is impossible to determine the exact year or month when "Seeing Off Yuan'er on His Mission to Anxi" was composed into music as "A Farewell Song at

Weicheng". However, there are historical records that "A Farewell Song at Weicheng" was already sung during the glorious age of the Tang Dynasty. The anonymous "Records of the Great Tang Dynasty" states,

> Li Guinian, Li Pengnian and Li Henian, the three brothers, were renowned for their talents during the Kaiyuan period. Li Henian's singing of the "Wei City" poem was particularly exquisite, while Li Pengnian was skilled in dancing, and Li Guinian excelled at playing the drum.

The "Wei City" sung by Li Henian was none other than Wang Wei's "A Farewell Song at Weicheng". The three Li brothers were active during the Kaiyuan and Tianbao periods. During that period, Li Henian was already singing "A Farewell Song at Weicheng", indicating that it had been composed to music during the Kaiyuan and Tianbao periods. In other words, shortly after Wang Wei's poem was published, it was already sung as a musical composition. During the Kangxi period of the Qing Dynasty, Xu Zeng once mentioned Wang Wei's shedding tears upon hearing someone sing "A Farewell Song at Weicheng" by the roadside. If this is true to the fact, it also indicates that the poem had been composed to music and sung in Wang Wei's lifetime.

8.2.2 Becoming a Popular Song in the Middle and Late Tang Dynasty

By the middle Tang Dynasty, "A Farewell Song at Weicheng" had already become a popular song that was widely sung. Bai Juyi often listened to and sang this song. When he met with friends, he would sing the song out of happiness, as was seen in his poem: "Let's not refuse to drink more when we meet, and listen to the fourth melody of 'A Farewell Song at Yangguan Pass'". When feeling depressed, he would sing "A Farewell Song at Yangguan Pass" to encourage wine drinking: "There is no other way to console ourselves, so let's sing 'A Farewell Song at Yangguan Pass' and have a drink". When reminiscing with friends, he thought, "The most memorable song is 'A Farewell Song at Yangguan Pass', which pours out like a string of pearls". During a singing event in the South Garden, there is the following description: "Everywhere there are high-pitched tones, silver notes, slow-paced lyrics, and the singing of 'Wei City'. Without drinking a cup, can it soothe my mood?".[29]

At that time, there were many professional singers renowned for their rendition of "A Farewell Song at Weicheng", such as Mi Jiarong and He Kan. In "*Lu Shi Za Shuo*", there are the following words:

> The beauty of singing has longly been praised in the history. During the Yuanhe period, there were excellent singers such as Mi Jiarong, He Kan, and more recently there is Chen Buxian. ... Liu Yuxi, in his poem "To Mi Jiarong", says: "In three reigns, Mi Jiarong was highly respected, for his capacity to transform new sounds into old ones. The younger generation today disdains the older generation, and he has to dye the hair to serve

the younger ones." In another poem entitled "My Depreciating Return to the Capital and Hearing He Kan's Songs" the poet says: "It has been over two decades since I left the capital city. Today, I hear again the old music from the palace, and my heart is filled with endless emotions. Of all the old acquaintances from those days, only He Kan remains, and I eagerly ask him to sing "A Farewell Song at Weicheng" once again".[30]

With the promotion of top singers like Mi Jiarong and He Kan, the song "A Farewell Song at Yangguan Pass" naturally became more popular. Shen Si, one of Bai Juyi's friends, also had a talented maid who was good at singing "A Farewell Song at Weicheng". For the line "the most memorable song is 'A Farewell Song at Yangguan Pass', which pours out like a string of pearls", Bai Juyi made some notes: "Shen has a maid who is skilled in singing the *ci* works such as the line 'West of the Yangguan Pass no more friends will be seen'".[31]

During the Mid-Tang period, "A Farewell Song at Weicheng" was not only sung by professional singers but also by ordinary people every day. Wei Xuan's "*Liubinke Jia Hua Lu*" recorded a pancake vendor who sang "A Farewell Song at Weicheng" every morning:

> Liu Yuxi's uncle, Liu Bochu (Liu Suzhi, with the courtesy name Bochu, an assistant minister in the Ministry of Justice), once said: "I used to live in Anyi town, where there was a vendor selling cakes. Every morning when I passed by his stall, he would happily sing his catchy jingle. One day, after chatting with him for a while, I learned of his poverty. So, I gave him ten thousand coins to expand his business and asked him to consider it as payment when I come daily to eat his cakes. However, from that day on, I no longer heard his singing when I passed by. I thought he had gone away, but when I called out to him, he emerged. I asked him, 'Why did you stop singing so soon?' He replied, 'With more capital, I need to put more thought into my business and have no time to sing the song of 'A Farewell Song at Weicheng' anymore.' Then I remarked, 'I suppose it's the same for those who aspire to be higher-rank officials.' This sparked a burst of laughter".[32]

Liu Bochu lived in the mid-Tang period,[33] slightly earlier than Bai Juyi. Bai Juyi's "Bai Kong Liu Tie" (Vol. 16) also included the story of this pancake vendor who "have no time to sing the song of 'A Farewell Song at Weicheng'", indicating that this story had been circulated for a long time during the mid-Tang period. From the singing of the song by a pancake vendor every morning, we can imagine how popular "A Farewell Song at Weicheng" was at that time. This story later became a commonly used anecdote for Song Dynasty poets.

During the late Tang Dynasty, the song "A Farewell Song at Yangguan Pass" remained popular. Li Shangyin mentioned singing "A Farewell Song at Yangguan Pass" twice in his poems. In "While Drinking, Playfully Given To A Friend" (*Yin Xi Xi Zen Tong She*), he wrote the following line: "The enchanting melody of the song A Farewell Song at Yangguan Pass captivated you all, leaving you mesmerized. The half-filled cup of pine-leaf wine in your hands remained untouched, as if frozen upon the jade cup". In his poem "Two Poems for the Singing Lady", he wrote, "The rosy cherry lips concealed pearly white teeth within, yet the song 'A Farewell Song at Yangguan Pass' was sung with such heart-wrenching sorrow and poignancy that it could break one's heart".[34] Zhang Hu's "Two Poems on Listening to Music" also mentioned the singing of "the first sound out of the west of Yangguan Pass" by "young boys".[35] Cui Zhongrong's "To a Singing Lady" also mentions the singing of "A Farewell Song at Weicheng" by a singing girl at a feast: "Please stop singing A Farewell Song at Weicheng, for all the listeners are guests far away from their homes".[36]

During the Five Dynasties period, people continued to sing "A Farewell Song at Weicheng". Feng Yansi's *ci* work "Poem to the Tune *Que Ta Zhi*" described the scene of drinking while listening to "A Farewell Song at Yangguan Pass". It says, "In drunkenness, do not decline a full gold-cup of wine; one song of 'A Farewell Song at Yangguan Pass' breaks my heart into a thousand pieces".[37] Tan Yongzhi once heard someone singing the nostalgic "A Farewell Song at Yangguan Pass" in a riverside pavilion, saying, "Who is singing 'A Farewell Song at Yangguan Pass' outside, which makes it impossible for me to have a nice dream in such solitude?"[38]

During the Tang and Five Dynasties, the song "A Farewell Song at Weicheng" was sung throughout the country, while the original poem – namely, Wang Wei's "Seeing Off Yuan'er on His Mission to Anxi" – had little impact. In "Selected Tang Poems", only Wei Hu's "*Cai Diao Ji*" included this poem, and other selections and reference books to Tang poems at the time did not include or mention the poem. Yin Fan, who lived at the same time as Wang Wei, compiled the "Heyue Yingling Collection" and claimed to have selected the most famous works of the time. He selected 15 poems by Wang Wei, but this poem was not included. Rui Tingzhang's "Guoxiu Collection" selected seven poems by Wang Wei, and this poem was not included either. It can be said that during the Tang and Five Dynasties period, "A Farewell Song at Weicheng" was well-known, but not the original quatrain poem "Seeing Off Yuan'er on His Mission to Anxi".

8.2.3 Classic Song at Farewell Banquets

In the Song Dynasty, a period known for the flourishing of long and short *ci* works, the classic song "A Farewell Song at Weicheng", which had been sung for two hundred years, not only managed to withstand the test of time against newer singers but also gained even more popularity. It became the beloved classic song at farewell banquets during the Song Dynasty.

Almost every farewell situation in the Song Dynasty was accompanied by singing and listening to the song. In a poem by Lou Yue entitled "Song Chen Jin Dao Cui San Shan", there are lines such as, "When parting ways, we sing 'A Farewell Song at Weicheng' while pouring wine to bid farewell".[39]

Zhou Fuxian's lyrics entitled "*Zhe Gu Tian*" ("The Partridge Sky") described, "We used to sing 'A Farewell Song at Yangguan Pass' when bidding farewell, and express our emotions with wines at the crossroads. Now, the wine gets bitter due to the affection, we sing the song to bid farewell to each other". In Su Maoyi's poem "To the Tune *Zhu Ying Tai Jin*", there are the following lines: "Approaching the wide road, we part and sing 'A Farewell Song at Yangguan Pass'".[40] Farewell scenes were commonly found everywhere, and the melancholic and poignant song "A Farewell Song at Yangguan Pass" could also be heard everywhere:

> At the farewell banquet we get drunk while appreciating the beauty's dancing, raising a cup and listening to "A Farewell Song at Weicheng". When old friends at Yangguan Pass bid farewell, we sorrowfully ask the sorrowful clouds when we will meet again.[41]

The song "A Farewell Song at Yangguan Pass" was continuously sung from the beginning of the Northern Song Dynasty until the end of the Southern Song Dynasty without interruption. Whether in Wei Ye's poem in the early Song Dynasty, in Mei Yaochen and Liu Ban's poems in the middle of the Northern Song Dynasty, in Li Zhiyi's poem in the late Northern Song Dynasty, in Wang Zhao and Zhou Zizhi's poems in the early Southern Song Dynasty or in Liu Kezhuang and He Yinglong's poems in late Southern Song Dynasty there are descriptions of the singing of the song. Even at the end of the Song Dynasty and the beginning of the Yuan Dynasty, the song was still sung by people. In Chen Zhu's poem "A Visit to Ciyun Temple on the Twentieth Day of the First Month of the Yiyou Year" (Part 2), there are lines, "Listen again to the song 'Three Farewells of Yang Guan (*Yang Guan San Die*)', I wonder when I will meet this old man again?" The year Yiyou refers to the 22nd year of the Zhiyuan era (1285). By this time, it had been almost ten years since the fall of the Southern Song Dynasty.

During the Song Dynasty, of those who sang "A Farewell Song at Yangguan Pass", there were professional singing and dancing girls, as stated in "maidens singing 'A Farewell Song at Yangguan Pass'",[42] or "a fair-skin beauty singing 'A Farewell Song at Weicheng'".[43] The famous girl Li Shishi of the Northern Song Dynasty was especially skilled at singing the song. Zhu Dunru once wrote a poem to praise her singing: "She who could sing 'A Farewell Song at Yangguan Pass' to the best, is none other than Lady Li of the previous dynasty".[44] There were also wandering singers who sang the song. Fan Chengda's "Song of the Singer in a Riverbank Market" goes:

> I could tell that you weren't singing "A Farewell Song at Weicheng" with a composed demeanor. Your voice was filled with discontent. It was pitiful to see your weary face and you endure the torment of hunger in this twilight hour. Yet, you forced a smile and sang as if you were a bird in spring, incessantly chirping in search of a companion.[45]

This singer who endured hunger and sang the song calmly in the streets indicates that it was a popular song widely known by the people at that time.

During the Northern Song Dynasty, many literati loved to sing the song and were skilled in it. Du Tingzhi, a friend of Mei Yaochen, was one of them. In Huan Wei's "Nanyang Collection", Volume 8, there is a note to the poem "Visiting Du Tingzhi (Du Mu) with Liu Chang": "Don't sing 'A Farewell Song at Yangguan Pass' in his front, for he has deep sorrow for so many years". In the annotation, the poet adds the following words, "Du Tingzhi is good at singing this song". Du Tingzhi's love to sing the song is also mentioned in Cai Xiang's poem. Jiang Xiufu, a friend of Du Tingzhi and the author of "Jiang Lin Ji Za Zhi", also loved to sing the song. A man with the surname Lu, a close friend of Qiang Zhi, also enjoyed singing the song at banquets. He sang so well that sometimes, the guests in the seats were moved to tears. Qiang Zhi once wrote a poem titled "On the Occasion of Mr. Lu's Wine Drinking and Singing of 'A Farewell Song at Yangguan Pass' at the Banquet":

When will the ancient people's grievances end?
The sorrowful sound of 'Yangguan' continues to this day.
Mr. Lu, intoxicated with wine, happily sings by himself,
While tears flow freely from the seated guests.[46]

Su Shi also loved to sing the song in his lifetime. In Lu You's "Notes from the Laoxue Study", Volume 5, there are the following words:

It is said that Dongpo cannot sing, so his composition of Yuefu songs does not show phonological of harmony. However, Chao Yidao once said, "At the beginning of the Shao Sheng years, we parted ways with Dongpo near the Bian River. Dongpo, intoxicated with wine, sang 'A Farewell Song at Yangguan Pass' loudly." Thus, it is not that the Su Shi cannot sing, but that he does not like to restrict the rhythm of his songs.[47]

Su Shi not only sang the song himself but also used the melody of the song in his own poems.

In the tenth year of the Xining reign (1077), Su Shi and Su Zhe, his younger brother, sang the poem "Mid-Autumn" to the Tune "A Farewell Song at Yangguan Pass" in Xuzhou. In the first year of the Shaosheng reign (1094), while he was in Jiangxi, he sang this poem again.[48] It can be seen that the song was what Su Shi was familiar with and deeply loved. Furthermore, Su Shi paid special attention to the singing style of the song and wrote a specific essay titled "The Fourth Tune of Yangguan" to discuss the singing style.[49]

During the Song Dynasty, the accompaniment instruments for the song were the *guzheng* (a 21- or 25-stringed plucked instrument in some ways similar to the zither) and bamboo flute. Wen Yanbo, a scholar of the Northern Song Dynasty, wrote in his poem "To *guzheng*": "The intricate strings move along the precious pillars, playing a few tunes of 'Yangguan'".[50] This indicates that the *guzheng* was used to perform "A Farewell Song at Yangguan Pass" at the time. In the poems of Lu You in the Southern Song Dynasty and the monk Xing Hai, there were also records of the use of flutes for accompaniment with the song. In the Ming and Qing Dynasties, the *guqin*, a seven-stringed plucked instrument in some ways similar to the zither, was used as an accompaniment instrument.

With the widespread of the song during the Song Dynasty, "Seeing Off Yuan'er on His Mission to Anxi" became a well-known masterpiece, which was even praised as a poetic masterpiece through the ages. Han Bian of the Southern Song Dynasty praised it as the "ultimate song of 'A Farewell Song at Yangguan Pass'"; Zhang Yan, in his work "*Ci Yuan*", also stated that if the sadness of separation could be expressed as in "drink one more cup of wine my friend, west of Yangguan Pass there's no one you know", it could be called an "unparallel song".[51] Liu Chenweng even praised this poem as the number one masterpiece of all time.[52] The song and the tune of "A Farewell Song at Yangguan Pass" became well-known phrases of parting among people in the Song Dynasty and were the most popular keywords in farewell poetry. According to database searches, there are 193 poems that use the imagery of "Yangguan Pass" and 75 poems that use the imagery of "Weicheng" in "Complete Collection of Song Poetry" (1999). There are 162 poems that use the imagery of "Yangguan Pass" and 33 poems that use the imagery of "Weicheng" in "The Complete *ci* Works of the Song Dynasty" (1965). Nowadays, a line from a popular song often becomes a popular phrase in society. In the Song Dynasty, the phrases "Yangguan Pass" and "Weicheng" were also the "collective memory" of poets and lyricists, which were popular phrases in poetry and lyrics.

8.2.4 Continuous Popularity during the Jin and Yuan Dynasties

The song "Three Farewells of Yang Guan (*Yang Guan San Die*)" was still popular during the Jin and Yuan Dynasties. Li Zhi, a poet from the late Jin and early Yuan dynasties, once learned to sing the song from someone else. In his work "Jing Zhai Xian Sheng Gu Jin Chen" (Vol. 4), he stated,

> In the poem "Seeing Off Yuan'er on His Mission to Anxi" written by Wang Mojie (Wang Wei), the lines go as,
>
> "Light dust was laid by the morning rain in Weicheng,
> The willows beside the guest inn look fresh and green.
> I urge you to have another parting wine again,
> When you go out of Yangguan Pass to the West it is hard to meet old friends."
>
> Afterwards, many farewell poems were accompanied by this poem and sung as "Xiao Qin Wang" or "Gu Yangguan Pass". When I was in Guangning, I learned to sing this song from an old musician named Mr. Yi.[53]

This account reveals at least three pieces of information. Firstly, there were old musicians who could sing the song "Three Farewells of Yang Guan (*Yang Guan San Die*)", indicating that the singing style was passed down among professional musicians. Secondly, it can be seen that there were multiple music scores circulating at that time, indicating that there were many people who could sing it. Thirdly, at that time, people who understood music could mostly sing this song, and after composing a new tune, it was easier to spread widely.

In fact, during the Jin and Yuan Dynasties, there were more people than the old musicians and Li Zhi who could sing the song. Yuan Haowen's friend, Xin Yuan, was an example. Xin Yuan once wrote a poem called "Accompanying Yuan Haowen to Xuzhou, at a Request to *Sing Yang Guan San Die*, Then I Undertook It".[54] This shows that Xin Yuan was good at singing the song. Therefore, his friends at the banquet asked him to sing it.

In the Yuan Dynasty, the popularity of the song might not have been as high as that in the Song Dynasty, but people still frequently heard it. For example, in the third year of the Zhida year of the Yuan Dynasty (1310), when Bai Pu left Wucheng, his friends bid farewell to him, "Raising the cups, we suddenly hear 'A Farewell Song at Yangguan Pass'. How much tear was shed on the faces? They soak the silk handkerchieves several times". When Hong Xiwen bid farewell to an old friend, he also "sang 'A Farewell Song at Yangguan Pass' with a cup of wine, bidding farewell to my lifelong friend". In *sanqu* (a type of verse popular in the Yuan, Ming and Qing Dynasties, with tonal patterns modelled on tunes drawn from folk music) and drama of the Yuan Dynasty, the song was also often heard. For example, in Ma Zhiyuan's play "Autumn in the Han Palace" (*Han Gong Qiu*), when Emperor Yuan parted with Zhao Jun at the Ba Bridge, he was reluctant to let her go. Therefore, he deliberately asked Zhao Jun to slowly sing the song to delay the time. Although this is fictional in the drama, it reflects the reality of life.

In "Regional Preferences in Singing Songs" in "*Nancun chuo geng lu* ('Nancun's Notes in the Intervals of Ploughing', Vol. 27)" written by Tao Zongyi, the author stated, "In Dongping, people prefer to sing '*Mu Lan Hua Man*'; in Da Ming, they prefer to sing '*Mo Yu Zi*'; in Nanjing, they prefer to sing '*Sheng Cha Zi*'; in Zhangde, they prefer to sing '*Mu Hu Sha*'; while in Shaanxi, they prefer to sing '*Yang Guan San Die*' and '*Hei Qi Nu*'".[55] The so-called phrase "regional preferences in singing songs" means that people of different regions have their own preferences in singing songs. For example, people in Shaanxi are fond of singing "Three Farewells of Yang Guan (*Yang Guan San Die*)", but it doesn't mean that they only sing this song. From this, we learn that the song "A Farewell Song at Yangguan Pass" was still popular in Shaanxi during the Yuan Dynasty.

8.2.5 Evolution into a Classic Qin Piece in the Ming and Qing Dynasties

After the peak period of communication during the Song, Jin and Yuan Dynasties, the song "A Farewell Song at Yangguan Pass" was comparatively less popular in the Ming and Qing Dynasties. However, it did not disappear completely and was still occasionally sung. In the early Ming Dynasty, Gao Qi heard the old musicians singing the song as described in the following lines, "After singing the song of 'A Farewell Song at Weicheng', I feel desolate, for it is not as appreciated as the new popular songs. Today, when the guests gather together in the princely mansion, who in Jiangnan still recognizes Li Gui Nian?"[56] It is just that the old musicians who sang the old songs were no longer appreciated anymore, unlike those who sang the new popular songs that were highly chased after. In the Ming Dynasty, not only the old musicians but also the common people could sing the song. Hu Yinglin once heard Zhao Wulang singing a song on the boat, "The boat is bright in the moonlit night, and Zhao Wulang sings a beautiful song. I eagerly listen to the song 'A Farewell Song at Yangguan Pass', forgetting that the boat is heading forward in Wuchang (Suzhou)".[57] This shows that in Hu Yinglin's lifetime in the Wanli era (1573–1620), there were still some people who could sing the song.

During the Jiajing and Longqing periods of the Ming Dynasty (1522–1572), Tian Yiheng wrote in the "*Yang Guan San Die* Atlas" about the singing of the song by a singer Liu Yiyi in Yangzhou:

> Liu Yiyi, with the courtesy name Yiyu, was a resident of Twenty-Four Bridges in Yangzhou. ... The mandarin ducks flew apart, and the farewell songs echoed each other. The girl Liu Yiyi sang the song "A Farewell Song at Yangguan Pass" for me. ... Her farewell words were quick and short, her voice choked with increasing sorrow.[58]

During the Kangxi's reign of the Qing Dynasty, Zha Shenxing once heard a Qin woman singing the song in Bianzhong (present-day Kaifeng, Henan):

> The horse neighs as the guest returns to the lane. Half-drunk, fumbling the head, his facial expression is changed. Feeling grateful to the farewells of old friends, he asks the Qin woman to sing "A Farewell Song at Yangguan Pass".
> (Note: there was a Qin concubine on the site)[59]

In the anonymous novel "Zhangtai Liu" of the Qing Dynasty, it was also written in the seventh chapter, "Throughout the history, when bidding farewell, many would sing the song 'A Farewell Song at Yangguan Pass'. Let me try singing the song to toast".

Generally speaking, during the Ming and Qing Dynasties, "*Yang Guan San Die*" as a song was not as popular as it was during the Song and Yuan Dynasties. It was only occasionally sung by the people. But as a musical tune, it remained popular. In other words, during the Ming and Qing Dynasties, it was transformed from a vocal song to instrumental music, with a shift from individual singing to instrumental performance.

Among the instrumental compositions in the Ming and Qing Dynasties, "*Yang Guan San Die*", performed with *qin*, was the most widely known and had the most music scores. The earliest surviving recorded *qin* score of the music is found in the "*Zhe Yin Shi Zi Qin Pu*", which was compiled before the fourth year of Hongzhi (1491). This indicates that at least during the Hongzhi period, the *qin* work of "*Yang Guan San Die*" had already become popular. There are around two hundred surviving *qin* scores from the Ming and Qing Dynasties,[60] and at least 30 of them include the score of "*Yang Guan San Die*". The inclusion of this music in so many *qin* scores demonstrates that it was a popular and frequently performed classic piece at the time.

The *qin* works of the Ming and Qing Dynasties can be roughly divided into two categories: *qin*-songs and *qin*-music. *Qin*-songs primarily involve singing with accompanying music, with lyrics and melodies. *Qin*-music, on the other hand, is mainly performed on the *qin* instrument without lyrics. The *qin* scores of "*Yang Guan San Die*" collected in the Ming and Qing Dynasties are mostly *qin*-songs, containing both lyrics and tunes.

The widespread popularity of the music "*Yang Guan San Die*" during the Qing Dynasty can also be seen from the descriptions in popular novels of that time. In Chapter 38 of Sixiang Jiuwei's *Hai Shang Chen Tian Ying*, there is a description of playing the *qin*-music of "*Yang Guan San Die*":

Xiufen, Yuehong and Shunhua are together under the sycamore tree, playing the *qin* there. ... Xiufen smiled and said, "With such dedication and consideration, he will eventually learn it. If Miss Shan wants to listen, I will play a piece." Then she tuned the instruments and played the "*Yang Guan San Die*".[61]

In Chapter 13 of Hua Yue Chi Ren's novel *Hong Lou Huan Meng*, the sequel to *Hong Lou Meng* (Dream of Red Chamber, or Dream of RedMansions), there is a description of Lin Daiyu and Miaoyu's play of "Yang Guan San Die" with the *qin* together:

The next day, all gathered at the Yan Yang Building in Lin's Garden. After drinking, Baoyu, Daiyu, Miaoyu, and several other sisters and close friends, along with Qingwen and others, took a boat to Cold Fragrance Spring. Miaoyu and Daiyu played the *qin* together, starting with "*Yan Hui Cao*" and "*Yang Guan San Die*". After tea, they played "*Ping Sha*" and "*Qiao Ge*". The sound of the *qin* and the rhythm of the spring echoed with each other. All kept silent, and even the fish and birds forgot about their activities. Baoyu was filled with indescribable joy.[62]

In addition to *qin*-music, during the Yuan, Ming and Qing Dynasties, there were also *pipa*[63] and flute compositions of "*Yang Guan San Die*". In Jiang Yikui's "Yaoshantang Wai Ji", there are the following words:

During the Yuan Dynasty, there was an official in Xuanfu who bought a girl Lu Huinu as his maid-servant. Lu wrote a poem on the window of the boat, saying, "My parents value wealth and make light of me, so I have to carry my *pipa* on the journey of ten thousand *li*. Whenever I play '*Yang Guan San Die*', they all applaud with great joy. However, who knows that it is out of my heartbroken sorrow." There is endless sadness in the performance.[64]

From the poem, we learn that the music "*Yang Guan San Die*" was played by a girl with a *pipa*.

In Chapter 18 of *Er Nü Ying Xiong Zhuan* (A Tale of Lovers and Heroes), a novel written by Wenkang of the Qing Dynasty, there is a description of how Ji Xiantang learns to play the *pipa*. Among the tunes he learns, there is "*Yang Guan San Die*":

After half a month of effort, he learned various tunes such as "*Chu Sai*" (Going Out of the Frontier Fortress), "*Xie Jia*" (Pulling Shield Down), "Xunyang Ye Yue" (Night Moon above Xunyang) and even two-tone *ban'er*, two-tone *chuan'er*, two-tone "Yue Er Gao" (Moon High in the Sky), two sets of *lingzi*, "*Song Qing*" (Green Pines), "Hai Qing" (Blue Sea), "Yangguan Pass", "Pu An Curse", "Five Famous Horses" and so on. He followed the score and learned them attentively, with his heart and hands in harmony.[65]

As for the flute tune of "*Yang Guan San Die*", Chen Weisong once wrote, "In the city full of willow trees, the flute has already been applied in performance of '*Yang Guan San Die*'. In the 20th chapter of Wei Xiuren's novel '*Hua Yue Hen*'" (The Flower and the Moon Trace), He Sheng has a poem as follows: "I bother you to compose the *Qiting* tune again, and have it played 'Yang Guan San Die' by flute". In the 29th chapter of the novel *Lei Zhu Yuan* (Tears of Destiny), written by Tianxu Wosheng (Chen Xu), there is a more explicit statement: "Played '*Yang Guan San Die*'on the flute".[66] Although these are fictional characters in novels, they also reflect real-life situations. In other words, if fictional characters in novels can play the "*Yang Guan San Die*" on the *qin*, flute and *pipa*, the performance must be a common occurrence in real life at that time. Even in modern times, "*Yang Guan San Die*" is still a frequently performed famous piece in various instrumental music.

In conclusion, "Seeing Off Yuan'er on His Mission to Anxi" was sung and performed in the glorious age of the Tang Dynasty and became a popular song in the middle and late Tang Dynasty. With the rise of *ci* works in the Song Dynasty, the new style did not replace the old tunes, and "*Yang Guan San Die*" was even more popular during the Song Dynasty, becoming a classic song of farewell banquets, a collective memory of literati and commonly used imagery in farewell poems. During the Jin and Yuan Dynasties, it was not as popular as in the Song Dynasty, but there were still some people singing it. In the Ming and Qing Dynasties, although the song "*Yang Guan San Die*" was occasionally sung by people, it was no longer popular and was replaced by a musical composition. In conclusion, "Seeing Off Yuan'er on His Mission to Anxi" is a poem that was turned into a song and further transformed into a musical composition. From the 8th century to the present day of the 21st century, it has been sung and performed, transcending thousands of years but remaining fresh as before. It can truly be regarded as an enduring masterpiece throughout the ages, a precious gem in the history of Chinese poetry and music.

Notes

1. Works such as Ouyang Xiu's *"Zui Weng Ting Ji"* ("Record of the Old Tippler's Pavilion"), Su Shi's *"Chi Bi Fu"* ("Ode on the Red Cliff"), Tao Yuanming's *"Gui Qu Lai Ci"* ("Going Home"), and Liu Yuxi's *"Lou Shi Ming"* ("An Epigraph in Praise of My Humble Home") have all been set to music and sung. Zha, Fuxi. 1958. *Cun jian guqin qupu ji luan* ("A Compilation of Ancient Guqin Music Scores"), People's Music Publishing House, 13–16, 28.
2. Fu, Xuancong et al. 1997. *Quan Song shi* ("Complete Poetry Works of Song Dynasty"),Vol. 18. Peking University Press, 12162.
3. Wang, Chang. 1985. *Li Boshi hua Yang Guan Tu* ("Li Boshi's 'Yangguan Paintings'"). *Jinshi cuibian* ("Selected Rubbings of Ancient Inscriptions"), Vol. 138. Beijing China Bookstore, 7. According to the quote from Su Shi's "Qiuchi Notes" mentioned in the text, the content of Dongpo's postscript can be found. Li Boshi's poem has already been quoted earlier, and Wang Chang probably said "unable to verify" because he had not heard of Li Boshi's work. In addition, Li Tao's "Continuation of the Comprehensive Mirror for Aid in Government" in Vol. 326 records the following:

   > In the fifth year of Yuanfeng, May, Zhang Shunmin, who was newly appointed as the Supervisor of Yizhou, said: "Yesterday, I followed Gao Zunyu in charge of military affairs in Huanqing Road. While accompanying the army on the expedition, there was disagreement with Zunyu regarding the reduction of supplies. I myself claim that no matter the size of the matter, none have been adopted. I think the court's appointment is given to the general, and the military command center has a subordinate position, merely an auxiliary duty. Furthermore, not listening to a single word, stepping back will result in severe reproach, and minor loyalty was overlooked, making it impossible to express one's opinions. Now, I am organizing the records of recent auxiliary affairs in the military and hope to investigate further." The superiors responded: "Submit a detailed investigation to Yuwen Changling." Shunmin was instructed to have a Kaifeng Prefectural Scholar accompany him to Fuzhou for a response.

   In the same book, in the 330 section, in the fifth year of Yuanfeng, October, it was recorded,

   > Zhang Shunmin, newly appointed as the Supervisor of Yizhou, was assigned to supervise the tea, salt, and alcohol taxes in Chenzhou. Shunmin worked in Gao Zunyu's military command center, responsible for military affairs, and accompanied the army on expeditions. He made no contribution to the painting and even wrote satirical poetry. He was later demoted and frequently praised Gao Zunyu, but his opinions were never heard several times. The superiors ordered a detailed investigation by Yuwen Changling and found that most of Shunmin's statements were true, so there was a slight adjustment (on May 6th).

   In May of the fifth year of Yuanfeng, Zhang Shunmin was demoted to the position of supervisor of Yizhou (present-day Nanning, Guangxi), but he did not take up the post. In October, he was reassigned as the supervisor of Chenzhou for tea, salt

and alcohol taxes. He accompanied the army to the border and entered Gao Zunyu's military command centre, which would have been in the fourth year of Yuanfeng (1081).
4 Li, Tao. 1985. *Xu Zizhi Tongjian chang bian* ("Sequel to *Comprehensive Mirror in Aid of Governance*"), Vol. 318. Taiwan Commercial Press, (319): 412.
5 In Shi Rong's "*Shangu waiji shi zhu* ('Annotations to Huang Shangu's Extra Poems')", there are records that Huang Tingjian (Huang Shangu) wrote the two poems when he was an officer in *Mishu Sheng* (Secretarial Department) and *Shi Ju* (Historiography Institute). See Shi, Rong. 2003. *Shangu waiji shi zhu* ("Annotations to Huang Shangu's Extra Poems"). Shanghai Chinese Classics Publishing House, 994. Zheng Yongxiao concludes that Huang Tingjian composed the poems in the second year (1087) of Yuan You years. See Zheng, Yongxiao. 1997. *Huang Tingjian nianpu xibian* ("New Compilation of Huang Tingjian's Chronology"). Social Sciences Academic Press, 199.
6 Chao, Yuezhi. *Jingyusheng ji* (Collected Works of Chao Yuezhi), Vol. 9. *Siku quanshu* (Complete Library in Four Branches of Literature, Wenyuange edition), Vol. 1118:174.
7 Chao, Yuezhi. *Jingyusheng ji* (Collected Works of Chao Yuezhi), Vol. 9. *Siku quanshu* (Complete Library in Four Branches of Literature, Wenyuange edition), Vol. 1118:105.
8 Fu, Xuancong et al. 1991. *Quan Song shi* ("Complete Poetry Works of Song Dynasty"), Vol. 25. Peking University Press, 16611.
9 Zhang, Chou. *Qinghe shuhua fang* ("Qinghe Studio's Collection of Paintings and Calligraphies"), Vol. 1. *Siku quanshu* (Complete Library in Four Branches of Literature, Wenyuange edition), Vol. 817: 12.
10 Wang, Keyu. *Shanhu wang* ("Collected Comments and Inscriptions on Calligraphies and Paintings"), Vol. 47. *Siku quanshu* (Complete Library in Four Branches of Literature, Wenyuange edition), Vol. 818: 894.
11 Lu, Shen. *Yanshan ji* ("Collection of Yanshan"), Vol. 88. *Siku quanshu* (Complete Library in Four Branches of Literature, Wenyuange edition), Vol. 1268: 572.
12 Xia, Wenyan. *Tu hui bao jian* ("Preciouos Mirror of Painting"), Vol. 4. In Yu Anlan. 1982. *Hua shi congshu* ("The Series of Painting History"). Shanghai People's Fine Arts Publishing House, 99.
13 Xia Wen Yan, Tu Hui Bao Jian, Vol. 4, Collection of Art History edition, Shanghai People's Fine Art Publishing House, 1982: 103. Xia, Wenyan. *Tu hui bao jian* ("Preciouos Mirror of Painting'), Vol. 4. In Yu Anlan. 1982. *Hua shi congshu* ("The Series of Painting History"). Shanghai People's Fine Arts Publishing House, 103.
14 Zhou, Mi. 2000. *Yunyan guo yan lu* ("Record of Clouds and Mist Passing before One's Eyes"). Liaoning Education Press, 30.
15 Tang, Guizhang. 1965. *Quan song ci* ("The Complete Collection of *ci* Works in Song Dynasty"), Vol. 24. Zhonghua Book Company, 15789.
16 Li Gonglin (1049–1106), with style name Boshi, was a great painter in the Northern Song Dynasty. His artistic creations covered a wide range, including Daoist themes, figures, horses, palaces, landscapes, flowers and birds. He excelled in the art of copying. Some of his surviving works include "Painting of Five Horses", "Copying Wei Yan's Painting of Pasture", "Image of Vimalakirti" and "Painting of Sages".
17 "*Xuanhe Huapu*" is a compilation of the paintings preserved in the imperial court during the Xuanhe era of Emperor Huizong of the Northern Song Dynasty (1119–1125). Since the establishment of the Song Dynasty, there has been a strong emphasis on the collection and search of ancient books and paintings. During Emperor Huizong's reign, the imperial collection grew increasingly rich, prompting the compilation of a catalogue of works by famous painters from previous dynasties, which resulted in the completion of the 20 volume "*Xuanhe Huapu*" in the year

Xuanhe Gengzi (1120). The volumes include a total of 6,396 artworks of 231 painters from the Wei, Jin and Northern Song dynasties. The works are categorized into ten sections: Daoist themes, figures, palaces, ethnic groups, dragons and fish, landscapes, animals, flowers and birds, ink bamboo and fruits and vegetables. Each section is accompanied by a short essay discussing the origin, development and representative figures of the category. The painters' biographies and their works are arranged chronologically. Although *"Xuanhe Huapu"* is primarily a catalogue of paints, it goes beyond a mere listing by providing discussions on each section and critical evaluations of individual painters. Thus, it serves as not only a record of the paintings preserved in the imperial court during the Song Dynasty but also as a biographical history of Chinese painting.

18 Wang, Chang. 1985. *Jinshi cuibian* ("Selected Rubbings of Ancient Inscriptions"), Vol. 138. Beijing China Bookstore, 7.
19 Zhao, Lanpo, with the courtesy name Yuqin, was a renowned collector of calligraphy and painting during the Southern Song Dynasty.
20 Zhang, Chou. *Qinghe shuhua fang* ("Qinghe Studio's Collection of Paintings and Calligraphies"), Vol. 8. *Siku quanshu* (Complete Library in Four Branches of Literature, Wenyuange edition), Vol. 817: 314.
21 Li, Ziliang. 1989. *Zhang Shunmin shiji jiaoqian* ("Anthology of Zhang Shunmin's Poems with Annotations"). Heilongjiang People's Publishing House, 34.
22 Wang Wei's original poem, entitled "Sending Mr. Yuan on His Way on a Mission to Anxi" (*Song Yuaner Shi Anxi*), goes as following: By the walls of Wei City the rain at dawn/ dampens the light dust,/all green around the guest lodge/the colours of willows revive./I urge you now to finish/ just one more cup of wine:/ once you go west out Yang Pass/ there will be no old friends. See. Stephen Owen. 1996. An anthology of Chinese literature: beginnings to 1911. Norton, 375.
23 Stephen Owen. The Poetry of Du Fu, Vol. 5. De Gruyter, 31.
24 Stephen Owen. 2016. The Poetry of Du Fu, Vol. 3. De Gruyter, 42.
25 Anonymous. *Xuanhe huapu* ("Painting Manual of Xuanhe Era"). Shanghai People's Fine Arts Publishing House, 1982: 75.
26 Wang, Shizhen. 1963. *Daijingtang shihua* ("Poetry Remarks from the Carrying-Classics Hall"). People's Literature Publishing House, 78.
27 Fu, Xuancong et al. 1991. *Quan Song shi* ("Complete Poetry Works of Song Dynasty"), Vol. 24. Peking University Press, 15807.
28 Li, Bi & Li Zhiliang. 2002. *Wang Jinggong shi zhu bu qian* ("Wang Jinggong's Poem with Annotations and Supplements"). Bashu Publishing House, 5.
29 Bai, Juyi. 1979. *Dui jiu* ("Drinking Wine"). *Bai Juyi ji* (The Collected Works of Bai Juyi), Vol. 26, 598; *Da Su Liu* ("Reply to Su Liu"). Vol. 27, 614; *Wanchun yu xiejiu xun Shen Si zhuzuo xian yi liu yun ji zhi* ("Visiting Shen on a Late Spring Day with Wine"). Vol. 33: 757; Nan Yuan shi xiao yue ("Appreciating Music in the South Garden"). Vol. 26. Zhonghua Book Company, 589.
30 *Taiping guan ji* ("Extensive Records Compiled in the Taiping Years"). Vol. 204. Zhonghua Book Company, 1551.
31 Bai, Juyi. 1979. *Bai Juyi ji* ("The Collected Works of Bai Juyi"), Vol. 33, 757.
32 Wei, Xuan. 2000. *Liu Bingke jia hua lu* ("Liu Yuxi's Talks"). *Tang Wudai biji xiaoshuo daguan* ("Grand View of Story-Telling Novels in Tang and Five Dynasties"). Shanghai Chinese Classics Publishing House, 794.
33 According to "Biography of Liu Bochu" in Vol. 153 of *"Jiu Tang shu"* ("Old Book of Tang"), Liu Bochu was appointed official position in 815 and passed away at the age of 61.
34 Peng, Dingqiu et al. 1986. *Quan Tang shi* ("Complete Poetry Works of Tang Dynasty"), Vol. 539. Shanghai Chinese Classics Publishing House, 1361–1362.
35 Peng, Dingqiu et al. 1986. *Quan Tang shi* ("Complete Poetry Works of Tang Dynasty"), Vol. 511. Shanghai Chinese Classics Publishing House, 1297.

36 Peng, Dingqiu et al. 1986. *Quan Tang shi* ("Complete Poetry Works of Tang Dynasty"), Vol. 801. Shanghai Chinese Classics Publishing House, 1964.
37 Zeng, Zhaoming et al. 1999. *Quan Tang Wudai ci* ("*ci* Works in Whole Tang and Five Dynasties"). Zhonghua Book Company, 654.
38 Tan, Yongzhi. 1986. *Jiang guan qiu xi* ("Nightfall at Riverside Inn in Autumn"). *Quan Tang shi* ("Complete Poetry Works of Tang Dynasty"), Vol. 764. Shanghai Chinese Classics Publishing House, 1896.
39 Fu, Xuancong et al. 1999. *Quan Song shi* ("Complete Poetry Works of Song Dynasty"), Vol. 47. Peking University Press, 29371.
40 Tang, Guizhang. 1965. *Quan song ci* ("The Complete Collection of *ci* Works in Song Dynasty"). Zhonghua Book Company, 3566, 2560.
41 Liu, Chang. *Ji Wang Geshi (shi yue shi yi ri Jizhou xiang bie shi yi yue shi yi ri wen guo Gubeikou)* ("Letter to Wang Geshi"). Fu, Xuancong et al. 1991. *Quan Song shi* ("Complete Poetry Works of Song Dynasty"), Vol. 9. Peking University Press, 5917.
42 Su, Shi. *Ci yun Wang Xiongzhou huanchao liubie* ("A Farewell Poem to Wang Xiongzhou"). Fu, Xuancong et al. 1999. *Quan Song shi* ("Complete Poetry Works of Song Dynasty"),Vol. 14. Peking University Press, 9494.
43 Liu, Chang. *Zen bie Changan ji Cai Jiao* ("A Farewell Poem to Cai Jiao in Chang'an"). Fu, Xuancong et al. 1999. *Quan Song shi* ("Complete Poetry Works of Song Dynasty"), Vol. 9. Peking University Press, 5941.
44 Zhou, Mi. 2000. *Haoran Zhai ya tan* ("Commentary on Poetry in the Haoranzhai Library"), Vol. 2. Liaoning Education Press, 40.
45 Fan, Chengda. *Yonghe shi ge zhe* ("Singer in a Riverbank Market"). Fu, Xuancong et al. 1999. *Quan Song shi* ("Complete Poetry Works of Song Dynasty"), Vol. 41. Peking University Press, 25994.
46 Qiang Zhi. *Lu Jun zhijiu wei yu chang Yang Guan* ("Lu Prepares Wine Drinking and Sings of 'A Farewell Song at Yangguan Pass' at the Banquet"). Fu, Xuancong et al. 1999. *Quan Song shi* ("Complete Poetry Works of Song Dynasty"), Vol. 10. Peking University Press, 6917.
47 Lu, You. 1979. *Lao xue an biji* ("Notes in the Laoxue'an Studio"), Vol. 5. Zhonghua Book Company, 66.
48 Zou, Tongqing & Wang, Zongtang. 2002. *Su Shi ci bian nian jiaozhu* ("Annels of *ci* Works of Sushi"). Zhonghua Book Company, 210.
49 Su, Shi. 1986. *Sushi wenji* ("A Collection of Su Shi's Works"), Vol. 67. Zhonghua Book Company, 2090.
50 Wen, Yanbo. *Yong zhen* ("To *Guzhen*"). Fu, Xuancong et al. 1991. *Quan Song shi* ("Complete Poetry Works of Song Dynasty"), Vol. 6. Peking University Press, 3477.
51 Zhang, Yan. 1986. *ci Yuan* ("Source of ci-Poetry"). Zhonghua Book Company, 264.
52 Tian, Yiheng. 2005. *Yang Guan San Die tu pu* ("*Yang Guan San Die* Atlas"). *Quan Ming shihua* ("Notes on Ming Dynasty Poetries"). Shandong Qilu Press, 1515.
53 Li, Zhi. 1995. *Jingzhai xiansheng gujin tou* ("Discussion of Ancient and Modern Poems"), Vol. 4. Zhonghua Book Company, 44–45.
54 Xue, Ruizhao & Guo, Mingzhi. 1995. *Quan Jin shi* ("Complete Poetry Works of Jin Dynasty"), Vol. 111. Nankai University Press, 5917.
55 Tao, Zongyi. 1998. *Nancun chuo geng lu* ("Nancun's Notes in the Intervals of Ploughing"), Vol. 27. Liaoning Education Press, 321.
56 Gao, Qi. *Wen jiu jiaofang ren ge* ("Hearing Someone Sing Songs in Old School for Court Musicians"). *Da quan ji* ("Complete Works of Gao Qi"), Vol. 17, 1230. This poem imitates Du Fu's "Meeting Li Guinian in Jiangnan", which goes as follows: "In the lodgings of the Prince of Qi I saw you commonly, at the head of the hall of Cui Nine I heard you many times. It's really true that in Jiangnan the scenery is fine, and in the season of falling flowers I meet you once again" (tr. By Stephen Owen). See Stephen Owen. 2016. *The Poetry of Dufu*, Vol. 6. De Gruter, 193.

57 Hu, Yinglin. *Tong Fangzhong guo yun yian zhouzhong ting Zhao Wushu yuan ye ge zuo* ("In a same boat with Fang Zhong, I listened to Uncle Zhao's distant night song during our journey through the clouds'). *Shaoshishan fang ji* ("Collected Works of Hu Yinglin"), Vol. 15, 542.
58 Tian, Yiheng. 2005. *Yang Guan San Die tu pu* ("*Yang Guan San Die* Atlas"). *Quan Ming shihua* ("Notes on Ming Dynasty Poetries"). Shandong Qilu Press, 1522.
59 Zha, Shenxing. 1986. *Bian zhong yu Cai Yuanshi ci yun liubie san shou* ("Encountering Cai Yuanshi at Bianzhou and composing three farewell poems in response"). *Jingyetang shiji* ("Collection of Poems at Jingyetang"), Vol. 20. Shanghai Chinese Classics Publishing House, 568.
60 *Cun jian gu qin pu ji luan* ("A Comprehensive Collection of Surviving Ancient *qin* Scores") written by Zha Fuxi contains 34 *qin* scores of Ming Dynasty and 69 *qin* scores of Qing Dynasty, totalling 103 scores (People's Music Publishing House, 2001 edition). "Catalogue of Chinese Music Scores" records a total of 200 *qin* scores from the Ming and Qing Dynasties (People's Music Publishing House, revised edition, 1994).
61 Zou, Tao (*Si Xiang Jiu Wei*). 1994. *Haishang chen tian ying* ("In Shanghai Dust"). Shanghai Chinese Classics Publishing Hoouse, 440.
62 Hua Yue Chi Ren. 1991. *Hong Lou huan meng* ("Illusionary Dream of the Red Chamber"). Zhonghua Book Company, 1927–1928.
63 The *pipa*, sometimes called the Chinese lute, is a pear-shaped and short-necked traditional Chinese musical instrument. It is one of the most popular Chinese instruments prominent in Chinese opera orchestras. It has been played for almost 2,000 years in China as a solo instrument or in ensemble settings.
64 Jiang, Yikui. 1995. *Yaoshantang wai ji* ("Records at Yaoshantang Studio"), Vol. 70. Shandong Qilu Press, 228.
65 Wen, Kang. 1983. *Er nü yingxiong zhuan* ("A Tale of Lovers and Heroes"). People's Literature Publishing House, 308.
66 Chen, Xu (*Tian Xu Wo Sheng*). 1991. *Lei zhu yuan* ("Tears of Destiny"), Baihuazhou Literature and Art Publishing House, 221.

Epilogue

This book is the result of a research project funded by the National Social Science Foundation titled "A Study on the Literary Communication of Song Dynasty". It is also a summary of my research on the literary communication of the Song Dynasty. Since the early 1990s, I have been focusing on the issue of literary communication. The accumulation of over 20 years of exploration and contemplation is somewhat modest.

What is consoling for me is that every part of this book consists of solid "dry goods" based on first-hand historical materials, without any empty content. Some chapters were obtained through independent exploration. All the content has been published in academic journals such as *Literary Review*, *Literature & Art Studies* and *Literary Heritage*. This time, only some technical revisions were made during compilation, such as changes in titles, adjustments to the introductory texts of each chapter and uniform formatting of annotations. The content and viewpoints remained largely unchanged. Since each article was written at different times, there may be variations in the editions of the same reference book, which have been retained, as they were to provide readers unfamiliar with the literature with some version information. A few chapters were previously abridged due to space limitations in the publications, but this time, they are published in their original manuscript form, and missing or incomplete citations have been supplemented as much as possible.

I would like to express my gratitude to my doctoral students Chen Xiaoqing and Tian Gan, and M.A. students Zheng Donghui, Yang Hua, Xin Qi, Ma Zhongyan, Hou Weilin and Wang Jie for their hard work in researching and verifying citations for me. I would also like to thank my senior fellow Xiao Peng for spending the time to have conversations and exchanges with me, providing many enlightening insights. Thanks to the peer reviewers of Routledge.

Wang Zhaopeng

Index

Pages followed by "n" refer to notes.

Bai Juyi 4, 13n8, 32, 40n80, 79, 88n71, 119n68, 183, 184, 195n29, 195n31
block printing 14, 31, 32, 34, 54n33, 75
Buddhist temple 32, 59, 62, 77, 85n35, 131

Cai Yong 23, 38n41
Chao Buzhi 11, 35, 52n16, 66, 85n36, 93, 143, 144, 150, 152
Chao Yuezhi 43, 171, 194n6, 194n7
Chen Qi 49, 50, 51, 54n44, 133
Chen Shidao 20, 44, 66, 67, 93, 114, 121n103, 131, 134
ci poetry 6, 7, 107, 121n109, 122n134, 147

drafting epitaphs 130–134
Du Fu 7, 8, 18, 160, 179, 195n23, 195n24, 196n56, 196
Du Tingzhi 187

Eastern Han Dynasty 12, 14n13, 19, 23, 38n41, 51n2, 56, 158
Emperor Huizong 3, 18, 28, 42, 61, 94, 111, 172, 194n17
Emperor Renzong 26, 72, 92, 94, 126
Emperor Shenzong 5, 94, 100, 128, 130, 169, 170, 171
Emperor Zhenzong 22, 79, 83n20, 92, 100, 129, 132, 133
engraving printing 3, 16, 18, 36n3

Fan Chengda 93, 94, 116n22, 186
Fan Zhongyan 11, 27, 93
Fan Zuyu 133, 134
Farewell Song 115n9, 182–190, 196n46

Han Yu 3, 8, 9, 13n5, 39n47, 77, 137n3, 141
Hao Qingchen 175, 176
Huang Tingjian 1, 5, 9, 11, 16, 19, 25, 26, 33, 35, 43, 44, 47, 52n16, 53n21, 69, 75, 76, 96, 132, 141, 143, 144, 145n4, 170, 171, 174, 175, 180–182, 194n5

Imperial Academician 125–130, 162
Imperial Academy 12n2, 26, 50, 65, 79, 92, 115n9, 127–130, 137n5, 152, 172
imperial court 13n5, 18, 57, 79, 80, 130, 131, 175, 194n17, 195n17
imperial edict 25, 45, 82n5–n10, 118, 129, 130
imperial examination 5, 32, 61, 62, 65, 71, 72, 79, 86n50, 93, 104, 105, 136, 170–172

Jia Dao 9, 66, 110
Jiang Kui 9, 68, 93, 94
jinshi degree 104, 120n100

Kou Zhun 34, 62, 74, 83n20, 99, 100, 104

late Tang Dynasty 4, 16, 23, 183, 184, 192
Li Bai 7, 9, 18, 32, 34, 143, 160
Li Gefei 11, 149–152, 162, 164n15, 164n23, 164n24
Li Gonglin 168–171, 173–181, 194n16
Li Guinian 90, 92, 183, 196n56
Li Henian 183
Li Qingzhao 6, 9, 11, 15n16, 15n17, 20, 35, 37n22, 59, 83n13, 111, 147–153, 158, 159, 161–163, 164n15, 167n55, 167n57, 167n58

Li Shishi 103, 108, 114n7, 186
Li Song 172, 173, 174
Li Zhi 90, 144, 186, 188, 189, 195n28
Liang Dynasty 51, 56, 82n4
Liu Cha 141, 170, 187
Liu Jiangsun 76, 77, 113
Liu Jisun 78, 87, 142, 143
Liu Kezhuang 27, 39n59, 46, 54n44, 150, 186
Liu Qi 29, 82n11, 97
Liu Songnian 172–174
Liu Xiang 21, 82n1
Liu Yong 5, 9, 95, 108, 113

Mei Yaochen 20, 63, 93, 186, 187
Meng Jiao 9, 141
Ming Dynasty 6, 7, 12, 144, 153–163, 164n28, 165n32, 166n44, 167n58, 172, 175, 190, 196n52, 197n58, 197n60
Mishu Jian 12n1
Mishu Sheng 12n1, 85n36, 134, 194n5
Mu Xiu 20, 131

Northern Song Dynasty 1, 3–5, 11, 18, 19, 21, 22, 24, 33–35, 37n19, 39n61, 44–47, 49, 54n41, 73, 74, 78, 82n5–n10, 83n20, 91, 95–98, 100, 101, 104, 108, 110, 113, 116n27, 130–132, 135, 142, 152, 168, 171, 174, 176, 180, 186, 187, 194n16, 194n17

Ouyang Xiu 5, 10, 11, 16–18, 24, 28, 29, 31, 35, 39n46, 39n64, 43, 45, 47, 49, 53n26, 83n13, 93, 104, 105, 112, 113, 126, 127, 133, 134, 142–144, 154, 193n1

poetry anthologies 6

Qin Dynasty 2, 4, 23, 166n45
Qin Guan 1, 11, 26, 33, 44, 52n16, 113, 114, 144, 150
Qing Dynasty 6, 7, 12, 30, 160, 163, 169, 180, 183, 190–192, 197n60
Qu Yuan 51, 56, 65, 81n1, 82n1

Shao Bowen 40n81, 41n92, 115n14, 132, 138n31
Sima Guang 46, 93
Sima Xiangru 165n37
Southern Song Dynasty 4, 6, 20, 21, 24, 27, 35, 43–50, 53n21, 54n44, 55n51, 60, 76, 79, 91–105, 110, 114, 121n106, 128–130, 132, 134–136, 139n41, 140, 142, 144, 147–150, 162, 163n1, 172–175, 180, 186, 188, 195n19
stone carving 24, 25, 31, 63, 64, 70, 75, 175
stone engraving 24–27, 31, 32, 34
stone inscription 1, 3, 4, 16, 22–24, 26–31, 35, 37n22, 38n39, 40n69, 148, 151, 162
stone tablet 14, 24–30, 32, 34, 35, 64, 127, 131, 175
Song Yu 51, 82n1, 122n146, 123n146
Su Shi (Su Dongpo) 1, 3, 5, 8–11, 16–18, 21, 22–28, 30, 31, 33–35, 36n8, 36n9, 36n12, 37n25, 37n29, 39n50, 39n56, 40n66, 40n67, 40n73, 40n77, 40n86, 52n7, 52n16, 63, 64, 66, 67, 78, 79, 85n32, 88n68, 88n71, 90–93, 95, 96, 98, 99, 105, 114, 116n19, 131, 138n23, 142–145, 146n16, 152, 156, 164n24, 169, 170, 175, 179, 180–182, 187, 193n1, 196n48, 196n49
Su Zhe 28, 43, 52n7, 63, 180, 181, 182, 187
Sui Dynasty 12n2, 33, 51, 68, 126, 137n1

Tang Dynasty 1, 4, 7, 10, 11, 16, 18, 19, 23, 27, 32, 34, 35, 36n3, 39n57, 42, 43, 52n3, 53n21, 57, 85, 90, 92, 97, 113, 115n14, 117n39, 120n92, 132, 137n2, 137n5, 141, 168, 183, 184, 192, 195n34, 195n35, 196n36, 196n38

Wang Anshi 11, 17, 35, 42, 43, 66, 75, 78, 87, 92, 93, 95, 142, 143, 181
Wang Chang 24, 169, 170, 171, 175, 193n3
Wang Dan 92, 115n13, 133
Wang Qi 33, 68, 69, 78
Wang Qinruo 79
Wang Wei 10, 168, 169, 171, 173, 174, 177–183, 185, 188, 195n22
Wang Yucheng 43, 77, 99, 119n67
Wang Zhuo 35, 90, 91, 100, 114, 147, 181
Wei Xiang 142, 143, 145n7
Wei Ye 22, 62, 98, 186
Wei Zhonggong 6, 148–150, 155, 156
Western Han Dynasty 19, 23, 51n2, 82n1, 165n37
woodblock printing 31, 32, 34

Xiangguo temple 19, 20, 37n19
Xiao Chang 107–110, 122n130

Xie Yunwen 171, 172
Xin Qiji 5, 9, 21, 73, 96, 100, 104, 144, 148
Xin Yuan 189

Yang Guan 110, 168, 172, 173, 182, 186, 188–193, 196n46, 196n52, 197n58
Yang Ningshi 63
Yang Shen 6, 167n58, 182
Yang Wanli 44, 45, 48, 54n34, 99
Yang Wengong 129
Yangguan Pass 171, 174–190, 192, 196n46
Yuan Dynasty 4, 12n1, 25, 76, 92, 94, 114, 115n9, 133, 153, 154, 157, 158, 162, 175, 182, 186, 189, 191

Zhang Gang 46, 49, 53n28, 54n40

Zhang Lei 11, 27, 35, 39n57, 52n16, 66, 85n36, 99, 119n68, 144, 145, 146n17, 152
Zhang Ruzhou 162, 164n15
Zhang Shunmin 169, 170, 177, 178, 179, 181, 193n3, 195n21
Zhang Xingzhong 156, 161
Zhao Mingcheng 15n16, 30, 151, 152, 162, 164n15
Zhao Tingzhi 132, 151, 162, 164n15
Zhou Bangyan 4, 33, 67, 113, 133
Zhou Bida 45, 47, 94, 116n22, 130, 132, 142
Zhou Mi 6, 21, 94, 108, 111, 174
Zhu Shuzhen 6, 11, 147–150, 152–162, 163n1, 163n13, 167n53
Zhu Xi 68, 85n42, 98, 118n60, 148, 161, 163n7

For Product Safety Concerns and Information please contact our EU representative GPSR@taylorandfrancis.com
Taylor & Francis Verlag GmbH, Kaufingerstraße 24, 80331 München, Germany

www.ingramcontent.com/pod-product-compliance
Lightning Source LLC
Chambersburg PA
CBHW061347300426
44116CB00011B/2027